DOUBLE DIASPORA IN
SEPHARDIC LITERATURE

INDIANA SERIES IN SEPHARDI AND MIZRAHI STUDIES
Harvey E. Goldberg and Matthias Lehmann, editors

DOUBLE DIASPORA

in

SEPHARDIC LITERATURE

JEWISH CULTURAL PRODUCTION

BEFORE AND AFTER 1492

DAVID A. WACKS

INDIANA UNIVERSITY PRESS

Bloomington & Indianapolis

This book is a publication of

Indiana University Press
Office of Scholarly Publishing
Herman B Wells Library 350
1320 East 10th Street
Bloomington, Indiana 47405 USA

iupress.indiana.edu

Telephone   800-842-6796
Fax   812-855-7931

Manufactured in the United States of America

Library of Congress
Cataloging-in-Publication Data

Wacks, David A.
   Double diaspora in Sephardic literature :
Jewish cultural production before
and after 1492 / David A. Wacks.
   pages cm — (Indiana series in
Sephardi and Mizrahi studies)
   Includes bibliographical
references and index.
   ISBN 978-0-253-01572-3 (cloth : alk. paper)
— ISBN 978-0-253-01576-1 (ebook) 1. Jewish
literature—History and criticism. 2. Spanish
literature—Jewish authors—History and
criticism. 3. Sephardic authors. 4. Spanish
literature—13th century—History and
criticism. 5. Spanish literature—Classical
period, 1500–1700—History and criticism.
6. Spanish literature—Foreign countries—
History and criticism. 7. Jewish diaspora in
literature. I. Title. II. Title: Jewish cultural
production before and after 1492.
   PN842.W33 2015
   809'.88924046—dc23

                                    2014044168

1 2 3 4 5   20 19 18 17 16 15

For Zev and Eitan

CONTENTS

ACKNOWLEDGMENTS

First I would like to thank the Department of Romance Languages and the College of Arts and Sciences at the University of Oregon for their ongoing support over the past ten years and, in particular, the efficient, hardworking, and ever-professional departmental administrators, Herlinda Leon, Kerry Schlicht, and Zach Lazar.

Support from various sources enabled me to bring the project to completion. I received a Harry Starr Fellowship in Judaica from the Harvard Center for Jewish Studies (2006), a Summer Research Award from the College of Arts and Sciences, University of Oregon (2010), and the Ernest G. Moll Fellowship in Literary Studies, Oregon Humanities Center, University of Oregon (2010). In addition, AHA International in Oviedo, Spain, provided administrative support and office space during spring semester 2013. I spent much of spring 2013 working at the offices of AHA International Oviedo, the library of the University of Oviedo, and especially Cafetería-Restaurante Flandes, where you can get the best *tortilla española* in town. Large portions of this book were researched and written while I listened to the channel "Drone Zone" on somafm.com, a nonprofit, listener-supported, commercial-free internet radio station.

I had the opportunity to present preliminary versions of a number of chapters at professional meetings, including the International Congress on Medieval Studies, the Modern Language Association, the Midwest Medieval Association, the Mediterranean Seminar (UC Multi-Campus Research Project), and in invited talks at the following institutions: the

Center for Medieval Literature at the University of Southern Denmark, the Department of Romance Languages and Literatures at the University of Notre Dame, the Department of Spanish and Portuguese at the University of Colorado, the Department of French, Italian, and Hispanic Studies at the University of British Columbia, the Abbasi Program in Islamic Studies at Stanford University, the Department of Romance Studies at Cornell University, the Department of Spanish and Portuguese at Princeton University, Consejo Superior de Investigación Científica (CSIC), and the University of Toronto.

Preliminary versions of a number of chapters have appeared in print. Material from chapter 3 appeared in "Vernacular Anxiety and the Semitic Imaginary: Shem Tov Isaac Ibn Ardutiel de Carrión and His Critics" (*Journal of Medieval Iberian Cultural Studies* 4.2: 2012, 167–184). Sections of chapter 5 appear in "Vidal Benvenist's *Efer ve-Dinah* between Hebrew and Romance" (in *A Sea of Languages: Literature and Culture in the Premodern Mediterranean,* ed. Suzanne Akbari and Karla Mallette, 217–231, Toronto: University of Toronto Press, 2013). Sections of chapter 7 are included in a chapter in an edited volume: "Reading *Amadís* in Constantinople: Imperial Spanish Fiction in the Key of Diaspora" (in *In and Of the Mediterranean: Medieval and Early Modern Iberian Studies,* edited by Núria Silleras-Fernández and Michelle Hamilton, Memphis: Vanderbilt University Press, forthcoming). Some material from chapter 7 is also included in "Translation in Diaspora: Sephardic Spanish-Hebrew Translations in the Sixteenth Century" (in *A Comparative History of Literatures in the Iberian Peninsula,* ed. César Domínguez and María José Vega, vol. 2, Amsterdam: Benjamins, forthcoming).

During the time I worked on this book I was invited to a number of venues to speak about preliminary versions of several chapters. My thanks go to the UC Irvine Department of Spanish and Portuguese, the Duke University Department of Romance Studies, the Consejo Superior de Investigación Científica, Princeton University's Department of Spanish, the Vancouver School of Theology, Cornell University's Department of Romance Studies, Stanford University's Abbasi Program in Islamic Studies, the University of British Columbia's Department of French, Hispanic, and Italian Studies, Colorado University's Department of Spanish and Portuguese, Notre Dame University's Department of Romance

Languages and Literatures, Southern Denmark University's Center for Medieval Literature, NYU Abu Dhabi, and UC Berkeley's Department of Spanish and Portuguese. Very special thanks go to the UC Multi-Campus Research Project in Mediterranean Studies/the Mediterranean Seminar, whose quarterly meetings served as workshop and incubator and whose members provided ample intellectual and moral support. Many individual colleagues helped me complete this project, by discussing, reading, commenting, and collaborating in a number of ways. My most heartfelt thanks are due to Suzanne Akbari, Barbara Altmann, Sam Armistead, Judith Baskin, Lars Boje Mortensen, Shamma Boyarin, Olga Davidson, Daniela Flesler, Leonardo García-Pabón, Amalia Gladhart, Margaret Greer, Elise Hansen, Matti Huss, Avi Matalon, Aída Oceransky, Regina Psaki, Kate Regan, Ángel Sáenz-Badillos, Judit Targarona Borrás, Khachig Tölölyan, Janie Zackin, and the anonymous reviewers from *Journal of Spanish Cultural Studies* and *Journal of Medieval Iberian Studies*.

Finally, I would like to thank my partner Katharine Gallagher for her support, advice, insight, and so much more.

A NOTE ON TRANSLATIONS, TRANSLITERATIONS, AND BIBLICAL CITATIONS

Translations are my own unless otherwise indicated. For transliterations of Hebrew and Arabic words I use modified versions of the systems used by *Jewish Quarterly Review* and *Journal of Arabic Literature.* In both languages the letter *ayin* is indicated by the character ʿ-, while Hebrew *alef* and Arabic *hamza* are indicated by a single apostrophe. In some cases I have opted for conventional transliterations of proper names and nouns that are more commonly known in Anglophonia (i.e., Abbasid vs. ʿAbbasid or Abdallah vs. ʿAbd-Allah). When a Hebrew poet has cited a biblical text directly, I indicate the citation in italics and reference the citation in a footnote.

DOUBLE DIASPORA IN
SEPHARDIC LITERATURE

Introduction

Jews in Christian Iberia in the medieval and early modern periods considered themselves to be living in diaspora, descendants of those Hebrews who were exiled from Judea and Samaria, first by the Babylonians and subsequently by the Romans. Their religious and literary culture expressed a diasporic consciousness. As Spaniards they shared many of the aesthetic and cultural values of their Christian neighbors, and as medieval Jews they understood their own history along prophetic lines: they were chosen to suffer the pain of exile, to keep God's law until the arrival of the Messiah. Sephardic poets such as Judah Halevi wrote passionately of returning to Zion, but at the same time these poets were also natives of the Iberian Peninsula, speakers of Spanish and other Romance dialects, and aficionados of local troubadour poetry, knightly romances, folktales and ballads.[1]

In 1492, when the Catholic monarchs Ferdinand and Isabella gave their Jewish subjects the choice between conversion to Catholicism or expulsion, many Sephardic Jews opted to leave their homeland, relocating to North Africa, the Ottoman Empire, or Western Europe. With the expulsion, the Sepharadim, who had always identified as a people living in diaspora from their Biblical homeland, now found themselves in a second diaspora from their native land where their ancestors had lived since before Roman times.[2] Spanish, their native language they once shared with the Christian majority, became a diasporic Jewish language spoken alongside

Turkish or Arabic or Dutch. These two diasporas, from the Holy Land and from Spain, would "echo back and forth" in the Sephardic imagination.[3] This double diaspora gave rise to a new historical consciousness formed in the crucible of Spain's imperial expansion and tinged with a new messianic urgency brought on by the massive changes afoot in the Early Modern Mediterranean: Protestantism, print culture, increasingly sophisticated trade networks, and the expansion of Spain's empire into Western Europe, North Africa, and beyond.

Sephardic Jews gave voice to the experience of double diaspora in their literary culture. Jonathan Decter has written on the transition between Jewish writing in Muslim and Christian Spain in the Middle Ages, and Monique Balbuena has written on diasporic consciousness in modern Sephardic writers.[4] Here my focus is on the transition between medieval Spain and the Sephardic diaspora against the backdrop of Spanish royal and imperial power.

Instead of focusing on the narrative of exile and diaspora as expressed by Sephardic writers, I study the ways in which they negotiate among Jewish, Spanish, and diasporic modes of cultural production. These authors are Jewish in Spain and Spanish abroad. They write troubadour poetry and courtly romances in Hebrew in Toledo; then later, from their homes in Turkey or Italy they write nostalgically about both Sefarad and Zion *as* Sepharadim. Some, whose families converted nominally in 1492 rather than leave their country, receive classical educations as Christians in Spain, later flee the Inquisition to Venice where they can live openly as Jews and write Jewish-themed poetry and plays in a crisp Castilian that might have come from the pen of Cervantes.

The year 1492 (poor, tired 1492) has served as a line dividing Sephardic culture into two distinct pre-Expulsion and post-Expulsion periods. Like gulls fighting over halves of a clam dropped from a distance onto a stretch of pavement, scholars have laid claims to one or another period according to subspecialty and discipline: the historian, the rabbinic scholar, the Hebraist, the Hispanist, the folklorist. My purpose in this study is to try to study the whole clam, to articulate a vision of medieval and early modern Sephardic cultural production that is not definitively split by 1492. The critical lens of diaspora, ironically, can bring together the cultural production of Sephardim before and after their 1492 expulsion from Spain.

In simple terms, *double diaspora* means exactly that: the Sepharadim living on the Iberian Peninsula were in diaspora; they imagined themselves as having come originally from Zion and eventually settled on the peninsula. Then, after 1492 they lived in a second diaspora, one from the Sephardic homeland, the Iberian Peninsula, Sefarad. When we think about diaspora and its relationship to Sephardic cultural production, we are dealing with a multilayered phenomenon, a double diaspora.

The organizing concept of diaspora is especially productive in this case because it allows for a continuity of thought that respects 1492 but is not ruptured by it. That is, 1492 is not, for the diasporic imaginary, an end, but a new beginning. By giving the diasporic imaginary the pride of place, and by celebrating the challenges of diasporic culture as a site of cultural work, we can avoid the tendency to place violence, disaster, and loss at the center of the discussion. When one thinks of cultural production in terms of diaspora, 1492 brings opportunity and growth. It adds a layer of diaspora to the mix. The result is a kind of symbolic synergy through which the tropes of diaspora are reenergized, reorganized, remixed.

In the centuries leading up to 1492 (and in this study I am dealing primarily with the culture of Sepharadim living in Christian-ruled Iberia as opposed to Muslim-ruled al-Andalus), diaspora is a lens through which to study Sephardic culture's engagement with the sovereign power and vernacular culture of Christian Iberia, the "hostland," and the interaction between this engagement and the symbolic attachment to and practice of the cultural structures oriented toward the historic Zionic homeland.

There are (at least) two bodies of scholarship that address the question. The first, carried out primarily by scholars working in the field of Judaic or Jewish Studies, is concerned with the diaspora of the Jews from Zion following the Babylonian captivity and the Roman destruction of the Temple in Jerusalem. Until fairly recently when one spoke or wrote of diaspora it usually meant the Jewish diaspora.

In recent decades, scholars (primarily in the social sciences) have applied the concept of diaspora to a wide range of other experiences: Armenian, African, Indian, Chinese, and so forth. This activity has generated a staggering amount of bibliography and a good deal of polemic. Most recently, a number of meta-studies have come out that critique the abuse of the diasporic lens of inquiry. Not all scholars are in agreement as to which experiences qualify as diasporic. A messy picture indeed, but one worth delving into in our discussion of a series of Sephardic intellectuals working between the thirteenth and sixteenth centuries: Jacob ben Elazar, Todros Abulafia, Shem Tov Ardutiel de Carrión, Vidal Benvenist, Solomon ibn Verga, Joseph Karo, and Jacob Algaba.

While most theorists of diasporas subsequent to the Jewish one are familiar with scholarship on the Jewish diaspora, the converse is rarely true. In this study I wish to demonstrate how insights gained in the study of non-Jewish diasporas can help to shed new light on Sephardic cultural production. In short, I want to make the point that the study of Jewish cultures can benefit from the study of non-Jewish cultures. In doing so, I am speaking to all who are interested in Sephardic and Hispanic history and culture, critical theorists, rabbis, Hebraists, Hispanists, and historians.

In chapter 1, "Diaspora Studies for Sephardic Culture," I provide an overview of critical thought on the idea of diaspora both in Judaic studies and, more broadly, in critical theory and the social sciences. This overview serves as an introduction to a discussion of the problem of *galut* (exile, diaspora) in a series of medieval Sephardic thinkers such as Hasdai ibn Shaprut (tenth century), Abraham ibn Daud (twelfth century), Moses Maimonides (twelfth century), and Judah Halevi (twelfth to thirteenth centuries). In the final section of the chapter, I discuss how an ecumenical theoretical approach to Sephardic culture can nuance our readings of Sephardic culture by approaching it not as specifically Jewish but as categorically diasporic.

The second chapter begins the series of case studies of texts by Sephardic authors. Jacob ben Elazar's thirteenth-century collection of tales shows us two faces of diasporic cultural production. His debate between the sword and the pen maps the specific intellectual and political concerns of the Jewish communities of Castile onto a genre of poetic debate that had long been cultivated to question the relative superiority of temporal versus symbolic power. Ben Elazar redeploys the sword-versus-pen debate of Andalusi literary tradition in the new political landscape of Christian Iberia. The debate is a literary performance of the diasporic community's mediation between Islamic al-Andalus and Christian Castile. In the second example, the tale of Sahar and Kima, Ben Elazar synthesizes the narrative conventions of courtly romance with the Andalusi Hebrew poetic tradition to produce a text with one foot in the Andalusi past and another in the Christian Iberian present, mediating between the biblical and the courtly imaginations. Both of his texts respect the ebb and flow of the local diasporic community while grounding his discourse in the language and habits of expression of the Zionic-centered Hebrew Bible.

Chapter 3 deals with Todros Abulafia (late thirteenth century), a Sephardic poet who worked at the court of Alfonso X ("the Learned") and whose poetry was at times in very close dialogue with the Provençal and Galician-Portuguese troubadours active at court. Like Ben Elazar, Abulafia as a diasporic writer mediated between the cultures of hostland and homeland, and his work is likewise a product of dual symbolic loyalties, to the literary cultures of the Iberian Peninsula and to the Zionic diasporic imaginary. His work is itself the product of two diasporas. The first is that of the Sepharadim, writing in Iberia while facing Zion. The second is the poetic diaspora of the Andalusi lyric tradition that, in exile from al-Andalus, inspired the vernacular lyric of the troubadours, which was later brought back to the courts of Christian Iberia. Abulafia was fully conscious of both of these diasporas and leverages this awareness to produce some of the most innovative Hebrew poetry in the Sephardic tradition.

As conditions for the Sepharadim in Christian-dominated Castile began to deteriorate, the writing of Shem Tov Ardutiel de Carrión (fourteenth century) mediated between the need to respect royal power and the desire to safeguard Sephardic cultural and linguistic autonomy in an age of increasing pressure to convert and assimilate. In chapter 4 I study two of Shem Tov's texts, the Castilian *Proverbios morales* and the Hebrew *Debate between the Pen and Scissors*. In them, Ardutiel expresses a Sephardic resistance toward literary vernacularization while simultaneously complying with the king's request that he produce a Castilian-language compendium of "Jewish" wisdom. In a feat of literary sleight of hand, Shem Tov uses both Hebrew and Castilian to critique the literary use of the vernacular, demonstrating the subtlety and adaptability characteristic of non-sovereign, diasporic cultures caught between two needs: to articulate their diasporic identity, and to acculturate to and accommodate the dominant culture.

In chapter 5 we discuss the work of an author who lived in increasingly difficult times for the Sepharadim. Vidal Benvenist wrote his tale of Efer and Dina at the turn of the fifteenth century, during a period of heightened persecution, when mass conversions to Catholicism were the norm in the Kingdom of Aragon. Like Ben Elazar and Abulafia, he consciously adapts the vernacular literary traditions of the hostland even while delivering a message that shuns the use of the vernacular. Benvenist instructs the reader to cleave to Jewish tradition and remain faithful to the Andalusi Hebrew literary tradition. He clothes his narrative in biblical dress, drawing from the Dina and Esther stories so well-known to his community. At the same time, he makes ample use of themes and motifs common to the vernacular culture of his times: the plaint of the *malmaridada,* or mis-married girl, the vernacular retellings of Dina and Esther, and cultural references specific to the Iberian context. These twin discourses of linguistic and religious resistance and literary and cultural assimilation are a further example of how Sephardic authors negotiated their position as a diasporic minority.

Chapter 6 takes us out of the Iberian Peninsula and into the Sephardic diaspora, the "double diaspora" in which authors such as Solomon ibn Verga and Joseph Karo (sixteenth century) are faced with the task of answering, yet again, "What happened?" In *Shevet Yehudah* (Rod of Judah) Ibn Verga's approach to the problem of diaspora is at once highly literary and social scientific *avant la lettre.* He laces his book, which details the historical persecutions and expulsions of Jewish communities from antiquity to the early sixteenth century, with novelized vignettes and dialogues that, had they been written in Latin or Castilian instead of Hebrew, might have come from the pen of a Christian humanist. At the same time he approaches the question of diaspora from a social scientific perspective, honoring the doctrine of galut and ge'ulah (redemption) while exploring the human psychology behind persecution and discrimination. In the end, for Ibn Verga, human history is more about human action than divine plan. Ibn Verga's contemporary, the great rabbinical scholar and kabbalist Joseph Karo, saw history almost exclusively as divine plan. For Karo, all human history is an earthly reflection of the divine romance between the male and female aspects of God. He and his circle of mystics were not concerned with histories of gentile kings and nations. However, Karo's revolutionary innovation in articulating the divine-human relationship was to place human agency at the center of the divine drama: according to him, God needed human assistance to reunite his male and female halves and bring an end to the Jewish diaspora. Despite their two very different approaches to understanding diaspora, both thinkers were characteristic of their times in that they, like many of their Christian counterparts, assigned a central role to human agency in understanding history.

Chapter 7 deals with Jacob Algaba's 1554 Hebrew translation of the Spanish blockbuster chivalric novel *Amadís de Gaula* (1508). *Amadís* was iconic for a Spain at the dawn of the imperial age, a kind of superhero of empire, onto whom Spanish readers projected their pride in having become masters of an enormous empire and their fears of losing that empire to the Ottoman Turks. Following their expulsion from Spain, the Sepharadim practiced their own form of imperialism as they came to dominate many of the important Jewish communities of the Ottoman Empire. Their cultural and technological superiority stemmed in large part from the high social rank their leadership had attained in Iberian courts. Algaba's Hebrew translation appropriates Amadís, transforming him from avatar of imperial desire into a mark of Sephardic supremacy, refashioning Spanish into Sephardic. Algaba's de-christianization and judaization of the text was a way for Ottoman Sepharadim to proudly identify with the land that had cast them out, but that remained for them the ancestral homeland that lent them their vernacular cultural identity.

Diaspora Studies for Sephardic Culture

[We] were pretending . . . that we had brought a kind of India with us, which we could, as it were, unroll like a carpet on the flat land.

V. S. Naipaul, *Literary Occasions*

The Torah is the portable homeland of the Jews.

Heinrich Heine, *Hebraeische Melodien*

DIASPORA STUDIES FOR SEPHARDIC CULTURE

Diaspora is a Greek word that describes the broad scattering of a people as if they were seeds scattered across several furrows in a field. In its original usage it described the colonization of people dispersing from metropolis to colonies in order to reproduce imperial authority in conquered lands. In the Greek translation of the Hebrew Bible (the Septuagint) it came to mean the dispersion of the Jews from Zion throughout the Mediterranean and Middle East. Since then it has come to be applied to a range of historical scatterings: African, Indian, Chinese, Armenian, and others. Ultimately diasporic culture is a discussion about Here (the hostland) and There (the homeland). What did we take with us from There? What are we doing with it Here? When (and under what circumstances) are we going back There? And what happens when history conspires to make Here a new There?

The seed metaphor is productive for thinking about diasporic culture, because it implies an originary culture (the seed or the DNA contained within it) and the varied expression of that culture when it responds to the resources of the local host culture.[1] Although we tend to emphasize the scattering, and especially the collective longing for the hand that scattered us, or perhaps the plant from which we were originally harvested, I think it is time we emphasized the germinating and taking root in the new soil, watching the unique chemical signature of the new soil give expression to the originary DNA of the seed in a plant that is neither all Here nor all There.

Jewish thinking about diaspora (Hebrew *galut,* exile) is eschatological and providential. The dispersion from There to Here is not merely a story of human action; it is divine plan. It accepts as a given two prophetic ideas: the first, that the Jewish dispersion from Zion is divinely ordained, and the second, that the Jews' eventual return will announce the coming of the Messiah. This approach, cultivated by rabbis and Jewish intellectuals for millennia, persists even in the modern discipline of Judaic studies. Theorists of other, non-Jewish diasporas have borrowed the metaphor but not the prophecy. Their analyses of, for example, Indian diaspora are grounded in the political, social, and psychological circumstances of diasporic cultures. This is not to say, as we will see, that they always move entirely beyond the paradigm of galut and ge'ulah (redemption), but that their starting point is historical and empirical rather than prophetic.

In the middle of the twentieth century, historians of mass migrations of populations of Armenian, African, and other (non-Jewish) populations began adapting the term *diaspora,* referring to the Hebrew abstract noun *galut* (or the concrete noun *golah,* Jewish communities in exile) to describe the experience of these peoples in dispersion. Since these first studies, the semantic field associated with the word *diaspora* has expanded to include a wide variety of groups—ethnic, religious, national, and racial. Indeed, diaspora studies has grown into its own interdisciplinary field—according to one critic, an "academic growth industry"—bridging literature, ethnic studies, anthropology, history, and political science. William Safran and Richard Baumann both complain that the term *diaspora* has been diluted by overuse, while Sudesh Mishra takes Safran to task for proposing overly monolithic, essentialist conceptions of diasporic experience, and James Clifford simply acknowledges the expansion of the term's reach in academic discourse.[2] Scholars have studied the Jewish diaspora for over a century and have recently turned their attention to the diasporas of Africa and India, to broadly conceived comparative studies, and, more generally, to theorizing the effects of diaspora on culture. Ironically, many of these scholars do not acknowledge the genesis of the term in Jewish history.[3] A third wave of studies has focused on mapping and critiquing the various strains and schools of critical thinking on the subject of diaspora.[4] The discussion of diasporic culture has had an important impact in the field of literary and cultural studies, witnessed by the recent publication of scholarly "Diaspora Studies" readers and handbooks.[5]

It is probably no surprise that scholars of diaspora cannot agree on a definition of diaspora. Some insist that it applies only to certain groups and not others.[6] They draw distinctions based on the nature of the dispersion from the homeland (*en masse* or ongoing, catastrophic or opportunistic), on the mode of group identification in diaspora (religious, social, ethnic, national, etc.), or on the discourse of return to the homeland (liturgical ideal, political program, personal goal), among other factors. Much of this argument hinges on the question of essentialism, or whether one can speak of a "diasporic culture" as a discrete unit with fixed characteristics. Critical responses to this question vary widely. Walker Connor confidently widens the semantic field of diaspora to mean "that segment of a people residing outside of the homeland."[7] Khachig Tölölyan finds this trend "problematic," and warns of a "certain danger of biologism," while Stéphane Dufoix's protests that this dilution of the term renders it "theoretically . . . useless."[8]

Brent Edwards points out that when British cultural theorists such as Stuart Hall began to use the term, it was in response to nationalist and racist theories of cultural production. Like Chicano studies or African American studies in the U. S. academy, it was a way to recognize and valorize habits of cultural expression of a given ethnic minority that were seen as at variance with the prevailing national norms formulated by the dominant majority. However, as Sudesh Mishra writes, some diaspora theorists "guardedly repeat [the] ideological ploy" to which Hall and his colleagues were reacting.[9] That is, they ascribe an essentialism to diasporic cultures that smacks of nineteenth-century nationalist discourse. They fall into the trap of reproducing categories of experience and cultural expression that they have inherited from earlier scholarship of national culture, without sufficiently interrogating those categories.

As a corrective, Edwards proposes that we think of diaspora as a "key site of *struggle* over competing articulations," rather than as a single articulation or a single mode of discourse.[10] Sudesh Mishra likewise emphasizes the emergent, iterative, polyphonic, and polysemic nature of diaspora. He inveighs against earlier critics whose "dual territorial" approach to diaspora essentially duplicates a paradigm of Jewish galut and ge'ulah that deprivileges the "itineraries consisting of serial detours and digressions" that for him characterize diaspora but that are disruptive to the "dual territorial" model of exile and return.[11]

For purposes of articulating a theory of double diaspora that spans pre- and post-1492 Sephardic culture, the approach of Khachig Tölölyan, who has written extensively on the Armenian diaspora, is most productive. He proposes a paradigm of diasporic culture based on the following elements:

1) a collective mourning for a trauma that shapes cultural production in diaspora
2) a preservation of elements of the culture of the homeland
3) a rhetoric of "turning and re-turning" toward the homeland (as opposed to an actual return or repatriation)
4) a network of diasporic communities that are characterized by differences among each other and over time[12]

Tölölyan's formulation combines the best of the dual territorial school with sensitivity to the dynamism and emergent nature of social systems. Whereas traditional Jewish scholarship writes of a return to the homeland, whether real or imagined, Tölölyan writes that diasporic people "turn and re-turn" toward the homeland while recognizing that they maintain dynamic attachments to both homeland and hostland.[13] His approach is also compatible with this project because he seeks to draw connections between earlier and later diasporas and, in a broader sense, to think about the social and cultural processes that obtain in diasporas as analogous to emergent forms of culture growing from other transnational, globalizing experiences where identification with a nation state competes with other forms of identification:

> At its best the diaspora is an example, for both the homeland's and the hostland's nation-states, of the possibility of living, even thriving in the regimes of multiplicity which are increasingly the global condition, and a proper version of which diasporas may help to construct, given half a chance. The stateless power of diasporas lies in their heightened aware-ness of both the perils and the rewards of multiple belonging, and in their sometimes exemplary grappling with the paradoxes of such belonging, which is increasingly the condition that non-diasporan nationals also face in the transnational era.[14]

In the same spirit of nuancing the dual-territorial understanding of diaspora, a number of critics have proposed the idea of "double diaspora." This occurs when a significant diasporic community experiences another diaspora from a hostland where they have significant history and to which they have developed a strong cultural affiliation. Some examples of double diaspora would be the diaspora of Indian Parsis or African Jamaicans throughout the Anglophone world, or Armenians or Israelis throughout Europe and North America. In some ways, the Sephardic diaspora has more in common with these modern double diasporas than it does with the original Jewish diaspora from Zion.

To return to Tölölyan's paradigm, there is a traumatic dispersion (the 1492 expulsion) that serves as focus for collective mourning and an inspi-ration for various forms of social organization and cultural production (Sephardic culture). Engagement with theories such as Tölölyan's can be productive for the study of the Jewish diaspora(s), and in particular to the Sephardic diaspora. Theories of non-Jewish diasporas begin with the premise that diasporic cultures are a product of human actions and mundane material and social conditions, which in turn generate symbolic, religious, or spiritual narratives. A diaspora studies approach to Sephardic history allows us to honor the prophetic discourse of traditional Jewish sources while keeping our understanding of cultural production grounded in historical record.

GALUT: HISTORY AS DIVINE PLAN

Galut and its companion ge'ulah are arguably the single most important concepts in Jewish history. The experience of exile in its material,
spiritual, and artistic inflections has made Jewish culture what it is. Major
historians of Jewish culture have made this point more authoritatively
than I. Yitzhak Baer, writing for a popular audience in his book *Galut*
(1947), put it very succinctly: "The problem of being a Jew is inseparably
bound up with the Galut."[15] Ten years later, Salo Baron concurred that
Jewish history is a history of galut and that the Jewish religion itself would
be "unthinkable" without the drama of "chosenness" that is essential for
redemption from exile.[16]

The concept of galut that is essential in shaping Jewish culture over
the centuries has also been the single most influential principle behind
modern Jewish historiography. This is no accident: it was also, not surprisingly, the single most influential principle behind premodern Jewish historiography. Although modern historians of the Jewish experience
imagined themselves as dispassionate scientific observers and interpreters
of Jewish history, they had (and continue to have) something in common with their predecessors, a residual understanding of Jewish history
as prophetic that has continued to influence modern academic thinking
about Jewish diasporas.

Jewish historical consciousness has always been bound up with no-
tions of prophecy and divine will. The Hebrew Bible is filled with scenes
in which God plainly states that Israel (the biblical nation, not the modern
nation-state) has been selected to carry out a divine mission and that the
existence of that nation *is* prophecy. This galut consciousness that becomes
so crucial to Jewish culture in diaspora is anticipated in the early books
of the Hebrew Bible (*Tanakh*). The themes of wandering and expulsion
dominate the book of Genesis through its series of narratives of expulsion,
wandering, and return.[17] Adam and Eve are expelled from Eden, but are
able to redeem themselves through work and childbirth. Cain is banished
from his home and condemned to wander the earth, but is protected by
God in his exile. Noah and his family are consigned to float aimlessly during the flood, but land at Ararat with a rainbow backdrop that portends

a good relationship between God and humankind. Abraham sets forth from Ur to find Canaan, a land that God claims to have reserved for him, pending the covenant of circumcision. Joseph's sojourns in Egypt end well for him but eventually his descendants are enslaved by the Pharaohs.

Deuteronomy is a more unified narrative that sets the stage for an eventual homecoming to the Promised Land, a metaphysical reversal of Adam and Eve's movement from Paradise to exile.[18] This narrative is continually updated in subsequent books that keep pace with historical realities of diaspora and colonial domination. For example, Esther deals with the problem of living as a minority community in diaspora in Persia. The rabbis pick up where the Old Testament leaves off, though their mode is more pragmatic (Leviticus) and less dramatic (Exodus). Living under colonial domination of the Holy Land requires a slightly different skill set, one to which the Mishnaic tractate Avodah Zara (Idol Worship) speaks. In it, the rabbis explain the how-to's of living among gentiles, even in the Holy Land itself.[19]

The rub has always been that it seems the Jews were chosen for a perfectly good reason, but that prophetic distinction does not necessarily carry over into social or material privilege. It hardly bears repeating that Jewish history, even in the most dispassionate retelling, is a history full of sorrows. This conflictive existence, born of divine blessing but lived as constant persecution, has been, according to Amos Funkenstein, a "source of perpetual amazement" to the Jews themselves, who generate new and improved explanations and interpretations for the marvel of their own survival.[20]

This historiographical tendency has deep roots in scripture and liturgy. The history of the Jews begins with the Hebrew Bible itself, which contains a whole series of books written in various genres that tell the history of Israel. They are, on the whole, narratives, some of them highly novelized, with only moments of somber chronicling such as the famously stultifying genealogical interludes popularly known as the "begats." The book of Chronicles contains a few accounts of major battles in addition to royal genealogies, but there is nothing in the Tanakh on the order of a Herodotus or a Livy. Even the books that are broadly historical are highly novelized, the best example of which would be the book of Esther. We might take these as early examples of what Amos Funkenstein calls "counterhistories." He writes:

Counterhistories form a specific genre of history written since antiquity.
... Their function is polemical. Their method consists of the systematic
exploitation of the adversary's most trusted sources against their grain.
... Their aim is the distortion of the adversary's self-image, of his identity,
through the deconstruction of his memory.[21]

In this study we will be talking about sovereignty and especially the
importance of the Jewish relationship to sovereignty for understanding
Sephardic cultural production. This question lies at the heart of the problem of diaspora and is particularly important in understanding the diasporic imaginary, the ways in which living in diaspora shapes the symbolic
work of the community. This is as true for historiography as it is for poetry
and belles lettres.

The dearth of premodern Jewish historiography hinges on the question
of sovereignty. The writers and compilers of the Hebrew Bible, especially
those who produced its Masoretic (canonical) text, lived in diaspora. They
were not working in the service of a royal court with temporal power.
Kings did not mobilize armies based on interpretations of their official
histories. Rather, they were religious scholars who were working to produce a stable, authoritative liturgy and jurisprudence. The history that
appears in their texts was not produced to serve the ideology of a kingdom
or a nation-state, but rather that of an ethnic group who lived under the
political domination of kingdoms and nations of different religions and
who believed themselves to be ethnically, and to varying degrees, culturally distinct from the Jews who lived among them.

Jewish history as it appears in the Tanakh, then, is not mediated by
royal or political institutions (that do not exist within the Jewish communities) but by religious institutions. Jews experienced their own history as liturgy, as exegesis, but not as history. When they read (or hear) in
1 Chronicles (29:26–27) that King David reigned for forty years, it is not
part of a narrative that aims to legitimize the reign of the current king,
for there is no current king, at least not a Jewish one. Instead, it is part
of the story of a people's relationship to God and their struggle to align
themselves with divine will.[22]

The liturgical and exegetical experience of what history is contained in
the Tanakh (Hebrew Bible) is also important in understanding why Jewish attitudes toward historiography evolved as they have. The first section
of the Tanakh (the Torah) is read aloud in the synagogue in weekly *para-*

shot (portions or sections) on Mondays, Thursdays, and Saturdays. This means that the observant Jew (and during the period in question we can assume a fairly high level of observance among literate Jews) associated history with worship, communal service, and the celebration of festivals. Not only were the events narrated in the Tanakh motivated by divine will, Jewish history itself was a divine commandment enacted through a cyclical liturgical calendar. In traditional Judaism, the communal study of Torah is required of every Jewish male, three times a week, every week of every year.[23]

Diasporic culture also gave rise to a particular sort of exegetic historiography by which rabbis, in the course of their systematic commentary of a given biblical text, subordinated historical material to organizing principles of biblical exegesis, usually abstracting lessons for moral or religious conduct from the exploits of patriarchs, matriarchs, kings, prophets, and other elite figures. But they did not engage in the kind of proto–political science that we see in historiographical texts written for temporal authorities.[24] For Jews, then, history was not history as we imagine it today. It was prophecy, divine writ, exegesis, and liturgy. With few exceptions (and important ones such as we will see further on), these experiences dominated Jewish historical consciousness until the nineteenth century. We should therefore not be surprised that modern academic practitioners of Jewish historiography persisted in some of the prophetic habits of thought developed by their rabbinic predecessors during long centuries of Torah study.

By the medieval period, when Christian and Muslim societies were very actively developing royal historiographies in the service of political ideology, very few texts that looked like chronicles and histories emanated from the Jewish communities of Christendom and Dar al-Islam. Yosef Yerushalmi writes, in his frequently cited study of premodern Jewish historiography, *Zakhor*, that Jews did not really cultivate historiography in the Middle Ages.[25] According to him, this was not due to any intellectual deficit or inability to produce historiography, for it is well documented that they made significant advances and innovations in other literary and theological genres, but rather to disinterest. The rabbis had long ago laid out the "essential contours of the relations between Jews and gentiles," and consequently there was "little or no [Jewish] interest in the history of contemporary gentile nations."[26] That is, if writing official histories was the purview of courts and sovereign states, then the stateless Jews had no reason to write them. Instead of cultivating historiography, Jewish communities encoded their temporal historical consciousness in *responsa* literature, the open letters written by leading rabbis in response to questions regarding the particulars of Jewish conduct.[27] The considerations of daily life (technology, political shifts, changing relations with non-Jews, the marketplace, the many-faceted engagement with the dominant cultures) that are largely suppressed in exegetical texts are all found here in robust detail, so much so that Jewish historians have exploited responsa as fertile sources for the study of Jewish communities.[28]

It is not insignificant that the birth of modern Jewish historiography (taking the sixteenth-century corpus studied by Yerushalmi as a starting point) was a reaction to the expulsions from Spain and Portugal, and therefore focused disproportionately on that aspect of the Jewish experience. History is not always written by the winners, and in the case of Jewish historiography, the experience in Spain cast a long shadow over Jewish approaches to modern history well into the twentieth century. Robert Chazan aptly points out that just as modern historians such as Salo Baron were questioning this tendency, the all-too-modern experience of Nazism and Holocaust reinforced the "lachrymose" approach.[29]

PROPHETIC HANGOVER: TAKING A SECOND LOOK AT JEWISH HISTORY AS GALUT

Amos Funkenstein, a highly influential Jewish historian who has trained a number of students who themselves became influential in the field, questions his nineteenth-century predecessors' claims to impartiality. He reminds us that Jewish historians, even those of the nineteenth century, were still Jewish, and as such shaped by intellectual habits they inherited from traditional Judaism. He asks, "[H]ow deeply did the radical historicization of Judaism separate scholars from 'collective' Jewish memory? [Yosef] Yerushalmi thought that this separation became almost total. I doubt it."[30]

Funkenstein's student David Biale challenges us to rethink the role of galut in our approach to Jewish history. His emphasis on a shift from "Judaism" to "Jewish culture" privileges human activity over divine revelation as an organizing historical principle. For him, the doctrine of chosenness that characterizes traditional approaches to Jewish history is translated, in the modern academic scene, into a form of institutional parochiality. For Biale, Judaic studies has become "careerist and conformist."[31] The academic enterprise should be about expanding the field of inquiry, about challenging received wisdom, not idolizing it, he argues. He challenges the field to take up the gauntlet thrown down by the towering figure of kabbalah scholarship, Gershom Scholem, who in Biale's words sought to "explode the comfortable myths in which modern Judaism cloaks itself." He asks us to "criticize the field of Jewish studies for both its antiquitarianism and conservatism."[32]

To this end Biale proposes that we focus our inquiry not on Judaism per se but rather on Jewish culture. Judaism as a religion will always privilege prophecy, and therefore a historiography focused on religion will always be out of step with the values of the contemporary academy. This focus on what he calls "the theology of Jewish uniqueness" results in a kind of intellectual solipsism, a tendency to imagine Jewish history as having "evolve[d] in some splendid isolation from the rest of the world, at the most pausing to fend off alien influences."[33] Likewise, the Spanish Hebraist Ángel Sáenz-Badillos has made similar remarks about the parochialism of Judaic studies, citing the field's "ideologically and nationalistically laden perspective" and its publication of studies based on "exclusivist" points of view that ignore all sources outside of the Jewish ones.[34] To counter this trend, Biale proposes a historiography focused on culture, on human concerns and motivations, on the activities of Jews as determined not by prophecy but by worldly vicissitudes: those of the crown, the state, the marketplace, the family, and so forth.[35]

ZIONISM AND GALUT

At just about the same time, Daniel and Jonathan Boyarin issue another challenge to the legitimacy of galut as a basis for Jewish historiography, this one more explicitly rooted in frustration with the shortcomings of political Zionism. For them, Jewish culture is incompatible with political hegemony, having been formed in periods of nomadism, settled tribal power-sharing, and finally diaspora outside of the homeland. They assert that the failure of political Zionism to establish a harmonious, stable, and equitable state in the homeland demands an alternative approach. They propose diaspora "as a theoretical and historical model to replace national self-determination."[36]

Boyarin and Boyarin argue that Jewish culture is a product of three stages of historical development, none of which included a successful hegemonic nation state. Abraham and the patriarchs were first nomadic clans in the Arabian desert and lands in the general area of what is today Israel, Palestine, and Jordan. After the life of Joseph and until the exodus, they lived as an ethnic and religious minority living in Egypt, and then again as desert nomads. Even after the Israelites entered the Promised Land they lived among other tribal cultures of the area and mixed with them. There was, according to them, no Jewish hegemonic political power in the region until the Davidic dynasty, which "symbolically overturned" the historical de-territoriality of Jewish culture.[37] Accordingly, Jewish culture is not equipped to provide the grounding for a hegemonic state such as modern Israel, because Jewish culture is far better at mixing with surrounding cultures, sharing power, and redefining itself emergently:

> The Rabbis produced their cultural formation within conditions of Diaspora, and we would argue that their particular discourse of ethnocentricity is ethically appropriate only when the cultural identity is an embattled (or, at any rate, nonhegemonic) minority. The point is not that the Land was devalued by the Rabbis but that they renounced it until the final redemption; in an unredeemed world, temporal dominion and ethnic particularity are impossibly compromised.[38]

Boyarin and Boyarin point out that traditional rabbinical authorities, until very recently, have always stressed that the House of David cannot be reestablished until the arrival of the Messiah. In light of this doctrine, any attempt to reestablish Jewish political hegemony in the homeland is "a human arrogation of a work that only God should or could perform."[39]

Diaspora is a productive model for the de-territorialization of identity. The uncoupling of national identity from political nationalism is a way out of many current political struggles. Boyarin and Boyarin provide an excellent example for how a reassessment of diaspora in Jewish history can generate radical and far-reaching new insights into existing data. For example, their reading of biblical history as the story of nomadism, permeable tribalism, and global diaspora that were not always the product of violent displacement turns galut on its head, substituting the temporal for the prophetic as an organizing principle. In particular, their assertion that rabbinic Judaism, even in Palestine, often preferred colonial political domination completely deconstructs one of the core tenets of the doctrine of galut, namely that diaspora and statelessness are a divine punishment and not a human phenomenon:

> Diaspora is not the forced product of war and destruction—taking place after the downfall of Judea—but that already in the centuries before this downfall, the majority of Jews lived voluntarily outside of the Land. Moreover, given a choice between domination by a "foreign" power who would allow them to keep the Torah undisturbed and domination by a "Jewish" authority who would interfere with religious life, the Pharisees and their successors the Rabbis generally chose the former.[40]

Rabbinic doctrine stipulates that Jewish statehood cannot recur until the arrival of the Messiah. There was a narrative of return, but it was a return that only God could set in motion. The role of the Jews (and this finds expression in messianic strains of Judaism from the Middle Ages forward) was to keep the commandments and wait patiently for the Messiah's arrival, at which time the Temple in Jerusalem might be rebuilt.[41]

Most recently, Robert Chazan has questioned the trend in Jewish historiography of focusing on the suffering and persecution of Jewish communities in medieval Western Europe. He follows Baron in this gesture. While taking care not to minimize the role of persecution and suffering in medieval Jewish history, Chazan argues that they cannot be the defining characteristics of Jewish experience. That is, while liturgy and the Jewish artistic imaginary represent galut as suffering and as a diminished state, the reality as Jews lived it did not always correspond.[42]

In light of these voices urging a reassessment of our understanding of the validity of galut as a lens for modern historiography, some scholars have returned to antiquity to take a second look at the sources. Even before Biale, Boyarin and Boyarin, and others issue their rallying cries for new approaches in Judaic studies, Gerald Serotta writes that according to rabbinical evidence from late antiquity, diasporic Jewish communities were not characterized by actual suffering and actual longing to return to Zion. Quite the contrary; Galut Bavel (the diasporic community of Babylon, whose descendants became Persian and then Iraqi Jews) was an affluent community that boasted the most authoritative rabbinic academies in the Jewish world. If, as Heinrich Heine so famously wrote, the Torah is the portable homeland of the Jews, then it follows that the most important center of Torah studies is the literal homeland of the community, and Zion the symbolic homeland. To wit, the Talmud Bavli (Babylonian) quotes one Rabbi Judah as saying that "whoever goes up from Babylonia to the Land of Israel transgresses a positive commandment."[43]

Babylon's prestige as a center for Jewish learning was so respected that it acquired the status of a kind of second Jerusalem, one born out in rabbinical decisions. In some cases, laws that were applied in Jerusalem were also applied equally in Babylon—but not in the rest of the diaspora.[44] Diaspora (even galut) turns out to be about politics. The Babylonian academy was more successful and more prestigious because it enjoyed more favorable political conditions under Parthian rule than did the Jerusalem academy under Roman rule. The exilarch (the chief rabbi of Babylonian Jewry) was a ranking Parthian official and commanded military force to execute his decisions. By contrast, the patriarch (chief rabbi of Jerusalem) had no Roman military command and was at the mercy of the Roman colonial government.[45] This contrast would not surprise any student of modern colonialisms and imperialisms; a powerful indigenous political and spiritual leader poses much more of a threat to a colonial government than a minority leader living in the metropolis. What is relevant for this discussion is that it goes against the galut narrative of Zion as the only authentic Jewish homeland, spiritual or otherwise.

According to Gerald Serotta, the Talmud is quite clear on the legal (rabbinical) question of Zion's purity; it derives from the presence of the *shekhinah*—God's feminine immanence on earth—in the land and from the sanctifying practice of the biblical commandments by Jews resident in Zion.[46] Serotta's approach is very useful for the study of Sephardic galut because it is sensitive to the importance of the relationship between the diasporic communities and imperial power. To the Romans, Palestinian

Jewry was an indigenous population with a long history of native sovereignty. They were less governable than the Babylonian Jews because their relationship to the imperium was always problematic (much like that of the indigenous Americans to their European conquerors). In short, they were not a diasporic population, and so their institutions had not evolved in a situation where they were subject.

MEDIEVAL SEPHARDIC VOICES OF GALUT

The doctrine of galut found expression in nearly every form of Jewish literature, from rabbinic writings to profane poetry. Most sources deploy traditional tropes of oppression, martyrdom, and suffering that form the building blocks of the discourse of galut.[47] Some of the medieval Sephardic sources, however, display a different disposition and occasionally belie the relatively comfortable circumstances of the Jewish communities of Sefarad.

One of the most striking examples is the letter of Hasdai ibn Shaprut to Joseph, the King of the Khazars.[48] Ibn Shaprut lived during the tenth century, the golden age of the Cordovan Caliphate under the reign of Abd ar-Rahman III. Ibn Shaprut rose to a very high position at court and was de facto minister of foreign affairs to the Caliph. In this capacity, he corresponded with Joseph, king of the Khazars, a nation in the Caucasus that had collectively converted to Judaism following the example of their king. This unique example of Jewish sovereignty captivated the Sephardic imagination. As Esperanza Alfonso notes, Shaprut's letter begins with the requisite tropes of galut (nomadism, statelessness), but also concedes that the situation of the Andalusi Jews (for the moment) is generally positive:[49]

> How, indeed, can an idea be expressed in fair words by those who have wandered, after the glory of the kingdom has departed; who have long suffered afflictions and calamities, and see their flags in the land no more? We, indeed, who are of the remnant of the captive Israelites, servants of my lord the King, are dwelling peacefully in the land of our sojourning, for our God has not forsaken us, nor has His shadow departed from us.[50]

But the section where Ibn Shaprut quizzes Joseph on the geopolitical realities of the Jewish Khazari kingdom is more revealing of Ibn Shaprut's fascination with the possibility of Jewish sovereignty:

What walled cities and what open towns it has; whether it be watered by artificial or natural means, and how far his dominion extends and also the number of his armies and leaders? Let not my lord take it ill, I pray, that I enquire about the number of his forces. May the Lord add unto them, how many soever they be, an hundredfold.... My lord sees that I enquire about this with no other object than that I may rejoice when I hear of the increase of the holy people.[51]

It is as if Ibn Shaprut can scarcely believe that the dream of Jewish sovereignty is real. All his life he has read about a Jewish kingdom in the Tanakh, has listened to rabbis discuss the loss of the Jewish kingdom, has lamented its loss during Tisha B'Av, has sung hopefully of its eventual renewal at Passover. Suddenly, he learns that far away, a Jewish king rules over a substantial territory between the Black and Caspian Seas. Apart from the usual interest in politics one would expect from a diplomat, his personal curiosity as a Jew is understandable. It shows us that the official discourse of galut was always in tension with political realities, whether dealing with the political vicissitudes of a diasporic community such as Andalusi Jews or with the possibility or impossibility of Jewish sovereignty in Zion (or elsewhere, as in the case of Khazaria). As we can see from Ibn Shaprut's letter, the example of the Jewish Khazari kingdom captivated the Sephardic imagination and was later, as we will see, the subject of an important treatise on religion by the eleventh-century intellectual Judah Halevi.

If Ibn Shaprut is concerned with sovereignty and conditions of Jewish life in diaspora, the following example from twelfth-century writer Abraham Ibn Daud speaks to the evolution of diasporic institutions, namely the establishment of four rabbinic academies in different parts of the Mediterranean. Ibn Daud was born in and lived in Toledo and is best known for his chronicle of rabbinic authority, *Sefer Ha-qabbalah* (Book of Tradition). The book's purpose is to legitimize the tradition of rabbinic Judaism in the face of Karaite skepticism. Ibn Daud's strategy is to document the transmission of Jewish religious authority from Moses to the most prominent Spanish rabbis of his day. It is very much the product of a diasporic culture. While it retains the structure of a chronicle, it is concerned not with gentile temporal power (kings and queens, successions and lineages) but with the highest authorities *within* the diasporic communities of Mediterranean Jewry: rabbis.

In one anecdote, Ibn Daud tells the tale of the four sages who founded four separate rabbinic academies around the Mediterranean. It explains how rabbinic authority migrated from the Babylonian academy (the seat of the exilarch, the rabbinic authority outside of Palestine) to four cities around the Mediterranean. This is significant because the result is the redistribution of religious authority throughout the region, creating a network of important academies in place of a centralized authority in Baghdad or Palestine.[52] The anecdote bears repeating in full here:

> The commander of a fleet, whose name was Ibn Rumahis, left Cordova, having been sent by the Muslim king of Spain, 'Abd ar-Rahman an-Nasir. This commander of a mighty fleet set out to capture the ships of the Christians and the towns that were close to the coast. They sailed as far as the coast of Palestine, and swung about to the Greek sea and the islands therein. [Here] they encountered a ship carrying four great scholars, who were traveling from the city of Bari to a city called Sefastin, and who were on their way to a Kallah convention. Ibn Rumahis captured the ship and took the sages prisoner. One of them was R. Hushiel, the father of Rabbenu Hananel; another was R. Moses, the father of R. Hanok, who was taken prisoner with his wife and son, R. Hanok (who at the time was but a young lad); the third was R. Shemariah b. R. Elhanan. As for the fourth, I do not know his name. The commander wanted to violate R. Moses' wife, inasmuch as she was exceedingly beautiful. Thereupon, she cried out in Hebrew to her husband, R. Moses, and asked him whether or not those who drown in the sea will be quickened at the time of the resurrection of the dead. He replied unto her: "The Lord said: I will bring them back from Bashan; I will bring them back from the depths of the sea." Having heard his reply, she cast herself into the sea and drowned.
>
> These sages did not tell a soul about themselves or their wisdom. The commander sold R. Shemariah in Alexandria of Egypt; [R. Shemariah] proceeded to Fostat where he became head [of the academy]. Then he sold R. Hushiel on the coast of Ifriqiya. From there the latter proceeded to the city of Qairawan, which at that time was the mightiest of all Muslim cities in the land of the Maghreb, where he became the head [of the academy] and where he begot his son Rabbenu Hananel. Then the commander arrived at Cordova where he sold R. Moses along with R. Hanok. He was redeemed by the people of Cordova, who were under the impression that he was a man of no education. Now there was in Cordova a synagogue that was called the College Synagogue, where a judge by the name of R. Nathan the Pious, who was a man of distinction, used to preside. However,

the people of Spain were not thoroughly versed in the words of our rabbis, of blessed memory. Nevertheless, with the little knowledge they did possess, they conducted a school and interpreted [the traditions] more or less [accurately]. Once R. Nathan explained [the law requiring] "immersion [of the finger] for each sprinkling," which is found in the [Talmudic] tractate Yoma, but he was unable to explain it correctly. Thereupon, R. Moses, who was seated in the corner like an attendant, arose before R. Nathan and said to him, "Rabbi, this would result in an excess of immersions!" When he and the students heard his words, they marveled to each other and asked him to explain the law to them. This he did quite properly. Then each of them propounded to him all the difficulties which they had, and he replied to them out of the abundance of his wisdom.

Outside the College there were litigants, who were not permitted to enter until the students had completed their lesson. On that day, R. Nathan the Judge walked out, and the litigants followed him. However, he said to them: "I am no longer judge. This man, who is garbed in rags and is a stranger, is my master, and I shall be his disciple from this day on. You ought to appoint him judge of the community of Cordova." And that is exactly what they did. The community then assigned him a large stipend and honored him with costly garments and a carriage. [At that point] the commander wished to retract his sale. However, the King would not permit him to do so, for he was delighted by the fact that the Jews of his domain no longer had need of the people of Babylonia.

The report [of all this] spread throughout the land of Spain and the Maghreb, and students came to study under him. Moreover, all the questions which had formerly been addressed to the academies were now directed to him. This affair occurred in the days of R. Sherira, in about 4750, somewhat more or less.[53]

This passage is key in establishing a narrative of diaspora in the Iberian context. First, it recalls other, biblical foundational narratives of dispersion that explain different typologies or taxonomies. The first is the Noahic story of the origins of ethnicities, in which each of the sons of Noah migrates to a different continent to father a distinct race (Genesis 10).[54] The next chapter of Genesis relates the Tower of Babel story (Genesis 11:1–9), which explains global linguistic diversity. The marriage of these archetypes in the story of the four captives to the folkloric motif of the false beggar who is actually of noble blood (with the patently Jewish twist substituting scholarly prowess for nobility) is particularly compelling.[55] Just as the Babylonian community looked for historical narratives that

would reinforce the authority of their academies vis-à-vis the Palestinian academies, Ibn Daud here establishes the authority of the Cordovan
academy and its independence from the Babylonian.[56]

This episode is particularly relevant to a diaspora studies approach to
Sephardic culture because it demonstrates two of the key facets of diasporic identity formation as defined by critics such as Robin Cohen and
Khachig Tölölyan: the relationship between the diaspora community and
the host sovereignty, and the relationship between the diasporic community and the other parts of the diaspora. The fact that this dispersion
was carried out by *force* (the four rabbis were captured by pirates) in the
context of a Mediterranean economic system is not coincidental, but consonant with previous narratives of the Babylonian captivity, with the idea
that the Jewish galut is a state of oppression, captivity, and expulsion.
While this is a longstanding commonplace, one with significant symbolic value, it is not necessarily historically accurate.[57] It is notable that
the (Muslim) king takes great pleasure in the new prestige of Cordova's
talmudic academy, and Ibn Daud's text registers a consciousness of the
political implications of this turn of events.

It would be irresponsible, in any discussion of diaspora and Sephardic
culture, to leave out the writings of Judah Halevi, the towering intellectual
figure of Spanish Jewry in the transition between Muslim and Christian
rule in Castile.[58] Halevi was a native of Tudela (not Toledo as some have
claimed) and is considered one of the most important poets in Hebrew
tradition. In addition, he was an accomplished philosopher and rabbinical thinker, whose Arabic-language religious polemic, *Kitab al-Kuzari*
(Book of the Khazari), dealt with the theological implications of galut in
a novel way: Halevi sets his discussion of the relative merits of Judaism,
Islam, and Christianity in a fictional dialogue between the King of the
Khazars (the same to whom Hasdai ibn Shaprut wrote his famous letter
cited above) and a rabbi, the fictional avatar of Halevi himself.[59] The king
of the Khazars is looking to adopt a new religion and interviews a rabbi,
a priest, and a faqi to aid him in making an informed choice. This way of
framing the debate belies Halevi's preoccupation with the question of
sovereignty, because it ingeniously sidesteps the question of galut and
prophecy by representing Judaism as a hypothetical state religion for a
state other than Zion. Halevi is not in danger of transgressing the traditional doctrine of galut according to which there can be no Jewish state

without the Messiah, because the state in question is not the traditionally imagined post-messianic Jewish state in Zion. The Jewish Khazari state is not, strictly speaking, diasporic.

Halevi in the *Kuzari* takes the original seed metaphor of diaspora seriously. Jews are the seeds that spread the true religion abroad to prepare the world for the Messiah. Even Christianity and Islam spring from the seed of Judaism, though the current adherents distance themselves.[60] With the arrival of the Messiah, the three monotheistic religions will be reunited: "The nations merely serve to introduce and pave the way for the expected Messiah, who is the fruition, and they will all become His fruit. Then, if they acknowledge Him, they will become one tree."[61]

This messianic narrative puts diaspora and the inevitable cultural assimilation in a positive light. Although it may seem that the Jews are assimilating and taking on the cultural identities of the lands where they make their homes, they are in effect undercover, waiting for the moment when they will marshal all the peoples of the earth into a new age, at which point the nations will assimilate to the Jews' divine mission. This narrative subverts the Christian doctrine of Israel's moral decrepitude. Medieval Christian doctrine understood galut as God's way of showing what happens to a people who denies the true Messiah. The Jews, according to many medieval Christian theologians, were allowed to persist in their faith only to serve as a negative example by which one might explain all the ill that was heaped upon them by Christian rulers and neighbors.[62]

In the *Kuzari*, the suggestion of a viable Jewish kingdom, even of one that was not part of biblical history, could be seen as a nod toward the messianic promise of a restored kingdom in Jerusalem, the fulfillment of the prophecy recited in the daily liturgy that one day all nations will "accept the yoke of Thy kingdom."[63] In the end, Halevi must have decided that life in galut was intolerable, for as he grew older he penned a series of (now very famous) poems expressing his longing for Zion and depicting his pilgrimage to Jerusalem. This amounted to more than poetic speculation. In the 1160s Halevi actually made the decision to leave Spain and to move to Palestine, after time spent in Egypt, where he lived out the rest of his days.[64]

Contrary to what one might think after reading Halevi's depiction of a Jewish state in the *Kuzari*, Halevi's pilgrimage or return to Palestine was in no way political. He did not advocate for the large-scale settlement of Palestine by Jews, nor does his Zionic poetry seem to call for a reconstitution of the Jewish kingdom or reconstruction of the Temple. Raymond Scheindlin notes that Halevi's poems of Zion (with the one exception of "Ode to Zion") are "devoid of messianic material" and give voice to a "personal religious vision" rather than a theological or political ideology.[65] We should not, however, read the *Kuzari* as a monolithic expression of Halevi's views on return to Zion. Yochanan Silman points out that Halevi contradicts himself on this issue even within the *Kuzari* itself, arguing at one point that (in accordance with prevailing rabbinic opinion) one should happily accept the burden of exile; in another section he argues that this acceptance will only delay the coming of the Messiah (and therefore the return to Zion).[66]

Given this personal religious orientation, it is helpful to read Halevi's poems of pilgrimage in the context of Christian poems and songs of pilgrimage to the Cathedral of St. James in Santiago de Compostela, which in Halevi's day was the second most important pilgrimage route in Western Christendom (after Rome) and which passed through the region of Navarre where Halevi is thought to have been born.[67] Rudolph writes that the "urge to undertake pilgrimage was at its strongest" precisely during the eleventh and twelfth centuries, when Halevi lived. [68] During this period, literature depicting and promoting pilgrimage to Santiago flourished, such as Gonzalo de Berceo's *Milagros de Nuestra Señora* and the *Codex Calixtinus,* known also as the *Libro de Santiago.*[69] This fact in itself suggests that even in the act of expressing a desire to return to the Holy Land, Jewish poets revealed the extent to which they were implicated in the artistic culture of their hostlands.

MOSES MAIMONIDES

If Halevi chose to leave a Spain that was on the balance a good place for Jews to live, Maimonides' experience was one of flight from persecution. In 1148 the intolerant Almohad dynasty conquered his hometown of Cordova, after which his family spent some ten years avoiding Almohad-controlled areas of al-Andalus. They eventually settled in Fez.[70] Moses ben Maimun (Maimonides, the Rambam) was a highly prolific and influential rabbi-philosopher from Cordova. Despite being a great champion of the rationalist philosophy that Halevi takes to task in the *Kuzari,* Maimonides nonetheless coincides with Halevi on several important points in his own understanding of galut.[71] He expands on Halevi's idea that Jews' collective mission is to serve as a witness for the true faith. In his *Epistle to Yemen,* Maimonides stresses that galut is a trial and that the persecutions and humiliations that Jews face living among gentiles constitute a process of purification by which only those who are strongest in their religion will prosper and live to prepare the world for the eventual coming of the Messiah. Spero reads this as the elevation of personal and collective suffering to a "theological principle . . . applied . . . to the historical posture of the Jewish people in *galut* as a whole."[72] All of this is divinely ordained by a God who has set Israel apart and made it different from the other nations for this very purpose:

> God has made us unique by His laws and precepts, and our preeminence is manifested in His rules and statutes, as Scripture says, in narrating God's mercies to us, 'And what great nation is there, that hath statutes and ordinances so righteous as all this law, which I set before you this day?' (Deuteronomy 4:8). Therefore all the nations instigated by envy and impiety rose up against us, and all the kings of the earth motivated by injustice and enmity applied themselves to persecute us. They wanted to thwart God, but He cannot be thwarted. Ever since the time of the Revelation, every despot or slave that has attained to power, be he violent or ignoble, has made it his first aim and his final purpose to destroy our law, and to vitiate our religion, by means of the sword, by violence, or by brute force, such as Amalek, Sisera, Sennacherib, Nebuchadnezzar, Titus, Hadrian, may their bones be ground to dust, and others like them.[73]

Despite his personal experience of exile from al-Andalus, Maimonides did not ever take the inward, mystical turn that was the reaction of many other Jewish thinkers to a political reality of powerlessness and persecution. Perhaps this was because as an adult Maimonides was always well situated as a court physician under the Mamluk Sultan at Fustat (Old Cairo). In any event, his *Epistle to the Jews of Yemen* would be very influential on further Jewish thought on the metaphysical discussion of living in galut.

For Jews who lived under less favorable circumstances, such as in Provence in the twelfth century, Catalonia in the thirteenth, and Castile in the late thirteenth and fourteenth, the kabbalistic tradition evolved as a spiritual response to life in diaspora. Rachel Elior writes that "a spiritual response to historical changes and iniquity was the only avenue left open to the Jewish communities that possessed neither political power nor military force throughout the course of their long exile."[74] The theosophical approach afforded by kabbalah held out the promise that human experience could not be explained by biblical commentary and rabbinical jurisprudence alone.[75] For the kabbalist, creation (and consequently human history, galut, etc.) was not simply the story of the relationship between God and humankind. There was a hidden narrative available to only the most learned and disciplined among Jewish scholars, a narrative that spoke of the relationship between the female divine presence (shekhinah) and the Jewish people. According to this narrative, the shekhinah is sent by God to accompany the Jews in their exile and to protect them until the redemption.[76] In the beginning, practitioners of this style of esoteric theosophy insisted that it be limited to only the most learned Jewish men of a mature age, for some of the imagery and ideas it employs would be considered heresies in the context of normative liturgy and *halakha* (Jewish law).

The catastrophic experiences surrounding the expulsions from Spain (1492) and Portugal (1497) caused Jews to rethink their experience. This had significant repercussions for how they conceived of prophetic eschatology as expressed in kabbalistic writing and also for Jewish law and the emergent genre of Jewish historiography. One such potentially dangerous element of the kabbalistic doctrine of *galut ha-shekhinah* that would develop after the expulsion from Spain, most notably in the writings of Joseph Karo, was its emphasis on human agency in divine prophecy.[77] Karo proposed that God, or the shekhinah, requires assistance (and not simple obedience) from the faithful. That is, instead of humans being completely dependent upon God to bring about the ge'ulah (redemption), the kabbalists suggested that God was in fact dependent upon humans to prepare the way for the coming of the Messiah, who would not appear until humanity reached a higher level of spiritual development.[78]

This gives us an overview of how medieval Sephardic Jews understood the question of galut and their place in human and divine history. The challenge for scholars of Jewish diaspora is, as we have noted, to move beyond this paradigm and to approach Jewish diasporas as another, non-exceptional example of human culture in diaspora.

BEYOND GALUT: DIASPORA THEORY AND
THE DIASPORIC IMAGINARY

Much of traditional Jewish culture and literature is an operationalization of diaspora, a performance of diaspora. Sephardic literature in particular gives symbolic expression to various aspects of living in diaspora: religious doctrine, social structures, customs, habits of thought. As is to be expected, many writers of the Jewish and Sephardic diasporas deal with the subject of exile/diaspora/galut directly. There are poetic laments for expulsions, historiographical treatments of series of persecutions and expulsions, personal accounts of the expulsions from Spain and Portugal.[79] These are a part of what I will call the diasporic imaginary, but only one part. The majority of the texts I study here do not deal directly with the subject of diaspora, yet they are a product of diasporic imaginaries. That is, they are written by authors who live in diaspora and whose diasporic condition finds expression in their work, in their choice of subject matter, in the linguistic and aesthetic traditions they continue or to which they react. They are not always participating in what we might call the discourse of diaspora (i.e., the representation of or discussion of diasporic life), but they give voice to a diasporic imaginary, a way of interpreting the world that is conditioned by their experiences of living in diaspora and by rabbinic, poetic, historiographical traditions of galut and ge'ulah.

This approach, with its focus on how diasporic experience finds expression in the artistic repertory, is productive for studying medieval Jewish authors through the lens of current critical theory of diaspora because aesthetic choices that are not directly related to the representation of diaspora are less determined by explicit galut thinking, but are still witnesses to diasporic culture. When Jacob Ben Elazar (Toledo, twelfth–thirteenth centuries) adapts narrative strategies from French romance in his own stories, or when Vidal Benvenist shifts the focus of his *Efer and Dina* from the male to the female protagonist, these authors are not making conscious statements about the position of a diasporic Jewish community in the Christian kingdoms of Castile or Aragon, they are *performing* these statements, realizing these statements in the aesthetic, poetic, linguistic, and thematic choices they make. They are not talking about diaspora, they are *doing* diaspora, and they are doing diaspora in ways that make sense to theorists of modern diasporas.

The Jewish example may be the starting point for historians and theorists of subsequent diasporas, but scholarship of the African, Armenian, Indian, Chinese, and other (early modern and modern) diasporas has developed quite differently. Due to their position in history, these modern diasporas develop a diasporic imaginary much later in the game. That is, the diasporic imaginary develops in full modernity, in an era of mechanical reproduction, of mass media, of modern nationalisms, social science, and everything else that modernity might imply. These representations of diaspora are formed by modern subjects whose discourse is informed by the novel, by modern symbolic orders, and less by the allegory, prophecy, and mystical visions that defined late antique and medieval discourses. This means that discourses of modern diasporas do not generally subordinate human actions to divine eschatology, as does the Jewish diasporic imaginary.[80]

While the discourse of diaspora studies has taken certain cues from the Jewish case (most notably its nomenclature), the Jewish example has not overdetermined critical approaches to Armenian, Indian, African, and other diasporas. On the contrary, theorists of these diasporas have been pointedly critical of the approaches of historians and political scientists working on questions of diaspora in modern Jewish history and particularly critical of Zionist ideologies that framed themselves as the answer to the problem of living in galut. Vijay Mishra, for example, notes that throughout history many Jewish communities have been far more significantly attached to their actual communities than to any Zion, real or imagined.[81]

Ironically, most of the founders of the modern Zionist movement have been secular and therefore did not openly profess a belief in *messianic* redemption of the Holy Land. It follows that the basis for their political program was more nationalist than anything else. It was a nationalism informed by biblical narratives and by historical migrations, but that does not adhere to rabbinic interpretations of these narratives. As we will see in our chapter on Solomon ibn Verga's *Shevet Yehudah,* it should not surprise that Sephardic Jews, after their violent engagement with incipient Spanish nationalism, might react with their own nationalist formulations.

In the following chapters we will see precisely how Sephardic writers demonstrate a diasporic consciousness in their aesthetic and discursive choices, in texts that deal both implicitly (Jacob ben Elazar, Todros Abulafia, Vidal Benvenist, Jacob Algaba) and explicitly (Shem Tov Ardutiel, Solomon ibn Verga, Joseph Karo) with themes of diaspora and galut.

2

Allegory and Romance in Diaspora:
Jacob ben Elazar's Book of Tales

Thirteenth-century Sephardic author Jacob ben Elazar lived and worked in Toledo, a city so often described as multicultural or diverse that it has become a bit of a cliché. Ross Brann, for example, writes of a "singularly Iberian cultural pluralism." Francisco Márquez Villanueva describes late thirteenth-century Toledo as a city that is "still Eastern" (*todavía oriental*).[1] Our aim here is not to go into a full accounting of the cultural life of Ben Elazar's hometown, nor to critique the various theories of *convivencia* that have leaned heavily on Toledo as a case study.[2] Rather, I aim to read two of Ben Elazar's *Tales*, written in the full flush of Toledo's "multiculturality," as a case study in diasporic literature. Seen from this angle, Ben Elazar's work is not only a site of transition between Arabic and Christian literary practice, or an example of a literary convivencia, but also an example of the cultural work of the diasporic writer.

Ben Elazar demonstrates his relationship to the literary culture of the dominant Christian society while simultaneously reflecting the values and priorities (and struggles) of the Jewish community of Castile of which he was a member. In his manipulation of the literary conventions of the Hebrew *maqama* (rhyming prose narrative), he carves out new literary space to give voice to the concerns of a diasporic community in transition between Arabic-dominant and Romance-dominant host cultures.[3]

In the first text, the debate between the sword and the pen, he deals more directly with the question of temporal and intellectual power. The genre of the debate between pen and sword had long been cultivated by Arabic authors writing from the perspective of a sovereign majority. Here Ben Elazar maps the conventional allegorical interpretation of the sword as military (concrete) force and the pen as intellectual (symbolic) power onto the internal struggle in the Jewish community between rationalists and antirationalists, two opposing theological camps in Castilian Jewry. In his debate between the pen and the scissors he maps the theological response to a community in transition between Sephardic and Ashkenazic religious traditions, a transition likewise occasioned by the change from Muslim to Christian sovereignty. The diasporic cultural work in his text responds, therefore, to political processes both internal and external to the Jewish community and deals both with shifts in relationships between sovereign (first Muslim, later Christian) and non-sovereign groups (Jewish rationalists and antirationalists), as well as with the internal theological and political ramifications of these shifts.

In the second example, the love story of the youths Sahar and Kima, Ben Elazar adapts the conventions of courtly romance to a text written in a heavily biblical register of medieval Hebrew that is redolent with biblical and rabbinic allusions. His text "turns and re-turns" toward the Zionic imaginary in both language and literary convention, while remaining squarely in Sefarad, a symbolic construct and historical homeland where Jews had long mediated between the values of their community and those of the dominant culture that exercised temporal power over them.

This is what we mean when we speak of an author *doing* diaspora. Ben Elazar does diaspora by adapting the literary models available to him from Arabic and Romance literatures to speak more directly to his experience as a member of a diasporic minority who enjoys a different relationship with sovereignty and with the learned culture of the majority. In *Love Stories,* Ben Elazar adapts the genre of the literary debate between pen and sword (cultivated by both Muslim and Christian authors in Iberia) to reflect a Jewish literary and cultural sensibility, a diasporic mediation between the conventions of Arabic and Hebrew literatures from which the author draws. In the same collection of tales, he adapts the literary conventions of courtly (but not, as we will see, *chivalric*) romance of the Christian world, thus giving voice to the emergent nature of a diasporic community that is en route from one cultural moment to another while remaining geographically in the Iberian Peninsula.

Critics have signaled the importance of the Romance-speaking context of authors writing in Christian Iberia, with particular reference to Ben Elazar's work. For Hayim Schirmann the reciprocal nature of the characters' love relationships, and the active role of the women in them, is reminiscent of the European *novella*.[4] Dan Pagis, who became one of the foremost authorities on Hebrew literature of the Middle Ages and the Renaissance, noted that the communities that produced the Hebrew maqamat were not knowledgeable in (spoken) Arabic, but were native speakers of the Romance languages and were familiar with the emergent literatures in those languages. According to Pagis, this was particularly true in the case of Ben Elazar's *Love Stories*.[5]

Jacob Ben Elazar was a typical polymath intellectual of his time, and in addition to the *Book of Tales* he is author of an Arabic-language grammar of the Hebrew language and a partial Hebrew translation of the Arabic frametale *Kalila wa-Dimna*.[6] Ben Elazar's work is part of a corpus of medieval Iberian Hebrew literature that has been underappreciated by scholars of Hebrew as well as by Hispanists. Hebraists have tended to downplay the contributions of prose writers of the twelfth and thirteenth centuries, favoring the verse of the so-called Hebrew Golden Age of the tenth and eleventh centuries. Ángel Sáenz-Badillos points out that critics have focused far less on the period of Christian rule, both for ideological considerations and because many researchers in the field have lacked preparation in Romance languages.[7] But Ben Elazar is writing *precisely* when Castilian is still very much emergent as a literary language, when Gonzalo de Berceo—often named as the first author to write in literary Castilian—writes his works of *clerecía* (religious narrative poetry), a full generation or two before the massive vernacularization project of Alfonso X comes to pass.[8]

Ben Elazar's *Book of Tales* (*Sefer Ha-meshalim* in Hebrew) is a collection of ten short pieces of narrative, not all of which are tales.[9] The author refers to each piece as a *mahberet*, the Hebrew equivalent of the Arabic word *maqama*, which came to be applied to any collection of short narrative written in rhyming prose interspersed with verse.[10] Ben Elazar situates his work in the corpus of Hebrew *mahbarot*, such as those of Judah al-Harizi,

Judah Ibn Shabbetay, and other Hebrew authors writing in the twelfth and thirteenth centuries in Christian Iberia.[11]

The Book of Tales survives in a unique manuscript. The text is corrupt, and critics have had a difficult time reading it.[12] Even if the manuscript tradition were stronger and the text more reliable, medieval Hebrew is not easy, and there are few specialists in medieval Hebrew who are also familiar with medieval Romance literature, and vice versa. In addition to its value as a testimony to Sephardic literary culture, his work provides the Hispanist with some interesting data points about the reception of courtly romance in the Iberian Peninsula.

DIASPORA AND LANGUAGE CHOICE

The choice of Hebrew as a literary language, especially for secular (or, if you prefer, profane) literary practice, is significant when thinking about diaspora and its impact on literary practice. By Ben Elazar's time, Sephardic writers had been debating the relative merits of Arabic and Hebrew for over a century. Their debate was in turn an extension of a previous debate, one internal to the Islamic community, over the relative merits of Arab and non-Arab Muslims vis-à-vis the inherent superiority of Arabic as the language chosen for the revelation of the Qur'an.[13] In the Jewish context, the question of Arabic's supremacy took on a different significance. While Arab and non-Arab Muslims contested the ethnic or cultural superiority of one group over another, Sephardic writers were conducting an internal debate that had more to do with the relationship of Sephardic intellectuals to the official language of the sovereign powers of al-Andalus.

The basic contours of the original debate on the superiority of Arabic are as follows: The Arabic language boasts a rich poetic tradition that predates Islam by some centuries. The revelation of the Qur'an in Arabic was further proof (for the Muslim community) of the superiority of their language, and by extension, their culture. When the community of Islam began to grow beyond the borders of the Arabian Peninsula where Arabic was a native language, large numbers of Persians, Assyrians, Berbers, and members of other ethnic and linguistic groups began to adopt Arabic as their literary language. Arabic therefore became an imperial language used by authors from a variety of ethnic and linguistic groups. In this pluralist Islamic society, during the first centuries of the Abbasid Caliphate (beginning in 762 CE), there developed a debate over the relationship between language and ethnic identity that was critical of the doctrine of 'arabiyya (also the word for the Arabic language), the idea that the superiority of the Arabic language flowed from the superiority of the Arabs themselves, a fact proven by their being chosen to receive the Qur'an.

Medieval Arab grammarians, attempting to clarify the meaning of obscure passages of the Qur'an, visited Bedouin tribes to do linguistic fieldwork. The dialects of the Bedouins were considered by the city dwellers to be purer and closer to the language of the Qur'an.[14] This contradicted the idea that the language of the tribe of Quraysh, of which the Prophet Muhammad was a member, was the superior dialect of Arabic at the time the Qur'an was received. In order to solve this dilemma, the grammarian Abu Zakariyya Yahya bin Ziyad al-Farra' (d. 822 CE) explained that the dialect of the tribe of Quraysh was superior because the Qurayshis were in constant contact with different Bedouin tribes.[15] This way, he reasoned, the Qurayshis were able to select the best features from each of the Bedouin dialects in forming their own poetic language. "We said: In the same way they [the Qurayshis] were accustomed to hear from the tribes of the Arabs their dialects; so they could choose from every dialect that which was the best in it. So their speech became elegant and nothing of the more vulgar forms of speech was mixed up with it."[16]

During the Abbasid Caliphate, Muslims of Persian background, many of whom were accomplished grammarians and poets in Arabic, criticized the doctrine of 'arabiyya, instead advocating for the superiority of non-Arabs. This was the shu'ubiyya (from Arabic sha'b, people or nation), the ethnic polemic between Arabs and non-Arabs. Shu'ubi writers attacked Arabs for their rustic origins as desert nomads, while they prided themselves as representatives of a cosmopolitan urbane culture that predated Islam. Thus the Persian poet Abu Sa'id al-Rustami wrote (in Arabic) in the tenth century CE:

> If I am asked about my descent I am of the tribe of Rustam
> but my song is of Lu'ayy b. Ghalib.
> I am the one who is publicly and secretly known
> as a Persian whom Arabianism (al-ta'rib) drew to itself.
> I know well when calling the parole
> that my origin is clear and my wood hard.[17]

Although the language of Abbasid-era shu'ubiyya speaks to ethnic origin, what was actually at stake for the writers and their audiences was the question of access to prestigious administrative positions at court and in the Abbasid administration. The elites of Abbasid society largely claimed Arab descent, while the great mass of middle-class functionaries more often identified as Persian. Ultimately, the shu'ubiyya debate was not about Persians being cultured and Arabs being primitive nomads, it was about class and economic opportunity.[18]

In al-Andalus this debate was reproduced by writers who identified either as descendants of the Arab elite that led the 711 invasion of Visigothic Hispania, or as descendants of the various other ethnic groups that lived in the Iberian Peninsula (Hispano-Romans, Visigoths, Franks, Slavs, Basques) and who converted to Islam and adopted Arabic as their literary language. Abu Amir ibn García al-Bashkunsi (i.e., *el vascuense,* the Basque) was one such author who resuscitated the shu'ubiyya debate in tenth-century al-Andalus. In his case, the ruling class of the kingdom of Denia considered itself to be of pure Arab lineage and discriminated against those it considered to be of non-Arab stock. Ibn García himself, as his name suggests, was born a Christian in Basque country, but was taken captive as a child and brought to al-Andalus where he converted to Islam and received a classical Arabic education. His shu'ubi treatise (ca. 1050) harshly criticizes the rulers of Denia for their ethnic arrogance and their rustic origins in the Arabian Peninsula:

> Your mother, O Arabs, was a slave to our mother. If you deny this you will be found unjust. There is no excess in remonstrating, for we never tended monkeys nor did we weave mantles, nor did we eat wild herbs; there is no cutting off your relationship with Hājar; you were our slaves, servants, enfranchised ones, and valets.... [19]
>
> [The non-Arabs] are clear, grave, not camel herders or diggers tilling the soil; great kings, not burners of camel dung for fuel.... These non-Arabs were warriors, not guardians of palm branches or planters of palm shoots....
>
> ... their drink was wine, and their food roasted meat, not the mouthful of colocynth seeds in the deserts or the eggs of lizards taken from their nests.[20]

During Ibn García's lifetime a parallel discussion was taking place within the Jewish communities of al-Andalus over the relative merits of

Arabic and Hebrew. The Jewish communities of al-Andalus (Muslim-ruled Spain) were highly Arabized, but many were also conversant in the Romance dialects of the Iberian Peninsula. In addition to their participation in the Arabic-language culture of the times, Andalusi Jews also left behind a tremendous legacy of Hebrew-language learning ranging from rabbinical treatises to secular poetry.

Some Andalusi Jewish writers, such as the poet Moses ibn Ezra, espoused a kind of Jewish ʿarabiyya that imitated the structures of the ʿarabiyya debate while substituting Hebrew for Arabic.[21] Ibn Ezra held Arabic to be a flawless model for Hebrew to follow. According to Ross Brann, the response of Hebrew authors in al-Andalus to the challenge of Arabic poetry's supremacy was a two-step process by which Jewish authors first "assimilate[d] Arabic paradigms" and later "render[ed] them into Jewish forms."[22] Ibn Ezra himself argues that Arabic poetics are the benchmark for Hebrew poets. He even goes as far as saying that biblical Hebrew poetry at its best sounds like Arabic poetry. Ibn Ezra's poetic ideal is a sort of amalgam of Arabic poetic sensibility and Hebrew language:

> And the poetry of Moses was true and kingly,
> Like an Arabic poem, in words of sweetness....[23]
> And one speaking in the language of the Jews,
> Spoken in perfect symmetry,
> And the power of the speech of Araby
> With its turns of phrase and eloquence....[24]
> Delightful sayings, in the Arabic tongue or the Hebrew,
> And wisdom to grasp on every side, from each direction....[25]

Even after Christian monarchs conquered most of the Iberian Peninsula, Arabic continued to be a prestigious language of secular and Jewish learning, particularly in the fields of grammar, poetics, and philosophy. A select elite of Jewish intellectuals living in Christian Iberia continued to study Arabic and to produce learned treatises in Arabic long after it ceased to be the language of government. The city of Toledo was conquered by Alfonso VI in 1085 CE, yet nearly a century and a half later Toledan writer Jacob ben Eleazar (fl. ca. 1220) would complete a treatise on Hebrew grammar, *Kitab al-Kamil*, in Arabic.

A contemporary of Ben Eleazar named Judah al-Harizi, who was a translator of Arabic literature into Hebrew as well as an author in his own right, begins his book *Tahkemoni* with a lament for the sorry condition of

Hebrew-language learning in the Jewish communities of the Arab world (including Spain) and calls for a Hebrew renaissance by which Jewish authors might lay claim to the literary greatness exemplified in the Hebrew Bible:[26]

> They have enslaved the tongue of the Israelites to the tongue of Kedar [i.e., Arabic] and they said: "Come let us sell her to the Ishmaelites." And they said to her: "Bow down, that we may go over." And they took her and cast her into the pit until she perished among them. And the tongue of Kedar blackened her, and like a lion, tore her. An evil beast devoured her. All of them spurned the Hebrew tongue and made love to the tongue of Hagar. They embraced the bosom of an alien. They desired the wife of a stranger. They kissed her bosom, for stolen waters were sweet to them. Their hearts were seduced when they saw how excellent was the poetry that Hagar, Sarai's Egyptian handmaiden, had borne. And Sarai was barren![27]

Like al-Harizi, Ben Elazar includes in his own introduction a refutation of Arabic's superiority and assertion of Hebrew's literary greatness. He explains that the reason he wrote his *Book of Tales* was to demonstrate Hebrew's virtues and to silence the doubters:

> Said Jacob ben Eleazar: The reason for this book of tales, and the composition therein of my words, is because the learned amongst the Arabs were troubling the Holy Tongue, who nonetheless boasted against it in their insolence, saying: "It should be fitting to write in our language every tale!" They were challenging Our Language, saying: We will prevail!" . . .

> Whereupon I began to compose, saying:
> You would mock me, saying: "Is not the Holy Tongue crude?"
> But no! She is a giant who silences all others,
> Run to her and do not falter,
> Whether elegy or invective, saw or anecdote.[28]

In these pro-Hebrew texts (*'ibraniyya* is the Arabic word for Hebrew), authors drew on some of the resources of the shu'ubiyya, but the context of their argument was different. Abbasid and Andalusi shu'ubi writers wrote in the dominant, official language of state that was common to both Arabs and non-Arabs. By contrast, Jewish writers of the 'ibraniyya wrote in Hebrew, which was read exclusively by their Jewish peers. Their debate was internal to the Jewish community. They were fighting to determine which language would emerge victorious as the prestige language of secular learning in the Jewish communities.

The Ibn Tibbons and others who endeavored to bring Arabic texts over into Hebrew were preserving the prestigious Andalusi curriculum for future generations of Jewish students who now lived outside of the Arabophone world and for whom Arabic had become a rarefied language of learning available only to the most elite of Jewish society. It is true that even Hebrew texts would have been read by a small elite, but by the midthirteenth century, Classical Arabic was known only by a small fraction of the most aristocratic Jewish families of Castile. Therefore, we can say that Shem Tov Falaquera's promise to publish a series of books opening the prestigious Andalusi curriculum to Hebrew readers is a "democratizing" gesture.[29] Henry Malter perhaps overstates the case when he says that Hebrew was a language "better understood by the masses"; however, it is true that Hebrew translations of Arabic works of philosophy might have reached broader Jewish audiences who lived in areas where Arabic was not a widely used language of intellectual inquiry.[30]

In a sense this debate was a rhetorical exercise. Thanks to the efforts of the Ibn Tibbon family of translators, Hebrew already boasted a large repertory of secular scientific and philosophical texts brought over from Arabic originals (mid-twelfth to the early fourteenth centuries). The Ibn Tibbons were Spanish Jews who migrated to Provence during the midtwelfth century, when the Almohad invasion of al-Andalus made life difficult for certain Andalusi Jewish communities. They translated scores of important works of grammar, Aristotelian philosophy, and science into Hebrew for diffusion among the Jewish communities of Europe and the Mediterranean who lived in countries where Arabic was not widely known.[31] Through their efforts, as well as those of others who wrote on secular topics in Hebrew, such as Abraham ibn Ezra, Hebrew became a language of secular learning as well as of rabbinics in the region.[32]

What is curious is that by the thirteenth century, authors living in Christian Spain such as Ben Elazar were still waging poetic war against Arabic, which by now was no longer a productive secular literary language in Christian Iberia. According to Ross Brann,

> though Arabic was still in use in fourteenth-century Toledo, direct,
> head-to-head competition with Arabic was no longer a reality but a
> haunting memory because, by 1200, Hebrew had essentially supplanted
> it as the language of scientific, philosophical, and religious discourse. For
> Hebrew literature in the post-Andalusian age, it was a battle against the

ghost of Arabic language, poetry, and culture and not against its looming presence.[33]

Why, then, continue the debate? Was it simply through force of habit, or had the repudiation of Arabic's superiority become part of the intellectual legacy of Sephardic writers? It may very well have been a performance of Sephardic literary identity to argue for Hebrew's superiority when writing in Hebrew, even though the challenge of Arabic as a rival had long become an afterthought. This is further evidence of how deeply seated the diasporic identity was in Jewish thought: it was difficult for Jewish writers (especially when writing on profane themes) to imagine Hebrew as a sovereign language whose superiority was backed by force of arms. Any such assertion had to be accompanied by a discussion of the literary language of the majority and Hebrew's relationship to it.

The choice of Hebrew as a literary language is significant, especially in the case of profane works such as the *Book of Tales* of Ben Elazar or the other rhyming prose compositions of his contemporaries. The idea that Hebrew is an acceptable (or even superior) literary vehicle for nonreligious matters carries an ideological charge. It suggests that it is important for Hebrew to develop the capacity to express scientific, literary, historical, and philosophical discourses. It is a choice that implies that Hebrew must make itself ready to one day take the stage as a language of state. If not, why not cultivate the sciences in the languages of the gentiles, just as Maimonides and other Andalusi Jews had done in Arabic?

To complicate matters, the Hebrew used by Sephardic writers in Ben Elazar's time was heavily biblical. This was a conscious choice. They had at their disposal the Mishnaic Hebrew of the Talmud as one option but chose instead to compose in a register of Hebrew that was copied directly from the Hebrew Bible; they lifted words and entire phrases directly from it. Nineteenth-century critics coined a term to describe this practice: *shibbutz,* literally "inlay," as a jewel is inlaid in settings of wrought silver or gold.[34] If the Hebrew Bible was the most authoritative source of poetic and rhetorical excellence, then surely the very words of the text were appropriate building blocks. If the choice of Hebrew as a literary language belied a diasporic consciousness, shibbutz belied the writers' *Zionic* imaginary, the projection of the places, names, and events of the biblical past onto the concerns of the present day.

We might say that shibbutz is 'ibraniyya in action—the direct deployment of biblical (authoritative) language following 'arabiyya's assertion
of the superiority of Arabic. Ross Brann explains that the concept of the
Hebrew Bible as a "Jewish Qur'an" was the lynchpin of the project to
adapt the Qur'anic paragon of Arabic rhetorical excellence for Jewish poets writing in Hebrew.[35] This relationship to biblical language is crucial for
understanding medieval Sephardic writers such as Ben Elazar. Medieval
Hebrew poets and writers drew on biblical Hebrew not just for the inert
materials, the building blocks of their texts, but rather felt that they were
infusing their writing with, in the words of Peter Cole, "a source of power
and a transfer of energy."[36] Neal Kozodoy explains that there was a met-
onymic connection between the characters and content of the Hebrew
Bible and the very language in which it was written:

> The poet regarded the Bible also as an aesthetic model, valid for all time.
> The Bible was an inextricable part of his mental life; it was second nature
> to his art. He looked to it constantly, and he incorporated it bodily—its
> phrases, its grammatical forms, its diction, its imagery, its characteristic
> attitudes and patterns of thought—into his poetry, charging the lines of
> verse with the electric potency of the sacred text.[37]

The words of the Bible carried a certain historical force that recalled a
lost Golden Age, one in which the Jews were not a disenfranchised minority living in diaspora. Kozodoy writes that "if the personages of the Bible,
and the narratives of the Bible, were alive and active in his mind, forever
recalling [the poet] to the impossible perfections of his past, the words
themselves of the Bible were no less so."[38] Every time a Hebrew poet deployed a phrase from the Hebrew Bible in his work, he was "turning and re-
turning" to Zion, both aesthetically and historically, refracting the world
and words of the Hebrew Bible through the literary styles, thematic material, and historical reality of the day. The frequent deployment of biblical
language is a poetic exegesis, one that engages the Zionic imaginary with
the diasporic, and is an artistic mediation between two symbolic centers.
Just as rabbinic thought mediates between biblical Israelitic religion and
diasporic reality by interpreting sacrifice, holy work, and pilgrimages into
symbolic ritual, so the literary gloss of biblical texts projects the scripture
into profane literary practice.

This deployment of Zionic language (in both its sacred and historical-prophetic valences) is easily fathomed in the case of a debate of arms and letters that centers precisely on the subject of political power and literary expression. What, however, does it mean in the case of a love story, a courtly romance such as the tale of Sahar and Kima, to which we are about to turn our attention?

DIASPORA AND LITERARY FORM

There is a certain measure of irony in the fact that Hebrew writers demonstrated the superiority of their own literary language by adapting genres and styles from *other* languages. If you are slavishly imitating the literary characteristics of an Arabic form such as the maqama, does this prove that Hebrew is an inherently superior literary vehicle or merely one capable of absorbing the habits and conventions of another language?

Generic transformation is one of the hallmarks of literary innovation. Itamar Even-Zohar writes that "through [translated works], features (both principles and elements) are introduced into the home literature which did not exist there before."[39] In the case of narrative, Ben Elazar and his peers accomplished this transformation through translations. Judah al-Harizi was an accomplished translator who brought into Hebrew the rhyming prose narratives of al-Hariri and the *Guide for the Perplexed* of Maimonides. One might even argue that his crowning achievement may not have been the composition of his original work *Tahkemoni*, but rather his bringing over into Hebrew the Arabic narratives of al-Hariri. Consider which would have had a broader impact on the intellectual culture of his times: bringing al-Hariri and Maimonides, respectively the two greatest names in philosophy and belles lettres of his time, into Hebrew? Or the composition of an original work *in the style of al-Hariri* whose aim was to repeat al-Hariri's exercise in rhetorical pyrotechnics for a Hebrew-reading audience? Bear in mind that al-Hariri's *Maqamat* were considered the paragon of Arabic literary style; the work was said to have had pride of place next to the Qur'an itself in the house of many a Muslim intellectual.[40] As important as al-Harizi's *Tahkemoni* may have become for later tradition, at the time it was the translations from Arabic, which opened the door to later innovation in Hebrew, that were the most innovative, most ground-breaking achievements. Al-Harizi and Ben Elazar, in translating Arabic works such the anonymous *Kalila wa-Dimna* and al-Hariri's maqamat, were doing important work of expanding the literary repertoire of Hebrew by rendering the literary genres, themes, and styles of their times into the language of the Hebrew Bible.

The translation and introduction of new genres is a measure of the viability and vigor of the new literature.[41] In the Sephardic case this is significant on two levels: on the first, the development of a sophisticated vernacular literature demonstrates that the diasporic culture is able to rise to the same levels of sophistication as the literature of the hostland, therefore raising the prestige of the group as a whole relative to the official culture of the sovereign power. At the same time it demonstrates this superiority to the other communities of the diaspora. While at first glance the discussion may seem to be internal to the Iberian Jewish community, it is a part of negotiating the position of a diasporic minority at home as well as in the context of world Jewry.

The literary debate genre is well suited to the concerns of a community in diaspora. It is a vehicle that allegorizes the divided concerns of a community that turns simultaneously toward two symbolic centers, the Zionic and the diasporic. The individual debates claim to deal with more specific aspects of communal life. The debate between Hebrew and Arabic (though never allegorized per se in a literary debate, as were other struggles), the struggle between different political and theological factions in the community, are all symptomatic, in the diasporic context, of the great vacillation between the Zionic and the diasporic. In our first example from Ben Elazar's *Tales*, the author makes use of the debate format to give voice to the struggle between two factions in the Jewish community whose theological disagreement had serious political implications. On the surface, his text continues the tradition of the literary debate between sword and pen, but as we will see, the allegoric struggle between temporal and symbolic power represented in the debate also speaks to the conflict between rationalists and antirationalists that would come to divide the Jewish community of Castile in the thirteenth century.

The debate over the relative roles of military force and political rhetoric in governance is very, very old. While the familiar dictum "the pen is mightier than the sword" may now be received wisdom, for hundreds of years it was a site of contention. In Spain during the twelfth to fourteenth centuries, authors wrote version after version of the literary debate between the pen and the sword in Arabic and Hebrew.[42] The arms vs. letters debate was well-covered territory during the Renaissance and on into modernity.[43] However, in the Iberian context the genre has its roots in Classical Arabic literature, in which poets had long rhapsodized over one or the other instrument. There are several such examples in the poetry of the Umayyad and Abbasid periods, as well as in the poetry of al-Andalus,[44] but it was not until the eleventh century in Spain when the pen and sword came forward to speak for themselves as protagonists in a literary debate by Ahmad ibn Burd the Younger.[45] Ibn Burd wrote his *Risalat al-sayf wa-l-qalam* (Epistle of the Sword and the Pen) as part of a panegyric dedicated to King Mujahid al-Muwaffaq of Denia around the year 1040.[46]

Ibn Burd, a Muslim writing for a king (who as a monarch would probably identify with the sword to some degree, even if he were a bookish kind of king), came to a safe conclusion: the pen and the sword are both worthy instruments, and both occupy an honored place at court. In his version, the two instruments trade barbs but eventually come to an agreement by which each recognizes the value of the other's contributions:

> What a beautiful mantle we don, and what excellent sandals! How straight the path we walk and how pure the spring from which we drink! A friendship, the train of whose garment we let drag and a fellowship whose fruits we pick and whose wine we taste. We have left the regions of sin a wasteland and its workmanship in ruins, we have wiped out every trace of hatred and returned sleep to the eyelids![47]

Ibn Burd's innovation of the development of the debate in which the pen and the sword are both fully fledged characters with their own voices inspired imitators among the Hebrew literati of Castile. In the first quarter of the thirteenth century, Judah al-Harizi adapted Ibn Burd's debate in chapter 40 of his *Tahkemoni*.[48] Al-Harizi wrote in Hebrew for a Jewish patron who, unlike Ibn Burd's patron King Mujahid, was not a military leader and whose relationship to sovereign political power was that of a minority courtier and member of a diasporic culture. Al-Harizi is writing some fifty years before Todros Abulafia would pen his troubadouresque verses at the court of Alfonso X, and unlike Abulafia, some of whose verse resembled courtly poetry written by Christian troubadours, al-Harizi's text is a rhyming prose maqama, which was never considered a courtly genre per se. James Monroe, referring to the Andalusi Arabic maqamat of twelfth century author al-Saraqusti, has called it "the literature of outsiders no longer welcome at [court]."[49]

While Jews did bear arms from time to time, and especially during the twelfth century when they were often charged with garrisoning and defending newly won towns in the Christian conquest of al-Andalus, they did not develop a culture of chivalry to the same extent as the Christian courtiers and noblemen who served the same kings. This is the case throughout the Christian period in Spain as well as in Italy. Majorcan Jews were prohibited from carrying arms in 1390 and Castilian Jews in 1412. Such prohibitions, of course, suggest that Jews *did* carry weapons, or at best affected courtly fashions involving weapons. To wit, Abrahams cites one mock tournament staged for Purim in Italy, in which participants tilted at Haman in effigy.[50] In the following century, Solomon Ibn Verga portrays a Spanish king named Alfonso chastising the Jewish community for teaching their children fencing despite the fact they don't go to war: "Why do you teach your sons to fence if you do not go to war? Is it not in order to more easily murder Christians?"[51] Historians are divided on the extent of Jewish participation in the actual *fighting*, a question of some importance to the discussion of the debates between pens and swords and the adaptation of chivalric literature in Hebrew. According to Yitzhak Baer, in the twelfth and thirteenth centuries Jews frequently garrisoned and "defended" towns recently conquered by Christian monarchs.[52] Salo Baron likewise cites a case of a Jewish resident of Orihuela who participates in the city's defense.[53] Jonathan Ray doubts that he actually bore arms, suggesting that he was simply a "functionary who found himself besieged along with the rest of the castle's inhabitants."[54]

What is clear is that chivalric experience did not stimulate the Jewish literary imagination as it did for Christian authors. Later in this chapter we will see what this means for Ben Elazar's adaptation of courtly, chivalric literary modes, but, in the case of the Hebrew debates between pen and sword, the Sephardic disposition was perhaps not that far off from that of the Christian clerks who wrote debates between clerks and knights. The clerks' reaction was to have the knights lose the debates in which they would have been at a natural disadvantage (lacking the training to win in a formal debate). They likewise appear to identify with the pen against the sword, mapping the allegory of temporal vs. symbolic power onto a debate current within the Jewish communities of Iberia and southern France.

It should not, therefore, surprise that al-Harizi's debate looks a bit different from that of Ibn Burd. He is writing for an audience whose members typically do not bear arms themselves and who have suffered violence at the hands of the majority time after time. The massacres of Jews in Granada in 1066, in France and Germany in 1096, and the periodic violence against Jews in Christian Iberia were very real reminders that swords were not just something to write about.[55] Accordingly, the pen is victorious in al-Harizi's version. This is not surprising—in Latin debates between clerks and knights (written by clerks), the winners were always the clerks.[56] But before ceding the field, the sword reminds the pen of the value of military force. This is particularly appropriate for the Jewish context in which the royal authority is sublimated into the rabbinate, who then bears certain forms of temporal power.[57]

> Every king guards his kingdom by means of me. Were it not for dread of me, his greatness would not for an instant endure. But I guard him from his oppressors. I send my wrath before him. I kill his foes, and all their troops. And as for all the people that come with them, were it not for dread of me, his enemies would subdue him and bring him down to Sheol; but when they see the edge of my sword in his hand, who then is it that is able to stand before me?[58]

The pen counters that he not only provides right guidance for those in power, but also is the instrument of Divine Will and of religion:

> My commands are a crown on the head of kings
> And the goodness of my metaphors brings heart's delight.
> Yes, because of me earth endures in justice.
> In my words and deeds there is no blight.
> Through me God graved the Ten Commandments,
> Gave my people their heritage at Horeb's height.[59]

Al-Harizi's narrator is in the end won over by the pen, whom he describes with sword-like attributes: "When I heard his dark sayings, and the parable of his rhetoric, I wrote the words upon my heart. I inscribed his utterance with an iron pen."[60]

Al-Harizi here is reworking Ibn Burd's debate in a diasporic key. The Jewish community, a class of administrators, financiers, scholars, and merchants, lives by the pen, yet sometimes dies by the sword despite a (usually) privileged relationship to sovereign political power. Their value as administrators and courtiers guaranteed their social position but was, absent any durable rights, subject to the whims of the king. David Nirenberg argues that in general, Jews in medieval Iberia suffered far less violence at Christian hands than did their Muslim neighbors because they depended on royal and not seigneurial protection. The monarchs they served protected their Jewish subjects jealously out of concern for their economic value.[61] Yitzhak Baer states the matter quite plainly: "Generally speaking, the Jews in Spain, as in all of Christian Europe, were regarded as the personal property of the King."[62]

This very direct metaphor of the sublimation of temporal sovereignty to intellectual authority is built upon a foundation of earlier examples that put into practice in the literary field the political theory of the rabbis. According to David Biale, in the absence of Jewish sovereignty, rabbinical discourse reproduced the structures of royal power, relegating to the rabbis and the religious courts the power that once dwelt in the Jewish state. For Biale, the rabbis become "a kind of substitute royalty, kings in exile."[63] Al-Harizi and Ben Elazar are simply dramatizing a process that was already some thousand years in the making: the symbolic transfer of power from sword to pen. Jacob Ben Elazar, writing in Toledo some years after al-Harizi, takes this diasporic interpretation of the debate a step further. His debate is more than a competition for superiority; it is a moral manifesto for what he perceived as a time of intellectual and religious decadence. His pen not only wins the debate, it serves as the moral compass for what Ben Elazar describes as a "generation of fools."[64]

The debate begins like the others, with each instrument denigrating and pointing up weaknesses and faults in the other. The sword calls the pen weak, empty, and inconsequential, while describing himself as the "glory of kings."[65] The pen tells the sword to "get back into your sheath and calm down," reminding him that he is abusive and unjust, he spills innocent blood and undermines justice. He holds that he has power that far transcends the temporal powers of the sword.[66] The pen, he explains, can form reality, teach history, morals, and law:

> My mouth will cause you to know what has happened in the past, the history of princes, kings, and priests who came before us, to the point that you will feel you have been friends with every one of them.[67] My mouth will speak to your mouth and will inform you about their justice and loyalty, their perversity and their sins. From my mouth you will learn doctrine and wisdom and it will teach you mysteries and deep knowledge.[68]

The pen then changes the rules of the game. He explains that what is at issue is not whether the pen is better than the sword, but whether humans can live righteously according to God's law. Both pen and sword are mere instruments and neither intelligence nor might are of lasting value.

Authors such as Ben Elazar mapped the concerns of the day onto these debate poems, which we may read as having (at least) two levels of allegorical meaning. In the first, the concrete pen and sword represent the abstract qualities of intellect and temporal power. In the second, they represent factions within the Jewish communities of Sefarad who were in disagreement over the writings of Maimonides.[69]

Part of the attraction of such allegories for the reader is the hermeneutic challenge they present. On the surface of the debate, the referents seem clear enough: the pen represents learning and intellectual (or perhaps spiritual) power, the sword temporal, military force. The diasporic context of Ben Elazar's pen/sword debate suggests a different interpretation, one that speaks to the values of a diasporic religious minority to whom the pen and the sword mean something different. Here Ben Elazar maps the current internal struggles of the Jewish community between Aristotelians and anti-Aristotelians onto the imagery of military and symbolic powers, equating the Aristotelians with the pen and the anti-Aristotelians with the sword.

In the second half of Ben Elazar's debate, the pen launches into an Aristotelian sermon on the unity of God dense with allusions to Sephardic scholarship and worthy of Maimonides, the Spanish-born rabbi and physician who changed Jewish life forever by continuing the work of Ibn Rushd

(Averroes) in reconciling Jewish religion and Greek philosophy: "The principles of all the unities are Eight, but only of he in whom there is no plurality you may proclaim that He is truly One, and is the only true God, who is a refuge since times gone by; He is not found in any place, only in the thoughts of the wise man and in the forge of Reason. . . ."[70] Here Ben Elazar is weighing in on a philosophical debate that was causing a serious political rift in the Jewish communities of Castile in the mid-thirteenth century: the Maimonidean controversy. This debate divided Jewish communities in Spain and southern France into two camps: those who favored a Judaism that could adapt to the advances in science and philosophy made possible by the translations of Aristotle's works into Arabic, Hebrew, and Latin (Maimonideans), and those who preferred a more traditional interpretation of Jewish law that shunned any reconciliation with Greek philosophy (Traditionalists).[71] This division split many communities into opposing camps, and in Castile, noted intellectuals and authors such as Judah ibn Shabbetay were banned by the dominant Traditionalists for espousing Maimonidean views that the former considered heretical.[72]

One Traditionalist doctrine that the Maimonideans found objectionable was the kabbalistic conception of the *sefirot*, the ten emanations or spheres of God's essence. To the Maimonidean mind, this imagery smacked of polytheism and thus struck at the root of Jewish belief as they understood it. The Traditionalists countered that such interpretations were beyond the understanding of the great majority of Jews, whose deficient learning did not qualify them to scrutinize the opinions of leading rabbis and judges.

It should be noted here that it was not just matters of faith that were at stake. The Jewish communities of Castile enjoyed a good deal of internal autonomy and operated a Jewish court system to deal with all internal legal matters. Therefore (and not unlike the U.S. judicial system), the doctrinal disposition of a given judge could have a significant impact on the life of the community in matters that had nothing to do with religion. In this context, one must consider the appearance of the *Code* (*Mishneh Torah*) of Maimonides, one of the first attempts to systematize Jewish law, which was structurally similar to the efforts of the Scholastics to provide research tools, indexes, and tables of contents for the benefit of Christian scholars. Before its appearance, in order to challenge the opinion of a given judge one would have to possess a level of learning (knowledge of Talmud, Torah, and key rabbinical texts) superior to that of the judge. Maimonides' *Code* had a democratizing effect. With the *Code* in hand, "anyone could open the book and dispute the law with the judge."[73]

Ben Elazar continues to expound on the unity of God, and his insistence in following this line suggests that he is circling back to yet another meaning of the pen versus the sword, one particularly suited to a diasporic Jewish audience living under Christian rule: "The Almighty truly must be called One, you cannot divide him into pieces, nor can you join him; all of him is that is called One is indivisible once it is united. The One that cannot be divided remains eternally, but the unity that is created, perishes."[74] Why, in the context of a debate between pen and sword, this insistence on God's essential unity? It doesn't seem to make sense for either of the interpretations we have so far discussed. The question of God's unity seems irrelevant to the traditional interpretation by which the pen represents letters and the sword arms. Even when the pen represents Maimonideans (science) and the sword Traditionalists (fundamentalism), it doesn't add up: neither side is advocating for a plural God. Ben Elazar here is suggesting a third interpretation: the pen is the diasporic Jewish community, and the sword Christian sovereignty, a double-edged sword (pun intended) that presents both a theological threat in the form of the Trinity (the division of God into parts) and a political threat in the form of the ever-present possibility of violence, perhaps violence in the name of same Trinity.[75] The restrictions placed on Jews by the Fourth Lateran Council of 1215 ushered in a new phase of programmatic official antisemitism that found expression in religious disputes and more aggressive proselytization that sometimes incited popular antisemitic violence.[76]

Throughout the text of his debate, Ben Elazar demonstrates a uniquely diasporic viewpoint. The introduction of his text (like that of al-Harizi) is a call to arms to shore up Hebrew learning in an era that finds it under attack from both Arabic and conversion to Christianity. In his discourse Ben Elazar turns and re-turns to the Zionic imaginary. His choice of biblical Hebrew roots the language of his text in the geography and semantics of power of the Hebrew Bible, part of which is a witness to a past era of Jewish sovereignty in Zion. When he writes about sovereign power, he uses language from the Hebrew Bible that speaks to ideas about royal power that are rooted in biblical realities, rather than those of thirteenth-century Castile.

Like al-Harizi, Ben Elazar accomplished this transfer, this carrying over of material from one language to another, even when he was writing original material in Hebrew. If translation opens the door to reading literary debates, imaginative narrative, and Aesopic fables in Hebrew, the next step is for Hebrew writers to cultivate original works in these genres. This is what we see in Ben Elazar's *Tales*. But there is more going on in this work. According to Jonathan Decter, "Hebrew rhymed prose narrative [is] a form that emerged through a complex interaction of Hebrew, Arabic, and European literatures (mostly in Romance languages but excluding Latin)." He also argues that Hebrew texts such as that of Ben Elazar, rather than being "derived singularly from one culture or the other" are more "fruits of authors aware of multiple literary models who created their texts through a process of negotiation."[77] Ben Elazar incorporates elements of genres of Romance language literatures from which he has not translated, but with which he was familiar and that he carried with him, alongside al-Hariri and the other Arabic classics, in his literary toolbox.

THE TALE OF SAHAR AND KIMA: ROMANCING DIASPORA

In the debate between the pen and the sword, Ben Elazar allegorizes the challenges of living in diaspora; in his tale of Sahar and Kima he performs them. Hebrew literature in the late Middle Ages was in a period of expansion, adapting new genres from both Arabic and Romance literary tradition and bringing these new examples under Hebrew's expanding tent. In the context of Christian Castile, some of these new examples were bound to come from the literary practice of the Christian majority, notably the Romance language poetry and prose that was written and read in the courts of Christian monarchs and nobles. Just as the Hebrew poets of the Jewish communities of al-Andalus succeeded in adapting Arabic poetics and literary mores for a Hebrew-speaking audience, Sephardic writers living in Christian Iberia drew on the literature of the Christian majority for inspiration. In the example presented below, Ben Elazar's adaptation of courtly romance is a diasporic literary strategy that draws both on the authority of Andalusi Hebrew literature and on the examples of the emergent Romance language styles (French chivalric romances, troubadouresque love poetry) that were becoming so popular in Castile during the thirteenth century.

By the close of the twelfth century, French writers had produced a substantial corpus of chivalric novels based on Celtic legends that sought to close the gap between antiquity and the current day.[78] This was a bit of symbolic *translatio imperii* by which local kings could transfer some of the authority of the great rulers and heroes of antiquity onto their own reigns. Iberian chroniclers followed suit, employing varying degrees of the literary flexibility and sleight of hand necessary to the task. As a result, Britannic characters were recast as players in Iberian history. Many of these characters were not represented as Iberians themselves, but some are married to Iberians, in a mimetic projection of the practice of marrying children of royalty to children of political allies in order to ensure international relations and maintain stability. There is a tendency to press fictional narratives set elsewhere into the service of narratives of dynastic (and later national) origins.[79]

What concerns us here, more than the tendency to knit together local history with that of Britain, Rome, or France, is the courtly and chivalric mode of discourse that developed in the French romance, glimmers of which we see in the prose of Ben Elazar. It is not particularly shocking in itself that a Sephardic writer would be imitating styles popular at court where he or his benefactor might have served. In this case, however, Ben Elazar's discourse of courtly love appears some years before writers working in Castilian begin to bring over the world of the French Tristan, Arthur, and Lancelot into their own languages. Ben Elazar's Sahar and Kima is a very early example—perhaps the first example—of an autochthonous Iberian writer adapting Arthurian courtly discourse in an original composition.[80]

It is clear that Arthurian and other romances cultivated by French writers reached Iberian audiences in the twelfth century. The first references are by Catalan troubadours. In a composition dated to 1154, Bernat de Ventadorn mentions Tristan and Iseault, and around 1170 Guiraut de Cabrera follows suit, mentioning a whole string of French romances in one of his songs.[81] Then follows a long silence until the end of the thirteenth century, when Alfonso X "The Learned" of Castile and León (1252–1284) incorporates the Floire and Blancheflor story in his ambitious chronicle project, the *Estoria de España*.[82] Elsewhere in his works, he makes mention of the Britannic legends of Brutus, Arthur, and Merlin in the *Cantigas de Santa Maria*.[83] It was not until the fourteenth century that Arthurian material took root and flourished in Castile. The anonymous *Novela del Cavallero Çífar*, while not strictly speaking an Arthurian romance, includes some Arthurian material.[84] The Castilian adaptation of *Tristan and Iseult* (*Tristán de Leonis*) dates from the early fourteenth century, roughly contemporary with the Castilian translation of Arthurian narratives (*Historia de la demanda del Santo Grial, Libro de Josep Abarimatia, Estoria de Merlín, Demanda del Santo Grial*) translated by Juan Bivas (or Vivas) around 1313.[85] According to Henry Thomas, the practice of chivalry in Spain, especially its "superficial and theatrical side," was imported by French and English knights who came "from other lands to help the Christians in Spain to fight the Infidel."[86] Similarly, Entwistle reports that "in the year 1343 or thereabout Castile was swarming with Englishmen and even with Englishwomen, who were attracted by the wars of the south and by the pilgrimages of the north of the Peninsula."[87] Since the eleventh century, even before the First Crusade, papal bulls of crusade created spiritual incentives for knights from outside the Iberian Peninsula, including many from England and France, to join Christian Iberian forces against Muslim armies.[88]

The impact of chivalric culture in Iberia also found reflection in the popularity of the courtly mores and entertainments depicted in the novels. This is as much due to the presence of French and English knights in the Peninsula who were involved with campaigns against Muslim kings as it was to the representations of courtly culture in the books themselves. Naming conventions of the times similarly reveal a popular fascination with Arthurian chivalric fiction. During the early fourteenth century in Portugal, Lusophone varieties of characters from the novels such as Lancelot, Arthur, or Guinevere became increasingly common across class lines.[89] Chivalric romance, and the practice of chivalry in general, grew steadily in popularity in Iberia thereafter. With the appearance of Garci Rodríguez de Montalvo's *Amadís de Gaula* (Zaragoza, 1507), the chivalric moves from courtly trend to popular phenomenon, and a mania for all things chivalric is unleashed. For the next hundred years until the publication of *Don Quixote* in 1605, chivalric culture, or at least chivalric culture as imagined by authors of chivalric novels, is king. Although somewhat outside the scope of our argument, the robust popularity of the chivalric romances tracks with the development of the increasingly sophisticated court culture of the fifteenth century, whose soundtrack is *cancionero* poetry. The corpus of this poetry (while a late example for our purposes) is peppered with references to the protagonists of Arthurian narrative.[90]

We have seen that, apart from the troubadouresque references to Arthurian narratives, the first Iberian narratives that bear significant Arthurian influence were those included in the Alfonsine histories, and these did not emerge until the mid- to late-thirteenth century, followed shortly thereafter by *Çifar* at the turn of the fourteenth. This means that the courtly discourse of Ben Elazar's two young lovers, Sahar and Kima, would mark the tale as one of the first Iberian texts to bear influence of courtly chivalric mores, some three-quarters of a century before the first Castilian language example. Reading Ben Elazar's Hebrew text in the Romance language context gives us more data points to bring to our consideration of the development of chivalric romance in Spain. He introduces elements of the courtly attitudes and behaviors (as well as the physical surroundings and props) of the world of chivalric romance while substituting feats of poetic and rhetorical brilliance (the pen) for that of arms (the sword), as is the norm among heroes of French and Castilian chivalric novels. Jonathan Decter points up this distinction in his comparison of Ben Elazar's book with the French and (considerably later) Castilian versions of *Floire et Blancheflor*. He concludes that "Ben Elazar does not create protagonists who embark upon chivalrous forest adventures or engage in tournaments to earn love and prestige. Yet his characters do embody the internal transformations characteristic of Romance protagonists."[91] In short, Ben Elazar picks and chooses from the narrative resources available to him in the chivalric romance; he keeps the courtly and discards the chivalric.

To sum up, if we overlook authors such as Ben Elazar, our view of Castilian literary practice is impoverished. The Sahar and Kima tale gives us an example of the practice of courtly romance in Castile well before the Castilan *Crónica de Flores y Blancaflor* intercalated in the Alfonsine *Primera Crónica General,* and some seventy years before the *Cavallero Çifar.*

One might think that since Ben Elazar is using biblical Hebrew to tell his tale he might graft bits of biblical feats of arms into the text to keep with the spirit of the genre. Maybe he would describe rhetorical heroics *using the language* of biblical heroics. He does not. He is more indebted to the Arabic sense of rhetorical prowess featured in the medieval maqamat. Since there is no Jewish class of warrior-nobles in Christian Iberia, the literature does not develop an inventory of imagery of the warrior hero. While tenth- and eleventh-century Andalusi Hebrew poets, and most notably Samuel Hanagid ibn Nagrela, wrote war poetry, the exemplary values of the poetry of the thirteenth and fourteenth centuries are poetic excellence and religious piety. For Ben Elazar's audience, the criteria for heroic values do not include feats of arms. Knights appear very infrequently in works by Sephardic and other Jewish authors, and when they do it is through translation from other languages, or when the knight is a subject of parody.[92] There is no autochthonous chivalric hero in Hebrew literature.

Barbara Fuchs describes romance as a genre that "stages over and over again the tension between the pursuit of love and the pursuit of arms, presenting the lover as essentially compromised by the erotic drive that takes him away from his obligations."[93] This distinction is obviated in the Jewish social setting, and arms as a category of excellence is often replaced by letters, whether secular or sacred. In Ibn Shabbetay's *Minhat Yehudah,* the protagonist Zerah (albeit in a farcical mode) enacts precisely the dilemma described by Fuchs, that of the lover whose erotic impulse distracts him from his heroic endeavors. In the case of Zerah, a Jewish protagonist who is judged by his excellence in study, romance distracts him not from arms but from study.[94]

In order to properly situate the Sahar and Kima tale in the discussion of romance we need to distinguish the courtly from the chivalric. In his definition of chivalric romance, Cesar Segre emphasizes the relation of the characters to the courtly setting, and while there is no doubt that Jews were players on the courtly scene, and occasionally went to war, there is relatively little of the chivalric in the medieval Jewish experience.[95] In their introduction to their 1985 collection of essays on romance, Brownlee and Brownlee note that the *Roman de la Rose,* which is contemporary with Ben Elazar, is the first work where courtliness edges out chivalry.[96] This move is moot for Jewish authors, who generally did not practice chivalry, real or imagined. Although Iberian Jews may have taken arms in some cases, Jewish elites were not raised in a culture that revered arms and chivalry as an essential component to aristocratic (or middle-class) male identity. Consequently there is no original Jewish literature of chivalry in the Middle Ages. Eberhard Hermes, in his introduction to his translation of Petrus Alfonsi's early twelfth-century collection of tales, the *Disciplina clericalis,* notes that in the world of Alfonsi, "the merchant plays a role which he had not before achieved, at least in the West, whereas the knight scarcely makes an appearance."[97] A generation before Ben Elazar, when the Toledan writer Judah al-Harizi writes his *Tahkemoni,* the knight makes a brief appearance in one of the tales, but by and large Hermes's assessment stands. Hebrew writers, some of them, are doing courtly, but they are not doing chivalric.

Gaunt also points out that the romance is a projection of troubadouresque ideas about courtly love, but an ironic play on them as well, refracted through the perspectivist lens.[98] The same might be said about the maqama and also the medieval Arabic romance *Bayad wa-Riyad,* which (at the same time) project and toy with the courtly love ideals of the Andalusi poets.[99] In Hebrew, and as exemplified in Ibn Shabbetay's *Offering of Judah,* love distracts you not from arms and adventures, but from scholarship. Again, in this case the courtly chivalric ideal is displaced by the mercantile or scholarly, but still courtly, ideal. This stands to reason when we think about the social context of Jewish writers and readers in comparison to what the scholarship on romance tells us about the social context of Christian writers of vernacular romances. The patrons of most Hebrew authors were not nobles, but notables whose fortunes hinged on royal contracts, or business deals, but not feats of arms (as with noble patrons).[100]

How does this nonchivalric yet courtly discourse play out in the text itself? The story begins with the young nobleman Sahar embarking from the port of Jaffa to Syria. There is a storm and a shipwreck, and our hero washes up on the shores of the land of Tsovah, which Decter identifies as Aleppo.[101] He wanders into the city, where all the local girls and women are stunned by his beauty. He stumbles into the palace, mistaking it for a synagogue, and is immediately detained and tied up by a pair of Ethiopian guards. When he recites an extemporaneous poem in protest, the crowd is so impressed by his poetic skill that he is released. Kima hears his poem and falls in love with him. She then tosses him an apple inscribed with a poem of her own and blows him a kiss. Sahar is escorted out of the court and tossed into the street, forlorn and pining for Kima. She sends a servant with a letter professing her love for him. The servant leads him back to the palace, where Sahar recites more poems of his love for Kima. After making him pass through a series of tests of his resolve and poetic prowess, Kima reveals herself to him, reproaching him for speaking openly of their love. There ensues a series of sung and written poetic exchanges, followed by a Bollywood-esque song and dance routine, and finally a romantic all-nighter in the *hortus conclusus* of the palace garden. The couple is discovered by Kima's father, the king, who threatens to kick Sahar out, but is so moved by laments of the young lovers that he agrees to allow them to marry. Shortly after the nuptials he dies of plague, conveniently passing his crown to Sahar and Kima, who live happily ever after.[102]

What most distinguishes this narrative among other Hebrew (and Arabic) love stories of the Middle Ages is its particular brand of *courtliness*. It is the details of the behavior of the young lovers that sets this story apart from its Hebrew analogues and moves it closer to medieval romances written in European vernaculars. Not all of the details of the *amores* of the protagonists are specific to courtly love *chez* Capellanus. Much of the nuts and bolts of the amorous discourse is common to both Andalusi and romance courtly traditions. Sahar falls in love with Kima from just hearing her voice.[103] He complains of her aloofness, constantly laments the mere possibility of being separated from her despite never really having been united with her. Ladies-in-waiting serve as go-betweens, carrying poetic messages between the lovers. Love letters and poems are not simply recited or written on paper. In one case Kima embroiders a poem to Sahar on a curtain behind which she hides from him.[104] And of course, the lovers complain of the impossibility of love and of the pain of separation.

However, there are many examples of amorous motifs that are anomalous in Hebrew and Arabic tradition and much more characteristic of vernacular courtly discourse. When Sahar sees Kima, he bows and kisses her hand.[105] He does this to avoid scandal in front of Kima's ladies-in-waiting. Her response to this advance is to wax lyrical about the value of chaste love, but she couches this idea in terms of class and in terms of an understood doctrine of courtly love. She explains to Sahar that the "laws and customs of true lovers" enforce chastity, while the sons of slaves yield to their passions. The narrator assures us that her words ennoble and edify Sahar, who then concedes to spend the entire night in the palace gardens with her, speaking of approved courtly topics but not actually touching physically. Particularly interesting is that this is all couched in biblical Hebrew, with all the stock imagery, phrasing, and allusions that implies. For example, Kima describes their amorous bond in the same terms that God explains the covenant to Noah. Much like his Christian counterparts, Ben Elazar speaks of love in religious language. When Sahar speaks of the "laws and customs" (*huqim u-mishpatim*) of courtly lovers, he uses language drawn from Exodus, where Moses's father-in-law Jethro is exhorting Moses to instruct the Israelites in the new laws received at Sinai (Exodus 18:20).[106]

Kima repeatedly chastises Sahar to be chaste in his love for her. She is not simply preoccupied with her honor, or with being haughty, which would be a perfectly recognizable posture for a courtly lover: *la belle dame sans merci*. However, Kima's objection to physical love is on moral grounds. She explains that "to love with passion is a sin" and does her best to stave off his physical advances.[107] This manifestation of troubadouresque chaste love is particular to the vernacular literary tradition of Western Europe and has no exact analogue in Arabic, although the figure of the suffering, chaste lover is found in the verses of the so-called '*Udhri* (pure) poets.[108] The nature of Sahar's devotions to Kima are more suggestive of ultrapyrennean examples such as the French Arthurian romances. Roger Allen's description of the love-sensibility of the 'Udhri corpus could easily be applied to the courtly love of the troubadours:

> The poet-lover places his beloved on a pedestal and worships her from afar. He is obsessed and tormented; he becomes debilitated, ill, and is doomed to a love-death. The beloved in turn becomes the personification of the ideal woman, a transcendental image of all that is beautiful and chaste. The cheek, the neck, the bosom, and, above all, the eyes—a mere glance— these are the cause of passion, longing, devastation, and exhaustion.[109]

Ben Elazar is doing things here that no other Hebrew author has done. He is adopting the local conventions for representing idealized heterosexual love and blending these sensibilities with conventions, ideologies, and habits of expression drawn from the Hebrew and Arabic poetic traditions. Hayim Schirmann notes that the women in Ben Elazar's stories have a more active role and are more agentive in the narrative.[110] This squares with the idea that the chivalric romance developed in order to speak to the concerns of a courtly audience (and perhaps to courtly patronage) that included powerful women. In light of all this, if we compare the Sahar and Kima tale to the Hebrew tradition alone, Ben Elazar looks like an outlier. But when we look at him next to his colleagues writing in romance, he looks like a writer who is simply up to date and writing the way people write in France and Spain at this time. It is, of course, noteworthy that Ben Elazar would be writing something that looks like courtly romance in the early thirteenth century in Toledo.

If it is not precisely chivalric, what is it about Ben Elazar's Sahar and Kima that looks like romance? According to Cesar Segre, the great achievement of medieval romance was to "link love to glorious deeds so as to make love the direct cause and heroic personal identity and social position the indirect consequences."[111] In the case of Sahar and Kima, the heroics are linguistic; demonstrations of feats of rhetoric are here substituted for feats of arms.[112] The tale is more orthodox in its operationalization of courtly love and its commonplaces. Kima is physically aloof not because she is cruel and manipulative like the merciless *belle dame* of the troubadours, but because she subscribes to a code of amatory behavior that is unique to nobility. The class anxiety of romance is present, even if the heroic values are different. On the face of it, there is a lot that is familiar in "Sahar and Kima" (there's a nice play on words: "Kima" is also the Hebrew word for Pleiades). The title alone, "The Love of Sahar and Kima," eponymous lovers so recognizable from French romances (*Erec et Enide, Tristan et Iseult, Aucassin et Nicolette*), is unheard of in Hebrew until Ben Elazar's work.[113]

Sahar's entree to court is precipitated not by a tournament, but by a display of poetic excellence.[114] The challenges that stand between him and his lady are not martial but poetic and intellectual. Little wonder, then, that Ben Elazar should include in his collection a debate between a pen and a sword, a metaphor for the tension between arms and letters as personified in the knightly and clerical classes, or perhaps, in the Jewish context, between Christian noblemen (who bore arms and whose power base was territorial) and Jewish courtiers (who did not, and whose power base flowed directly from the throne).

In "Sahar and Kima," the courtly chivalric ideal is displaced by a scholarly, but still courtly, ideal. While critics tend to characterize the tension in romance between the clerkly and the knightly, this dichotomy is obviated in the Jewish context. We have in "Sahar and Kima" a case of courtly ideals refracted through a diasporic experience, where courtly heroics are framed in terms of excellence with the pen, as opposed to the sword.

3

 ~~~✑~~~

Poetry in Diaspora: From al-Andalus to Provence and Back to Castile

The poetry of Todros Abulafia, who wrote at the court of Alfonso X of Castile-León (1252–1284) is the product of two diasporas, one human and one poetic. As a diasporic poet, Abulafia is very much in the tradition of Jacob ben Elazar and other Sephardic poets before him, who negotiated between the Andalusi and biblical Hebrew poetic imaginaries. The troubadour style of poetry has its roots in the Iberian Peninsula, in the highly refined Andalusi lyric brought to Provence by William IX of Aquitaine at the close of the eleventh century. Troubadouresque poetry later returned to the Peninsula as a prestigious export from beyond the Pyrenees, setting the standard for courtly poetics in Christian Iberia. We find in Abulafia's poetry a curious mixture of Andalusi Hebrew and troubadour poetics that is the product of the diaspora of Andalusi poetics itself, of its sojourn in southern France and its return to Castile at the court of Alfonso X.[1]

Todros Abulafia was author of an extensive corpus of Hebrew poetry, which he himself collected in his *Diwan* titled *Gan hameshalim ve-ha-hidot* (The Garden of Saws and Parables).[2] He enjoyed the direct patronage of Alfonso X, "The Learned," and his diwan contains a number of poems addressed to the king himself.[3] Abulafia is a rare if not unique case of a Jewish poet writing in Hebrew under royal Christian patronage, and his poetry, like that of the Provençal and Galician-Portuguese troubadours at Alfonso's court, is not typically included in scholarly overviews of literary practice at the court of the Learned King. To modern scholarship,

Abulafia has been a diasporic poet who is a shadowy outsider from any angle. In Spain he is virtually unknown, despite having written the most significant corpus of poetry and having produced the only known *diwan* (collected poems of a single author) at the court of that country's most intellectually important medieval ruler. He is not mentioned in any of the studies of the Christian troubadours who wrote and performed at the court of Alfonso X. He scarcely appears in historical studies of Alfonso's reign, even in those that deal specifically with the boom in arts and letters for which Alfonso X is famous (hence "the Learned"). Abulafia is absent in Evelyn Procter's discussion of Provençal and Galician poets of Alfonso's time.[4] Norman Roth mentions him in passing in his discussion of the Jewish translators who collaborated with Alfonso X.[5] Joseph O'Callaghan gives an overview of the Galician-Portuguese troubadours active at Alfonso's court but does not mention Abulafia.[6] Salvador Martínez makes brief mention of one verse of the poet in his discussion of the detainment of Alfonso's Jewish tax farmers.[7] Jewish scholars of medieval Hebrew poetry have viewed Abulafia at times with admiring curiosity, at times with disdain. He is still a bit of an enigma. Peter Cole aptly sums up the diverse opinions scholars have formed of Abulafia: one called him "one of the greatest poets of whom the Jews can boast," while others dismiss him as a "mediocre epigone."[8]

Abulafia lived at a time when the upper classes of the Jewish community of Toledo were waging a sort of culture war, in some ways a continuation of the Maimonidean controversy that, as we have seen in the previous chapter, figured so prominently in Ben Elazar's debate between the pen and the sword. One side leaned toward assimilation and materialism, another toward traditionalism and piety. This division was personified in Todros ben Yehudah Halevi and his relative, the "other Todros": Todros ben Yosef Halevi Abulafia, a prominent Talmud scholar and chief rabbi of Toledo.[9]

The story behind the discovery of the manuscript containing the collected poems (diwan) of Abulafia is something that Cervantes (that master of the "found manuscript" conceit) might have written. Carroll Johnson points out that the found manuscript trope is not only a fictional conceit, but is less a fictional conceit than a reflection of how texts were disseminated around the Mediterranean in the Middle Ages.[10] If the story of the Abulafia manuscript seems Quixotesque, it is simply because they are both (*Don Quixote* and the story of Saul Abdallah Yosef's Abulafia mansucript) tales of manuscript transmission that seem anomalous. In the age of print we expect industrial-scale (or at least artisanal-scale) systematic diffusion of large, sometimes vast print runs, not the hand-to-hand, irregular transmission patterns typical of manuscript culture.

Up until the late nineteenth century, scholars of Spanish Hebrew poetry were familiar with Abulafia's name and had edited a handful of his poems, but he was a minor player, a footnote in the medieval Sephardic repertoire. As it turns out, he had written and compiled a vast poetic corpus—some twelve hundred poems. Abulafia was one of the first poets in Hebrew or the Romance languages to compile his own diwan, although this was standard practice among medieval Arab poets. In the seventeenth century, an Egyptian Jewish scribe made a copy of Abulafia's diwan. It passed from one antiquities dealer to another and eventually found its way into the hands of Saul Abdallah Yosef (1849–1906), a Baghdadi Jewish businessman and accomplished amateur scholar. Yosef made a copy of the manuscript and brought it back to his home in Hong Kong. The Romanian-British Jewish scholar Moses Gaster published a facsimile edition of Yosef's manuscript, which David Yellin used as the basis for a 1932 critical edition. Yosef's discovery of the manuscript fairly doubled the corpus of Hebrew poetry from the time of Alfonso X and radically changed our understanding of the poetry of thirteenth-century Spanish Jewry.

Abulafia was a notable of the Jewish community of Toledo, which at the time was a very well established community that boasted a centuries-long history and had been regularly represented at court since long before the Christian conquest of Muslim-ruled Toledo (*Tulaytula* in Arabic) in 1085. Under Alfonso's administration there were several court Jews who served as financiers, outfitters, tax collectors, and the like.[11] Abualfia's poetic production occupies an important place in the history of Sephardic literary culture for its originality, for his unique status of a Hebrew poet receiving direct royal patronage, and for his diasporic aesthetics by which he negotiates between royal Christian court, Hebrew Andalusi poetic tradition, and the troubadour poetics of his day. Though the overwhelming majority of Abulafia's poetry builds upon Arabic and Andalusi Hebrew models, two of Abulafia's more troubadouresque poems shed light on the connection between Andalusi courtly lyric and troubadour poetry. At a time when Arabic literary culture is in decline and the Romance vernaculars are emergent, Abulafia's troubadouresque poems are a microcosm of the larger literary historical movements of the times in Christian Iberia.

Our approach to Todros Abulafia as a diasporic writer, and in particular as a Hebrew poet influenced to some degree by troubadour poetics, begs us to back up a bit and consider two larger, interrelated questions. The first is that of Eastern and Western culture in medieval Iberia: to what extent did the troubadours draw on Andalusi lyric and musical traditions and how is this heritage reflected in Abulafia's adaptation of troubadour poetics? The second is how modern scholars, themselves diasporic subjects like Abulafia, have responded to the expression of this subjectivity in Abulafia's poetry.[12]

Scholarship on Romance languages has long considered the question of the Romance debt to Andalusi literary culture. The broad contours of the debate have centered on the influence of Arabic courtly styles on the nascent tradition of troubadour poetry in Provence and the concomitant questioning of how modern literary historiography, especially of national literatures, has constructed grand narratives that obscure important cultural processes and products that do not fit its categories. This has led critics to question the dominant narratives of French and Spanish literary history to come to a more nuanced understanding of the development of courtly lyric in Iberia and southern France during the late Middle Ages.

The story of the development of troubadour lyric is one that has attracted a good deal of controversy.[13] What should be, on the face of it, a straightforward story of artistic innovation and imitation has been distorted by nationalist, sectarian, and racist bias. The basic narrative is as follows: William of Montreuil (Normandy) was tasked by Pope Alexander III to lay siege to the Muslim city of Barbastro, then held by al-Muzaffar as part of the Taifa of Lleida. William VIII of Aquitaine served Montreuil as commander in the siege, which was successful. As part of the booty, William took home with him to Aquitaine a group of *qiyan*, highly refined slave women who specialized in singing and playing instruments, more like indentured conservatory professors than domestic servants. These qiyan were practitioners of a prestigious tradition of courtly performance that has no equal in continental Europe, even in the sophisticated centers of the western Mediterranean on what is now the coast of France and Italy. William IX of Aquitaine, whom literary historians typically regard as the first troubadour, grew up at the court of his father listening to the songs and melodies of the qiyan. His earliest compositions, written in Provençal in clear imitation of the Andalusi lyric tradition in which he was raised, are claimed by European scholarship as the first lyric poetry in any Romance vernacular, and the troubadour corpus (together with that of the Germanic *minnesingers*) as the originary lyric of Western European lyric poetry.[14] This troubadour style then replaces the Andalusi tradition as the prestige form of courtly lyric in the Iberian Peninsula, with Christian monarchs in Portugal, Castile-León and the Crown of Aragon regularly inviting troubadours of various regional origins (French, Italian, Catalan, Portuguese, Castilian, etc.) to work in their courts. Meanwhile, the Andalusi courtly lyric is exported to North Africa and the East, where it becomes, in parallel fashion, the prestige idiom of courtly music in the Arab world. In this way the troubadour style is a kind of prodigal son of Andalusi courtly lyric that returns to the Iberian Peninsula in Provençal and Portuguese dress.[15]

What does all this mean for our reading of Abulafia's poetry? We find in the poems we read here a curious mixture of Andalusi Hebrew and troubadour poetics that is in some sense the product of the diaspora of Andalusi poetics itself, of its sojourn in southern France and its return to Castile at the court of Alfonso X. It is as if Abulafia recognizes troubadour poetry as a kin and welcomes it back home in his verses, in which the troubadouresque and the Andalusi mix and mingle freely. Seen from this angle, Abulafia's flirtation with troubadour poetics is more family reunion than performance of exoticism or, for that matter, colonial mimicry.[16]

Why would Abulafia be better able to understand this than a poet working in Galician or Provençal? He worked in Hebrew, a Semitic language and close relative of Arabic. He demonstrates familiarity with Andalusi poetics, though it is not clear if he has firsthand knowledge of Classical Arabic verse or if he knows only some Andalusi vernacular Arabic. As we have seen in our discussion of vernacularity and translation as a context for Ben Elazar's *Love Stories,* and as we will develop further in this chapter, in Christian Iberia, Hebrew is the natural meeting place of the Andalusi and the Romance, a third space where Arabic and European poetic traditions blend and produce new forms, new poetic repertoires, and, in the case of Abulafia, a new poetic voice.

It is a commonplace of scholarship on medieval Hebrew poetry to state that it is a melting pot of Hebrew and Arabic poetics. David Yellin refers to Arabic poetry as the "sister" of Hebrew poetry.[17] Dan Pagis writes of the "typical Andalusian blend of Jewish and Arabic culture."[18] According to Raymond Scheindlin, the Jewish community of al-Andalus so thoroughly assimilated the "Arabic literary tradition that they eventually synthesized it with their Jewish literary heritage."[19] For Ross Brann medieval Hebrew poetry is a "Hebrew subcultural adaptation of Arabic verse."[20] It is likewise true that Hebrew is a mediating vehicle between Arabic and vernacular Romance traditions. This is particularly so in the broader systemic sense of Arabic-speaking Hebrew writers producing texts that would then be read and adapted by Romance-speaking Hebrew writers and readers. The greater textual community bound by Hebrew literary practice includes participants with native proficiency in Arabic, in Romance, and sometimes in both.

The converse question—that of the Romance influence on Andalusi Arabic and Hebrew literature—has not been explored with the same rigor.[21] In the previous chapter we discussed the relative conservatism of the scholarship on the Hebrew literature of Christian Iberia, the tendency, decried by Angel Sáenz-Badillos and other contemporary scholars of medieval Hebrew literature, to imagine Hebrew poets as somehow ignorant of or impervious to the literary and artistic trends of their Christian counterparts.

DIASPORA AND POETRY

But what of Abulafia himself? What is his diasporic moment? In a sense, it is not dissimilar from the case of Jacob ben Elazar. Abulafia was from a Castilian Jewry that still revered Arabic as a classical language of learning; his poetry by and large is representative of the Andalusi Hebrew poetic tradition as it was practiced in the context of Christian rule.[22] Like Elazar, Abulafia is between literatures, and his innovations tell us much about how he negotiated the spaces between the Andalusi past and the Christian present.

In fact, just as the debate over the origins of troubadour poetry leads us to question such neat categories as past/present and Andalusi/Christian, Abulafia's poetry, and in particular his poems on *fin'amors* or troubadour-esque love, similarly bid us call into question the categories around which we tend to organize cultural production at the court of Alfonso X. Neither is he alone in this respect. A number of forms of cultural production at the court have been minimized or cut out of the more mainstream cultural histories of the thirteenth century in Castile.

The musical tradition, so vividly represented in the miniatures of Alfonso's *Cantigas de Santa Maria,* is largely lost to us, and we can only attempt to reconstruct the music that was performed at his court.[23] The work of the Provençal and Catalan troubadours who performed at court has been preserved in manuscript, but we have no *cancionero* (poetic anthology) of the poets sponsored by Alfonso, no material record that brings together the Provençal, Galician, French, Hebrew, and Arabic songs sung in his court. Even within the narrow scope of Alfonso's own poetic production, the canonical, devotional *Cantigas* nearly completely eclipse the corpus of his invective poetry, the now-scurrilous, now-obscene compositions included in the piquant *Cantigas d'escarnho e mal dizer.*[24] Perhaps the greatest irony of the material record of Abulafia's poetry is that among the poets at Alfonso's court, he is the only one to have left us a collected works, and yet he has left the lightest of traces among literary historians and has eluded almost entirely the gaze of the Hispanist.

ALFONSINE COURTLY CULTURE

All of the above gives us a sense of how modern scholars have read (or not read) Abulafia's poetry. If the city of Toledo during the early thirteenth century was the backdrop for our study of Ben Elazar's stories, for Abulafia it is the court during the second half of that century, during the rule of Alfonso X.[25]

Alfonso, as has been written, may not have been the most effective statesman and military campaigner, but was successful in creating an indelible legacy for himself in the area of the arts and sciences. He reformed the chancery, elevated Castilian to the level of an imperial language, and conducted a massive vernacularization project of which the translation of many Arabic works into Castilian was only one part.[26] In addition he left behind a law code, the *Siete Partidas,* parts of which are still on the books in some Hispanic countries (as well as in some U.S. states) and directed the composition of a universal history spanning from biblical history to the reign of his own father, Fernando III.[27] He is said to have composed, himself, in Galician-Portuguese, a hymnal of over two hundred songs dedicated to the Virgin Mary, one manuscript of which contains hundreds of miniatures documenting (or perhaps imagining) life at his court; to this day, it remains one of the most important sources for both material culture and musical notation in thirteenth-century Iberia.[28]

As we will see, Alfonso revolutionized courtly culture in Christian Iberia, effecting a sort of *translatio imperii* of Arabic *adab* literature into Castilian. María Rosa Menocal writes that "the whole of the Alfonsine era, including its texts and its ideologies, is best understood in terms of an Arabic tradition converted into a Castilian one."[29] Alfonso's aim was to reproduce the Andalusi curriculum, the standard education of an Andalusi courtier, in Castilian.[30] He wanted his court to equal the cultural refinement of that of the Andalusi Taifa kings of Seville and Cordoba conquered by his father Fernando III, and he saw this best accomplished by putting the Andalusi curriculum within the grasp of Castilian courtiers, nearly all of whom lacked proficiency in Classical Arabic, in which the most important learning was currently available. His goal was to elevate the general level of education and discourse at court, to make his courtiers "increasingly more courtly."[31] In doing so, Alfonso perhaps may have indeed exceeded the standard of greatness that, as legend would have it, Fernando set for his son on his deathbed: "I leave you the whole realm from the sea hither, which the Moors won from Rodrigo, King of Spain. All of it is in your dominion, part of it conquered, the other part tributary. If you know how to preserve in this state what I leave you, you will be as good a king as I was, and if you win more for yourself, you will be better than I was, but if you diminish it, you will not be as good as I was."[32]

While he may not have surpassed his father in territorial expansion, he certainly trumped him in expansion of intellectual capital, for he provided for his court a quality of education that as yet was unavailable in Paris, Bologna, or London. Alfonso therefore sought a shift in the very values that shaped courtly life, to elevate the arts and sciences above the chivalric and military values that had sustained courtly life in Castile-León up to his rule—values that had enabled his father to bring almost all of al-Andalus under Christian control.

The Andalusi curriculum was, in a way, part of the spoils of war, spoils that would only further his claims on broader imperial power. His aspirations to the throne of Holy Roman Emperor placed him in competition with other monarchs such as Frederick II of Hohenstaufen, whose patronage of the arts and letters was part of a larger imperial project.[33] This self-consciousness imbued Alfonso's activities with a sense of grandeur and destiny that were a precursor of the imperial image projected by Carlos V during the sixteenth century.[34]

Part of the imperial cultural project of Alfonso was to employ poets at court who would promote his image and further his interests. In the thirteenth century there was effectively no courtly lyric poetry written in Castilian. Instead, poets from Castile and elsewhere composed courtly lyric in either Galician Portuguese or Provençal, both of which had come to be poetic *linguae francae*.[35] In light of Alfonso's massive vernacularization project, this exclusion of Castilian as a language of courtly lyric poetry is curious. Why would Alfonso espouse a linguistic policy that embraced Castilian for purposes of history, law, science, philosophy, and didactic fiction, but exclude poetry? He wrote his own poetry, *Cantigas de Santa Maria*, and the collected invectives and panegyrics known as the *Cantigas de escarnho e mal dizer*, in Galician Portuguese. The poets who worked at his court composed lyric in a number of languages, but not in Castilian. Why not?

In order to answer this question, we must return to the first glimmers of vernacularism in Castile. Carlos Alvar points out that while Alfonso VIII was patron to some twenty or more Provençal troubadours, Fernando III shut the door to courtly poetry.[36] In this respect Alfonso X clearly excelled in comparison to his father. A number of troubadours celebrate or otherwise mention the Learned King in their verse. Bonifacio Calvo warns Alfonso against idle sycophants and hangers-on who lack knightly valor and who

> prefer to remain in their houses
> drinking fine wines and eating rich foods
> than to take castles with vigor.[37]

Calvo also celebrates the Learned King as a patron of arts:

Here survive song and pleasure,
for the King Alfonso maintains them.[38]

Folquet de Lunel (1244–ca. 1284), who traveled to Toledo in 1269 for
an audience with King Alfonso, celebrated the enlightened environment
at Alfonso's court, a place where, according to him,

No good man waits in vain for his recompense,
a court without larceny and violence,
where one listens to reason,
a court without pride and villainy,
in which there are a hundred donors who bestow
rich gifts without even being asked.[39]

Guiraut Riquier (1254–1292) similarly celebrates Alfonso's court as a
place "where learning is listened to and esteemed."[40] Peire Cardenal (ca.
1205–ca. 1272) sang that Alfonso was "the [king with the best] judgment
. . . so much so that his deeds were esteemed."[41]

Why, then, did none of these poets celebrate the Learned King in Castilian, the language of the impressive corpus of translations and prose
works for which Alfonso enjoyed so much fame? There are two possible
explanations. The simplest is that the great body of Alfonsine prose was
translated from the Arabic, a language that, while respected as a vehicle
of prestigious learning, was not widely known at court. It was functionally *necessary* to translate it into a vernacular in order for the texts to be
intellectually fungible. If such great prestige was accorded to Arabic learning, why did Alfonso's project not include the lyric poetry of al-Andalus?
Was poetry considered untranslatable in the thirteenth century, as some
consider it to be today?[42] Given the tremendous smorgasbord of Andalusi
poetry available to Alfonso, why would he not even experiment with translating some of it into Castilian? When it comes to poetry in medieval Iberia and Provence, it is not a question of translation of texts, but of genres.[43]

We have seen the example of the translation of Andalusi poetry to Hebrew, through which the poetic values of Andalusi poetry were brought
over into Hebrew by poets who reproduced the imagery, the habits of
expression, and even the metrical structures of Arabic into original compositions in Hebrew. Something similar perhaps happened in the court of

William IX, who, a century and a half after Dunash ben Labrat composed his first lines of Andalusi verse in Hebrew, brought Andalusi poetics over into Provençal. In Alfonso's court, while there was a need to translate the Arabic scientific and philosophical corpus into Castilian, there was no *need* to translate the Galician Portuguese and Provençal lyric into Castilian, as (unlike Classical Arabic) these were languages that were readily understood at court. This familiarity made it possible to delay bringing courtly lyric poetry over into Castilian.

TROUBADOUR POETRY AT ALFONSO'S COURT

Troubadours were Western Europe's first highbrow poets to sing in the vernacular as opposed to in Latin. Troubadours did not *invent* vernacular poetry. People have always sung in whatever language they spoke.[44] What was new about the troubadours' work was that they wrote and performed songs in the vernacular language for royals and other elites. Why was this new, all of a sudden, at the end of the eleventh century? Before that time, sophisticated poetry written by educated people was written in a classical language such as Latin, Greek, Hebrew, or Arabic (depending on the location in Europe of the author). Songs sung in the languages that people actually spoke in daily life were everywhere (as they are now), but they were not acceptable to perform at court, and even if they had been, no kings were paying poets to write down and perform original songs in French or Portuguese or Italian. Not until the troubadours.[45]

The first courts to support troubadours who wrote and sang in the vernacular were in the south of France, in places like Aquitaine and the Midi. The first such poet was himself a nobleman of very high rank, William IX of Aquitaine. Like modern pop stars, the troubadours cultivated dynamic stage persona, penned autobiographies or had them written by others (*razós*), and tended to embellish their personal lives in their songs. And much like our hip-hop artists, they matched wits in poetic battles (*tensós*). In addition to composing poems celebrating troubadouresque fin'amors, Abulafia himself also traded Hebrew invective poems with members of the Jewish literary elite of Toledo.[46] The troubadour style spread from the south of France north into Germany and south into Catalonia and Castile.[47]

It was common for powerful kings and nobles to retain intellectuals, poets, and artists at court. A powerful king had a refined court, and in the twelfth and thirteenth centuries poetry still had pride of place as a high art form that also served very immediate political purposes. In medieval Europe, court poets were more like high-profile media figures whose verses communicated political propaganda and shaped the habits of speech and thought of the upper classes; they were rewarded with generous salaries and bonuses. While today we might trot out a poet laureate once or twice a year to recite a few lines at a presidential inauguration or another ceremonial event, medieval troubadours were in the public eye (or ear) constantly.

Alfonso's court was an important center of troubadour poetry.[48] Some of the poets who served at his court include Bonifaci Calvo, Arnaut Catalan, Guiraut Riquer, Peire Cardenal, Cerverí de Girona, and Airas Nunes.[49] Alfonso regularly employed troubadours as a sort of propaganda corps. Galician-Portuguese troubadours promoted Alfonso's various political projects on the Peninsula, while those writing in Provençal publicized his designs on the Holy Roman imperial throne.[50]

HEBREW AND POETIC VERNACULARITY

In the context of Christian government, the Andalusi literary legacy of Sephardic Jews was foreign—prestigious, perhaps, but ultimately foreign to the great majority of Christian elites, who valued Arabic learning but were most likely to consume it in Latin or Castilian translations. The diasporic moment had changed, and the cultural terms of engagement needed to be renegotiated. At this very moment of renegotiation, a new Romance vernacular poetic practice is emergent in Castile. Just as Sephardic poets are no longer practitioners of the dominant intellectual tradition, they are becoming practitioners of the emergent poetic tradition, by virtue of their Romance language nativity. While to us this may seem like a boon, to them it was a conundrum. Before Abulafia's time, Andalusi Jews were both connoisseurs and producers of Arabic poetry. Nonetheless, when writing in Hebrew they sometimes made a show of denigrating Arabic tradition, in an effort to exalt Hebrew. In the Andalusi context this bluster was mostly a rhetorical trope that authors deployed as an accessus in introductions to works of Hebrew poetry and prose. Though motivated by a linguistic protonationalism, it was ultimately the kind of good-natured brinksmanship one might read in medieval debate poetry of any tradition.

In Christian Iberia this exaltation of Hebrew poetics took on a new urgency, now that Sephardic intellectuals were estranged from the dominant intellectual tradition. It may well have been sour grapes: in Toledo, for example, between the Christian conquest of 1085 and the beginning of the reign of Alfonso X in 1252, there was no thriving poetic scene in which a Jewish poet might participate. By the late thirteenth century, poetic production in Arabic outside of Granada and Valencia had virtually ceased, and Sephardic poets had not, for whatever reason, taken to composing courtly poetry in the vernacular. Even Abulafia, whom his Jewish peers considered a notorious assimilationist and who did not hesitate to socialize, and fraternize, with Christians, did not, as far as we know, compose in the vernacular. Although he experiments with the dominant *poetics* of his day, he did not seem to have adopted the dominant poetic *language*.[51] Perhaps the vernacular had not yet achieved enough prestige or historical weight for Jewish poets to adopt it wholeheartedly. It may be that Jewish poets, as a diasporic minority, felt insecure about adopting the dominant poetic language because they had no history of participating in Latin intellectual life. Perhaps the admonishments of their grandparents' generation kept them away. In any event, it was not happening. Abulafia's renegotiation of the Sephardic diasporic poetics was going to be different. And, while he did not appear to have composed in the vernacular, he did participate in vernacular poetics. By this I mean that he expressed his orientation toward hostland poetics by adapting the themes, habits of expression, and poetic ideologies of his peers who composed in the Romance vernaculars. As we will see, Todros creates a new poetic voice that grows naturally from both the Andalusi Hebrew and vernacular troubadour traditions of courtly love. Some of this innovation is original and probably unrelated to what was going on in vernacular troubadour poetry. Todros was very creative in his reworkings of the stock imagery and poetic strategies of Andalusi Hebrew tradition.[52] However, in some cases it is clear that he is a sort of Hebrew troubadour.[53] On a more formal and specific level, Abulafia adapted some of the same generic conventions used by the troubadours. The Spanish Hebraist Ángel Sáenz-Badillos has demonstrated that some of Abulafia's invective poetry is structurally and thematically very similar to the *tensós* and *sirventeses* of the troubadours among whom he moved at court.[54] The one critic to thoroughly tackle the question of Todros's involvement with vernacular poetics is Aviva Doron, who in 1989 published a Hebrew-language monograph titled *A Poet in the King's Court*.[55] Doron deals with a few different aspects of Abulafia's work, focusing mainly on his poems dedicated to Alfonso and his love poetry. Abulafia's poetry is in dialogue with the troubadouresque discourse of courtly love. His adaptation of the conventions of fin'amors is where he is at his most innovative and where he least resembles his predecessors in Hebrew poetry. Abulafia's engagement with the poetics of the hostland is an important example in our study of diasporic literature.

ALFONSINE LITERARY CULTURE AND THE JEWISH ROLE

As we have seen above, Alfonso X "The Learned" of Castile-León is well remembered, even lionized, as a patron of arts and letters. Among medieval European monarchs he stands out as one who placed great value on science, literature, and poetry. Even when compared to the prodigious Louis IX of France he occupies a category of his own as a patron of learning.[56] His efforts to make Arabic (and to a lesser extent, Hebrew) learning available at his court is one of the most important chapters in the early development of Castilian as a literary language.[57] The previous, unwritten chapter of Castilian's development as a learned language was, ironically, the translation project of Archbishop Raymond of Toledo, carried out in the first half of the twelfth century by teams of Christian and Jewish translators who brought over Arabic texts into Latin. Their working language, the common language in which they would have discussed the Arabic terminology, concepts, and intellectual content, would have been Castilian. Therefore, the Alfonsine translations depend linguistically on the collaboration sessions of Archbishop Raymond's translators in the previous century.[58] It was this workshop in which a consciousness of Castilian as a language of secular learning was first cultivated.

At precisely the same time that Berceo and his peers were forging a literary legacy for Castilian with their saints' lives and adaptations of classical
narratives, Jewish scholars in Castile were bringing over important works
of Arabic learning into Hebrew, simultaneously expanding the horizons of
secular Hebrew prose literature. The linguistic situation for Castile's Jews
at this time was in flux as the community adapted to the sociolinguistic
realities of Christian rule. Evidence for vernacular usage among Castilian
Jews at this time is limited, but given the fact that the Mozarabic (Christian Arab) communities of Toledo were almost completely monolingual
Castilian speakers by the mid-thirteenth century, we can assume that the
situation of the Jewish communities was comparable.[59]

In any event, Hebrew was by no means a vernacular language in the
Middle Ages, and the Jewish communities of Sefarad spoke Romance
dialects or Andalusi Arabic. Hebrew was, like Classical Arabic and Latin,
a language of religion and learning, of speech-giving and reciting poetry,
but not in any sense a mother tongue. It may have been used in limited
contexts as a lingua franca between Jews whose vernaculars were mutually
unintelligible, but nobody was bawling for Mommy in Hebrew.[60]

The translation project of al-Harizi, Ben Elazar, and the Ibn Tibbons
(late twelfth-early thirteenth century) aimed to bring Andalusi learning
over into Hebrew for an audience of Jews in Christian Iberia and other
Christian kingdoms. It was in a sense the model for Alfonso's vernacularization project. Even before he ascended to the throne, Alfonso X commissioned a Castilian translation of the very popular Arabic work of prose
fiction, *Kalila wa-Dimna*. He underwrote (or perhaps directed) translations of scores of scientific works and commissioned (or perhaps wrote)
original works of law (*Siete partidas*), history (*General estoria*), and devout
poetry (*Cantigas de Santa Maria*).[61]

The Alfonsine project has been described as a kind of intellectual Reconquest or *translatio studii*,[62] the porting of science and learning from
Arabic to Castilian. But like the historical study of the Christian conquest
of al-Andalus, the question of the development of the Alfonsine literary
vernacular is less an "us vs. them" situation than a nuanced, layered negotiation of language choice and literary practice. Alfonso's project, much
like the great innovations of William IX in courtly lyric, was not the product of an individual genius who created a translation movement *ex nihilo*,

but rather a phase in a longstanding culture of translation in Iberia and Provence. In the first stage, that of the Arabic–Hebrew translations of the Ibn Tibbon family and others, Hebrew negotiated its way through fields and genres once the sole province of Arabic.[63] This brought secular learning into Hebrew practice (1100–1200). The children of this generation of translators collaborated with Alfonso to duplicate the exercise, this time into Castilian. It is possible to view these as two phases, the Tibbonid and the Alfonsine, as a single broader translation movement.[64] This means that the Arabic–Hebrew project provided the models and the habits of thought for the Arabic–Castilian project. Alfonso's achievement was not simply the translation of Arabic to Castilian; it was the adaptation of translation methods, and in a broader sense, of ways of thinking about and producing knowledge.[65]

The introduction of official vernacular literature created a secular literature not just in terms of its content, but in that for the first time there was literature being written in a language to which no single religious tradition could definitively lay claim. Granted there was plenty of Christian literature in the vernacular. It is well known that the need to preach in the vernacular (and the subsequent legitimization of vernacular preaching at the Fourth Lateran Council in 1215) was a great factor in the development of a literary vernacular in Spain and elsewhere in Europe.[66] But unlike Berceo's Christian didacticism in his works of *clerecía*, Alfonso's project was (largely) protohumanistic in that it did not purport to promulgate specifically Christian knowledge, nor to communicate with a specifically Christian (or potentially Christian) audience. Castilian was common to all subjects of the Crown of Castile and León, a royal and soon to be imperial language. Any Castilian speaker with enough patience to learn the Roman alphabet could read (or listen to) learned literature in Castilian, provided they had access to manuscripts.[67] Because of its importance for the historical idea of Castilian as a national and imperial language, literary history has tended to view the Alfonsine project as the product of an exceptional individual or, at best, of an exceptional kingdom and court, rather than as part of a broader vernacularization project that ultimately was to be far more significant in its impact, given that Latin translations of Averroes and other authors had already had their greatest impact in Paris and elsewhere.

As in the case of Jacob Ben Elazar, the missing piece in the scholarly discussion has been the question of the significance of Romance vernacularization for the Sephardic literary elite. How does the elevation of Castilian (or any of the other vernaculars) to official language of the chancery and the court affect Hebrew literary practice? As we will see, much of this change observed in Todros Abulafia has to do with patronage and working environment and the larger, murkier question of Jewish vernacularity.[68]

TODROS ABULAFIA *EN SU SALSA*

Abulafia was received at court by Alfonso X while still quite young. To mark the occasion he gave the monarch a golden cup inscribed with the following verses in Hebrew:[69]

> Faith's vengeance on falsehood was taken
> the day Alfonso was crowned as King—
> and so, coming to serve you, I bring
> a cup for your glory, with this small hymn.
> For the Lord commanded in Scripture: Ascend
> to sacred feasts with a gift in hand.[70]

This poem (apart from the fascinating material detail of the cup inscribed with Abulafia's verses) sheds some light on Abulafia's relationship to the Learned King and the importance of this relationship for his poetry. It also begs the question: What does Hebrew (or any other minor language) *mean* at a court where it is a minority language?[71] Abulafia here is writing in the language of the minority to demonstrate to leadership of that minority his relationship with (and allegiance to) the dominant political power. We should note that at Alfonso X's court, Hebrew was not widely understood, but it had visual symbolic value both as the language of the Old Testament (the Christian name for the Tanakh or Hebrew Bible) and as a language of scholarship at court. It is not insignificant that Alfonso ordered the translation of the Hebrew Old Testament as source material for the Castilian *Fazienda de Ultramar*.[72]

It is significant that in Christian Iberia, as opposed to al-Andalus, Sephardic poets no longer shared a courtly poetic language with those of the dominant majority. Andalusi Sephardic poets such as Samuel Hanagid Naghrela and Moshe ibn Ezra mastered the Classical Arabic poetics of their time and wrote beautifully in the language. It was their language of matters of state and of secular learning. In this environment, there was no barrier to their full participation in the poetic culture of the host-land majority; they had a place at the table and read, wrote, and recited alongside their Christian and Muslim counterparts. By sharp contrast, Sephardic poets of Christian Iberia largely shunned composing poetry in the vernacular, and very few Jews had a working knowledge of Latin. At the courts of Christian monarchs, courts at which there was certainly no shortage of Sephardic courtiers, Jewish poets did not have a place at the table, nor does it appear that they sought one. This is significant for a number of reasons, and we would do well to bear this in mind in our reading of Abulafia's verse as a discussion between these two poetic cultures mediated by the social realities and symbolic repertory of diaspora.

Andalusi poetic culture at Alfonso's court would have been considered prestigious, perhaps even autochthonous in some way,[73] but ultimately opaque, consumable only as a tangible form of heritage. To be certain, there were those at Alfonso's court who were highly proficient in Classical Arabic and probably many more who had passable command of the Andalusi Arabic vernacular. By and large, however, if an Arabic *muwashshah* or *qasida* were performed at Alfonso's court, it is safe to say that the majority of those present would not be able to understand the words.

Hebrew poetry at this same court would have been even more opaque to the majority. Aside from the Jewish courtiers present, precious few Christians would have been able to grasp even the gist of Abulafia's poems, were he to have performed them at court.[74] This does not mean that he did *not* perform them, however, or that his Christian counterparts at court would not have been able to enjoy them on *some* level. As Aloysius Nykl has argued in his discussion of Andalusi Arabic poetry in the Christian courts of southern France, you do not need to understand the words in order to enjoy the song.[75] Neither is it impossible, though again we lack documentary evidence, that there might have been some form of simultaneous translation or interpretation practiced to facilitate appreciation of compositions performed in languages less commonly understood at court: "Now he is saying that your coronation marked the victory of generosity over miserliness, and now he says that all who come to court must bear gifts, meaning, Sire, the very cup from which he reads the inscription I now relate to you," etc.[76]

Earlier in the thirteenth century, the writer Judah Ibn Shabbetay dramatizes such a scene. In his introduction to his maqama titled *The Offering of Judah,* he describes himself at court reading his work aloud to a previous "King Alfonso," who is so pleased with Ibn Shabbetay's composition that he grants the poet three hundred pieces of silver and five fine outfits to wear, and invites him to stay at court indefinitely.[77] Even if this representation were entirely fictional, it is suggestive of the ways in which Christian audiences, at least the ones that mattered most, experienced Sephardic literary culture. If, on the other hand, Christian audiences had no access to the *meaning* of Abulafia's verses, whether inscribed on cups, parchment, or elsewhere (let's not forget the example from Ben Elazar's "Sahar and Kima" of the verses embroidered on curtains), we must assume his audience was limited to the Jewish community, and that his references to his relationship to Alfonso were a way of demonstrating his position at court to his Jewish peers and perhaps to promote royal interests within the *aljama* (Jewish community) of Toledo.[78] Hebrew poetry had considerable authority within this community and would have more traction with Jewish notables than if Abulafia were to write in "mere" Castilian.

ABULAFIA BETWEEN TRADITIONS

The diasporic approach is one that pays special attention to the relationship with the hostland and, in particular, the differences and relationships between the various diasporic communities. The transition from Muslim to Christian society was a significant one for Sephardic poets, as it meant that their poetics was no longer an extension of the dominant literary culture. While Andalusi Hebrew poetry was a close second cousin to Andalusi Arabic poetry, the Hebrew poetry of Christian Iberia was far more distant linguistically and artistically from the poetries performed at the courts of Christian monarchs. The linguistic distance of Sephardic poetic production from that of the sovereign majority heightened the sense of living in diaspora.

In the eleventh century, Moshe ibn Ezra's celebration of Arabic poetics shows how closely integrated Sephardic poets were to the poetic culture of their times. By the thirteenth century, even Judah al-Harizi, who was a master of the Arabic language, recognizes that it is Hebrew, not Arabic, that is the future of Sephardic letters. This is not surprising, given that Arabic had by his time ceased to be a language of state in Castile. That the languages that replaced Arabic at court were not considered appropriate vehicles for Sephardic belles lettres means that Sephardic literary culture in Christian Iberia was more diasporic and looked increasingly toward the biblical linguistic past and the realities of the Hebrew-writing present than to Andalusi models.[79]

Hebraists, primarily those working in Israel, have shown progressive interest in the relationship of Abulafia's poetry to that of his Romance language contemporaries. While earlier criticism tended to frame Abulafia's innovations in terms of an abandonment of Andalusi Hebrew style, later critics celebrate it as one of the hallmarks of his innovation, perhaps as a measure of his Western-ness or as evidence of his poetic assimilation to Christian norms. Hayim Schirmann observed (without going into detail) that his poetry displayed certain formal aspects of the work of his Christian contemporaries, but always retained classical Hispano-Arabic prosody.[80] Dan Pagis goes a bit further, suggesting that the poetry of Abulafia structurally resembles that of the troubadours.[81] Sáenz-Badillos concludes that the invective poetry of Abulafia is a sort of hybrid of Andalusi linguistic features and some Romance-influenced ideation and imagery.[82] Aviva Doron argues that the main affinity of Abulafia with his Christian peers is in his individualized, personal poetic voice calling on God to intercede in personal problems, in which she sees the influence of Marian poetry, especially the *Cantigas de Santa Maria* of Alfonso X.[83] For Ross Brann, it is the love poetry of Abulafia (and not the devotional poems as per Doron) where he is most innovative, breaking with the stock tropes of Andalusi Hebrew love poetry and "cultivat[ing] the persona of the libertine" who writes not of stock, archetypical "gazelles" of the Andalusi school, but rather of specifically Arab, Spanish, or Slavic "maidens and wenches."[84] Most recently Peter Cole follows Brann, but adds that Abulafia "was likely influenced by the troubadour tradition" and was especially adept at reinventing, subverting, or simply rejecting many of the formal and stylistic conventions of the Andalusi school.[85] In general, when critics have written about Abulafia vis-à-vis the Romance language poetry of his times, most have not gone into specific textual detail.[86]

As a poet, Abulafia was heir to a very rich tradition of Sephardic He-brew poetry that dates at least back to the tenth century, when Andalusi courtier Dunash ben Labrat first began to adapt classical Arabic poet-ics to biblical Hebrew language. This combination, something that was possible only in a tolerant, sophisticated courtly milieu such as that of ninth-century Córdoba, was cultivated by a series of major eleventh- and twelfth-century Andalusi Sephardic poets who are now considered the grandfathers of Hebrew literature: Moses ibn Ezra, Samuel Hanagid, Ju-dah Halevi. When Abulafia wrote of love, he often used a Hebrew style that was based on the Andalusi Arabic poetry written in Spain in the tenth through twelfth centuries.

Abulafia himself points out that he employs popular poetic styles (literally, "daughters of the songs of the nations of this land made into Hebrew").[87] His experimentation with troubadour style was significant. Jewish poets in the area around Toledo had been living in a Christian-dominated society for over a hundred fifty years when Abulafia wrote. Despite this, they largely adhered to the Andalusi style they had inherited from Andalusi Jewish poets. In the eyes of most Jewish writers, the vernac-ular was not a language appropriate for writing poetry, and so they tended to downplay the importance of the troubadours, even if their Christian kings and queens thought otherwise. Abulafia was the exception. He was a master of the old Andalusi style, but was also an innovator who was not afraid to go out on a limb artistically. This did not impress some of his modern critics, but it did not appear to have slowed him down when he was living and working at court. Quite the contrary; he was popular at court and even accompanied King Alfonso on diplomatic missions abroad.[88]

ABULAFIA'S TROUBADOURISM

Aviva Doron has called Abulafia a "Hebrew troubadour."[89] She presents a few specific insights on how Abulafia's love discourse springs largely from Andalusi values, but with some key differences.[90] There are some elements of the spiritual love of the troubadours in his verse, such as the *dai li* (it is enough for me) trope that, according to Doron, recalls the selflessness of spiritual troubadour love.[91] Two of Abulafia's poems (numbers 714 and 715 in Yellin's edition) are particularly suggestive of troubadour poetics in the context of the poetry of troubadours who worked at Alfonso's court and of later works of courtly love lyric and narrative produced in southern France at the time Abulafia lived.

Troubadours wrote about love in a way that has come to be known as *courtly love,* a kind of poetic game with strict rules about how lovers behave and how they talk about the experience of love. Elements of this style have survived in popular poetic genres, and today one can hear songs on the radio that still use some of its language and tropes. The courtly lover served his lady as a knight serves a king. He sometimes sang of being her slave, of submitting himself completely to her. This adoration sometimes went over the line into a kind of heresy where he actually took to worshipping the lady instead of God.[92] He would perform any service for her to prove this love, even if she never granted him physical affection. Troubadours sang of a spiritual love that made them better people, more noble and pure. This set of rules was famously codified by the French cleric Andreas Capellanus in his three-part book *De Amore.*[93]

This doctrine, the amorous poetic imaginary of its times (and still, in many ways, of our own), continued to develop and transform in the pens and on the lips of courtly poets and writers in Provence and Christian Iberia. By the time of Alfonso X, we are dealing with a tradition some hundred and fifty years in the making. During the life of Alfonso we have, in Provence, at least two examples of chivalric and chivalric/courtly narratives written in verse that put into narrative practice the amorous ideations and imagery of troubadour love poems.

When we look at the poetry written by troubadours who passed through the court of Alfonso X, we see some striking similarities between their verse and that of Abulafia. The examples that follow all focus on aspects of troubadouresque amorous discourse that have no direct equivalent in Andalusi Hebrew tradition: chaste love with spiritual value, the heresy of courtly love by which the beloved is transformed into a deity, the focus on the nobility of lineage and of spirit of the beloved, and the refutation of any who would denigrate the lover's enterprise. With his reworking of these troubadouresque conventions, Abulafia is bringing something new to Hebrew verse that has not yet existed. Given the apparent divergence of Abulafia's formulations of courtly love from the love discourse of the Andalusi Hebrew tradition, it seems inevitable that he is doing so as a direct and deliberate artistic response to the literary fashions of the times.[94]

One of the characteristic commonplaces of courtly love in troubadour poetry is the idea of chaste love, that the lover can be sustained in his suffering by the mere sight or mention of his beloved, or by hearing her voice.[95] This is not the case in the verses of the Romance-language troubadours, in which the suffering itself is an indispensable part of the love experience of which they sing. It is precisely the suffering resulting from unrequited desire that ennobles the soul of the courtly lover and distinguishes him from a lusty commoner.[96] Peire Cardenal, writing in Provençal, maintains that the act of desiring his lady is *even better* than kissing her:

> I have desired, and desire still,
> and I wish to go on desiring
> rather than to hold my lady and kiss her
> in a place where I might enjoy her![97]
>
> Though she never grant me pleasure,
> I should still be her man forever![98]

Abulafia echoes this concept, suggesting that it is more important to desire than to achieve union, despite the emotional stress involved:

> I shall not think ever to touch her
> even though I spend my life sobbing over her.[99]

In the same poem he is quite clear that his love for the beloved is a spiritual phenomenon by which his soul is drawn to hers. Physical love, he says, is not a priority.[100]

> I have no desire to have her, to delight in
> her body, only to delight in her soul.[101]

This is consonant with the idea that it is the suffering of the lover that ennobles him and raises his love to a higher, spiritual plane. After all, if you are able to be together with your beloved, there is nothing to sing about.[102]

Again, Abulafia is in close step with Bernardet's *Flamenca*, in which the
protagonist likewise swears up and down that even the mental image of
his beloved is enough to sustain his desire:

> It is enough for me the sweet sound of her speech,
> and the pleasant image of her breasts.
> It is enough for me, when I think of it,
> that the image of her is a picture in my heart[103]

> I will hope for nothing from her,
> only to see her or to delight in the memory of her[104]

And Bernardet:

> Could I but have speech
> With you, or see you oft, 'tis true
> I would not say these things to you.
> Your precious presence and the sight
> Of you would satisfy me quite[105]

The spiritual nature of love is taken to the next level in what some have
called the heresy of courtly love, the moment in which the beloved begins
to take on a divine aspect, and the poet, in a vain effort to give voice to the
emotional intensity of his feelings, substitutes the language of religious
devotion for that of human love in an effort to express himself. It is in this
spirit that Bonifacio Calvo is able to speak of his beloved as so beautiful
and noble that even God himself might take her for a lover:

> If it pleased God to love a woman of the world,
> he would have a pleasant delight in her whom I have chosen[106]

Not content to describe her in terms of a divine being such as an angel,
Calvo brings God himself into the picture in a neoplatonist move by which
the beauty of the beloved is so otherworldly that it reaches a perfection
more characteristic of God than of humanity. Abulafia commits a similar
heresy, one perhaps more specific to Judaism, which unlike Christianity
saw the representation of the divine in human form as a heresy of the worst
order, punishable by excommunication. Abulafia's creative response is
to equate his devotion to his beloved to that of a religious holiday. The
specific reference here is to one of the three major biblical Holy Days,
the *shalosh regalim* (Shavuot, Sukkot, and Passover), or three occasions

on which the Hebrews would go in person to the Temple in Jerusalem, locating his amorous desire in the symbolic realm of the liturgically based turning and re-turning to Zion:

> My soul celebrates her as a holiday!
> See how, for her sake my soul sings the name of God!
> And so on this holiday I will visit her Temple,
> and perhaps I will steal a word from her![107]

> How will I ever choose another,
> while God himself exalts her?[108]

The troubadours also sang of the beloved's exceptionality among humans, namely her noble character, expressed both in terms of lineage and of individual behavior and speech. Because one could not attain a truly spiritual love with a commoner (who lacked the refinement to separate physical urges from the higher love that ennobles), it was necessary as part of the game of courtly love to establish the social bona fides of the beloved. This is particularly alien to the Andalusi tradition, in which poets spoke of the beloved's beauty, and of her cruelty and aloofness, but did not typically comment on her social class or represent class-specific behaviors. Again, it is Calvo who praises his beloved for her performance of courtly manners:

> Her honored conduct
> is so much more noble than the noblest[109]

In adapting this particular convention Abulafia resorts to a well-known passage from the Song of Songs, one of the most important sources of poetic language on the topic of love in biblical Hebrew. After establishing that he is drawing a class distinction and that his beloved is noble and therefore capable of inspiring the sort of emotions that are worthy to be expressed at court, he goes a step further:

> [When I was young and foolish]
> I did not distinguish between commoner and high born,
> or even the daughter of a nobleman, *awesome as bannered hosts.*[110]

Abulafia's insertion of the descriptor *awesome as bannered hosts* (Heb. *ayumah kanidgalot*) reinforces the idea that his beloved is of noble birth by suggesting that her father commands a large army (i.e., an army with many divisions, each carrying a banner). But at the same time, it points up that a Hebrew poet of the thirteenth century, when pressed for language to communicate the high birth of his beloved, must reach back into a biblical past in order to find a historical example of Jewish *nobility*. Though the Jewish notables of Abulafia's time certainly lived luxuriously and commanded wealth, they were not by any means considered noble. This glass ceiling at court was a constant reminder that Jewish sovereignty was a thing of the biblical past and that the political realities of the present, no matter how favorable they might be at times, were other. Nonetheless, as part of his assimilation to courtly culture, Abulafia adopts the convention of the nobility of the beloved, assuring us that now that his youthful days of chasing common girls are over, he is indeed ready to settle down with "a real damsel ['*almah*], an honorable girl, with a noble soul."[111]

Such a damsel's nobility is characterized not only by her lineage and conduct, but also by her speech, the type of speech that would get one noticed at court: eloquent, measured, refined. Once again, this description goes beyond the Andalusi repertory, in which a poet might speak of falling in love from hearing the beloved's voice, but only because that voice belongs to the beloved, not because it is a voice that carries an exemplary or exceptionally refined manner of speaking. The Andalusi beloved is not a courtly subject, and so her excellence is not measured by the criteria of courtly behavior or characteristics. Pero García Burgalés writes that his beloved is

> the lady whom God gave greater beauty,
> and whom he endowed with more eloquent and judicious speech,
> than all the other ladies in the world.[112]

He describes her as excelling all others in her speech, not in terms of her beautiful singing voice, but in terms of content: she knows how to speak at court, and that is part of what makes her a superior choice of beloved, aside from her beauty, high birth, and noble (for which we should read "courtly") conduct. Bonifacio Calvo similarly praises his beloved for *Sos senz e sas granz lauzors* (for her noble speech, [and] her intelligence).[113] Abulafia, for his part, writes that "her speech raises up the fallen," again borrowing from Jewish tradition, here the daily liturgy, comparing the power of the beloved's verbal skills with that of the word of God himself, in a creative bit of heresy.[114]

Abulafia's playful use of the Hebrew liturgy here, along with the biblical intertextuality that characterizes his poetry, contributes to a sense of polyphony and intertextuality that is richer and more nuanced than one finds in the classical troubadour corpus. In addition we notice, in this next composition, that Abulafia is novelizing the lyric, expanding the narrative capacities of the courtly love lyric as a genre. Abulafia's version is an expansion or gloss on a poem of Pero García Burgalés dealing with the same theme; a comparison of the two works highlights Abulafia's novelization strategy. In both compositions, the poetic voice complains that a friend is rebuking him for pursuing his beloved, that he is wasting his time. It is implied (in the Galician-Portuguese version) that the woman is out of his league and that he would be better served to find a more common girl who would more readily give him what he wants. The poetic voice becomes indignant and refutes the friend. If only he could see the beloved, he sings, "he'd be speechless just like me"

> when I see her, for I do not in any way know
> what to say to her then: and the same thing will happen to him!
> If, by chance, he wanted to tell her
> something, as soon as he found himself
> in her presence, everything would slip from his mind![115]

Abulafia's poem appears to be glossing Burgalés in a kind of *contrafactum* (Ar. *mu'arada*), by which he expands and elaborates on the theme introduced by the Christian poet.[116] In his version, he dramatizes the scene between the poet and his friend who thinks he is wasting his time on a woman who won't even talk to him. There is more narrative texture than in Burgalés's version, and Abulafia explores more extensively the depths of the torment suffered by the hopelessly enamored poetic voice, who is nonetheless vindicated by the fact that his friend shows himself to be equally powerless before the charms of the beloved:

> When he saw her, even as he spoke ill of her,
> His soul began to enter into her light . . .
> Suddenly, his soul was bound to hers
> And his heart was locked in the heart of her prison
> And even the splendor of her cheek, in its radiance, prevented
> his pupils from looking upon her brilliance.
> Then I fell upon my face, and my soul

was like a woman in her first childbirth who fears the pain
And I would have died, had he not
Reminded me of her, and I woke up thinking of her,
When he said: *What is with you, sleeper?* Look:[117]
There goes "that certain lady," Arise! Behold her beauty!
I give praise and confess to your beloved hind,
I am her ransom and her sacrifice!
Truly, it is enough for the man who loves her
to see her or to hear her words!
It is doctrine for every nobleman to make his life
a treadstone for her, and to lick the dust from her foot!
To suffer completely for her love,
for truly then God shall multiply her reward!
I shall set my heart to serve my love for her forever
Never shall I ask for her to set me free!
As long as the sun rises in the East, or
As long as the birds sing of her![118]

Here Abulafia does more than follow the lead of the troubadours with whom he served at court. He takes it to the next level, describing the scene in great detail, exaggerating, even parodying the skeptical friend who is converted to the same religion of love the poet practices. Aside from the obvious similarities in the scenario described, several of the details in this passage are tellingly characteristic of troubadour poetry and fairly absent from previous Hebrew tradition.[119] The image of the friend's heart being locked in a prison is, by the late thirteenth century, hopelessly cliché in Romance poetry, but is unheard of in Hebrew.[120] Equally characteristic of troubadour poetry is the *senhal* device used to indicate a known but anonymous beloved, here rendered by the Hebrew *plonit*, itself a loan from the Arabic *fulan* which in Castilan yields *fulana*, the rough equivalent of the English "what's-her-name"[121] The *nature* of suffering for the beloved is likewise more reminiscent of troubadour poetry than of Andalusi Hebrew tradition. While it is not at all uncommon in Hebrew to suffer from the effects of unrequited love, to complain of the beloved's cruelty and even to speak of or demonstrate one's inferiority and subordination to the beloved, the idea that such suffering should form a rule, a code, or a formal doctrine to be obeyed, is straight from the pages of Capellanus' *De Amore*.[122]

The combination of the presence of competing models of romantic love (the Andalusi and the troubadouresque) and the heightened sense of narrative and novelistic detail in the poetry of both Abulafia and his contemporary Bernardet both point up two broader, related trends in the Romance poetic culture of the thirteenth and early fourteenth centuries: the narrative turn in courtly lyric and a concomitant development of pro-tonovelistic polyphony in poets whose transformation (and parody) of courtly lyric styles point the way toward an authorial consciousness more characteristic of the modern novel in terms of its mimetic ambition and the scope of subjectivities it seeks to represent.

AUTHORIAL CONSCIOUSNESS AND THE NARRATIVE TURN

Three specific, overlapping sites of innovation can help to shed light on Abulafia's relationship to the vernacular culture of his hostland, Castile: the role of authorial consciousness in the development of the vernacular literatures; the innovative poetic voice that Abulafia brings to Hebrew; and his adaptation of the tropes of troubadouresque fin'amors. All three help us to better understand the nature of diasporic literary practice.

The late Middle Ages saw an important shift in the way that poets and authors imagined themselves. Olivia Holmes argues that the expansion of literacy and a shift in literary culture from oral to written modalities brings about a new authorial consciousness. She sees this as evidenced in three related developments: the poetic anthology, the *vida,* and the single-author collection.[123] While Petrarch is the most famous early example of the single-author collection, the trend starts quite a bit before the compila-tion of his *Canzoniere* in the late fourteenth century. It is also significant, particularly for our discussion of Abulafia's Hebrew poetry, that this shift occurs precisely during the emergence of the vernacular as a legitimate vehicle for upper-register literary activity.

The innovation of the single-author codex as an index of increased au-thorial consciousness may work in the Romance context, but must be understood differently in the case of a Hebrew poet. Abulafia compiled his own diwan, or collected poems, in 1298. While this may not yet have been standard practice among vernacular poets, Arabic and Hebrew poets had been doing so for centuries. The diwan of the late Abbasid era poet al-

Mutanabbi dates from the tenth century.[124] In Spain, Joseph Hanagid, the son of the poet Samuel Hanagid, completed his father's diwan in 1056.[125] As Petrarch would in the next century, Todros compiled his own diwan, titled "The Garden of Anecdotes and Saws," in 1298. He describes his compositions as a "flock without a shepherd" and explains that he put them together in no particular chronological order, opting instead to arrange them by genre and thematic content.[126] The first diwan of a poet working in a Romance vernacular is that of Peire Cardenal (fl. 1205–1272), one of Alfonso's troubadours whose verses Abulafia echoes.[127]

If, as Holmes argues, the emergence of authorial consciousness depended on an expansion of secular literacy and literary culture, it would stand to reason that it emerged much sooner in Arabic and Hebrew literatures, which had been developing secular literary traditions for centuries when troubadour poetry was beginning to emerge. Holmes mentions that the single-author codex coincides with an increased emphasis on autobiography in poetry and in texts about poets. Many of Todros's critics have dwelt on the uniquely autobiographical nature of his verse. Yitzhak Baer, in his history of Jews in Christian Spain, writes that "[Abulafia's] diwan is, in effect, a compilation in verse of the poet's personal memoirs and his observations on his times and contemporaries."[128] Hayim Schirmann, editor of the seminal anthology of Hispano-Hebrew poetry, calls his work "personal" and "confessional."[129] Peter Cole sees a "vivid personal dimension."[130]

Abulafia's poetry evinces a sort of protopolyphony, the first blush of that characteristic that would come to define the modern novel.[131] According to Bakhtin, the novel brings together various voices to represent a more complex, polyphonic experience than had been the case in earlier forms of prose narrative before the emergence of the novel. A single-author collection brings together different genres, tones, messages, and poetic voices.[132] Abulafia's diwan, and the authorial consciousness it demonstrates, might be conceived (as some have theorized about the cancionero of Juan Ruiz in the following century) as a kind of protonovel, a polyphonic, loosely autobiographical work that represents many aspects of the author's poetic voice(s). This would seem to put Todros ahead of his Christian peers in developing a more defined authorial presence, both in the 1298 compilation of his own collected poems and in the distinctly autobiographical flavor of his verse. I would not, however, argue that Arabic and Hebrew poets *influenced* their peers who wrote in the vernacular to move in this direction. Structurally, it makes sense that the conditions that gave rise to authorial consciousness simply existed earlier for Arabic and Hebrew poets than for the vernacular troubadours. The mid-thirteenth century seems to be the exact moment in which authors working in the European vernacular begin to assemble their compositions into single-author codices.

In addition to demonstrating a more developed authorial consciousness, Abulafia also moves his verse further into the territory of narrative, a step closer to contemporary works such as the Provençal Bernardet's verse narrative *Flamenca*.[133] He seems to be responding directly to his fellow troubadours by expanding and fleshing out in greater narrative detail scenes that the troubadours only sketch out indexically. Sarah Kay calls this trend in twelfth- and thirteenth-century poetry a "drift toward narrative."[134] This narrative impulse is accompanied by a tendency to develop primitive dialogue in the context of the lyric *cansó*. Kay writes that these moments are "not ... regular exchanges methodically attributed to two or more participants (as in the *tenso* or *partimen*), but ... irregular interjections which interrupt the first-person voice, and which come perhaps from within the 'self,' perhaps from outside it."[135] Abulafia's poem number 715, the novelization of the poet's rebuke of the nay-sayers, echoed in the verses of Pero García Burgalés, presents a fine example of this "drift toward narrative." Todros is novelizing the troubadours' lyric sentiments in a sort of contrapuntal imitative composition, known in Arabic as *mu'arada* or in Latin as *contrafactum*. Andalusi poets regularly engaged in such imitation as a way of proving their mettle and impressing or parodying the composers of the originals.[136]

Abulafia's poetry, when compared with the Andalusi Hebrew tradition, is best characterized by what Peter Cole has called its "vivid personal dimension."[137] While prior Andalusi poets wrote ostensibly biographical poetry, their poetic personae were more like types, like the masks of Greek theater that replaced the individual expressions of the actors with a standard image from the dramatic repertoire of personae. And while poets such as Solomon ibn Gabirol, Samuel Hanagid Naghrela, and Judah Halevi all had discernible poetic personalities, Abulafia managed to create a new, more immediate kind of poetic persona.[138]

The practice of fiction, and especially of new versions of Latin fictions brought over into the vernacular, changed forever how writers and readers understood the role of the author. According to Michel Zink, the authorial consciousness of fictionality that was a product of the translation of romance from Latin to the vernacular was responsible for the "appearance" of the author.[139] The authorial-narrative turn in thirteenth-century troubadour poetry is a result of this process. In the case of Abulafia, two things contribute to the autobiographicality of his poems. The first is that he distances himself from Andalusi tradition. The second is that he approximates the authorial persona of the troubadours of Kay's "drift toward narrative."

In a sense Abulafia anticipates the fourteenth-century trend of exaggerated pseudo-autobiographical verse that gives us such works as Guillaume de Machaut's *Voir Dit* and, in Castile, Juan Ruiz's *Libro de buen amor*.[140] Like these poets writing in Romance, Abulafia, in Ross Brann's words, "straddles the fine theoretical line between love poetry and love life."[141] He describes his poetic love objects with realistic touches that are more Juan Ruiz than Judah Halevi.[142] We can observe this tendency in all the major literary languages of the Iberian Peninsula and in the Western Mediterranean in general.

From the diasporic perspective, Abulafia's engagement with troubadour poetics was a small but highly significant portion of his total output. His poetic persona overall is highly intriguing, to say the least, but these poems in which he adapts troubadour poetics to Hebrew are of particular significance for a study of diaspora and literary practice because they are evidence of a diasporic writer's engagement with the literary practices of the dominant culture of the hostland. The fact that this type of adaptation was the norm for the Arabic-language poetry of al-Andalus and considerably more rare in Hebrew poetry in Christian Iberia supports the ideas of Khachig Tölölyan and others who stress the emergent and variable nature of diasporic culture. The shapes of diasporic culture change over time and from community to community. The political structures that obtained in al-Andalus accorded a protected place for religious minorities. The official language was that of a religion that recognized Judaism and Christianity as valid (if inferior), and this inclusion extended to the social and poetic cultures of the times. In Christian Iberia, Latin had never been cultivated by religious minorities, who were afforded neither social nor political stability by the laws of church and state.[143] There was, as a consequence, no common courtly poetic culture shared by Christians and Jews, though Alfonso made great strides in expanding the courtly function of the Castilian and Galician-Portuguese vernaculars.

Ultimately, the reasons for the inclusion or exclusion of Sephardic poets in the courtly poetic culture of al-Andalus and Christian Iberia were rooted in, or at least justified by, theology. The Qur'an made a space for Jews; the New Testament did not, unless those Jews wanted to become Christians, in which case they were welcome to join the dominant culture—until they weren't.[144] Theological disposition of the hostland aside, it is the question of vernacularity that makes the case of Abulafia and other Sephardic authors living in Christian Iberia so interesting. Once the vernacular becomes an acceptable vehicle for belles lettres at court, and especially given Alfonso's relatively enlightened approach to governing religious minorities, one would think that Sephardic writers, who had just as solid a command of the vernacular as any other native speaker of Castilian or Aragonese or Catalan, might have begun to experiment with writing refined poetry and prose in their native language. Some undoubtedly did, but by and large, and as we will see in the coming chapters, the rise of the vernacular as a literary language at court did not inspire a significant body of Sephardic literature in the vernacular.

As we have seen, Jewish intellectuals were key players in the Iberian vernacular revolution and were active in retooling the vernacular for learned cultural production, even before Alfonso's ambitious translation project. Still, they do not appear to have embraced the literary vernacular, choosing instead to champion the value of Hebrew as a superior literary language. They exhorted their peers to choose it, and not the vernacular, over Arabic, which by this time was largely a classical language of learning and not a language of significant new poetic production at Christian courts.

The Anxiety of Vernacularization: Shem Tov ben Isaac ibn Ardutiel de Carrión's Proverbios morales *and* Debate between the Pen and the Scissors

DIASPORA AND THE LITERARY VERNACULAR

Diasporic communities construct their identity in different ways, and language choice plays a large role in determining the boundaries among, as well as the relationships with, the hostland, the homeland, and the diverse communities of the larger diaspora.[1] We have seen how Sephardic writers mediated between the classical literary languages of the hostland (Arabic) and the homeland (Hebrew) and their participation in the development of a literary vernacular, especially at the court of Alfonso X of Castile-León. In this chapter I will address what happens when a Sephardic author steps into the literary limelight of the hostland, writing in the literary register of the vernacular that is common to both diasporic minority and dominant majority. Shem Tov ben Isaac Ardutiel (Sem Tob or Santób in Castilian) is a key figure in this discussion because he wrote significant original secular literary works in both Castilian and Hebrew. In this aspect he is perhaps unique in medieval Iberia, and the relationship between his *Proverbios morales* (*Moral Proverbs*; *Proverbios* hereafter) and *Vikuah ha-'et ve-ha-misparayim* (*Debate between the Pen and the Scissors*; *Debate* hereafter) tells us much about the significance of language choice in diaspora.

Already in the thirteenth century, Christian Iberia was emerging as a leader in developing a secular culture.[2] The kings of Castile were not anointed nor crowned by clergy as they were in the rest of Western Christendom.[3] Alfonso X's radical decoupling of the liberal arts from Latin, while it did not exactly render Latin obsolete as a language of secular study, was a powerful symbol of the crown's desire to create a secular space. This trend toward secularity elevated the prestige of the Castilian court and bolstered Alfonso's claims to the throne of the Holy Roman Empire. It also introduced an element of linguistic secularity into a literary world dominated by classical languages that were definitively identified with a specific religious group. Latin belonged to Christianity, Hebrew to Judaism, and Arabic to Islam.[4] But Castilian was, by virtue of its vernacularity, a common patrimony. Or was it? Here it is useful to distinguish between the different uses of the vernacular in the fourteenth century. It was, for the vast majority of those who spoke it, a language of colloquial, oral communication. Literacy levels, even when taking into account the fact that literary vernacularization opened the possibility of literacy to those who were ignorant of Latin, were very, very low by today's standards.[5] Before the widespread availability of printed editions, very few people had access even to texts written in the vernacular. By the numbers, most people's experience of texts in manuscript was one more characterized by an oral/aural experience than by a visual one. That is, when Ardutiel wrote, more people heard texts read to them than actually read the letters on the page.[6] This will not be news to any student of medieval literature, but it bears repeating in a discussion of the relative valuations of the literary vernacular in the Christian and Jewish communities. For just as religion served as a boundary marker between social groups in Ardutiel's time, so did the use of the literary vernacular.

In order for this argument to make sense, it is important to distinguish between the colloquial vernacular and the literary vernacular. It is quite true that by the mid-thirteenth century there were very few, if any, primary speakers of Andalusi Arabic in the Jewish communities of Castile. Jews and Christians spoke the same language at home but composed literary texts in different languages (with some significant exceptions such as the text in question). There was no question as to whether the spoken vernacular belonged to Jews or to Christians.[7] This was an incontrovertible fact of life in diaspora, and it is significant that there was no Jewish diasporic vernacular, no language that Jews had brought from their land of origin and continued to speak as a natural language at home. Whatever

Hebrew the Babylonian exiles had brought with them from Judea was quickly replaced by Aramaic, and the same held for Judeans exiled (or voluntarily dispersed) during the Roman period.[8] The diasporic tongue was nearly always a pen. Therefore it is choice of literary language, and not spoken vernacular, that is at issue here.

Somewhat after Ardutiel's lifetime, toward the end of the fourteenth century, the massive conversions of thousands of Jews to Catholicism in the wake of the pogroms of 1391 introduced a new class of Christians whose ethnic Judaism challenged established markers of identity. This destabilization of the semiotics of identity caused no little anxiety among the communities of Old Christians.[9] A similar effect occurred with the spread of vernacular (Castilian, Catalan) literature that, unlike Latin, Arabic, or Hebrew, could no longer be definitively associated with any of the Peninsula's religious traditions. To write in one's own mother tongue instead of the classical language of one's religion was at once a great leveler and a great source of anxiety. Jewish and Christian voices both in Spain and abroad have since spent centuries debating the meaning of a secular vernacular literature in a culture where identity had long been expressed primarily in terms of religious affiliation or heritage.

The anxieties resulting from the increasingly tenuous situation of Spain's Jewish communities in the late Middle Ages, the social transformations brought about by massive conversions in the late fourteenth and fifteenth centuries, the ensuing obsession with ethnic purity demonstrated by the statutes of *limpieza de sangre*,[10] and Spain's eventual modernization all crystallize around the work of Shem Tov ben Isaac Ardutiel de Carrión.[11] I will explain how Hispano-Hebrew writers voiced their anxieties over the use of the literary vernacular, then argue that Ardutiel's texts contained a veiled critique of the literary vernacular, a critique couched in specifically diasporic terms.

DIASPORIC LITERATURE IN A TIME OF DECLINE

While it is difficult to generalize about Jewish-Christian relations in Castile and impossible to do so for all of Christian Iberia during the late Middle Ages, it is safe to say that Christian monarchs found some of their Jewish subjects tremendously useful, but they were also bound by loyalty to the church to hold the Jewish *religion* in disdain publicly. It hardly needs to be repeated that generations of Christian monarchs and nobles of Castile and Aragon relied on Jewish courtiers for the daily administration of their courts and estates.[12] As in al-Andalus, Jewish subjects served their kings as administrators, financiers, physicians, diplomats, and trusted advisors. The fact that they enjoyed no legal protections or power base apart from the good favor of their king made them an excellent strategic choice to serve in highly placed positions. Unlike Christian nobles, whose alliances with other high nobility sometimes pitted them against the crown, and Muslim subjects, who were suspected of having conflicting allegiances to Granada or other Muslim states, Jewish courtiers' only source of political power was to remain in the good graces of the king.[13] This working relationship between Jewish courtier and Christian monarch existed side by side with the Christian theological contempt for Judaism. Unlike the Islamic doctrine of *dhimma*—protected Christian and Jewish minorities—that in theory guided the actions of Muslim caliphs and kings, Christian monarchs had no scriptural or theological directive to tolerate Jewish subjects. Any tolerance they practiced was predicated on the Jews' status as a useful minority and on customary practice. The situation was a far cry from contemporary ideas about cultural diversity in the context of a representative democracy.[14]

The fourteenth century in Castile was, for all Castilians, a difficult period marked by political strife, economic hardship, and social unrest. At mid-century the Black Death (1348) decimated all of Europe, and in 1369 the tyrant Pedro I ("the Cruel") of Castile was murdered by his illegitimate half brother, Enrique of Trastámara, who then assumed the throne in his stead.[15] Don Juan Manuel, the author of the canonical story collection *El Conde Lucanor* and a contemporary of Ardutiel, characterized this period as a *"doloroso et triste tienpo"* (a painful and sad time).[16]

Minorities, even privileged ones, do not fare well in such times, and the experience of the Jewish communities of Castile was no exception.[17] In general there was increased dissatisfaction with the privileged role of certain Jews at court, where they served, among other positions, as tax collectors. Such sentiment boiled over both at court and in the popular sphere when disaster or mass hysteria struck the general populace. In 1320–1321 there were a series of accusations of well poisonings against the Jewish communities, and in 1321 a band of shepherds from southern France who had been inspired by anti-Muslim crusade preachers crossed the Pyrenees, sacking the Jewish quarter of Tudela. Anti-Semitic violence likewise accompanied the Black Death of 1348 and the Trastámaran revolution of 1369.[18] Anti-Judaism both theological and political thrived. The Christian courtier Gonzalo Martín concerted the downfall of a number of Jewish courtiers, until his own fall from favor in 1339.[19] At the same time, the converso polemicist Alfonso de Valladolid (*olim* Abner de Burgos) preached against Judaism tirelessly. He succeeded at one point in convincing Alfonso XI to order the deletion of the *birkat ha-minim* (prayer for heretics) from the daily Jewish liturgy on the grounds that it discouraged Jews from converting to Christianity.[20] This is the state of affairs that obtained when Ardutiel lived and wrote the *Debate* and the *Proverbios*.

ARDUTIEL BETWEEN HEBREW AND CASTILIAN LITERARY PRACTICE

This downward trajectory in Jewish fortunes coincided with the upward trajectory of the success of Hispano-Romance vernaculars as successful literary languages, and Jewish writers' negative attitudes toward the vernacular reflect increased anxieties over fear of discrimination and persecution on the one hand and the temptations of conversion and assimilation on the other. During his reign in the second half of the thirteenth century, Alfonso X ("the Learned") institutionalized Castilian as a courtly language, displacing the previously dominant languages of church (Latin) and state (Arabic). This set Castilian on the track to the status of imperial language that it would ultimately assume in the age of the Catholic monarchs, with its own grammar, navy, and missionary force. Critical discussion of Alfonsine vernacular literary practice has tended to focus either on its competitive relationship with Latin or on its function as a vehicle for the dissemination of Arabic learning in translation.[21] The vernacular revolution in Spain coincided with a shift in the role of Hebrew writing and of the expansion of Hebrew literary practice to occupy more secular spaces left vacant by the translation and exile of Arabic. In al-Andalus, Jews wrote scientific and philosophic works in Arabic; in Christian Iberia they used Hebrew. This means that both Castilian and

Hebrew were moving into territory once held by Arabic, sharing space with each other, and to a lesser extent with Arabic, in a sort of medieval literary "contact zone."[22]

While there are dozens of Alfonsine-era translations into Hispano-Romance by Jewish translators, before Ardutiel there is no surviving original vernacular work by a Sephardic author.[23] Jewish authors during this period were more concerned with enriching Hebrew as a literary language and had little incentive, unlike Christian writers, to write in Castilian. Hebrew was considered the language of literature and of rhetoric, and while Castilian Jews who could write in either Roman or Hebrew characters were more than able to write competently in their native language, Castilian was not valued as a serious literary language in the Jewish community. Furthermore, Jewish and Christian writers were responding to quite different legacies. Generally, literary Castilian as a sovereign language strove to define itself against both Latin and Arabic, while literary Hebrew had to deal mostly with the lingering legacy of Arabic.[24] Although Castilian drew a great deal of material from Arabic sources, Castilian literary practice was never in competition with Arabic, as Hebrew had been for centuries in al-Andalus.

As we have seen in our discussion of Jacob ben Elazar, Sephardic authors of the eleventh and twelfth centuries saw the development of secular literary Hebrew writing as linked to Arabic. Moshe ibn Ezra in the eleventh century argued that literary Hebrew should reflect the best traits of Arabic (*'arabiyya*), and later authors argued for Hebrew's intrinsic superiority (*'ibraniyya*). This debate echoed and transformed the debates within Islam over the inherent superiority of the Arabic language vis-à-vis the Arabic or non-Arabic ethnicity of Muslims. In the late thirteenth century, with Arabic no longer a language of state, of court, or of new literary production, it was not a viable choice for Sephardic authors to write in Arabic. Their audience was a Hebrew-reading, vernacular Romance-speaking audience for whom Classical Arabic was at best a passive language of learning.

A contemporary of Todros Abulafia named Isaac ibn Sahula wrote a book that is useful for thinking about Sephardic authors' involvement at court and how this involvement relates to language choice. Ibn Sahula lived in Castile during the second half of the thirteenth century. He is the author of several kabbalistic works, including a commentary on the Song of Songs. His magnum opus, however, is *Meshal Haqadmoni* (Parable of the Old Timer), a frametale collection of short narrative and treatises on various scientific and philosophical topics, written in rhyming prose interspersed with verse.[25] The work is best known for being the first text to make mention of fellow Castilian Moses of León's *Zohar,* the foundational text of medieval Kabbalah. *Meshal Haqadmoni* is organized (like *Kalila wa-Dimna* and the *Conde Lucanor* after it) as a discussion between two characters, the Cynic and the Moralist. In his introduction, Ibn Sahula repeats the call of al-Harizi to rally around the cause of Hebrew letters, endangered by Jewish interest in Arabic and Castilian books.[26] Despite his protestations, by the late thirteenth century it is fairly clear that writing in Hebrew does not entail rejection of vernacular culture per se, even if Hebrew remains the preferred literary vehicle. While Ibn Sahula advocates a Hebrew-only policy for his fellow Jews, he does not hesitate to borrow from non-Hebrew sources, whether vernacular, Arabic, or Latin.[27]

Neither does his dedication to Hebrew as a literary language mean that Ibn Sahula turned his gaze away from the greater Christian society in which he lived. We should in no way mistake his nationalism for atavism or escapism. Like today's traditionalists, Ibn Sahula did not shun modern society; he chose to participate in it in hopes of promoting his own particular ideological program. In Ibn Sahula's case, this meant an emphasis on traditional rabbinic Judaism with a strong Kabbalistic bent and a protonationalist appeal (similar to that of al-Harizi) to his readers to turn away from Arabic and Castilian literature and to cultivate Hebrew as language of both secular and Jewish learning.[28] Raphael Loewe suggests that a substantial segment of *Meshal Haqadmoni* can be read as a political allegory for the Castilian court of Ibn Sahula's day, which means that (if we accept Loewe's reading) his interest in courtly affairs was not limited to the type of gallantry or scandalmongering associated with his contemporary Todros Abulafia, but rather took the shape of serious political commentary.[29] This engagement with current courtly culture, taken together with Ibn Sahula's Hebrew linguistic nationalism in the context of the vernacularization program of Alfonso X, means that although Ibn Sahula may have shunned the literary vernacular in theory, his own practice was very much engaged with vernacular literary practice and the court from which it emanated. Like Abulafia, who situated his writing in the royal court and whose literary voice moves between the Jewish and secular worlds, Ibn Sahula's writing, even while championing the superiority of Hebrew, does so in a work that likewise moves between the Jewish and Christian worlds, if only to establish the superiority of the former.

The case of Shem Tov Ardutiel reflects this trend, with the critical difference that Ardutiel wrote his vernacular work *Proverbios morales* at the behest of the king. While Abulafia and Ibn Sahula portray themselves as being involved in or interested in the goings on at court, Ardutiel is the first Sephardic author whose writing is the product of being called upon by the king to speak, as it were, and to do so in Castilian (and not Hebrew). We have in the dual examples of *Proverbios* and the *Debate* the first example of Sephardic literature by royal request, a literary record of Sephardic cultural and social integration that bears a royal *imprimatur*.

Already as early as the mid-thirteenth century, a Castilian writer such as Isaac ibn Sahula might well have spoken Castilian exclusively at home, even if he read Classical Arabic (which he certainly did) or was proficient to some degree in the Andalusi Arabic vernacular.[30] At the height of Alfonso X's glorification of the Castilian vernacular, Ibn Sahula touts his Hebrew *Meshal Haqadmoni* as a bastion of true Hebrew learning among impostors who simply repackage Arabic and Christian vernacular works: "Strong as a lion, / his poetry will surely blot out / the songs of the Christians / His poem resounds, / while yours grows bitter and silent."[31] He later states unequivocally: "I have not leaned upon the words of the Edomite [Christian], Ishmaelite [Muslim], Moabite [Christian], or Hagarite [Muslim]."[32] Here it is interesting to note that while Hispano-Romance was spoken (and written) by Christians, Muslims, and Jews alike, Ibn Sahula still refers to "the books of the Christians." These Hebrew-voiced assessments of literary uses of Hispano-Romance came during a period of intense literary vernacularization in Castile-León and Aragon, in which Jewish writers scarcely participated. Ardutiel himself makes this point: "No·m desdeñen por corto, que mucho judió largo / non entrarié a coto fazer lo que yo fago" (Let them not disdain me as short of learning, for many an important Jew would not venture to a hand's breadth of doing what I am doing).[33] What he is doing, and what "many an important Jew" would not, is undertaking to write an *original* moral treatise *as* a Jew that will succeed in being morally authoritative for a Christian audience at a time when Jewish fortunes in Castile were on the wane. To make matters even more sensitive, this treatise (in order to reach this Christian audience) would have to be written in the vernacular, a language considered by Jewish intellectuals to be an unacceptable choice for serious writing.

Whereas Andalusi Jews were well versed in, and wrote many important literary and rabbinical works in, the literary language of the dominant culture (Classical Arabic), most documented Jewish literary production in Hispano-Romance from this period is popular, paraliturgical, or homiletic.[34] In light of this absence of Jewish voices *in* the literary vernacular of Christian Iberia, what do Jewish authors have to say *about* the vernacular? The issue is certainly not Jewish ignorance of the various Romance languages spoken in the Peninsula (Galician-Portuguese, Castilian, Aragonese, Catalan, etc.), known collectively as Hispano-Romance. Spanish Arabist Julián Ribera lists several Andalusi authors who attested to Jewish and Muslim fluency in Hispano-Romance, and Samuel Stern wrote that it "might almost be taken for granted [that Andalusi Jews] made everyday use of the Mozarabic [Romance] of its Muslim and Christian neighbors."[35] In the eleventh century, Solomon ibn Gabirol lamented the sorry state of Hebrew letters among the Jews of Zaragoza, noting that "half of them talk the language of the Christians (*adomit*), and the other half Arabic (*bilshon benei kedar*)."[36] In the twelfth century, Maimonides makes reference to Andalusi Jews composing original poetry in Hispano-Romance.[37] Samuel ibn Sasson, a contemporary of Ardutiel, scolded the author of the *Proverbios* for composing verse in Castilian.[38] A generation later, Solomon ben Meshullam de Piera wrote a letter to Astruc Rimokh, chiding his fellow poet for having written him a letter in the vernacular.[39]

These critiques are consonant with medieval Hebrew and Arabic scholarship that associated clear speech and reason with classical languages such as Hebrew and Arabic, in contrast to the "stammering" and "babbling" of those who wrote in the vernacular.[40] Such is the atmosphere in which Ardutiel writes his *Proverbios* some time after 1351.

Given this voiced Jewish disdain for the literary vernacular, it must have been liberating and even a bit transgressive for Ardutiel to write something serious in his native language. Although he may have drawn criticism from the Jewish community for composing a moral treatise in the vernacular as opposed to in Hebrew, he would have had the cover of *having been coerced to do so* by King Pedro's request. Surely no member of the Jewish community, so dependent on royal patronage and protection, could fault Ardutiel for complying with the royal demand that he compose such a treatise? The fact of this royal interpellation, even if it is a fiction, provides Ardutiel with license to write freely in Castilian and may explain to a certain extent the total lack of attribution to Jewish sources of any of the content of the *Proverbios*. As long as he did not write anything identifiably *Jewish*, his experiment in vernacular writing would not qualify as transgressive, for it did not attempt to move the Jewish mind away from Hebrew literary practice, did not abandon the call to arms issued in the prior century by Judah al-Harizi and Isaac ibn Sahula.

"CLERECÍA RABÍNICA"

The case of the *Proverbios* is therefore unique among Castilian didactic poetry (excluding the small corpus of works written in Hebrew-character *aljamiado* and meant for an ostensibly Jewish audience) in that it was written by a Jew for an audience not exclusively Jewish. This calls into question the ideological function of the poem. As Paloma Díaz Mas has argued, the *Proverbios* are a kind of *"clerecía rabínica"* (priestly-rabbinic verse narrative).[41] While the idea of any rabbinic-priestly genre seems an oxymoron, it cannot be denied that the *Proverbios* have much in common with the verse narrative works of Gonzalo de Berceo and the less easily classifiable *Libro de buen amor* of his contemporary Juan Ruiz. A more productive term than clerecía rabínica for thinking about Ardutiel's text in a diasporic key is *cuaderna vía* (the quaternion way), which according to Colbert Nepaulsingh identifies the genre as inherently literary, naming it for the quaternion (*cuaderno*), a large folio of parchment folded twice, the basic unit of bookmaking in the manuscript era. Nepaulsingh argues that the term *cuaderna vía* also refers to the four-verse unit that, like the quaternion for the book, is the basic structural unit of the text of *mester de clerecía*. For Nepaulsingh, the structural unit of four verses is appropriate to the Christian didactic disposition of the authors of clerecía, who sought to explain their narratives in terms of worldly and heavenly significance: "For the poet, this is a quaternion way to tell a story because a single moral is taught in two senses, just as a single sheet of paper or parchment is folded twice. The poet takes care to 'unfold' both senses of his story so that the reader can appreciate the whole moral."[42]

This concept supports Díaz Mas's idea of clerecía rabínica in that while a rabbi would not be concerned in the same way with the duality soul/body, he *would* be (according to many critics of the *Proverbios*) interested in demonstrating the bivalence or bisemy of a given example or "lesson." The diasporic turn in the cuaderna vía, then, is that Ardutiel adapts the dominant verse form that (if we follow Nepaulsingh) takes its structure from Christian theological cues (body/soul) and adapts it not to a related Jewish theological problem, but rather to addressing the *political* reality resulting from living in galut: the need to advocate, carefully, the position of the diasporic community before the sovereign power. In the vernacular literary sphere, particularly in a text that is understood as *petitorio* or as in the voice of a minority speaking to power, the task of the text is more to negotiate power dynamics than to disseminate doctrine.

In fact, the very notion of clerecía rabínica is typical of majority understandings of minority religious culture. There is a tendency to think of the institutions, doctrines, and practices of the minority religion as versions or adaptations of Christian institutions. In Christian sources, for example, it is not uncommon to represent Muhammad as an object of adoration (as if he were a Muslim Jesus), or to refer to a synagogue as a Jewish church.[43] In this case, however, the analogy is truer than in that of the Muslim Jesus, for Ardutiel *is* adapting the clerecía genre—though it is safer to say that his text is a *secular* rather than *rabbinic* brand of clerecía, for nowhere does he explicitly attribute any part of his poem to biblical or rabbinic sources. In any event, a text *by* a rabbi, when directed toward a Christian (or at least non-Jewish) audience, is no longer a *rabbinic* text, because that is not what rabbis did in the fourteenth century. Rather, they taught Jewish religious tradition to Jews. In the *Proverbios*, Ardutiel does neither: neither his content nor his audience is meant to be specifically Jewish. If it were otherwise, the poet would not need to excuse himself for *being* Jewish, nor beg the audience's indulgence for the same reason:

> Even if my discourse is not great, it should not be despised because spoken
>   by a modest person: for many a sword
> Of good and fine steel comes from a torn sheath, and it is from the worm
>   that fine silk is made.

And a miserable catapult can be most accurate, and a torn skin can [still
manage to] cover up white breasts;

And a conniving messenger can bring good news, and a lowly lawyer can
introduce faithful arguments.

For being born on the thornbush, the rose is certainly not worth less, nor
is good wine if taken from the lesser branches of the vine.

Nor is the hawk worth less, if born in a poor nest, nor are good proverbs [of
less value] if spoken by a Jew.[44]

It is clear that Ardutiel is conscious of his position, of the difficulty of a
living member of a marginalized religious minority proposing to speak (or
write) authoritatively on moral matters. This being the case, what *did* Ardutiel hope to accomplish with this vernacular didactic work? Julian Weiss
has written eloquently on the ideological function of the works of mester
de clerecía in the thirteenth century. According to him, the vernacular
genre of the clerecía "enabled these clerics both to affirm their learned
cultural traditions and to disseminate them to a wider audience" (i.e., a lay
audience that did not understand Latin). The adoption of the vernacular
as a literary vehicle allowed these Christian clerics to serve as intellectual intermediaries, "adapting material from written Latin and French
sources, but also from popular legend."[45] According to this vision, then,
the clerecía was a kind of translation, of bringing over learned knowledge
to the unlettered, very much in line with, and flowing from, the decision of
the Fourth Lateran Council to authorize the vernacular for preaching to
the masses. But to what end? For Weiss the clerecía text is an instrument
of church hegemony, meant to overcome popular religious traditions and
"to present itself as the sole representative of unmediated truth."[46] In this
sense the *Proverbios* are horribly out of step as an example of clerecía as
ideological instrument. As a text written by a Jew for a non-Jewish audience, the *Proverbios* can hardly be read as an exercise in hegemony. Their
vernacularity must be understood differently.

According to Julian Weiss, Christian authors of clerecía, while purport-
ing to write in the language "en qual suele el pueblo fablar con so vecino,"
(the language in which the people speak with their neighbors) the listeners
[actually] found themselves walking a tightrope, balancing precariously
between the familiarity of the vernacular and a verse form, syntax, and
frequently a vocabulary that would have appeared quite wondrous.[47] That

is, the vernacular of the clerecía was not really the common vernacular, but a priestly register imbued with much of the wonder and authority of the priestly office, an otherworldly voice that sounded like language of the "people" but at the same time delivered an experience that inspired awe and wonder. One might say the same of the *Proverbios*. Written in a register of Castilian bearing features that places it alongside other contemporaneous examples, it seems to stand apart in many of its formal traits and must have made an impression upon Christian audiences similar to that of the clerecía.[48] However, the wondrousness and awe that inspired it were not rooted in ecclesiastical authority but rather in its opposite: a voice that challenged the very idea of hegemony, that invited the audience to consider a world of relativism and pluralism, to hold the contradiction that there may be more than one way to understand the world.

> What one man denigrates I see another praise; what this one considers
>   beautiful another finds ugly.
> The measuring rod that the buyer calls short, this same rod is called long
>   by the seller.
> The one who throws the spear considers it slow, but the man that it reaches
>   finds it speedy enough.[49]

Readers and listeners responded enthusiastically to Ardutiel's text, which was well received by the Castilian-speaking establishment.[50] In writing what Paloma Díaz Mas calls a "texto petitorio" (petitionary text), Ardutiel's primary goal would have been to win the favor of his sponsor, if not literary fame.[51] However, quite unlike the Jewish Alfonsine translators, who were all but anonymous, Ardutiel could take the credit for his original work in Castilian. In writing a learned, secular text in Castilian, Ardutiel anticipated the critiques of both his Christian and Jewish readers, the former of whom were liable to discount the teachings of a rabbi, the latter to shun a rabbi's vernacular writings.

This condition of outsider to both Jewish and Christian audiences opens up a new space for Ardutiel in which he is not bound by either religious tradition. Unlike other works of clerecía he does not (and as a Jew cannot) claim to represent Christian authority. As a Jewish author writing an entirely profane work he is similarly free from the conventions and expectations of Jewish religious texts. Even if he includes paraphrased material from, for example, the biblical book of Ecclesiastes, his failure to cite his source frees him from any responsibility he might have toward Ecclesiastes when writing as a religious authority. His text somehow manages to be *religious* without being sectarian or doctrinal. That is, he does not explicitly espouse the doctrine of any specific religion nor invoke its authorities, yet he deals seriously with concepts, such as sin, that are patently religious as opposed to moral or ethical, in that they are an aspect of the relationship between God and humanity, and as such are built upon a revelation-specific understanding of sin.

> Being in the anguish of fear over my sins—for I have committed many, without number, small and large—
> I considered myself as dead. But a very reassuring comfort came to mind, which made me happy:
> "Foolish, senseless man, it would be an insult to God for you to weigh your own malice on the scale of His forgiveness."
> He has given you life, you live [only] through His mercy. How could your deeds surpass His?[52]

According to Theodore Perry, this section of the poem on repentance is the most problematic for critics who would like to read the *Proverbios* as a completely secular "practical handbook of social and physical survival" and who argue that Ardutiel's "religious references are perhaps insincere or at least purely perfunctory concession to the time and its literary styles."[53] The section on repentance is too lengthy and too sincerely religious for this to be true.

Díaz Mas and Mota follow Perry in pointing out that the distinction Ardutiel makes here is a Jewish one, citing rabbinical authorities. Díaz Mas suggests that most Christian readers would not have been able to recognize this distinction. This may be so, as the common lay person was likely not well versed on the theology of sin and redemption; but what definitely would have struck a Christian reader as odd would have been the absence of Christ's salvation from any discussion of sin. The text is different in this respect from other works of translated wisdom literature, not only in that it is contemporary and associated with a historical author whose influences and interests we can identify positively, but in its nonsectarian approach to specifically religious concepts such as sin. The author does not claim to be representing Christian or Jewish doctrine, yet he still speaks of God and of the relationship between God and humanity. This makes it unique.[54]

Ardutiel's *Proverbios morales* is not responsible to any religious tradition and is bound perhaps only to avoid offending Judaism or Christianity. The author is effectively off the grid of literary and sectarian expectations and therefore unencumbered by them. This freedom allows Ardutiel a sense of play that is absent in the thirteenth-century Castilian translations of Arabic wisdom literature and is more characteristic of the ludic atmosphere of the Hispano-Arabic and Hispano-Hebrew maqama or of the *Libro de buen amor* of Ardutiel's contemporary, Juan Ruiz. Some critics have suggested that the mester de clerecía and the Hispano-Hebrew maqama share certain formal traits, such as a didactic (or at least pseudo-didactic) orientation and perhaps some similarity between the twelve-syllable line of the *clerecía* and the convention (in Arabic and Hebrew rhyming prose) of rhyming at least once every eleven syllables. Others have suggested that Ardutiel employs in the *Proverbios* the frequent homeoteleuton (near rhyme) characteristic of the Arabic and Hispano-Hebrew maqama. Paloma Díaz Mas discredits this idea, while still admitting some affinities between the maqama and Ardutiel's *Proverbios*, if not the entire mester de clerecía.[55] Raymond Scheindlin notes that although the *Debate* is technically a maqama, "it shows significant independence from the maqama tradition and from literary techniques appropriated from Arabic."[56] This formal departure from the classical maqama, begun already in the twelfth century, supports the idea that Romance, Hebrew, and Arabic authors were beginning to converge in some conventions. We have an example of a late Arabic maqama from fourteenth-century Granada, the *Maqama of the fiesta,* by Ibn al-Murabi, that displays similar independence from the classical maqamat of al-Hariri and, like other fourteenth-century works, has a narrator with a more distinctive individualized presence.[57]

THE TEXTUAL PERFORMANCE OF PERFORMANCE

What is certain is that the poetic voice of the *Proverbios,* of some of the later works of clerecía (especially Juan Ruiz's *Libro de buen amor*) and of a number of similarly pseudo-autobiographical/poetical works of the late thirteenth and fourteenth centuries does bear resemblance to the poetic voice of the maqama. Far from coincidence, the affinity of the literary voice of these and other related genres is reflective of a broad movement in vernacular literary culture toward an authorial consciousness manifested increasingly in written, rather than live, performance. Troubadours, authors of didactic works of mester de clerecía, of poetic autobiographies and autobiographical poetry, as well as Hebrew and Arabic maqamat, all converge in this trend.[58] The key to this similarity lies in its relation to verbal performance and the role of the literary composition in transforming live literary practice into durable form. Sylvia Huot writes that this voice, exemplified in the French *dits* (pseudo-autobiographical poetic narratives) of Jean de Froissart and Machaut, is a result of the entextualization of the troubadour's performance, of a "voice projected into writing."[59] Jacqueline Cerquiglini writes that the French dit is a genre that entextualizes poetic performance.[60] It represents the performance of poetry, and reproduces some of its conventions and formal aspects.

Before one composed in the vernacular, the vernacular was a language of performance, and not of written composition, even if the texts in question were literary. Theodore Perry notes that this performativity is what distinguishes Ardutiel's text from the corpus of vernacular wisdom literature (*Bocados de Oro, Poridat de Poridades,* etc.) written in prose. By virtue of having been *written* in verse, "the aphorisms of the *PM* were recited and became part of a living, oral tradition."[61] This example challenges the oral/literary dichotomy that Walter Ong proposes in *Orality and Literacy.* Ruth Finnegan has responded to this distinction by calling for more specific discussion of literary and oral "characteristics or consequences likely to be associated with orality and with literacy," rather than to posit (as Ong has done) two distinct cultures, one oral, another literate.[62]

The result is a sort of textual performance of performance, a simulacrum of performance in which the poet reproduces certain aspects and formal conventions of live performance while making amply clear, through literary-reflexive references, the "bookness" of his text.[63] This is also true of the works of clerecía that consciously borrow from the discursive conventions of the oral epic while at the same time invoking their authority as products of a learned written tradition (one that includes languages such as French and Latin that would have been out of the reach of the great mass of the

Castilian-speaking target audience). In both cases, dit and clerecía, the author invokes the authority of traditions of live performance and of the written tradition (and the authority that flows from the manuscript itself, with all the material wealth and privilege that form implies).

In one sense, these authors are borrowing some of the structural traits of verbal performance, recreating it in the context of a book.[64] Richard Bauman has posited that verbal art identifies itself as such by pointing out its difference from ordinary pragmatic speech.[65] Authors of dits, works of clerecía, and maqamat are doing something analogous in writing; their texts call attention to their own literary metaperformativity by simultaneously invoking and parodying (in the most literal sense) their performativity. Just as a parody of an established genre calls attention to its defining characteristics by their exaggeration, the entextualization of verbal performance calls into question the defining characteristics of poetic performance by reproducing them in a context (the written composition) the circumstances of which do not demand or produce the same results. Ardutiel's contemporary and neighbor in Castile, Juan Ruiz, makes great use of this type of generic parody in his *Libro de buen amor* in confusing boundaries between the "bookness" and the performativity of his own text, with frequent references to the material reality of the book itself and to his own persona as performer of lyric and connoisseur of multiple lyric traditions.[66]

The playfulness and parodic possibility inherited from the maqama and expressed in the parodic manipulation of the conventions of verbal performance, coupled with the freedom from authorial responsibility to any particular religious tradition, leaves Ardutiel ample space to assert an original authorial presence, one that is frequently ironic, despite the serious subject matter at hand. In one notable example, Ardutiel dedicates no fewer than fifty-two couplets to the value of knowing when to stop talking, beginning his discourse by reminding the reader that:

> It is bad to speak too much, but it is worse to be silent; for, in my opinion, the tongue was not given to be speechless.
> However, the superiority of silence cannot be denied; it is always suitable to speak about it.
> In order that we might speak [only] half of what we hear, for that reason we have one tongue and two ears.

He who wishes to speak much without great wisdom would surely do better business in keeping silent.
The sage who wished to praise silence and denigrate speech said as
follows:
"If speech were figured by silver, silence would be represented by gold."[67]

In some ways, Ardutiel was in virgin territory. Writing in Castilian, he was
mostly free of any anxiety of influence. He did not stand in the shadow of
Judah al-Harizi, or Isaac ibn Sahula, as he did when writing in Hebrew.
He was not constrained by obedience to either Christian or Jewish doctrine or exegetical tradition.[68] Thus unmoored from convention, he was
at liberty to develop an individual poetic voice—an unusual opportunity
at a time when writers were valued for their command of stock tropes and
stylistic conventions.[69] Ardutiel was free to pick and choose materials as
he wished. He could, for example, include salty bits of folk wisdom such as
the following proverb: "It's true enough, the old proverb: The houseguest
and the fish both stink by the third day."[70] This freedom to pick and choose
among popular, classical, or Judaic sources had long applied to authors of
maqamat working in Hebrew. Joseph ibn Zabara incorporated folkloric
narratives, biblical references, and snippets of classical medical texts in
his *Sefer Sha'ashu'im* (Book of Delights).[71] Isaac ibn Sahula likewise drew
upon popular tales and Aesopic fables in *Meshal Haqadmoni*. But this was
the first time a Sephardic author was at his liberty in this fashion in a vernacular text. However, as I will demonstrate in the following pages, if we
take the *Proverbios* alone we have only one part of the picture. We stand
to gain a far better understanding of this work of rabbinical clerecía, and
in particular of Ardutiel's problematic relationship with the literary vernacular, when we read it together with his work of Hebrew belles lettres,
the *Debate between the Pen and the Scissors*. There is a certain reciprocity
or intertextuality between the two texts. *Proverbios* contains references to
Debate both in a short segment debating the relative superiority of arms
versus letters (in the tradition of similar debates written in Hebrew by
Jacob ben Elazar and others, and in French by the clergie/chivalrie debates mentioned in our discussion of Ben Elazar's *Stories*) and in another
segment debating the relative merits of the pen and the scissors as writing instruments.[72] Both texts are therefore present in the other in ways

that help us achieve a more nuanced understanding of Ardutiel's artistic intervention.

ARDUTIEL'S *DEBATE BETWEEN THE PEN AND THE SCISSORS*

The type of comparative work necessary to bring the *Debate* together with the *Proverbios* does not happen very often. The fragmentation of the medieval Iberian corpus has been the historical standard from which we are now happily learning to deviate. If Hispanists have emphasized the difference of Ardutiel's literary voice in the *Proverbios,* scholars of Hebrew have downplayed the distinctiveness of the *Debate* and almost entirely segregated it from the *Proverbios* and the greater context of fourteenth-century Hispano-Romance literature. Neither are they in consensus as to the literary quality of the *Debate.* Hayim Schirmann, for example, maintained that Ardutiel was merely typical of the "inferior literary tastes of his time," but Peter Cole admires his "fluid rhymed prose."[73] What is clear is that unlike his *Proverbios,* Ardutiel's *Debate* lacks the status of novelty act. It is, when studied as an example of the late medieval Hebrew maqama, an original example of a demanding literary genre, but stands in good company with a long series of such texts by other Peninsular Jews.[74] Here, for better or for worse, Ardutiel is just another Hebrew fiction writer, not a "Castilian Theognis" or a writer whose Hebraic background "invades" Castilian poetry.[75]

While there is a sizeable bibliography on the *Proverbios,* Ardutiel's *Debate* has attracted relatively little attention.[76] The few critics who have studied the poem have read it as an allegory representing either individual historical figures or personifications of various ideologies. Sanford Shepard reads it as a critique of the prominent converso and anti-Jewish polemicist Alfonso of Valladolid (formerly Abner of Burgos).[77] The editors of the complete Hebrew edition, Nini and Fruchtman, read it as a critique of a general "cultural decline" in the Jewish community of Ardutiel's day, in which the scissors represent ignorant but powerful men who come to dominate positions in the Jewish community traditionally held by scholars and rabbis.[78] Einbinder discounts these readings, suggesting the alternatives of either a debate between kabbalists and rabbinists, or perhaps between written and oral law, or more generally a commentary on polysemy and the human tendency to come up with differing narratives of a single event.[79] Most recently, Blackwelder-Carpenter has suggested that the *Debate* is a blueprint for cross-cultural understanding, while Zackin, in an erudite and penetrating study, reads the text as an indictment of the irresponsible uses of philosophy without proper grounding in traditional religious thought.[80] Einbinder has suggested that perhaps none of these readings can ever be definitive, because ultimately the *Debate* is more about the predicaments of writing itself than about any specific histori-cal or intellectual phenomenon.[81] In the same vein, Cole argues that "a straight one-to-one allegorical reading seems to be inconsistent with the details of the story itself."[82] Taken this way, rather than as a snapshot or critique of a historical reality, we can understand Ardutiel's text as a sort of manual for critical thinking about writing and reading. Before advancing my own reading, I'd like to summarize the text here:

The debate takes place one cold winter's day in which the narrator's inkwell freezes solid, so that the narrator breaks his pen's tip on the hard surface of the frozen ink. The scissors come forward to take the pen's place, which leads to a debate between the two in which the pen and the scissors both extol the virtues of their respective techniques of writing. Unable to settle their differences, they agree to find a third party to judge which of them is the more fitting utensil. The pen goes out into the town and returns with a wise old man, who is told to look around the house and determine the purpose of each item in it. He picks up the pen and writes with it, then picks up the scissors and uses them to trim his hair, fingernails, and moustache, thus settling the dispute.

Again, unlike the *Proverbios,* the *Debate* has a clear literary genealogy. It is a parody of the medieval Arabic and Hebrew literary debate between the pen and the sword such as that written by Jacob ben Elazar, couched in the stylistic conventions of the Hebrew maqama.[83] If we map the bias of almost every version of the sword vs. pen debate onto Ardutiel's text, the pen is likely to win, just as the pen or clerk emerges victorious (nine times out of ten) in the sword vs. pen and clerk vs. knight debates that Ardutiel is spoofing. The idea is that if you are attempting to write with scissors, *you are doing it wrong.* The scissors are not meant for writing, the pen is; and so whoever is meant to be represented by the scissors is incorrect in their thinking or in their actions, but more specifically in their selection and application of a given doctrine, philosophy, or way of thinking to a real life situation. This is where the *Debate* differs from its models. In the Arabic and Hebrew debates between pen and sword, the pen writes and the sword applies military force, but both are the right tool for the job. Ardutiel's *Debate* introduces the idea of decorum, that there is one correct way to write, and to do so you must use a pen.

This shift from comparing apples to oranges (as in the arms vs. letters tradition) to judging both fruits by the same criteria echoes the debates between the lovers of knights and clerks that spun off from the earlier French chivalrie/clergie debates between clerks and knights. In the lovers' debates (represented in Castilian by *Elena y María,* late thirteenth century), the two women judge the knight and the clerk not by a general categorical comparison (i.e. "which is better, knights or clerks?") but by a single criterion: their ability to satisfy a woman.[84] The obvious bias in favor of the clerks in these debates—owing in no small part to the fact that they were all written by clerks at a time when fighting men (at least in Castile) did not typically write poetry—indicates a shift in the target audience and in the perspective represented by the debate. If the arms vs. letters and pen vs. sword debates are directed toward a larger audience, the debates between lovers of clerks and knights and that of Ardutiel between pen and scissors suggest a more specialized audience that by its specific disposition is biased toward a particular outcome. Similar to the oafish, brusque, fatigued, and frequently absent knights decried by the lovers of clerks in the French debates, the scissors, which were never meant to write, cannot possibly win. The game, as it were, is rigged against the sword/scissors, since the criteria by which they are judged inherently favor the pen. For an audience of clerks, the knight cannot emerge victorious; for a Hebrew-reading or -listening audience of Jewish notables and writers, the pen must always win out over the scissors in a contest of writing.

Ardutiel's choice of scissors to stand in for the traditional sword in the debate is also significant, especially when taken together with the setting of his maqama in the home. Traditionally the maqama is set in a series of cities, giving the impression of the narrator's itinerary through known or fictional cities. Ardutiel's setting is in what appears to be the narrator's own home, in a region where it gets cold enough for ink to freeze inside the house (Ardutiel lived in Soria, where temperatures drop below freezing during the winter months). This shift from public to private settings happens somewhat later in Castilian literature, and by the end of the fifteenth century we see scenes in Fernando de Rojas's *Celestina* regularly taking place indoors in the homes of the protagonists.[85] The scissors likewise can be understood as the domestic counterpart to the sword, and in some cases can stand in metonymically for a person. We have one such (later) example in the Catalan poetry of Francesc Moner, who fantasizes that his beloved's scissors (whose handle is engraved to resemble the head of a bird) transforms into a live bird and flies away.[86] In this case the accoutrements of the lady, which represent such courtly refinements as needlepoint, provide a counterpart to that of the man, the sword. Finally, in reading the scissors, and in continuing to explore the symbolic values of sword and pen vis-à-vis the courtly realities inhabited by Christian and Jewish courtiers, we should note that Ardutiel was, in addition to a man of some considerable learning, a sheep rancher. For him, the scissors would be a symbol of his own métier (as would a sword to a nobleman) and just as representative as the sword for the nobleman for how he made his way in the material world. If the nobleman historically earned his keep at court with the sword, assisting the king in the defense of the realm, the middle-class Jewish courtier had to earn his keep with the pen or, in Ardutiel's case, the scissors. I am not suggesting that Ardutiel meant for the scissors to have any allegorical value in this sense (though I am about to offer a slightly different allegorical reading), but merely that for a sheep rancher, the scissors would be a wholly familiar instrument, one that served to convert one's assets into fungible woolen form.

TWO WAYS OF SEEING OR TWO WAYS OF WRITING?

The key to understanding the *Debate* may be found in the *Proverbios*. Although the *Proverbios* is essentially a compilation of wisdom literature, the circumstances and identities of its author and its putative audience(s) are unusual for the late Middle Ages in Western Europe. In the introduction to his *Debate,* Ardutiel adopts a posture of deference toward the culture of the majority while at the same time making a case for his own position as a minority author. We should bear in mind that Ardutiel famously invokes his subaltern status in his own *accessus ad lectorem* when he excuses himself for *naçer en mal nido* (having been born in a poor nest, i.e., being of inferior/Jewish origin). This makes him different from his contemporaries who, in similarly formulaic ways, beg the reader's indulgence due to their lack of learning or moral turpitude.[87] He is presenting himself as a different type of writer, one whose personal situation gives him a perspective that differs from that of his audience. Therefore, when he writes about relativism (or, if you prefer, dual perspectivism), we must read him in light of his avowed difference. For him, the question of relativism is not simply a universal one, but one that bears directly upon his fortunes as the member of an embattled minority.

> When the wind comes up, first I agree then disagree: it puts out the candle but also kindles a great fire.
> I immediately render the judgment that it is good to grow in strength and show great diligence in order to become active;
> For it is because of its weakness that the flame of the candle has died, and because of its strength that the great fire lived.
> But within a short time I appeal this decision, for I see the weak escape and the strong perish.
> For the same wind that acted upon those two [i.e., the candle and the great fire] in the same day destroyed this other one:
> The same [wind] shattered a very great tree, but the grass of the meadow was not terrified at its passing.
> He who is being burned up in his house receives great pain from the wind; [but] when he winnows his grain he is very delighted with it.
> Wherefore, I am never able to attach my opinion to a single stake; nor do I know which [shade] will avail me more, dark or light.[88]

As we have seen above, this applies equally, if not more so, to Ardutiel's *Proverbios,* with its cascade of metaphors of unstable or ambivalent meaning. True to his own observations in *Proverbios,* Ardutiel appears to give voice to (at least) two different understandings of the literary uses of dual perspectivism itself. In the *Proverbios,* it is an appeal for his Christian audience to consider the perspective of the Jewish minority, a sort of lesson in political protopluralism (two ways of seeing the world). However, in the *Debate,* it is a critique of vernacular learning relative to classical learning (two ways of writing about the world).

Despite the text's seeming resistance to definitive allegorization, I believe there is convincing evidence for another possibility: that the debate is one between Hebrew and Romance, with the pen representing the holy tongue and the scissors the vernacular. If one reads the *Debate* without reference to the *Proverbios,* this is unlikely to come to the fore: a Hebrew scholar (narrowly defined) tends to think in terms of Hebrew, and the reverse is true of the Romanist who reads the *Proverbios* without reference to the *Debate.* However, when we read the two as interrelated parts of Artudiel's repertory, we see a veiled critique of the literary vernacular begin to emerge. It seems as though Ardutiel experienced some anxiety over the *Proverbios,* to which he gives voice in a series of comments made in both the *Debate* and his vernacular text. In these comments he claims that the vernacular is a sort of last resort, an inferior alternative to writing in Hebrew that should not be considered the literary vehicle of a serious writer. This reading puts the famous *accessus* of the *Proverbios* in a new light. Ardutiel begs the indulgence of the vernacular reader to pay heed to his words, though they come from the pen of a Jew. At the same time he himself undermines the authority of his own words for having been written in the vernacular. He is at once "el que tira la lança" (he who throws the lance) and "al quien alcança" (he who his struck by the lance), putting into practice the dual perspectivism so lauded by readers of the *Proverbios.*

Einbinder's observation that the narrator resorts to writing with scissors only because he is concerned "with finding some means of expression in a situation where conventional methods have failed" supports this reading, if we understand the "conventional" methods as Hebrew and the "failure" as the "worsening relations" (Perry's words) between Jews and Christians in Castile during the second half of the fourteenth century.[89] Ardutiel, like most of the Jewish writers of his times, writes the *Proverbios* in the vernacular *because he has to,* because Hebrew is not an acceptable language for use at court, or simply because he has been asked to do so by the king himself. Likewise, the narrator of the *Debate* writes with scissors because he cannot with a pen. The vernacular, for him, is not his first choice, but given the situation, it is his best choice. The pen is an honored instrument for writing; the scissors, a utilitarian tool pressed into service as a last resort only when the pen's tip is broken against the frozen surface of the inkwell.[90]

Let us turn to the internal evidence in the *Debate* itself. Much like his peers in the Jewish community who would eventually disparage vernacular literature as "stammering" and "babbling," Ardutiel seems to argue that writing with scissors is not really writing at all, but rather insubstantial nonsense. The scissors boasts that his writing is pure "form without matter" and "spirit without a body."[91] He adds that his "letter alone ran to speak with you," unaccompanied by ink or even paper.[92] Ardutiel is here concretizing the metaphor of writing that "lacks substance." For Ardutiel, it is the vernacular—whose words are *meant* to be spoken (but not written)—that lacks substance, while Hebrew, never a vernacular language in Spain, is always written and carries the authority of biblical tradition.[93]

Even more convincing evidence for this allegorical reading is the pen's invective poem against the scissors, in which he compares the ink with which he writes to divine blessing, seemingly claiming that God is on his side and not that of the scissors: "Your writing," he taunts, "returns empty and thirsty, / but mine is sated with God's goodwill, and filled with his blessing."[94] This identification of the pen with Jewish religious authority and the scissors with the language of the Christian government also resonates with the origins of the debate as a parody of the tradition of debates between the pen and the sword.[95] The scissors are made of iron and are likened to two swords. In these debates the sword represents the nobility, and therefore temporal power, and the pen the clergy and divine (or perhaps symbolic) power. In a Jewish context, the twin "swords" of the scissors would likewise represent temporal power of the crown of Castile and, metonymically, the official language of its court, while the pen would represent the Jewish clergy and its own official language, Hebrew.

Official vernacularization contributes to the sense that *written* Castilian is largely a Christian phenomenon.[96] Although already by the eleventh century Ibn Gabirol refers to the Romance vernacular as *Edomit* (Edomite, i.e. "the Christian language"), it was official vernacularization and the elevation of Castilian as a language of state and of courtly literature that solidified for Jewish authors the notion of Romance as a specifically *Christian* language, the language of a Christian court, even if most of the vernacular texts emanating from that court were not religious in nature (though there are obvious exceptions such as Alfonso X's *Cantigas de Santa Maria*). This complicates the notion that, according to Francisco Márquez Villanueva, Alfonsine vernacularization was a secular, nonsectarian project that sought to give official form and exalted status to a vernacular culture shared by adherents of all three of the realm's monotheistic faiths. This may have been Alfonso's intention, but from the Sephardic point of view the situation was different. For Jewish writers, the literary vernacular was a tool used in certain religious contexts to reach those who did not understand Hebrew, and little else. In Ardutiel's day, writing *secular* texts in the learned vernacular was largely the province of Christian writers. Sepharadim, when writing serious secular texts, wrote in Hebrew. This is the point Ardutiel makes quite forcefully in his *Debate*, and in a more veiled manner in *Proverbios*. The vernacular is a last resort, an unnatural and less desirable option than Hebrew.

At the end of the *Debate*, the scissors and the pen bring in a third party to settle their dispute. Ardutiel describes him as a "needy man, a wise man full of wisdom, knowledge, and subtlety."[97] Readers of classical Arabic and Hebrew maqamat would have recognized this figure as Ardutiel's version of the rogue antagonist of the narrator, typically an old man, a beggar, a student, or another economically marginalized yet learned individual whose intelligence and rhetorical skill dazzles his audience. Here Ardutiel's *hakham* (sage) is a man whose word is authoritative. He surveys the situation before passing judgment:

> Whereupon the pen led him to his tent, saying to him: "Sir, let it be pleasing to your eyes: here is the house before you, look upon its length and width, and upon all of the wares, the large and the small, within it. Put every utensil in its place, every *raven according to its kind*.[98] Whereupon the man came leaning on his cane, turning this way and that, and he saw a jug of olive oil with a lamp in the back of the house. He made wicks and lit their lights. He found a needle (his clothes were torn) and he sewed up all the tears. And then, using his eyes as spies[99] he saw in the midst of all the tools a gold-shimmering pen,[100] flashing like lightning. Suddenly he became a quick scribe; he rushed to take it out from among the other

utensils and wrote in a book before their eyes. And so, *groping at noon*,[101] he found the scissors, pared his fingernails, cut his hair, and trimmed his moustache.[102]

This hakham or wise man, without uttering a single word, demonstrates the commonsensical conclusion that a pen is for writing and a scissors for cutting. The Hebrew language is fit for the writing of a sage and the vernacular for more utilitarian purposes, like cutting your nails and trimming your moustache (i.e., business correspondence and other pragmatic communication). Though the pen is victorious, the author later praises the scissors (for cutting) and, in a move reminiscent of the authors of Arabic and Hebrew maqamat who undermine their own narrative authority,[103] admits that he has written the treatise using scissors—the illegitimate writing instrument—and not with a pen. "The entire thing," he informs the reader, "was written very nicely without a pen in hand."[104] This recalls the liar's paradox ("This sentence is not true"). That is, if writing with scissors is illegitimate and this treatise, which proves that assertion, is written with scissors, what does this suggest about the reliability of the narrator and of the text itself? This undermining of the credibility of the narrator, like the figure of the shabby but eloquent *rhaetor,* is typical of the maqama, in which the narrator often contradicts himself, or eventually is interrupted by the author himself, who then takes credit for the narration.[105] As I have mentioned, the resistance of this "slippery" text to a definitive reading, allegorical or otherwise, suggests that, like the *Libro de buen amor* and Iberian maqamat, it is a sort of workbook for critical reading, a case study in ambiguity.[106] This would put Ardutiel in league with other late medieval Iberian writers whose aim was to point up the instability of a single truth in an age when several flavors of Averroist and Maimonidean rationalism wrestled with monotheistic doctrine.[107]

Ardutiel gives us a clue to this reading of the *Debate* in the episode of scissors writing found in the *Proverbios*. In it, he is unequivocal about the value of writing with scissors. It is a vain, empty enterprise that provokes a cynical response. It is not really "writing" at all, and the person who writes with scissors is a fool not to be taken seriously. In this passage, Ardutiel describes how he mischievously sends a letter of scissors writing to an arrogant and foolish correspondent, in order to deprive him of the benefit of real writing, which is of course done with a pen:

A wretch once thought [himself wise], and, to show him I was
Slick, I sent him scissors writing.
The idiot didn't know that I faked him out,
Because I didn't want to waste the ink on him;
So as not to dignify him, I made the full empty
I didn't want to give him a good, whole letter:
Like the one who takes the meat of the hazelnut
For himself and gives the next guy the empty shells,
I took out from the paper any meaning it had in it,
I kept it for myself, giving him an empty letter.[108]

Here Ardutiel boasts that in writing with the scissors, he "removed the discourse" from the text, like the meat of a nut from its shell.[109] If we can read the pen as Hebrew and the scissors as Castilian, then Susan Einbinder's suggestion that the *Debate* could be a kind of protonationalist Hebrew text rings all the more true and would place Ardutiel next to other Hebrew authors of the thirteenth and fourteenth centuries who espouse what we might call protonationalist positions on the superiority of Hebrew over Arabic or the vernacular.[110] Einbinder likewise identifies the pen as instrument of angelic discourse, which foreshadows Solomon Bonafed's view of Hebrew as the most fitting literary vehicle because it was the language in which the angels spoke to God.[111]

If this is true, and keeping in mind that Ardutiel did in fact write the *Debate* (ca. 1345) before the *Proverbios* (after 1351), what is he saying about his own vernacular writing? Is he really reclaiming the vernacular as a secular space where Jewish writers can write morally authoritative verse for a Christian audience? Or, as his parody of the scissors suggests, is it a cynical exercise in addressing the court in their own, inferior language? It is not likely that he would write in Hebrew for a Christian king, so he would here be falling back on Castilian by necessity, just as the man who needs to trim his nails must use a scissors and not a pen.[112] If we read the critique of the vernacular in the *Debate* as a key, available only to a Hebrew-reading audience, the scissors-writing episode in the *Proverbios* becomes a coded satire of the very man to whom Ardutiel dedicates the text. The *astroso* or wretch is Pedro I himself, and the "carta vacía" devoid of reason and substance (by virtue of being written in the vernacular and not in Hebrew) is nothing other than the much celebrated *Proverbios*.

POLYSEMY AND DIASPORA

There are different ways to read this semiotic instability or emphasis on multiple perspectivism. It could be, as several critics have argued, that Ardutiel is attempting to explain the minority position to a majoritarian audience, to generate sympathy for the situation of the Jewish community and to use the vernacular in order to (much as the mendicant orders did in preaching to the *vulgo*) "preach to them in the fields," that is, in their own language, thus increasing the likelihood of his message being well received. A writer is unlikely to capture the attention of the audience by writing in a language that readers do not understand and with which the audience may have quite negative associations. How do we read Ardutiel not just as a minority voice, but as a specifically *diasporic* minority voice?

The culture of diaspora that emerged in Judaism was only one possible response to the historical realities of the Babylonian captivity and the Roman occupation and dispersion. It might have been otherwise: the Babylonian and Judean Jews might just as well have assimilated into the cultures of the hostlands where they lived, and this book would have had to be written on a different topic. If you do not accept a divinely ordained framework for the Jewish diaspora, then the story of Jewish culture is not that of a people struggling to remain in God's good graces, biding their time until an eventual redemption. Rather, it is another human story of people attempting to make sense of human history, a history that is structured and motivated by power and by politics.[113] This is where post-colonial discourse is useful for thinking about Sephardic diaspora, even before the fifteenth and sixteenth centuries, when the stage on which Sephardic authors play becomes one of imperial expansion, exploration, and colonization.[114]

Matthew Raden was the first critic to read Ardutiel as a postcolonial author writing from the periphery, in an essay comparing him with his contemporary, the powerful nobleman Juan Manuel, author of the canonical, widely read (and taught) *Conde Lucanor*.[115] Ardutiel himself dedicates many verses of the *Proverbios* to explaining this fact, though he would not likely agree with my valuation of galut and ge'ulah as symbolic constructs in the service of a protonational ideology. As a devout Jew, for him diaspora *was* divinely ordained, and while he would not likely have rationalized the orthodox narrative of galut, he was clearly sensitive to the political realities that resulted from his community's status as religious minority. Several critics have written on the value of the *Proverbios* as a guide for negotiating cultural difference. How does a diasporic reading change the way we understand Ardutiel's adventures in the vernacular? What's more, how does the availability of the literary vernacular as an option, albeit a problematic option, change the position of Hebrew as a linguistic choice for Sephardic writers? History, or at least its material legacy, tells us that very little vernacular writing by Sephardic writers has survived. Hebrew continued to be their literary language of choice well into early modernity, and it is not until the late sixteenth and early seventeenth century that we see any significant Sephardic literary activity in the vernacular.[116]

Ardutiel's critique of the vernacular in the *Debate* sheds new light on the meaning of the vernacularity of the *Proverbios* and on medieval Sephardic authors' use of the literary vernacular in general. It is as if Ardutiel is saying, "Fine, I'll write you some 'Jewish' learning in the vernacular, but on my terms, and hardly anything authentically 'Jewish.'" He is not about to fall into that trap. Experience had proved that talking rabbinics to royalty was a dangerous undertaking.[117] Jewish participation in the literary vernacular was mostly limited to religious texts such as biblical translations or songs sung at religious holidays such as Purim and Passover. Jewish writers themselves were ambivalent about the validity of the vernacular as a literary language and (though much more markedly so in the fifteenth century, as we will see in the next chapter) guilt-ridden over abandoning Hebrew at a time when conversion to Christianity seemed a gathering threat to the Jewish community.[118] At the same time they were wary of a Christian public that was equally ambivalent about Jewish (and converso) participation in the dominant, vernacular culture. Both of these concerns, the decline of Hebrew as a literary language and the increasing pressure to convert to Christianity, are borne out in the fifteenth century, with cataclysmic results. Ardutiel's anxiety was the product of an increasingly unstable environment that led first to the pogroms of 1391, the watershed Disputation of Tortosa in 1413–1414, and ultimately to the expulsions of Jews from Castile-León, Navarre, and Portugal.

5

Diaspora as Tragicomedy:
Vidal Benvenist's Efer and Dina

By the turn of the fifteenth century, the anxieties expressed by Shem Tov Ardutiel over assimilation and pressures to convert to Catholicism had been realized dramatically. The violent pogroms of 1391 affected nearly every Jewish community in the Iberian Peninsula. Thousands of Sepharadim converted to Catholicism in their wake, creating for the first time a substantial class of conversos, the presence of which would eventually inspire the *estatutos de limpieza de sangre* (the statutes of blood purity) and finally the expulsion of Jews from Castile-León and Aragon. The communities were very much preoccupied with dealing with the events at hand, and things were only to go from bad to worse with the Disputation of Tortosa in 1413–1414, a public religious debate that culminated in the conversion of many of the Jewish notables of Aragon.[1] Benvenist's *Efer and Dina,* written sometime between these two events, is at once a moralizing treaty, a medieval gender novella, and a biting social parody. It was a carnivalesque literary release valve in a time when increasing assimilation and pressure to convert were putting unprecedented strain on the social fabric of Sephardic life. Benvenist's text, the story of a tragically mismatched May-December marriage, is a moral allegory, a wake-up call to the Jewish communities of Aragon to shun materialism, resist the temptation to convert, and cleave to traditional values. Yet at the same time, and much as is true of Shem Tov ben Isaac Ardutiel of Carrión, Benvenist is, despite his religious and political message, a member of a linguistic and vernacular cultural community that includes both Christians and Jews.

He participates in the vernacular culture of the times that include popular lyric, tales, proverbs, and so forth. Given that he was one of the few Jews of his day who could both read and write Latin, it is not at all unlikely that he was familiar with Latin and Romance literatures as well. His warning message to the Sepharadim of his day is delivered in a Hebrew that bears the marks of his experience as such. He makes use of a number of themes, conventions, motifs, and narremes that are prevalent in the vernacular culture of the day.[2]

It is clear that Benvenist's text speaks to the concerns of a *minority* population under siege, but what can *Efer and Dina* teach us about diasporicity? From a formal standpoint, Benvenist's liberal use of biblical allusion and textual borrowing (*shibbutz*) roots his text in the Zionic language of the Hebrew Bible and projects the concerns of the diaspora onto the places and people of the originary homeland narrative. But this is hardly unique to *Efer and Dina*; Ben Elazar, Abulafia, and Shem Tov all make liberal use of biblical materials. The language of the Hebrew Bible was, as noted, just about the only poetic model available in Hebrew for medieval authors. The juxtaposition of two biblical narratives within Benvenist's text, one quintessentially Zionic and the other quintessentially diasporic, bring out the diasporic orientation of Benvenist's tale. *Dina*, after all, is named for the biblical Dina, Jacob's only daughter, who is abducted and raped by the Caananite prince Shehem and whose story is itself an allegory for diasporic concerns over intermarriage and assimilation.[3] The second, more classically diasporic narrative that Benvenist brings into play is that of Esther, the diasporic heroine par excellence who saves the Jewish community of Persia with her cunning and sharp political acumen.[4]

Dina and Esther are narrative avatars of the Zionic and diasporic consciousnesses that define the cultural life of a community in diaspora. They are the two layers or fields between which the diasporic imaginary is generated. The interplay of the biblical stories of Dina and Esther, itself a diasporic textual dialogue, has its counterpoint in Benvenist's recourse to the narrative resources of his own theater of the diasporic imaginary, late medieval Aragon. Benvenist, like other Sephardic (and more generally, like other diasporic) authors, duplicates the diasporic concerns over miscegenation and assimilation in his own literary practice. Even as he exhorts his readers to cleave to tradition and shun the benefits of assimilation, he is mixing his biblical Hebrew with local traditions and tastes. The question remains (for the critic) whether his text, and by extension the texts of all Jewish writers in diaspora, is Dina or Esther.[5] Dina's narrative presents a vision nostalgic for Jewish sovereignty in the homeland, where threats to Jewish cultural autonomy are neutralized by military force, cut down by the swords of Simon and Levi.[6] Esther's narrative is more about working within the political framework of the hostland to further the interests of the community. These two approaches to the diasporic condition are allegorized in the biblical figures of Dina, the biblical namesake of Benvenist's protagonist, and Esther, the heroine of the Purim story with which *Efer and Dina* is paraliturgically associated. *Efer and Dina* is, in a way, a local Purim story, one told in the allegorical mode so popular with authors (both Christian and Jewish) in Benvenist's day.[7]

Benvenist drew upon vernacular sources (Esther) and themes while simultaneously arguing (as did many of his peers) for a return to tradition and a more siege-mentality approach (Dina) to living in the hostland. Such dynamics are characteristic of cultures in diaspora, and theorists of modern diasporas have pointed out that part of the challenge of studying these diasporas is to note the differences in how different communities within a diaspora approach these issues and how these approaches change with shifts in the historical, political, and economic circumstances of the communities.

EFER AND DINA AND ROMANCE LITERATURE

Vidal Benvenist lived in Zaragoza at the end of the fourteenth century and the beginning of the fifteenth, during very difficult times for the Jewish community of Aragon. He belonged to a group of Jewish intellectuals, the so-called Circle of Poets (*'adat noganim*) that included, among others, Solomon de Piera and Solomon Bonafed.[8]

At about the turn of the fifteenth century, Benvenist wrote a *mahbe-ret*, the Hebrew term for the originally Arabic maqama genre of rhyming prose narrative interspersed with poetry. Between the twelfth and fifteenth centuries, similar mixed prose/poetry narrative genres flourished in Hispano-Arabic (the maqamat of al-Saraqusti and the anonymous *Hadith Bayad wa-Riyad*) and in Romance (the anonymous *Aucassin et*

Nicolette, Dante's *Vita nuova*) throughout Europe. In Spain, the Toledan scholar Judah al-Harizi popularized the genre in Hebrew beginning with his translation of al-Hariri's Arabic maqamat, and following this with his own original composition, *Tahkemoni.* Several other authors in Spain and elsewhere, including our Jacob ben Elazar and Shem Tov Ardutiel de Carrión, wrote mahbarot in the two centuries before Benvenist wrote *Efer and Dina,* during which time many strayed considerably from the stylistic requirements demonstrated by the classical Arabic maqamat of al-Hariri.[9]

We would do well to understand Benvenist's use of the term in light of contemporary romance practice. Printed editions have given it various titles such as *Melitsat 'Efer and Dina* (The Rhyming Prose Tale of Efer and Dina) and more commonly *Melitsah le-maskil* (A Rhyming Prose Tale for the Scholar).[10] However, the title in the manuscripts is simply *Ma'ase Dina* (The Deeds of Dina), or *Ma'ase Dina ve-Toldot 'Efer* (The Deeds of Dina and History of Efer), after the first line of the composition.[11] The term *ma'ase* (lit. deeds), which had long been used to describe tales, eventually became associated with the European novella. There is a late thirteenth-century tale collection from southern France titled simply *Sefer ha-ma'asim* (The Book of Tales), which contains various types of narratives, about one quarter of which are Hebrew novellas.[12]

In addition to its identification of the term ma'ase with European novella, *Efer and Dina* adopts the practice common to the European romance narrative of naming the text after the lover protagonists. Benvenist's text is in fact the first to do so among medieval Hebrew narratives. While collections of tales were cast as maqamat typically named for the author, the practice of titling entire works after the names of the characters was new and specific to works produced in areas where the dominant language was Romance as opposed to Arabic. In Spain, such texts are represented by the French *Floire et Blancheflor* (an alternate version of which had flourished in Spain since at least the thirteenth century), the (somewhat later) Castilian *Grisel y Mirabella* (ca. 1480) and *Grimalte y Gradissa* (ca. 1485) of Juan de Flores, and the Hispano-Arabic *Hadith Bayad wa-Riyad* (late thirteenth or perhaps early fourteenth century).[13] Against this background, it is altogether likely that Benvenist understood his work not only as Hebrew mahberet, but also as European novella or romance. He does not, however, give us any explicit indication that this is his intention. What he does tell us is that his work is meant to be an enjoyable allegorical morality tale in which the arrogance and spiritual decadence of the protagonist lead him to ruin. We read in the first stanza:

> Learn clear words and sayings of books,
> Behold the deeds of Dina and the history of Efer.
> In it is a delightful lesson for the children of Time
> To read about the vanities of sin and the parables of mortality.
> In it you will find moral admonishments,
> A vision for those wise of heart and erudite.[14]

Efer is a very wealthy and morally corrupt man of a certain age whose virtuous, long-suffering wife falls ill and passes away. Shortly thereafter, Efer falls desperately in love with the young and lovely Dina. Her father, eager to benefit from his daughter's beauty, arranges for her to marry Efer, who has promised to provide a comfortable lifestyle for both Dina and her father. After the wedding, Efer finds he is unable to perform his conjugal duty. Hoping to mask the truth of his impotence, he obtains an aphrodisiac, and by misadventure, administers himself a fatal overdose. This comedy of errors in moral allegorical clothing has baffled critics when it has not evaded their gaze altogether. Before the excerpts included in Schirmann's landmark anthology *Hebrew Poetry of Spain and Provence*, there existed no modern edition, and it would be another fifty years before Matti Huss brought out his complete critical edition in 2003. Hayim Schirmann has described *Efer and Dina* as a "curiosity."[15] It sits at the nexus of several different Hebrew and vernacular Romance textual genres and traditions of practice.

Benvenist's work reflects the tensions and intersections of a unique cultural moment in Spain. The violent pogroms of 1391 that ravaged the Iberian Peninsula resulted in the deaths of thousands of Jews and the conversion of thousands more.[16] The Circle of Poets of Zaragoza consisted of a number of Jewish intellectuals from Catalonia who found refuge in Zaragoza, where King Juan I effectively quelled the anti-Judaic violence that ravaged the rest of the Peninsula in the summer and fall of 1391. These poets, including Vidal Benvenist, the "last great Hebrew poet of Spain"

Solomon de Piera, and others, found protection in the house of Don Gonzalo Benvenist (de la Cavallería), who was a notable at court and enjoyed considerable political influence with King Juan.

Juan's successor, Fernando de Antequera, was not so favorably disposed to his kingdom's Jews, and during his reign their fortunes took another turn for the worse. The Disputation of Tortosa occasioned another wave of conversions, including those of many of the religious leaders of the Jewish communities of the crown of Aragon.[17] During this period of terror, in which the community lived with the constant threat of violence, several of Benvenist's family members and close associates converted, including his own teacher Solomon de Piera.[18] The conversions of so many prominent leaders of the Jewish communities of Aragon must have been tremendously disheartening. Some understood these events in a messianic key and saw the conversions and the persecutions as harbingers of the ge'ulah, the redemption. Others, their resolve eroded by watching their beloved rabbis and leaders abandon the faith, were overcome with fatigue and saw in conversion a preemptive way to avoid what they must have understood as an inevitable turbulent end game. We have eyewitness accounts of the violence. In a letter to the Jewish community of Avignon, Hasday Crescas, a prominent scholar and leader of Catalan and Aragonese Jewry, lamented—and greatly exaggerated—the events of 1391: "And all the others [who were not killed] changed their religion. Only a few fled to the places of the nobles . . . a child might count them . . . but they were notables. And for our many sins there is not this day a single Israelite to be found in Barcelona."[19] The future of the Jewish community in the crown of Aragon seemed grim at best.

In these apocalyptic times, the Zaragoza poets saw themselves as the guardians of the Hebrew poetic tradition, manning the literary ramparts of a community under siege. They took refuge in literary conservatism, cultivating the styles of the Hebrew poets of al-Andalus. Turning their back on innovation, they exhorted their peers to shun the vernacular as a literary language.[20] In a letter to fellow poet Astruc Rimokh, De Piera chides his fellow poet for having written him a letter in the vernacular:

> The language of the Torah alone gives forth poems;
> It rectifies the babbling of those of barbarous tongue
> I have been given the laws of poetry; what do I care for

the language of Yael or the dialect of the chief of Qenaz?
The Hebrew language is my intimate; what do I care
for the language of the Arameans or the musings of Ashkenaz?
I shall anoint the Holy Tongue as my priest
What could I possibly care for the babbling of the babblers?[21]

This kind of protonationalist rhetoric was hardly new for Sephardic writers. We have seen similar examples from Ben Elazar and Ibn Sahula in the thirteenth century. By Benvenist's day, however, the stakes had risen. Nationalist rhetoric tends to amplify in times of crisis. In an environment so hostile to Jews, it was a predictably defensive rhetorical gesture to proclaim the superiority of Hebrew over Romance. De Piera and his peers were simply continuing the 'arabiyya/'ibraniyya polemic in which Jewish intellectuals of al-Andalus had championed the Hebrew language vis-à-vis Arabic.[22] In Christian Iberia, where the Romance vernaculars were gaining traction as literary languages, the debate continued. A generation before De Piera and Benvenist wrote, the Castilian poet Samuel ibn Sasson had similarly scolded his much better-known colleague, Shem Tov ben Isaac ibn Ardutiel, for composing verse in Castilian:[23]

Accept the gift of the language that is as close to you as a son,
in which only the most learned can jest;
Accept the poetry that encompasses cosmic wisdom,
and cast aside the banner of *their* language.[24]

During this time the fortunes of Castile's Jewish community had decreased considerably since the more liberal practices espoused under Alfonso the Learned. While there were still Jews at court, they did not enjoy the same level of support they once did. There was no Todos Abulafia–like figure active in 1400 of whom we know. The Zaragoza poets did not appear to have been able to assimilate *and* cultivate sophisticated poetry at the same time. They did not have that luxury in a post-1391 world. Their focus shifted away from court, and they turned inward toward their own community. Abulafia had enjoyed the direct patronage of the king, and others before him such as Joseph ibn Zabara were supported by prominent court Jews. Benvenist and his peers did not have access to court in the same way. Accordingly, their literature began to reflect the values of the bourgeois, as opposed to courtly, patronage enjoyed by Hebrew writers in the fourteenth century.[25] In this sense Benvenist's text is a Hebrew harbinger of a process that was about to take place in vernacular Iberian literature and that would famously bear fruit in works by bourgeois authors such as the lawyer Fernando de Rojas, whose *Celestina* openly challenged and even ridiculed the traditional literary values of the love literature favored by the aristocracy, and the anonymous *Lazarillo de Tormes* that likewise parodied the courtly conventions of the medieval chivalric romance.[26] In the Jewish case *courtly* is always a secondarily courtly aesthetic, one that represents the experience of authors working under the patronage not of the monarchs themselves, but of the court Jews whose tastes mirrored, to some extent, those of their Christian counterparts. Nonetheless this distancing from the center of power, taken together with the post-1391 atmosphere of fear and demoralization, had its effect on the Sephardic literary practices of the time.

By De Piera and Benvenist's time, the situation had worsened, and the Hebrew poets of Zaragoza were rallying for the preservation of the legacy of Hebrew poetics during a period not simply of decline, but rather of "universal ruin."[27] The result, at least for De Piera, is a sort of religious linguistic nationalism whose goal is "the defense of a world view and its symbols" against rival forces.[28] Though it may be anachronistic to speak of nationalism in a time before the existence of nations per se, we can at least understand this protonationalism in terms of the active and pro-grammatic formation of group identity, rather than political or territorial affiliation as in modern nationalisms.[29] In any event, the goals of De Piera's ideology coincide with those of modern linguistic nationalisms, to "derive unifying and energizing power from widely held images of the past in order to overcome . . . fragmentation and loss of identity."[30]

The formal literary conservatism of the Zaragoza Circle of Poets, to which Benvenist belonged, was, according to Judit Targarona Borrás, "an exercise in resistance," a predictable reaction to the increasingly dire situation in which Aragonese Jews found themselves, but it still did not mean that they ceased to be Aragonese.[31] While power can force vernacular culture into the service of political or religious ideology, and marginalize its enemies or perceived enemies by denying them access to the official cultures of its institutions (i.e., universities, church, court), it has not yet found a way to exclude an individual or group from a common vernacular culture. As any German Jew who came of age in the 1920s or 1930s or any exile anywhere whose government has turned against them can attest, the lullabies and riddles, local legends and ballads one learns in youth have a life span and a personal significance independent of political events.[32]

THE ROMANCE TURN

Such literary protonationalism notwithstanding, this was a Jewish community that shared a common vernacular culture, language, and literature with their Christian neighbors, and their literary practice reflected this reality, even if they did not seem to have been interested in creating an upper-register literary vernacular as were their Christian counterparts.[33] Even without taking into account the Romance language production of Spanish Jewish authors that has been lost to us, it is clear even from the Hebrew, and particularly from *Efer and Dina,* that these are authors working in the Romance world. The Zaragoza poets' jealous cultivation of Hebrew and condemnation of the vernacular did not ensure their isolation from the literary practice of the Romance world in which they lived, and Vidal Benvenist's *Efer and Dina* bears this out.

Benvenist's involvement with the literary practices common to authors writing in Romance languages is not readily apparent. We must look beneath the surface characteristics of his text, into the thematic material and narrative sensibilities of *Efer and Dina* in order to grasp the relationship between him and his Romance-writing counterparts. Benvenist wrote in the type of clever rhyming prose typical of Spanish Hebrew authors, linguistically conservative and rich in biblical allusions and inlaid phrases or shibbutzim. The setting and the characters bear biblical names, and we see none of the geographic and cultural specificity that one associates with the vernacular Romance prose fiction of the times. Stylistically, then, *Efer and Dina* does not seem to have much in common with the vernacular novella of the times. The biblically inspired (but ultimately imaginary) literary setting is more akin to the fantastic geographies and toponymies of the medieval romances that blended historical geography with place names and character names of the author's own invention.[34]

What is it, then, that places Benvenist's text within Hispano-Romance literary practice? We might start to answer this question by asking another: for what purpose and for what audience did Benvenist write? The introduction of Gershom Soncino to his edition of *Efer and Dina* (Rimini, 1523) describes it as a Purim entertainment for young people.[35] Whether or not Benvenist himself intended *Efer and Dina* to be performed during Purim, the fact that Soncino presents it as such suggests that readers and audiences understood the work as belonging to the tradition of Hebrew parodies practiced as part of the Purim celebration. Even if Soncino's aim was to characterize the text as a Purim parody for marketing purposes (the paraliturgical imprimatur likely would have moved more copies), the fact that the narrative easily lends itself to such characterization is significant. As we will see, the work's identification with the celebration of Purim is key to understanding *Efer and Dina* as diaspora literature per se, including its relationship to both Jewish scripture and liturgy on the one hand, and regional Romance literatures on the other.

The Jewish festival of Purim commemorates Persian Jewry's narrow escape from destruction in the fourth century before the Common Era. It is based on the biblical book of Esther, which is arguably the most highly novelized and "modern" narrative in the Bible. In it, the beautiful Esther conceals her Jewish identity in order to win a beauty contest, the winner of which gets to marry the Persian king Ahashverosh (perhaps Xerxes II). Esther wins and becomes queen. Meanwhile, the evil high minister Haman is plotting to destroy the Jews of Persia. Esther's virtuous uncle Mordechai foils the plot, the evil Haman is hanged, and both Jews and Persians live happily ever after. Needless to say, the story has resonated deeply with minority groups both Jewish and gentile, but was particularly popular with conversos, Iberian Catholics of Jewish background who identified with the problems of secrecy, dual identity, and the threat of violent persecution.[36]

In addition to its liturgical function as the occasion for the reading of the biblical scroll of Esther, the Purim celebration is a sort of Jewish Carnival, a day in which the natural order of things is reversed or suspended. Children boss their parents around, the baker dresses like a king, and drunkenness is tolerated, even encouraged. Like Carnival, the Purim festival provides an opportunity to release some of the tensions that build up in the course of a typical year, an antidote to the stress of family life, economic struggle, and the business of being human in a dangerous and

unforgiving world. But Purim is a *diasporic* carnival as well, and its trium-
phant narrative speaks to the specific concerns of a population struggling
with the demands and social realities of living in diaspora. According to
Daniel Boyarin, it is "the holiday of Diaspora par excellence."[37] In its broad
contours it can be understood, in its medieval European context, as a kind
of Jewish fairy tale, where the line between boy-meets-girl and Happily
Ever After has more twists and turns (and hairpin curves) than in the
vernacular folktales familiar to Sephardic audiences.[38] Esther does get to
marry the king, but she must first conceal her true Jewish identity, changing her name from the Hebrew *Hadassah* to the Persian *Esther* (cognate
with *Ishtar* or *Astarte*). The wicked stepmother is replaced by the scheming
minister Haman. The knight in shining armor is replaced by the brave and
wise uncle Mordechai, who arrives in the nick of time not with a sword,
but rather with a crucial piece of intelligence. Instead of forests, valleys,
and courts typical of the European folktale, the scene is urban, the walled
city of Shushan.

In addition to a public reading of the biblical scroll of Esther, Purim
celebrations have historically included the performance of original works
of parody, usually based on biblical or exegetic texts. Vernacular versions
of the Esther story have been read alongside the Hebrew since at least the
ninth century,[39] and in Spain, Rabbi Isaac ben Sheshet Perfet (Ribash)
cites Nahmanides (Ramban) and other Catalan and Provençal rabbis re-
porting that such vernacular readings of Esther were widespread during
their lifetimes (thirteenth–fourteenth centuries). He also chastises one
of his peers for allowing vernacular readings of the Esther story to the
women of his community.[40] In fifteenth-century Spain, Provence, and
Italy, there were two traditional genres of such paraliturgical Purim literature. One was the performance of original, lighthearted versions of the
Esther story in both Hebrew and Romance vernacular. Of these, the best
known are the fourteenth-century Provençal and Hebrew Esther poems.[41]

Alongside the Esther narratives there also exists a tradition of biblical and exegetical parody, such as the Bacchic spoof of the Book of the
Prophet Habakuk titled *Sefer Habakbuk Hanavi* (The Book of the *Bakbuk*,
[bottle] of the Prophet), or the Talmudic parody of Kalonymous ben Kalonymous, *Masekhet Purim* (The Tractate of Purim). In the carnivalesque
spirit of Purim, these texts celebrate the pleasures of this world: drunken-

ness, gluttony, and indulgence in general.[42] Like Benvenist's *Efer and Dina*, they make frequent use of irreverent biblical references, at once honoring and mocking the textual tradition in which they participated.

SHIBBUTZ AND DIASPORIC ANXIETY

In their direct use of the language of the Hebrew Bible, Sephardic authors were able to draw on the linguistic and symbolic resources of the Bible to give voice to contemporary concerns and artistic forms. It was one way in which they negotiated between the Zionic and diasporic imaginaries, one way in which their work gave voice to a specifically diasporic experience. This use of the language of the Hebrew Bible, while habitual, was also a way of connecting the present experiences of the authors with their symbolic homeland Zion. The people, places, flora, and fauna of the biblical Judea-Samaria are mapped onto the tales and songs they wrote in Barcelona and Zaragoza, creating a web of references that links Jerusalem with Zaragoza, Jaffa with Valencia, and so forth.

Like authors of other maqamat such as Judah al-Harizi, Joseph ibn Zabara, and Judah ibn Shabbetay, Benvenist often uses ironic shibbutzim to humorous effect. He does so in different ways; at times, he places the biblical language to create a double entendre, by which the new context assigns a meaning to a word that is different from that in the biblical context. There are many such examples in *Efer and Dina*. We find one in Dina's lament for her upcoming marriage to Efer, in which she bemoans her fiancé's advanced age and lack of vitality: "Father, my father, just look at his weakness and his character! He has to walk around outside with his cane, for his power and might are finished, *and his staff speaks to him!*"[43] Here, the shibbutz is from Hosea 4:12, where the prophet describes how Israel has alienated itself from God through its practice of harlotry, idolatry, fornication, and other types of poor behavior.[44] The first resonance of this description of Efer is that of the morally irresponsible Israel described in Hosea, who "consult their stick," that is, who puts their faith in divining and sorcery rather than in the Israelite God. In addition, there is a double entendre: Efer's "staff" speaks to him, or rather, he is thinking with his penis, his actions are motivated by lust, not by correct moral values.

Other ironic shibbutzim likewise play on the difference between biblical and medieval contexts, but without changing the meaning of the words themselves. The description of Efer and Dina's wedding party is one such example: "And so it was that on the next day Efer gathered up all the elders of his nation; all the inhabitants of the town, to rejoice in the *simha* of his nuptials, on the day of his wedding. And they went to Dina's house with tambourines and dancing, and *the whole town heard the sounds of celebration.*"[45] Here, the celebratory noises of the wedding party are juxtaposed with the biblical context, the unnatural sound of thunder coming from Mount Sinai in Exodus 20:15: "all the nation *saw* the sounds" (*kol ha'am ro'im et ha-qolot*). In the biblical passage, the unnatural sounds strike fear into the hearts of the Israelites, but here, the sense is that the wedding party sees marriage between the old man and the young girl as unnatural and views it with disgust.[46] Benvenist ironically characterizes what should be a happy, natural occasion by using language describing a scene of fear of the unnatural. The implication that the inappropriate union will end poorly is imbued with divine significance (if only ironically). The allusion to the thunder emanating from Sinai suggests that the mismatch will be not simply unfortunate, but a mistake of biblical proportions. If, as Benvenist suggests, we read Dina as an allegory for the moral integrity of the Jewish community of Zaragoza, her marriage to Efer is not just a bad marriage, but a communal disaster that affects "the entire nation" (*kol ha'am*), the collective referenced in the allusion to the thunder at Sinai.

ESTERISMO AND SEXUAL MIXING

According to Benvenist's allegory, Dina represents the integrity of the Jewish community, which is compromised by the arrogance and greed of Efer. The idea that the integrity or fate of the community resides in the bodies of its female members is not an innovation and is common to many narratives known to medieval Iberians. The foundational myth of Christian Iberia itself hinges on the violation of the daughter of Rodrigo, the last Visigoth king to rule in the Peninsula before the Muslim invasion of 711. In such narratives, the idea of family honor, always based on the sexual conduct of the women of the family, is adapted to represent the interests of a larger social group, be it religious (in the case of the Iberian Jews), national (in the case of the Rodrigo/La Cava narrative), or other.[47] The fears that motivate these national narratives of sexual impurity are the same ones that fuel the Dina and the Esther narratives, namely the fear that social (and sexual) intercourse with non-Jews poses an existential threat to the community.[48] David Nirenberg has pointed out that sexual politics frequently catalyzed and focused the broader anxieties of the Jewish communities of Aragon onto specific cases of Jewish-Christian or Jewish-Muslim intermingling. While there was no way to generally vouchsafe the well-being of the community (provided one reads well-being as "genetic purity"), community leaders could take measures to punish and deter dalliances between Jews and non-Jews. This served as a form of purity ritual by which the more global threat of total annihilation might be displaced or temporarily held at bay.[49] The biblical references provide the antidote for the erosion and feared absorption of the community through intermarriage and assimilation.

Benvenist maps these concerns, as novelized in the Esther narrative, onto his own Dina narrative, enacting an intertextual *esterimso*: the attribution of characteristics of the biblical Esther to the story of Efer and Dina. Certain aspects of Dina's situation, when read in light of *Efer and Dina* as a festive Purim entertainment, recall that of Esther. She is a young woman who marries for material advantage, whose marriage turns out to be problematic. For Esther the problem is the scheming Haman and his plans to destroy the Jewish community, for Dina it is the impotent Efer and his failure to expand the Jewish community. In both cases the continuity of the community is at risk, and the narratives hinge on the resolution of the problem.

The Jewish communities of Aragon at the turn of the fifteenth century were faced with similarly dire circumstances, and the Esther theme of near-destruction would likely reflect their own insecurities. In fact, this historical identification has given rise to a tradition of local Purim celebrations, in which Jewish communities celebrate their own close encounters with disaster. The best known such Purim is coincidentally that of Zaragoza, which actually commemorates events in Siracusa, Sicily, but has become conflated with Zaragoza in popular memory. The Zaragoza Purim even has its own narrative, the *Megillat Zaragoza*, which is modeled after

Megillat Esther.[50] This tradition of the celebration of local Purims shows that Jews identified on a deep level with the Esther narrative, to such an extent that they saw themselves reenacting it on the historical stage. The book of Esther had literally become a roadmap for negotiating life in galut, and ironically, an example of achieving a sort of worldly ge'ulah, a redemption that might be earned while still living in exile from Zion, a temporary reprieve or at best a hint of the final redemption toward which they believed themselves to be striving.

Efer and Dina, then, can be seen as an allegorical parallel text to the *Megillat Esther* in which Efer represents the threat to the integrity of the community and Dina the virtuous resistance to this threat. It is noteworthy that the Esther narrative would, in the generations after Benvenist, take on heightened significance among the descendants of the many Iberian Jews who converted to Christianity under pressured circumstances in the wake of 1391, 1413, and 1492. The elements of persecution, secrecy, and identity in the story of Esther resonated with conversos and *anusim* (the Hebrew term for those Jews who were converted forcibly) for hundreds of years. For example, we have late seventeenth-century Inquisitorial documents from Mexico in which accused Judaizers give testimony to their enthusiasm for the story of Queen Esther.[51]

On the surface, *Efer and Dina* does seem to fit with the ludic spirit of this Purim paraliturgy. Like paraliturgical versions of the Esther story, it is a highly novelized morality tale, yet unlike them, it cannot be read as a retelling of Esther. The levity of the Purim holiday is deemed appropriate for the obligatory merry-making prescribed by the Talmud for a wedding celebration (Ketubot 8:2a), and so a literary parody of the public reading of the *ketubah*, or wedding contract, is a natural topic for a Purim entertainment.[52] This parody of the performance of Efer and Dina's ketubah displays much of the same linguistic playfulness and irreverence as the other Purim parodies mentioned above. The text rendered in italics below may be understood as the whispered commentary of invited guests as they listen to the public reading of the traditional text of the ketubah. One can easily imagine a live Purim performance of the passage, with actors playing the parts of Efer, Dina, the presiding rabbi, and witnesses, the audience as guests, and a narrator in the wings interpreting Benvenist's snarky narration. In this passage, Benvenist plays on the practice of translating each phrase of the Aramaic of the traditional ketubah into the vernacular as it is read aloud, for the benefit of guests unable to understand the original.[53] But instead of translating, he inserts the voice of the narrator, who provides us with a blow-by-blow commentary on what is happening during the reading itself.

> Then one of the witnesses came beside him, and raised his voice, saying: "On the sixth, on Shabbat," *the noise of the groomsmen's drinking ceased,* "on the ninth day of the month of Av," *the bridesmaids were fainting, they felt Dina's pain in their own flesh;* "whereas [this man] Efer is the groom," *emanating profanity, radiating vanity, the desolation of his face terrifying the crowd,* "he said to Dina," *who was surrounded by her bridesmaids, all singing her praises,* "you shall be my wife" (*she appeared to be in mourning, like an oak tree with withered leaves*), "and I will honor, maintain, and serve you," (*He is like a filthy, abominable branch, considered [as ineffectual as] smoke and wind*) "and to go into you as is the custom of all lands." *Don't put your trust in vanity.* "And this is the dowry that the bride brings." *Horns and whistles are heard.*[54]

Although such broad comedy would seem to place *Efer and Dina* squarely in jocular Purim traditions of text and performance, Benvenist makes it clear that his moral message is deadly serious. In a lengthy excursus at the end of the tale, he explains that *Efer and Dina* is not just the bawdy tale of the sexual arrogance of one old man; rather, it is an allegory for the human soul's struggle with the temptations of the material world, couched in the type of saucy prose favored by young readers who would otherwise not pay attention to its moral content:[55]

> And now, wise and sage men, who fill your verses with knowledge and fear of God, take this parable to heart, and God will be with you. Listen attentively, come into the house of hidden meaning and enter into the chambers of its ornament, so that you might experience its hidden benefit and enjoy its exalted brilliance. I have not set down the words of this parable for my own good, my thoughts for any vain purpose. God forbid I should write foolishness within my precious words, my glory. Let my good name not depend on the surface meaning of my words, for there are useful teachings within my parable, hidden and occulted away. They are a medicine for the soul and an elixir for the body. [The apparent and the hidden] complement one another; if the words at first seem shoddy, soon their fragrance changes and their taste alters. Come to know their secret,

and you will catch a different breeze. As the wise man said: do not trust in the surface meaning of ideas, in their form. Rather, focus on what is within them, for there is a difference between a word's form and what is buried in its bosom, between the shell of the nut and its meat. However, in order to entice young readers, who enjoy a good jest, and who are not motivated by moral teachings alone, and whose mouths run with the delights of vanity, after which men chase, I have said: I shall open my mouth and speak words of deception, as is their manner, as an offering to entice them, in order to fill their hearts with wisdom. I shall bind them and lead them with their own ropes and cords: those of vain desires, they who would make a mockery of love.[56]

According to these words, Benvenist's purpose is clear: he wants to speak to the youth "in their own language," much as current-day clergy strive to deliver their spiritual messages in music and other media popular among their younger congregants. As he goes on to explain, the allegory is to be understood as follows: Efer represents man's earthly existence, his deceased first wife represents the wise soul who guides us on the narrow path, and the beautiful young Dina represents man's earthly desires and pleasures that ultimately lead to spiritual ruin.[57] In explaining the allegory, Benvenist uses the well-worn metaphor of the shell (exoteric form) and meat (esoteric meaning) of the nut, so common to both the Jewish and the Christian literature of his era, and famously so to readers of the Castilian *Libro de buen amor* (Book of Good Love), that appeared some seventy years before *Efer and Dina*.[58]

The historical context suggests that while perhaps inconsistent with the carnivalesque tone of traditional Purim literature, Benvenist's moral gravitas is sincere. These were, after all, disastrous times for the Jewish community, and Benvenist's peers used prophetic language to lament the calamities of 1391 and 1413.[59] According to them, the conversos became rich but abandoned Hebrew poetry and Jewish religion, and brought disgrace to the community.[60] Even before the catastrophe of 1391, Jewish sources stridently denounced those who abandoned the ancestral faith. The introduction to the 1354 *takkanot* (ordinances) of the union of Jewish communities of the crown of Aragon has the following to say about the conversos from their community: "Fire and sulphur and a scorching wind is the portion of their cup; to shoot the upright in the heart [the loyal

Jews] they bend the bow and make ready according to their desire their arrows. . . . Therefore, children of transgression [conversos] have become great and grown rich, and those who are borne from birth have changed their glory and that which they promised for shame."[61] The accusation that the conversos were selling out their community for personal gain was not unfounded. Long after the Disputation of Tortosa, Pedro de la Cavallería, a relative of Benvenist who converted in the second half of the fifteenth century, justifies the accusations made in the takkanot of 1354. In his testimony before a tribunal of the Inquisition, he freely admits, even boasts, that money and status were powerful considerations in his decision to convert: "Could I, as a Jew, ever have risen higher than a rabbinical post? But now, see, I am one of the chief councilors [jurado] of the city. For the sake of the little man who was hanged [Jesus], I am accorded every honor, and I issue orders and decrees to the whole city of Saragossa."[62] In the face of such motivation, at least some of Spain's Jews saw themselves *entre la espada y la pared*, between the sword and the wall: between the rewards of this world and of the world to come; between a difficult but virtuous life as a Jew and a more comfortable but pernicious life as a converso.[63]

In light of this predicament (and given his explicit moralistic reading of his own tale), it is altogether likely that although he is working in a parodic genre, Benvenist's message is dead serious and speaks to the anxiety in the Zaragoza Jewish community over the deleterious effects of money on moral judgment. Schirmann suggests that *Efer and Dina* may well have been based on actual stories of older men who were forced to dissolve marriages to younger women based on their impotence, meaning that Benvenist would have been addressing a social problem—and not simply a literary motif—familiar to his readers.[64] This moralizing intention is consistent with the serious messages of much of the poetry of his peers De Piera and Bonafed.[65] Yet even in answering De Piera's poetic call to Hebrew arms, Benvenist does not hesitate to draw on some of the generic conventions and narrative materials of the vernacular literature held in such disdain by his fellow poets. Despite the professed conservatism of the Zaragoza poets, Hebrew literary practice was continuing to exist in dialogue with the literatures of the vernaculars spoken by Hebrew authors. In order to fully understand what is going on in *Efer and Dina,* we must read below the surface and beyond the Hebrew context, into the vernacular practices of the times.

According to Raymond Scheindlin, the Zaragoza poets' preference for conservative style and mannerism resonates with the literary tastes of the Castilian and Aragonese nobility in the fifteenth century. He maintains that their poetry espoused the values of courtly love as codified by Ibn Hazm in the eleventh century and Andreas Capellanus in the twelfth, values that inspired the lyrics of the troubadours and of the Italian poets, that became the common currency of the discourse of poetic love in medieval Europe.[66] This is certainly true of much of the courtly lyric poetry of the cancionero corpus.[67] And while many of the middle-class *letrados*—educated courtiers and functionaries—who wrote this poetry consciously upheld the poetic values of the nobility, others (and especially those who did not depend on royal patronage) parodied or subverted medieval ideals of love and sexual behavior.[68]

In the late Middle Ages, the class system of Aragonese (and Castilian) society was in flux, witnessing an increasingly influential middle class made up of merchants, notaries, and clergymen.[69] Some of these were authors who produced works undermining courtly and ecclesiastical standards for sexual behavior. In the fourteenth century, Juan Ruiz, archpriest of Hita in neighboring Castile, famously lampooned the doctrines of both clerical celibacy and courtly love in the *Libro de buen amor*.[70] In the following century, the physician Jaume Roig chronicled the fruitless quest of a self-made Valencian burgher to marry happily in a scathing satire of bourgeois life titled *Spill* or *Llibre de les dones* (The Mirror, or Book of Ladies, ca. 1450).[71] This trend is already anticipated in the thirteenth-century Andalusi Arabic *Hadith Bayad wa-Riyad,* a tale narrated by a go-between woman whose clients flout courtly convention both in their behavior and in their verse.[72] These authors pointed up the irrelevance of idealized codes of sexual behavior in a new world in which mercantile culture threatened aristocratic values. In Castilian, this intrusion of a mercantile middle-class sensibility into the world of courtly love found its culmination in the *Celestina,* or *The Tragicomedy of Calisto and Melibea,* by the converso lawyer Fernando de Rojas, published as the fifteenth century drew to a close. Calisto's efforts to carry out the ideals of courtly love in a world where the old rules no longer apply makes for excellent broad comedy and biting social satire.[73]

While by 1400 there was in Aragon a sizeable middle class, it is not until the turn of the fifteenth century, and after introduction of print as a medium of diffusion for popular narrative, that we begin to see works that give voice to the values of the middle class that are in competition with (or that outright mock) the literary and social values of the old aristocracy. By the middle of the sixteenth century it was possible for the author of the picaresque novel *Lazarillo de Tormes* to blatantly ridicule the concept of male honor that was a mainstay of medieval chivalric romance and other courtly genres. In the context of the Hebrew literature of Christian Iberia, this type of satire was nothing new. Already in the early thirteenth century Judah ibn Shabbetay and Judah al-Harizi made a mockery of both courtly and middle-class behavior. But this was not yet the case among Christian authors in 1400 (with the notable exception of the *Libro be buen amor*), and so when we read *Efer and Dina* in the context of the broader literary culture of Castile and Aragon, it is an early example of middle-class, gendered social parody that would only later find expression, at mid-century in Catalan and at the turn of the following century in Castilian.[74]

Like his Christian counterparts who portrayed the failure of courtly values in a world governed more by money than by aristocratic ideals of romantic love, Benvenist portrays the conflict between mercantile society and medieval rabbinic ideals of love and marriage. The Jewish doctrine of *'onah* (conjugal rights) holds that a married woman is entitled to regular sexual relations and that a man who cannot provide this has no business getting married.[75] These conjugal rights of women are guaranteed in both Torah (Exodus 21:10) and Talmud (Ketubot 61b–62).[76] The *Iggeret Hakodesh* or Holy Letter, a thirteenth-century Hispano-Hebrew treatise on conjugal love, is quite explicit on the topic of a man's duty to his wife. He must engage in foreplay both verbal and physical, must allow her ample time to become aroused before engaging in intercourse, and should allow her to climax first.[77] The rich but impotent Efer is unable to fulfill these obligations and must resort to an aphrodisiac, of which he receives a fatal overdose. As in the *Libro de buen amor* and the *Celestina*, the protagonists rely on technology (potions and aphrodisiacs) to remedy their shortcomings in affairs of the heart, both with tragic results (Schirmann actually refers to the work as a "tragi-comedy").[78]

These works signal an important change in the literary discourse and practices of love. Whereas the works of Juan Ruiz, Jaume Roig, and Fernando de Rojas point up the impossibility of living out ecclesiastic and courtly ideals of love in a post-feudal society, Benvenist depicts the interference of mercantile values with rabbinic ideals of conjugal duty. This would place *Efer and Dina* in step with Castilian and Catalan reactions to the realities of middle class life. This trend in Castilian and Aragonese Jewish authors goes as far back as the *Disciplina clericalis* of the converso Petrus Alfonsi (early twelfth century), in which stories of merchants abound, but the nobleman "scarcely makes an appearance."[79] In the following century, authors of Hispano-Hebrew maqamat parodied the excesses of bourgeois life (in particular as practiced by women) as a distraction from a life of pious study.[80] One may read Dina as a metaphor for the materialism that Solomon De Piera denounces in the conversos who—in his opinion—had sold out their community. This allegorical reading resonates with the literary debate on women that flourished in Spain in Hebrew in the twelfth and thirteenth centuries and in Castilian and Catalan in the fourteenth and fifteenth.[81]

The debate on women in Christian Iberia spans the literature of the Virgin cult, the various pro- and antifeminist works of the time, including the Castilian *Corbacho* of Alfonso Martínez de Toledo (the archpriest of Talavera), and the Valencian *Spill* (Mirror) of Jaume Roig. In Hebrew, it is represented by texts such as Judah ibn Shabbetay's *Minhat Yehudah, Soneh Hanashim* (The Offering of Judah the Misogynist) and *Ezrat Hanashim* by an author known only as Isaac. In some of these texts, as in *Efer and Dina*, the woman is symbolic of man's weakness before the temptations of the secular world.[82] We also therefore read the debate as an allegory of contemporary social problems. For example, in Ibn Shabbetay's *Minhat Yehudah*, the misogynist Zerah is tempted away from his studies by the beautiful young Ayala, whose physical beauty and honeyed rhetoric make short work of Zerah's vow of scholarly celibacy. As in *Efer and Dina*, the fleshly pleasures represented by the beautiful young woman are ultimately the ruin of the protagonist, who is duped into marrying not the beautiful Ayala, but the hag Ritzpah.[83] This literary topos reflected an ongoing debate within the Iberian Jewish community over the moral dangers of intellectual assimilationism and materialism that came to a head in the Maimonidean controversy of the mid-thirteenth century.[84] In this way, Dina is part of a tradition of allegorical temptresses who embody the seductions and false promises of the material world as opposed to the durable rewards of Torah study and good works. What sets Dina apart from other temptresses in medieval tradition is that she is in no way complicit in the scheme to use her beauty to separate Efer from his money. Her natural right to a happy marriage with a man who can fulfill her needs falls prey to her father's greed and Efer's arrogance.

Unlike Ibn Shabbetay's Ayala, who is merely a decoy used to lure Zerah away from his studies, Dina ultimately bends to her father's will and in marrying Efer, joins the ranks of the unhappily married young girls of vernacular Romance tradition. In both oral tradition and in literary genres that draw heavily upon it, the theme of the young girl married to the much older man is well represented in medieval Romance literature. There are examples in the *Lais* of Marie de France, as well as in French *chansons de malmariées*.[85] The theme is especially well-represented in Spanish tradition as the *malmaridada* or *malcasada* (mis-married young girl), several of whom appear in popular songs preserved in cancioneros, compilations of courtly poetry, from the late fifteenth and early sixteenth centuries.[86] In the popular Spanish ballad of *La bella malmaridada*, the young bride's husband cheats on her; she retaliates by taking a lover of her own, and when her husband finds out, he kills her. The ballad probably dates back to the thirteenth or fourteenth century and first appeared in print in the mid-sixteenth century.[87] In Sephardic oral tradition, it has persisted into the twentieth century.[88] Students of Spanish literature will also recognize the theme of *La bella malmaridada* from the mid seventeenth-century play by Lope de Vega bearing the same title, or perhaps from the very popular novella by Cervantes, *El celoso extremeño* (The Jealous Man from Extremadura), in which a frustrated younger wife of a much older and obsessively jealous husband smuggles a lover into the house, to great comic effect.[89]

Less known are the contributions of Sephardic writers from Christian Iberia to the literature of the *malmaridada*. Roughly contemporary with *Efer and Dina*, a Judeo-Catalan wedding song, *Piyyut Na'eh* (Festive Hymn), lampoons the *malmaridada* theme, with a Talmudic twist (Hebrew words in italics):

> He broke the law *"Do not profane woman"* when he gave
> his daughter to an *old man,* who made her a *whore.*
> The *old man* lay down at *the head of the bed;*
> the *girl* woke him up with great *vigor.*
> The *old man* said to her: "Are you a *slut?*
> *Money and clothes* you will have, but no *sex!"*[90]

Here the girl's plight is similar to that of Dina: she is forced to marry a man who cannot perform his conjugal duty.[91] We have seen that rabbinic tradition guarantees a married woman sexual gratification. Furthermore, a man who will not or cannot gratify his wife sexually is partially responsible for any adultery resulting from his wife's frustration. This understanding of the sexual rights of married women informs Jewish interpretations of the *malmaridada* theme, in which older, less qualified grooms are taken to task for their vanity and arrogance. Vidal Benvenist's novelization of the *malmaridada* theme in *Efer and Dina* is exactly contemporary with this song, is likewise predicated on a woman's right to sexual gratification within her marriage, and similarly ridicules the older groom for not providing it. Benvenist's treatment of the *malmaridada* is a decidedly Jewish, literary take on a theme prevalent in the Hispanic and Romance world.[92]

The final vernacular tradition to which *Efer and Dina* responds is, in turn, of biblical origin. Benvenist named Dina for the biblical Dina (Genesis 24:1–31), the only daughter of Jacob, who is raped by Shehem, prince of the Canaanite city of the same name. In retaliation for Shehem's affront to the family's honor, Dina's brothers Shimon and Levi destroy the city and put all its male inhabitants to the sword. This story apparently resonated deeply with the famous Spanish sense of honor and was novelized in the medieval ballad "El robo de Dina" (The Rape of Dina).[93] Not surprisingly, Lope de Vega also wrote a play based on the ballad (*Robo*). Several of Lope's plays, including *La bella malmaridada* and *El Robo de Dina,* were based on popular ballads, and this suggests that the ballad of the Rape of Dina was popular with both Christian and Jewish audiences before and after the 1492 Expulsion. In all likelihood, Benvenist chose the name Dina for his protagonist in homage to the Dinas of his vernacular tongue, as well as to the biblical original.

Benvenist's tale of an ill-fated marriage occupies a unique space in the Hebrew and Romance literatures of its time. Linguistically, Benvenist is in keeping with the conservative ideological program of the Zaragoza poets, but his adaptation of the Hispano-Romance *malmaridada*, his critique of bourgeois morality, his participation in the current vernacular literary debate on women, and his nod to the Hispanic ballad tradition of the Rape of Dina all indicate that he was very much a Hispanic author in addition to a Jewish one. And despite the open disdain of some of his peers for the literary uses of the vernacular, Benvenist's use of contemporary thematic material, some of it drawn directly from the oral tradition of his own speech community, places him squarely among the vernacular writers of his day. However, this relationship of the Sepharadim to the vernacular culture of their homeland would soon change.

As the political situation continued to deteriorate for the Sepharadim, they converted and emigrated in higher numbers until 1492, when they were finally expelled from Spain (and five years later, from Portugal as well). After this point, after being Sephardic meant not living *in* Spain but being *from* Spain, they began to live a second diaspora, a specifically Sephardic diaspora in which Sefarad, or its memory, became a second layer of the historical diaspora from Zion. With the change came a shift in their relationship with the vernacular culture of the Iberian Peninsula. Spanish and Portuguese became specifically Jewish languages in the Sephardic diaspora, and the vernacular culture of the Sepharadim became a Jewish culture. Sephardic writers such as Solomon ibn Verga and Jacob Algaba traded on their Peninsular pedigrees and leveraged their Sephardic cultural legacies as intellectual currency in the context of a double diaspora from both Zion and Sefarad.

6

⁓

Empire and Diaspora: Solomon ibn Verga's Shevet Yehudah and Joseph Karo's Magid Meisharim

Diaspora is not a uniform experience, and each author's work refracts the experience of Sephardic diaspora in very different ways. Both Solomon ibn Verga and Joseph Karo were born in Spain and left in 1492 while still quite young. For both of them, the experience of expulsion and displacement was a major influence on their worldview and shaped their intellectual innovations in ways that had a profound impact on later Jewish thought. Ibn Verga, a historiographer, is author of the book *Shevet Yehudah*, a chronicle of ancient and medieval persecutions and expulsions of European Jewish communities. The rabbinical thinker and kabbalist Karo is best known as the author of a highly influential code of Jewish law, the *Shulkhan Arukh*, but it is his mystical treatise, *Magid Meisharim* (The Preacher of the Righteous) that we will consider here. In both cases, the diaspora of the Sepharadim from the Iberian Peninsula was key in their intellectual and spiritual formation and left a profound imprint on their work. Though the exile from Spain and Portugal was hardly the only such trauma to take place during the Middle Ages, it was a disaster on an unprecedented scale and as such provoked very strong reactions in the Jewish world.

One response to the trauma of the diaspora from Sepharad was to turn inward, to shun the dominant culture and the promise of cosmopolitanism it represented. Some fifteenth-century rabbis interpreted Jewish acculturation and materialism as having invoked God's punishment of expulsion. Yitzhak Baer writes that Isaac Abravanel framed the expulsion in precisely these terms: "Those Jews are deceived who think they can merge in the nations, take part in their causally determined fortunes, and escape the supracausal intervention of God."[1] Others sought to make sense of the new, Sephardic diaspora using the tools and intellectual habits of the dominant culture; they continued to participate in Spanish vernacular culture while attempting to come to a rational understanding of what had happened to them. Our two authors represent both of these reactions: Joseph Karo's mysticism and exacting jurisprudence is a turning inward, while Solomon ibn Verga's analytical (if somewhat fanciful) approach to history and engagement with the intellectual culture of the mainstream are a form of turning outward.

The matter of diaspora is not so simple as there-and-here. The privileged narratives of exile and return that diasporic communities historically tell about themselves are in reality far more complex. Part of the work of diaspora criticism is to pull on the loose threads of simplistic historical and cultural schemata so that the individual threads of the weave are revealed as such and to recognize that the peculiar nature of each individual thread does not have to contradict or give the lie to a broader narrative that allows for such recognition. Solomon ibn Verga is one such thread, and in *Shevet Yehudah* he works through (though does not deal with explicitly) many of the burning questions surrounding the expulsion and the rediasporization of the Sepharadim. What does it mean to be Spanish when your religious identity is officially excluded from the national culture? When the national histories composed at court no longer represent your king? What does it mean for Spanish to go from being a language uniting Christians, Muslims, and Jews to being a Jewish language? When your "Oriental" nature (Jewish) becomes "European" in the Ottoman context? And, in the case of Ibn Verga and many other Sepharadim who spent some of their lives as Christians, how does it change one to have seen through the looking glass of religious and cultural identity? How does having lived as part of the sovereign majority culture affect your understanding of the relationship between minority and majority? All of these questions are framed by the broader question of Spanish imperial culture and the role of the Sepharadim within—and more frequently without—a Spanish culture in transition to modernity, a transition made possible in no small measure thanks to their own exclusion from that culture.

Despite their very different approaches, both authors represent and transform on the pages of their work (and in very different ways) the experience of persecution suffered by their generation and that of their parents. Ibn Verga does this based on the principle that history, while set in motion by God, is carried out by human action. Karo the kabbalist sees human history as an allegory for exile and return of the Shekhinah, the female presence of God on earth. In his writing, the Shekhinah appears to him in personified form, guiding him toward a more perfect fulfillment of God's law, that will in turn help to restore the Shekhinah from exile and hasten the redemption. Both authors demonstrate very different expressions of a key innovation in sixteenth-century thought: the idea that human agency is as important as divine providence in the drama of human history. Karo does this by predicating divine redemption upon human action; Ibn Verga by recognizing that human decision and action are the primary engines of history.

Some influential Sephardic thinkers actually experienced increased agency through conversion to Christianity. The process profoundly affected their own thinking; it complicated spiritual practice and political identity, making it even more difficult to generalize about the converso and the Sephardic experiences. This question of conversion constituted one of the most important factors in the cultural history of the Sephardim of the post-1391 period. As we have seen in the previous chapter, the violence of 1391 occasioned a massive wave of conversions of Castilian and Aragonese Jews, and a second wave followed on the heels of the Disputation of Tortosa in 1412–1413.

As in the study of immigration—another type of crossing—there is a tendency to view conversion as a liminal experience by which one crosses over into a different state of being.[2] Popular narratives of immigration (especially those of immigration to the United States that stress self-sufficiency and pioneer imagery) tend to omit the experience of those who returned, who changed their minds, who could not or did not wish to make it in the new land, or who simply missed their homes. The real picture of the immigration experience reflects these nuances: some immigrants return after a short stay in the new land, some migrate back and forth for decades, some return in old age to die in their native land. Some immigrants relate their experience in positive terms; others are embittered or simply resigned. The same might be said of the history of Jewish-Christian conversion in late medieval Spain. The problem was not that the Jews were too alien or too different from their Christian neighbors, or that they themselves posed a threat to Christianity. We must remember that except in very rare circumstances, the Spanish Inquisition did not concern itself with the affairs of non-Christians.[3] No; the Jews were not the problem in the end for the Isabel and Ferdinand. Rather, it was the lack of hard bright lines dividing Christians and Jews that was the problem.

In the Alhambra Decree, the document promulgating the order of expulsion, Catholic Monarchs explain that it is not the *Jews themselves* that are the problem, but the fact that the existence of a large class of conversos still maintained social and familial ties with unconverted Jews, and this contact encouraged backsliding and Judaizing among the recently converted. The Edict of Expulsion makes it very clear that its primary motive was not hatred of Jews per se, but rather "the great harm to Christians which has resulted from and continues to result from their participation, conversation, and communication with Jews that they have had and continue to have."[4] As much as this "conversation and communication" was of concern to Christian authorities, it is also a consideration for students of Sephardic history. As history has proven, the expulsion did not solve Spain's Jewish problem. Neither does it serve as a firewall between Sephardic history and Spanish history. Scholars of Sephardic history have demonstrated that just as 1492 is not a hermetic seal between Spain and Sephardic diaspora, neither is it a firewall between Judaism and Christianity for those who converted rather than leave Spain.

The most significant debate among scholars of the Inquisition has hinged precisely on this question: were the conversos on the whole primarily sincere Christians who rejected their ancestral faith, or were they scofflaws whose (forced) conversions were purely cynical and who were bent on maintaining their original religion at all costs, Inquisition be damned?[5] The answer, in as far as we can arrive at one, is probably *yes* to both. Some were sincere, some were purely cynical in their Christianity, and most were probably conflicted. We cannot essentialize the "converso experience" any more than we can essentialize the "Christian experience" or the "African American experience." José Faur establishes a spiritual typology of conversos comprising "four classes: those who wanted to be

Christians and have nothing to do with Judaism, those who wanted to be Jewish and have nothing to do with Christianity, those who wanted to be both, and those who wanted to be neither."[6] I would go further to say that a given converso might drift or alternate between Faur's categories, or experience more than one at the same time. Additionally, the converso experience was lived in a social and familial context that complicated matters. A "sincere" converso might live in the same house with a "false" one, and so forth.[7] Individuals react to circumstances in their own way, a diversity that is amply born out in Inquisitorial records, in which examples abound of families in which some family members convert while others refuse, and one sibling practices orthodox Catholicism while another makes a show of attending mass on Sunday while still practicing Judaism (to the extent possible) at home.

The converso phenomenon has particular importance for the study of Sephardic diaspora (and re-diaspora) in later medieval and early modern Spain because it points up the problems resulting from the incipient nationalism of the Catholic Monarchs. It created a massive class of former Jews who were no longer technically Jewish (according to both the church and the Jewish community) but who were not accepted—in many cases—as genuinely Christian and therefore as genuinely Spanish. Official proclamations notwithstanding, it is safe to say that (unconverted) Sepharadim, conversos, and Christians old and new all felt equally Spanish (or perhaps it is less anachronistic to say equally Castilian, Aragonese, Catalan, etc.). It is this dissonance among cultural, religious, and national (or protonational) identity that I would like to explore here. As the literary examples of Ibn Verga and Joseph Karo will demonstrate, Sepharadim reacted variously to the expulsion and to the experience of conversion that many undertook (sometimes tentatively or equivocally) to avoid going into geographic (as opposed to spiritual) exile. Specialists on the subject of conversos have written on the presence or absence of a distinctive converso voice, on the halakhic (jurisprudential) status of conversos, and on the historical documentation that survives pertaining to the lives of conversos. Here I would like to explore how the experience of (temporary) conversion affected the textual practices of two exiled Sepharadim, Solomon ibn Verga and Joseph Karo. In particular I am interested in how the twin experiences of exile and conversion refract the larger issues of

Spanish imperial culture and the role of the Sepharadim in the cultural processes of imperial Spain, set against the struggle for Mediterranean hegemony between Spain and the Ottoman Empire.

EMPIRE AND SEPHARDIC DIASPORA

Recent critical efforts to reframe the study of Spanish imperialism after 1492, despite efforts to be inclusive and paradigm-altering, have overlooked the Sephardic postcolonial. In 2003, Barbara Fuchs proposed an overhaul of the study of the early modern Mediterranean, moving beyond the transatlantic discussion to revisit the question of Spain's imperial project in the Mediterranean itself:

> One of the central obstacles to developing a nuanced, well-rounded picture of early modern *imperium* within literary studies has been the relative lack of attention to Spain's position in the Old World. Spain's relations with Moors in North Africa and the Mediterranean, with the *moriscos* or "little Moors" who remain in Spain after the fall of Granada, with its Italian and Dutch possessions, and with its Genoese bankers are all important aspects of Spain's *imperium*.[8]

Notably absent from this inventory of proposed postcolonial engagements of the imperial Spanish Mediterranean are the Sepharadim. This makes a certain amount of sense, given the logic of university disciplinarity. On the one hand, the study of literature and cultural studies tends to reproduce the structures of national languages in microcosm. This means everything that happens on the Iberian Peninsula tends to fall into either Spanish Literature or Spanish Cultural Studies or Jewish or Judaic Studies. One of the problems with this tendency, especially in an age when scholars strive to represent and restore voices from the peripheries of national cultures, is that the structures of academic inquiry have not kept pace with the postcolonial imperative to resist state narratives of exclusion. In some cases, the creation of new spaces for the study of "minority" cultures can lead to a form of academic ghettoization, by which the minority cultures are (even in their study) relegated to the periphery. To quote James Young, "Postcolonial cultural critique involves the reconsideration of . . . history, particularly from the perspectives of those who suffered its effects, together with the defining of its contemporary social and cultural impact."[9] One logical way to rectify this omission would be to listen to the voices of the Sepharadim themselves, to expand the inquiry into "Spanish" culture to include, as Fuchs suggests, those groups who were part of the imperial experience but who have since been excluded from the discussion.

One such voice comes to us in the very curious form of Ibn Verga's *Shevet Yehudah,* or the *Rod of Judah.* The book is, among other things, an account of the persecutions of European and Iberian Jews throughout the Middle Ages and of the disastrous effects of the pogroms of 1391 and the 1492 expulsion. Ibn Verga was born in Seville, moved with his family to Portugal in 1492, and lived in Portugal (ostensibly as a Christian after the 1497 Portuguese expulsion of the Jews) until the 1506 massacre of conversos in Lisbon, when he fled to Naples. After living through subsequent expulsions from and reconciliations to that city, he returned to Judaism, settling in Turkey (perhaps Adrianopole), where his son Joseph edited the manuscript, finally publishing *Shevet Yehudah* in 1550.[10]

In studies of *Shevet Yehudah,* critics have tended to keep faith with traditional readings of Jewish historiography, in which the Jewish relationship to sovereignty is understood as an essentially paternalistic relationship, one backgrounded against traditional Christian and Jewish doctrines and understandings of history. And while on the surface the content of Ibn Verga's work might seem to hew to this model, his narrative and linguistic strategies speak to a subjectivity more characteristic of modern ideas of Spanish national and imperial identity.

In Judaic studies, traditional approaches to *Shevet Yehudah* have centered on the relationship between the Jews and the Christian kings portrayed in the book and on situating Ibn Verga's work in the context of other early modern works of Hebrew historiography, most of which also focus on persecutions and expulsions.[11]

The so-called lachrymose school of Jewish studies, that focused on the suffering of diasporic Jews, has dominated criticism of *Shevet Yehudah* until recent years.[12] This perspective is not so far removed from the prophetic explanations that medieval and early modern Jews themselves used to interpret their repeated misfortunes: the Jews suffered because they were bad Jews and because they embraced worldly courtly cultures that privileged material wealth and secular learning over traditional Judaism.

Several Sephardic voices of the fifteenth century speak of a desire to leave the corruption and impurity of Iberia behind and emigrate to the Holy Land.[13] Others writing in the aftermath of the violence of 1391, such as Hasday Crescas, pointed out that excessive Aristotelianism eroded the Jewish faith and called for a return to traditional biblical values.[14] José Faur points out that materialism in and of itself is not a sin of the variety that prolongs exile, but rather because it exposes the community to accusations by Christians, making the current exile more burdensome.[15]

This approach does not sufficiently explain *Shevet Yehudah,* in which Ibn Verga constructs an early modern Sephardic identity that refracts a more modern sense of Spanish-ness. That is, he makes free use of materials, genres, and perspectives that are drawn from outside of Jewish rabbinical and literary tradition and that demonstrate a high level of identification with (or at least *entanglement* with) the dominant intellectual culture of Christian Iberia. His involvement with Spanish identity, even as he is writing in Hebrew, is more characteristic of a modern diaspora set against the discourse and problematics of imperial posturing and a nascent national identity than it is of a medieval, prophetic understanding of Jewish suffering. Ibn Verga is engaging in discursive strategies and literary practices that in some sense belie the ideology he espouses.

It is precisely here that the postcolonial perspective can help us to elucidate two aspects of *Shevet Yehudah:* the Sephardic relationship to Spanish imperial power and Ibn Verga's adoption of some of the intellectual habits of humanism. Scholars of Ibn Verga have addressed both of these problems. For example, Yosef Yerushalmi's analysis in his 1976 monograph on the royal image in *Shevet Yehudah* does not take into account configurations of Spanish imperial power as such. For him, the fortunes of Spanish Jews were intimately bound with those of the king as an individual as opposed to the symbolic center of an imperial system. He writes that the Jews were "the one group in Spain that worked heart and soul for the aggrandizement of the king and the increase of his power."[16] The Christian kings portrayed in *Shevet Yehudah* are "ever ready to protect the Jews . . . [but] are sometimes prevented from doing so by their own subjects."[17] After reading Barbara Fuchs's essay on imperium studies, one begins to think of Ibn Verga differently, as a kind of by-product of the imperial process. Seen in the light of a decentered nationalism, the Sepharadim are not simply rejects who no longer figure in the equation of Spanish culture, but rather an important piece of a system of imperial cultural formation and history.

Likewise, insights from postcolonial critical theory can be useful in reading *Shevet Yehudah* in the broader context of Spanish imperial culture. Eleazar Gutwirth argues that "one has to come to grips with the proximity of the book to fifteenth- and sixteenth-century Hispanic (Jewish, converso, and Christian) non-historiographic sources, in order to place it in the context to which it belongs."[18] Elsewhere he points out the historiographic similarities between Ibn Verga's work and that of his Christian counterparts.[19] If we read Eleazar Gutwirth's comments about the presence of Spanish and Italian humanism in *Shevet Yehudah* in the light of theories of colonial mimicry, Ibn Verga's deliberate humanism is not merely a vestige or symptom of his [putative] converso education, but a form of symbolic resistance to the imperial power that forced him into exile. Imperial Spanish chroniclers tended to legitimate imperial authority in Roman precedent.[20] Ibn Verga breaks with the prophetic historical vision and roots the Sephardic experience of diaspora in the Judeo-Roman discourse, citing the *Yosippon* (the medieval Hebrew translation of Josephus) frequently.[21]

Eleazar Gutwrith has observed Ibn Verga's "attempt to mimic in Hebrew a Spanish Christian mentality and its image of the Jew."[22] This subjectivity differs from Franz Fanon's idea of mimicry in colonial elites in that it takes place in cultural forms that are expressed in the language of the diasporic minority, not in the imperial language (Spanish). If there is a colonial (or imperial) masking at play, it is a mask that one puts on in order to look in the mirror. This recalls the double consciousness of W. E. B. Du Bois and later of Paul Gilroy, the idea that one has two competing self-images, one "native" and one reflected by members of the majority. In Du Bois' words, it is a "sense of always looking at one's self through the eyes of others, of measuring one's soul by the tape of a world that looks on in amused contempt and pity."[23] Gilroy adds that this state of consciousness is also "diasporic or hemispheric, sometimes global and occasionally universalist."[24] Walter Mignolo similarly writes of a "double consciousness . . . in those who occupy a subaltern perspective."[25] According to Nadia Altschul in her discussion of Franz Fanon's work, such "mimicry is not merely an appropriation but a form of mis-imitation; and in contrast to imitation it shows ambivalence between deference and defiance."[26] Ibn Verga's adaptation of humanist models of historiography demonstrates this ambivalence in constructing a narrative whose viewpoint shifts constantly between diasporic and imperial.

Dialogue with other areas of diaspora studies can help to bring Sephardic cultural history up to date. Critics of the Indian and African diasporas are not working in the shadow of the doctrine of chosenness, and so are more at liberty to view history not as inherent or divinely ordained, but as a construct of a given political, socioeconomic, cultural, and historical moment. This is precisely where Ibn Verga's work breaks with the medieval tradition of Jewish historiography and what gives us our opening into the postcolonial. The problematic relationship of Ibn Verga with Spanish national identity is fundamentally characteristic of diaspora in the postcolonial context.

Daniel Boyarin explains that diaspora "disrupts and threatens cultural practices of nationalism as well as disciplinary practices in the cultural sciences, which assume a unitary culture more or less bounded in space."[27] This idea is particularly useful in theorizing the differences in Sephardic cultural production pre- and post-exile. In the late medieval Christian Iberian kingdoms, Jews (leaving aside the converso question for the moment) were effectively a minority culture, whose loyalty to the king assured their security and whose vernacular culture did not differ significantly from that of their Christian neighbors. After the expulsion we see a diasporic turn from peninsular minority to imperial abject, from second-class courtier to a sort of phantom colonial elite that extends Spain's cultural sphere of influence while at the same time disrupting the idea of a Spanish national identity in the very moment of its formation. One can make the argument for diasporic, subaltern readings of peninsular Jewish and converso cultural production. Gregory Kaplan contrasts the converso struggle for radical assimilation into a majority that sought to resist them with the "postcolonialist marginal voice [that] accentuates its cultural differences in order to avoid assimilation."[28] Michael Gerli suggests that postcolonial theoretical concepts are useful for nuancing some of the essentializing tendencies of earlier critics such as Américo Castro and Claudio Sánchez Albornoz.[29] Bruce Rosenstock points out in his study of Alonso de Cartagena's pro-converso writing that Cartage-na's subversion of the Visigothic origin myth "[demonstrates] forcefully" Bhabha's idea that nationalism is always "imbricated with a colonialist project."[30] I would argue that post-exilic Sephardic production such as that of Ibn Verga and Karo is particularly relevant to theories of postco-lonial diaspora.

In the time of the Catholic Monarchs, the nascent Spanish national identity is predicated on the elimination not just of a Jewish voice or of Jewish political power, but of a Jewish existence. It scarcely needs men-tioning that non-Jewishness is a *sine qua non* of Spanishness, by nothing less than royal decree. Diasporic Sephardic consciousness is constructed alongside a national identity from which the Sepharadim are excluded. What sets the Sephardic diaspora apart from earlier Jewish expulsions and re-diasporas is that they were exiled in the framework of a nascent modern nationalism, at a time in which their diasporic national identity could be articulated according to the structures of a national imaginary. Jews exiled from France, or England, or the Yiddish-speaking Ashkenazim ex-iled from German principalities never achieved this type of postnational diasporic imaginary because the majoritarian communities from which they were expelled were not constituted symbolically in the same way. The resulting identity is inherently dissonant: Ibn Verga enacts a reworking of an identity that is predicated on his abjection. His is a diasporic mimicry in which the imperial abject mimics the literary forms, rhetorical prac-tices, and linguistic praxis of the metropolis.

EMPIRE AND HISTORIOGRAPHY

Already in the thirteenth century, Alfonso the Learned very purpose-fully justifies his claims to the Holy Roman imperial throne by linking his lineage to that of Rome and Charlemagne's to that of Byzantium.[31] In the fifteenth century, the Catholic Monarchs Ferdinand of Aragon and Isabella "the Catholic" of Castile-León likewise framed their rule in imperial Roman terms.[32] They did this in order to strengthen their imperial claims in the Mediterranean, Africa, Asia, and the New World, to legitimize their role as evangelizers and defenders of the Christian faith, and to unite their temporal and religious authority in the figures of the Christian Roman emperors. While the pagan Roman emperors had sought to unite the known world under the civilizing influence of imperial Roman culture, the Christian emperors' goal included uniting said world in Christian salvation as well.[33]

The Vatican had long been cultivating Christian Iberian monarchs as champions of Christian holy war. This trend found its culmination in the reign of Ferdinand and Isabella, whose efforts to rid the Peninsula of Islamic political power and convert Jews and Muslims led Pope Alexander VI to coin for them the sobriquet "Reyes Católicos" (Catholic Monarchs) in 1474. A new series of Papal bulls promised absolution of sins for all those who aided them in their campaign against the Muslim Nasrid Kingdom of Granada, which as we know concluded successfully in 1492 when the Catholic Monarchs so famously marched into the Alhambra. Once the Peninsula itself was firmly in Christian hands, the Catholic Monarchs could turn their full attention to imperial designs elsewhere, and Columbus's voyage and territorial claims in the name of the Spanish crown created for them a vast new theater of imperial expansion and concomitant evangelization. In honor of this new endeavor, in 1493 Pope Alexander VI wrote a series of five new bulls that extended the indulgences associated with holy war at home to the New World, whatever that turned out to be. It was, in effect, a blank theological check legitimizing Spain's imperial claims to her neighbors in Europe. Royal propagandists referred to the bulls collectively as a Papal Donation, in conscious reference to the Donation of Constantine, the better to further link Spanish imperial power to its Christian Roman precedent.[34]

The symbolic work of grounding Spanish royal and imperial authority in Roman precedent had already begun during the reign of Juan II (r. 1406–1454), where court intellectuals who surrounded the Marquis of Santillana began to articulate the transfer of humanism from Italy to Spain, echoing the *translatio studii* of Greek learning to Rome.[35] Diego de Burgos makes this explicit in his *Triunfo del Marqués de Santillana*, comparing Apolonius's lament of Tully's appropriation of Greek wisdom to the contemporary transfer of learning from Italy to Spain: "For if Apolonius was pained that the Greeks, through the work of Tullius, brought eloquence from them to the Romans, how much more—and with reason—the Italians must feel the loss of and complain that the brilliance and genius of this man [Santillana] has taken it from them and brought it to our Castile."[36] As with the classical example, the transfer of humanistic learning from Italy to Spain went hand in hand with the *translatio imperii*, the transfer of political supremacy. The disorganized Italian city-states that supported humanist intellectuals and artists could hold up their cultural achievements as a counterpoint to their failures in the political sphere. Despite the chaotic state of affairs in Italy, leaders could claim to have equaled or excelled imperial Rome in cultural refinement. In Spain, however, the humanist acumen served a massive imperial project that aspired to claim the very legacy that Italy, in all its political disarray, could not.[37]

This analogy reached into the classical past as well, and the incipient nationalism of the fifteenth century made Spaniards of authors who had hailed from the Roman province of Hispania.[38] Thus Alonso de Cartagena, in the introduction to his 1491 translation of Seneca's *De providentia Dei*, anachronistically suggests to Juan II that Cartagena has translated Seneca (who was from the Iberian Peninsula), "so that one might read in our national language that which your subject composed in Antiquity."[39] In so doing, Cartagena adduces Seneca to the national patrimony while at the same time arguing for the value of Castilian as a royal (perhaps imperial) language. Authors also framed their classical references in terms of contemporary political struggles with other states. Fernán Pérez de Guzmán, in the introduction to his *Loores de los claros varones de España*, explains that while the classical authors of Rome excelled in rhetoric and ornamentation, Peninsular Latin authors produced "useful and wholesome works" (*fruto útil e sano*). This characterization of Peninsular authors as hardworking and sensible versus aesthetically superior jibes with the Castilian humanist tendency to recast the classical translatio imperii as taking place between Italy and Spain. In this scheme Italy plays the philosophically and aesthetically advanced Greece to Spain's efficient and effective Rome, the land of "useful and wholesome" works.[40]

Another tactic aimed at justifying imperial aspirations of Spanish monarchs was to compare them with Roman emperors. This transfer of imperial authority from Italy to Spain involved some adaptations and revisions to suit Iberian historical circumstances. For example, the invasion of the barbarian Goths that Roman historian Livy painted as heralding the end of Roman supremacy did not sit well with the fifteenth-century "Gothic Thesis," which posited the Iberian Visigoth kingdom as the historical prec-edent for the Christian conquest of al-Andalus.[41] The fifteenth-century chronicler Alonso de Cartagena solves this dilemma by analogizing the "barbarian" Goth invasion of Rome to the Muslim (and not Visigoth) invasion of the Iberian Peninsula.[42]

Comparisons of Juan II to Caesar Augustus strengthened the legitimacy of recent Castilian conquests in Italy. As Juan had in Iberia, Augustus had first pacified Italy before his great imperial conquests outside the Italian Peninsula. There was a logical analogue in Juan II's Italian conquests, and the comparison to Augustus legitimized Spanish domination of Italy while at the same time keeping the door open to further Mediterranean conquests.[43] It becomes clear, then, that Spanish monarchs consciously and programmatically cultivated a pre-history to what they imagined as a grand imperial moment, one in which the current exploits of Castile and Aragon were heirs to the legacy of the great emperors of imperial Rome. This trend begins at the court of Isabella and Ferdinand and reaches its full expression with the reign of Carlos V, whose reign coincides perfectly with the literary career of Ibn Verga and the young adulthood of Karo. It follows that we try to understand Ibn Verga's view of history against this background as a sort of Jewish response to the humanist historiography of his age, and Karo's messianism as its theosophical counter, the spiritual counterpart to Ibn Verga's historiographical gesture.

JEWISH HISTORIOGRAPHY IN THE SIXTEENTH CENTURY

Before 1500 there is virtually no tradition of Jewish historiography per se.[44] While European courts retained chroniclers to reinforce the politi-cal status quo and bolster their legitimacy, European and Mediterranean Jewish communities had no such textual tradition. Instead, historical con-sciousness was recorded more often than not in collections of *responsa*, legal case law written by authoritative rabbis that circulated throughout the Jewish world.[45] During the first half of the sixteenth century, Jewish writers began to write chronicles and histories that recorded events of importance to Jewish communities—wars, calumnies, expulsions, and so forth. Samuel Usque published his *Consolaçam ás tribulaçoens de Israel* (Consolation for the Tribulations of Israel) in 1553 (Ferrara).[46] Elijah Capsali, a Romaniote (Greek-speaking) Jew from Venetian-controlled Crete wrote a chronicle of the events surrounding the expulsion, *Seder Eliyahu Zuta* (The Minor Tractate of Elijah) in 1523, and a history of the Venetian empire and its Jewish populations titled *Divrei ha-Yamim le-Malkhut Venezia*(Chronicle of the Kingdom of Venice) in 1517 (these texts are published together in the modern edition of *Seder Eliyahu Zuta*). Moses Almosnino, a resident of Salonika, wrote *Crónica de los Reyes Otomanos* in Spanish (but in Hebrew letters) in 1567. Part of Almosnino's work was transliterated into Roman letters and published in Spain in 1638 by Jacob Cansino, royal interpreter in Spanish Oran, with the title *Extremos y grandezas de Constantinopla.*

It has been said that the expulsions from Spain and Portugal shocked world Jewry into the practice of writing history. This is an oversimplification, and scholars such as Jonathan Ray have begun to correct and nuance this idea.[47] In some cases, such as those of the historians Joseph Hakohen and Solomon ibn Verga, who both wrote in the sixteenth century, the historiographic turn in their writing can be explained by the fact that they lived for a time as conversos, as Christian intellectuals with access to the literature of the court and the universities. For them, the impulse to write histories "in the style of the Christians" would have been second nature.

Another aspect of the market for Jewish intellectual production was that in the Ottoman context (as in the Spanish), a good courtier, tax farmer, or merchant would be current with the affairs of the court. In the age of print, exploration, and complex international trade networks, global politics and history was now part of the dossier of a good Jewish courtier in the Ottoman Empire. This is evident already at the end of the fifteenth century in Isaac Abravanel's attitude toward history. According to Abravanel, history is not (*contra* Maimonides) a "waste of time," but rather a natural activity for the elite of any nation. Every nation, he remarks, desires to know its past and to chart the passing of time through a reminiscence of kings and their deeds. The biblical historical books record the days of kings of Judea, while the histories written by diasporic writers record the deeds of gentile kings toward other gentile kings and especially toward their Jewish subjects.[48] This explains why a writer such as Joseph Hakohen wrote one book recording persecutions of Jews and another recording the reigns of gentile kings. Both of these genres, according to Abravanel's reckoning, have a place in Jewish literary practice. The historiographical turn in the Jewish literature was not simply a reaction to bad news, it was a way to update one's curriculum vitae, to retrain in light of an increasingly global playing field where information and ideas traveled rapidly in the form of printed books and pamphlets along increasingly sophisticated intercontinental trade networks.

We can observe in Ibn Verga's narrative and linguistic strategies a subjectivity more involved with the discourse of Spanish national identity at the beginning of the sixteenth century. In his history of expulsions and persecutions he writes like a humanist, substituting both authors of Hebrew antiquity (Bible, rabbis) for Latin and Greek authors favored by Christian humanists, but he also draws on classical and medieval Iberian authors, lending his prose a more sophisticated, cosmopolitan tone.[49] He cites Josephus frequently, creating a Jewish humanist precedent in the Roman author who plays Virgil to his Dante.[50]

Both Hakohen and Ibn Verga point out the fact that they have consulted works by Christian authors in their research, which suggests that these histories are intended to be, if not universal, at least more cosmopolitan than prophetic, and that it pays to understand the works of the gentiles. Ibn Verga in particular, despite his claims of recording the persecutions for memory's sake, seems altogether too interested in Christian courtly culture and in the Christian perspective generally for this claim to be wholly authentic.[51]

THE IMPERIAL ABJECT

How do the Sepharadim fit into the imperial Spanish picture? They are no longer Spanish subjects after 1492.[52] As we have seen, Spanish imperial culture is constructed largely in the realm of the symbolic. On a domestic level, it would be difficult to say that individual subjects of Castile-Leon and Aragon considered themselves Spanish or identified in any meaningful way with the Spanish Empire. Local affiliation would, as Henry Kamen argues, prevail over the national or imperial until well into the nineteenth century, and modern regionalisms would then begin to deconstruct anew any national sentiment that had been achieved in modernity.[53] However, it is empire that is most responsible for a coherent sense of Spanish national identity.[54] The Sepharadim, although officially (and concretely) excluded from this identity, were abjected from the symbolic order of empire.

The imperial imaginary was a symbolic enterprise, one articulated on the stage of international politics, trade, and war. The construction of a collective identity calls for the establishment of a symbolic order, a set of boundary markers that shape consciousness. This symbolic order gives form to a collective consciousness that is articulated on the personal level of individual subjectivity.[55] As part of the process of the formation of a Christian Spanish imperial subject, the Sepharadim had to be either assimilated by conversion or "radically excluded" by expulsion. They are neither friend nor foe, neither Spaniard nor Turk. They share "only one quality of the [Turk] object—that of being opposed to *I*."[56] They are, in Kristeva's words, the "'something' that I do not recognize as a thing."[57] They are the imperial abject, that which had to be sacrificed in the creation of a national and imperial subjectivity and that which serves as a reminder, a disruptor, and a shadowy alternate self now free, in its own turn, to construct a parallel imperial subjectivity predicated in equal parts on its identification with, and official exclusion from, Spanish imperial identity.[58]

How did Sephardic intellectuals react to this exclusion? By refashioning the tropes and traditions of imperial humanism in their own image; by producing a Sephardic humanism that refracted their love for and alienation from Spain through a mixture of humanist and Jewish habits of expression.[59]

SOLOMON IBN VERGA AND HIS WORK

Ibn Verga's biography is stuff of epic adventure movies. He was born in Spain in the late fifteenth century, went into exile to Portugal as a child, left Portugal for Italy as an adult, lived for some years in Italy, and eventually found his way to the Ottoman Empire, settling in Adrianopole (modern day Edirna in Turkey near the border with Bulgaria). This itinerary, one shared by many other Sepharadim of his time, exposed him to a series of experiences and trials that must have seemed to him a sort of microcosm of the vast sweep of Jewish history he encompasses in *Shevet Yehudah.*

Ibn Verga is hardly the only historiographer of the Sephardic expulsion and the historical circumstances surrounding it. We have a number of texts that appear in the mid-sixteenth century that deal with the question of the expulsion from Spain, its analogues throughout history, and more broadly the question of persecutions and expulsions of Jews, along with some works of secular history.

What distinguishes Ibn Verga from these authors is his approach to interpreting historical events. While still working within the traditional framework of Jewish historiography that interprets historical events as divinely ordained, Ibn Verga demonstrates a social scientific interest in human motives that surround and propel historical events. He is, by all accounts, alone in this approach among Jewish historiographers of the sixteenth century. This plays out in the text in two contradictory ways. The multiple or cumulative authorship of his book reinforces the idea that historiography, like history itself, is a cumulative, collaborative project: God proposes and man disposes. Or rather: God sets the course, but man steers the boat. In addition to this important modification to traditional Jewish historiographical theory, Ibn Verga develops a very unique and distinct historiographical voice. His portrayal of Jewish-Christian relationships and his Sephardic humanist intellectual personality paint a picture that differs considerably from the lachrymose, prophetic view of Jewish history, despite the fact that his narrative, like that of many other works of Jewish historiography of the sixteenth century, is overwhelmingly a lament of persecutions suffered by Jewish populations of Europe in ancient and medieval times. Critics are divided as to whether or not *Shevet Yehudah* is actually a work of historiography. Heinrich Graetz derides it as a "martyrology" that is "not a unit, but a medley without plan or order, destitute even of chronological sequence."[60] Abraham Neuman praises Ibn Verga's analytical, scientific approach to history and calls *Shevet Yehudah* "the earliest sociological study of the Jewish question."[61] Yerushalmi argues the contrary, that Ibn Verga twisted the historical record to preserve the archetype of the Just King, as when he blames the edict of expulsion on Isabel, when (according to him) it was clearly a joint decision between her and Ferdinand.[62] Gutwirth praises the "richness and ambiguity of its motifs."[63]

Ibn Verga's literary creativity, so evident in his protocinematic dramatization of the events he narrates, extends to the way in which he frames his narrative. According to him, his text is a collaboration with his older relative Judah ibn Verga of Seville, which he has expanded and revised. Solomon ibn Verga's manuscript was later edited and revised by his son Joseph ibn Verga, who brought it to press in Turkey in 1550.[64] This representation of cumulative authorship is a reflection of Ibn Verga's own multi-segmented experience of expulsion and exile.

JEWISH HISTORIOGRAPHY AND MESSIANIC MYSTICISM

Jews from Spain had been settling in the Ottoman Empire since at least the fourteenth century, and after the expulsion of Jews from Spain in 1492 the populations of Sephardic Jews in the cities of the Ottoman Empire increased significantly. Messianism was in the air in those days, and Jewish hopes of returning to Zion in anticipation of the arrival of the Messiah coincided with Ottoman imperial designs on Palestine.[65] After the Ottomans annexed Palestine in 1516, Jewish and especially Sephardic immigration to Palestine surged, fueled both by favorable immigration policies and by messianic fervor.[66] The reconstruction and settlement of Tiberias (an ancient site prophesied to be the arrival point of the Messiah) by Doña Gracia and Don Joseph Nasi during the 1550s, against the backdrop of the gathering of messianic kabbalists in nearby Safed at the same time, provides us with a snapshot of the twin discourses of de-diasporization, of a physical return from the diaspora from Zion: the prophetic and the political. While these two positions are practically polar opposite reactions to the problem of restoring Jewish sovereignty in Zion, both nonetheless work to *resolve* the same problem of lack of sovereignty, while Ibn Verga's project is more to enhance our understanding of history than to try to move it forward.

The expulsion from Spain was a collective trauma superseded in Jewish history only by the destruction of Jerusalem by Titus Andronicus in the year 70 CE. Since Roman times, the rabbis had developed a sophisticated (if varied) doctrine of galut or diaspora that both explained the loss of a sovereign Jewish homeland and provided a structure for community governance and daily life both as colonial subjects in Roman Palestine (in the Talmudic tractate *Avodah Zarah*) and as a diasporic minority elsewhere. Expulsions and persecutions of Jews in various countries over time were fit into this scheme, rationalized as divine punishment for the Jews' lax observance of religious law or excessive acculturation, latter-day examples of the golden calf episode in Exodus.

Sephardic writers who witnessed (directly or otherwise) the events of 1492 gave voice to the trauma of the expulsion and the privations suffered by the expelled. They mostly followed rabbinic tradition but also drew on more modern-looking historical parallels with Roman and medieval examples. It was, after all, the sixteenth century, and the world was at the brink of modernity, a place characterized increasingly by global trade networks, rapid diffusion of ideas in print, and complex patterns of international migrations. Sephardic reactions to expulsion in the sixteenth century were bound to be different from Judean reactions in the second. Ibn Verga includes a number of vignettes of what befell the exiles:

> Some of them sought a path by sea amongst turbulent waters, but there also the hand of the Lord was with them to confound and exterminate them, for many of them were sold as slaves and servants in all of the lands of the gentiles. Many sank into the sea, drowning, at last, like lead. Others came to perish in fire and water, as the ships caught fire, and thus the fire of the Lord burned against them.[67]
>
> I heard from the mouths of one of the elders who went out of Spain that in one ship they declared an epidemic of plague, and its captain threw the passengers onto the beach in an unpopulated area, where the majority of them died of hunger. Some decided to go on foot to find a settlement. One of those Jews, his wife, and their children decided to go; his wife, not accustomed to walking, grew weak and perished. The man and his two sons that he had with him also passed out from hunger and, when he regained consciousness, found his two sons dead.[68]

One of the strategies Ibn Verga uses is to place his own opinions on the role of Jews in society in the mouths of his Christian characters.[69] Often this occurs in dialogues between a king and a high-ranking cleric, who is advising his king on how to best deal with the troublesome religious minority in their midst. These dialogues are written in the style of the humanist dialogue of the times, with lengthy discourses and frequent reference to Classical antiquity. Yet in the case of Ibn Verga's text, it is a view of classical antiquity seen through Jewish eyes. More often than not, the cleric comes down on the side of the Jews. In a discussion between a certain king Alfonso and a cleric named Thomas, the latter explains that hatred of Jews is not characteristic of the nobility, but rather of the commoner:

> Never have I seen an intelligent man hate the Jews, only the poor hate them. They have good reason.
>
> First: the Jew is proud and always seeks power; they do not consider themselves as exiles and slaves, expelled from one foreign nation to the next. They seek to present themselves as Lords and nobles; that is why the people are envious of them. The sage has said that hate engendered by envy can never be quelled.[70]

Thomas then goes on to explain in detail the social and political phenomena underpinning anti-Semitism, refuting a series of typical calumnies reported by King Alfonso. Ibn Verga also goes into depth in examining Jewish–Christian relations and what it means to be a member of a diasporic population struggling to stay in the good graces of a temporal power that holds Judaism and often Jews themselves in open contempt. In a fictional debate between the Spanish king and delegates from the Jewish community, the king accuses the Jews of being dishonest thieves, who have been welcomed into Spain only to repay their hosts with crimes and dishonesty. The delegates respond:

> As to the question of thievery, what can we say? Certainly we are like rats: one of them eats the cheese and all of them bear the blame. Naturally, there are good and bad [Jews], but the sins are borne by all of us. Are there not robbers and thieves among the Christians? Despite the fact that excellent and superior personal qualities are to be found among the Christians, we still see daily hangings for robbery and thievery. But sovereignty covers up many things, as the veil on the woman covers up many imperfections. Diaspora is the opposite, for it uncovers and makes a stain as small as a mustard grain seem as large as the orb of the sun.[71]

The protorealpolitik in Ibn Verga's historical imagination represents a new direction in Jewish history. On the surface he respects the prophetic tradition. He explains that the Catholic Monarchs Ferdinand and Isabella act merely as instruments of Providence. But he also brings a new, more modern approach, experimenting with representations of the Christian perspective and analyzing the political processes that drive key events.[72]

THE TEMPLE IN JERUSALEM AND THE
QUESTION OF SOVEREIGNTY

The question of (the loss of) Jewish sovereignty, its importance for understanding the persecutions, and its messianic value take concrete form for Ibn Verga in the image of the Temple in Jerusalem. In chapter 63 Ibn Verga poses a key question: why have the Jews suffered their particular fate, when (if their exile is to be understood as the wages of sin) they are no more sinful than any other group of people? He answers his own question with a quote from Amos 3:2, "You alone have I chosen," explaining that the Jewish doctrine of the chosenness of Israel explains the exceptional suffering of the Jews. When they were chosen to and agreed to receive the Torah, they were given special responsibility for upholding it, and particular liability for not keeping it. Ibn Verga then reviews six traditional explanations of Jewish suffering: sins of the fathers, the hatred of the gentiles, the murder of Jesus, materialism/assimilation, bearing false witness (it is possible he is referring here to insincere conversion to Christianity), and pride.

It is notable that in this list Ibn Verga combines calumnies common to Christian sources with those drawn from Jewish tradition. What follows directly is an excellent example of Ibn Verga's unique historical perspective and historiographical style. Apropos of this long list of justifications for Jewish suffering in exile, he offers a palliative: a description of the Temple in Jerusalem as a reminder of Israel's past sovereignty.[73] "Given that such matters destroy morale, I see it fit to introduce here a happier one, and that is the magnificence of the Temple and its building, as I have found it written by Versoris the Great, when Alfonso the Pious requested it from him. I have translated it from Latin into our Holy Tongue."[74] Alfonso then states that he has heard Versoris was in possession of a copy of Titus's description of the Temple in Jerusalem (actually that of Josephus, here perhaps via the Hebrew *Yosippon*). He explains that he plans to erect a temple in honor of Jesus and wanted to base his design on that of the original Temple in Jerusalem; therefore his recourse to the Jewish sources: "From where shall I take counsel if not from the words of the ancient sages, and all the more so if this image represents the construction of Solomon, of whom it is said: 'He was wiser than any.' Inform me of all this in a letter, in comprehensible language; and then ask, for I will give you what you desire."[75] Leaving aside the fact that Versoris's letters to King Alfonso are absent from the historical record and are most likely an epistolary fiction invented by Ibn Verga, the notion of a Christian ruler basing a new, Christian "Temple" in Rome after the Temple in Jerusalem is a historical fact. In his last bull (1513), Pope Julius II wrote that the model for papal leadership was not Moses and Aaron, but Solomon.[76] This is fitting in an age when the Papal States combined temporal and religious leadership in the figure of the Pope. In fact, several humanist writers described Julius II as a new Caesar, ruling over the Papal States.[77] These same authors linked Julius's ambitious construction projects with Solomon's Temple in Jerusalem.[78]

So, whose Temple is it? Medieval Jewish tradition had long revered Ezra's description of the Temple, augmenting it with that found in *Yosippon* via Josephus and reinforcing it with a robust tradition of manuscript illustrations of the temple vessels destroyed by Vespasian that would be restored at the redemption.[79] Writers of the Christian Renaissance lay claim to the legacy of the Temple, on the one hand according to standard Christological operating procedure, and on the other as part of their humanist interest in the description of *vetera vestigia* or classical ruins.[80] Ángel Gómez Moreno writes that humanists regarded classical ruins as the "admirable remains of a classical past elevated to the category of cultural myth for the present."[81] Both traditions used the image of the Temple as a messianic symbol. Both Jews and Christians believed that the construction of the Third Temple would herald the messianic redemption.[82] This messianism was, as we have seen, conflated with the idea of renewed Jewish sovereignty. This was true even (or perhaps even more so) in Roman times. The Bar Kokhba rebellion against Roman rule in Judea minted its own coinage with an image of the Temple, inspired by Ezra's vision, on the obverse.[83] It is not insignificant that Ezra was the first biblical prophet to write in diaspora, and therefore for him the restoration of the (first) Temple was already symbolic of imagined, as opposed to actual, Jewish sovereignty.[84]

However, while other writers of Ibn Verga's generation rely, in humanist fashion, on the Latin Josephus himself rather than on the medieval Hebrew *Yosippon* or *Sefer Bin Gorion*,[85] Ibn Verga goes a step farther, portraying his reliance on a (fictional) Latin, Christian source. It is almost as if his version of the historical record is more legitimate for its Christian origin, as if Ibn Verga wants to make the point that if the Christian record validates his point, his case is even stronger than if it were built solely upon Jewish sources.

The exiles reacted variously to the events described by Ibn Verga, and immigration patterns bear out the disconnect between the importance of Zion as a symbolic versus real homeland. Historically, very few Jews emigrated to Palestine from the diaspora, and those who did were typically supported by charitable donations from abroad, there being little to no Jewish commerce or industry in the Holy Land. In the Ottoman period, the more favorable relations between the sultan and his Jewish subjects resulted in an increased Jewish presence in Palestine. Jewish immigration to Palestine was only a trickle compared to the far larger settlements in important trade centers such as Salonika and Constantinople, but for Jews, Palestine had unparalleled historic and spiritual appeal. Some sought refuge in the protection of the Ottoman Empire, seeking to recreate the life they had enjoyed in Spain. For them, the move to Palestine was a double diaspora, a return to the days of Roman Palestine, living in the Zionic homeland under a foreign king—a situation, we should remember, that was in perfect accordance with the rabbinic thought of the times.

After the (disastrously) failed Bar Kokhba rebellion in Roman Judea, the rabbis adopted a careful attitude toward messianism. Their main contribution was to temper the ever-present popular messianic idea (the same idea that gave rise to the many prophets who lived in the time before and after Jesus) with rabbinic moral and theological values. Nonetheless, the general resurgence of popular messianism in the sixth through seventh centuries CE in the Mediterranean required a rabbinic response to temper the zealotry and militarism that inevitably accompanied popular messianism. It is for this very reason that while there is a Talmudic tractate on Purim, a holiday that celebrates a Jewish victory over tyranny in diaspora, there is no Talmudic tractate on Hanukkah, a holiday that celebrates a Jewish military victory over an occupying force in Palestine itself, and one "almost inevitably bound up with messianism and militarism."[86]

TWO REACTIONS TO EXILE

We can discern two different reactions to the expulsion from Spain in the intellectual and political gestures made by various Sepharadim during the sixteenth century. The common response was to turn inward, to shun the vernacular culture and cosmopolitanism that many rabbis interpreted as having invoked God's punishment of expulsion. Others sought to recreate their Spanish experience by taking full advantage of the benevolence of the Ottoman sultans and gaining prominence at the Sublime Porte (the court of the sultan) just as they once had at the courts of Christian monarchs in Spain and Portugal. Many Sepharadim who lived in Palestine had spent some time living as conversos (Jews converted to Catholicism) in Spain, Portugal, and in Italy.[87] This experience had given them a taste of life as a member of the dominant culture. They were more familiar with the intellectual and religious life of the Christian majority than their unconverted Jewish counterparts. As we will see, some conversos who then returned to Judaism in Italy or in Ottoman lands suffered terrible guilt for having chosen an insincere conversion over expulsion or martyrdom at the hands of the Inquisition. This drove some to an extreme form of pious asceticism that ironically bore clear marks of Christian influence. In the case of Karo, this guilt manifested as an intense desire to be martyred by the Inquisition, the fate met by the self-styled Messiah Solmon Molkho, whom Karo admired. Karo gives voice to this desire frequently in the *Magid Meisharim*.[88] Werblowsky notes that for Karo, Molkho's "death at the stake assumed the significance of a coveted privilege," but one that was, living as Karo did in the Ottoman Empire and not in Christendom, ultimately impossible to realize.[89] For other ex-conversos, the experience made them hungry for more—not more Christianity, but more of the relative freedom and power that comes with a majority identity. Some toward God, others toward material and political security.

Both Karo and Ibn Verga internalize the historical harangues and persecutions suffered by their generation and that of their parents. Ibn Verga intellectualizes and externalizes, personifying in literary form the persecutors and defenders of Jews in Europe. His righteous gentiles are a dramatization of a role fulfilled in mystical discourse by the Shekhinah. Karo internalizes and personalizes the struggle, manifesting his harangue mentality in the form of his *magid,* an angel who speaks with the voice of the Shekhinah, lecturing him on spiritual correctness in the form of a series of biblical commentaries on the *parasha* or weekly reading.

Both examples are products of a specific time in history. Though it may sound cliché, the turn of the sixteenth century was in many ways the "Dawn of Modernity," especially with regard to the innovation and development of new intellectual currents and ideas such as were at stake in the work of our authors. The dispersion of the Sepharadim occurred in the age not of the scroll and tablet, but of print, and in the exact same year as the first voyage of Columbus to the new world. Some of the same aesthetic trends that critics have identified in the vernacular belles lettres and philosophical writing of the times are evident as well in Karo's mystical diary and in Ibn Verga's historical writing. In their work we see the same emphasis on the psychology and interior spirituality of the individual, the same exploration of cause and effect in human behavior that drove the development of the novel in works such as *Cárcel de Amor* (1492), *Celestina* (1499), and *Lazarillo de Tormes* (1545).[90] The relatively rapid circulation of ideas and people afforded by print technology and improved navigation and shipbuilding turbocharged the intellectual ferment of the Sephardic world in the sixteenth century. No matter that much of the circulation was owed to expulsions and displacements; if anything this only lent more urgency to intellectual discussions that touched on history, religion, and philosophy.[91] Such was the atmosphere in which Karo and Ibn Verga lived and wrote.

JOSEPH KARO'S *MAGID MEISHARIM*

Joseph Karo (Toledo 1488–Safed 1575) turned toward God. Karo was a highly respected expert in Jewish law and is best known as the author of the definitive synthesis of Jewish law, the *Shulkhan Arukh* (Set Table). He migrated from Spain to Portugal to the Ottoman Empire, passing through Adrianopole, Fez, and Salonika, before settling in Safed in Palestine. There he joined a group of pious mystics who concerned themselves with putting the spiritual house of Jewry in order.[92] For Karo and the circle of mystics who had gathered at Safed in northern Palestine, the expulsion was divine retribution for the sins of the Sepharadim. Their project was the spiritual refinement of all Jews, to be achieved through rigorous observation of the law and tireless pursuit of the mystical dimensions of the Torah and the commandments. Karo and his companions dedicated themselves to the compulsive refinement of religious law and mystical practice. For them, the road to redemption was the path of righteousness, exacting fulfillment of the divine commandments and rigorous contemplation of the nature of God. They were not concerned with reestablishing Jewish political power—this would be accomplished only after the arrival of the Messiah. The best way to prepare for this, according to Karo and his circle, was through fastidious observation of the commandments and penetrating contemplation of their mystical meaning.

The theosophical approach afforded by Kabbalah held out the promise that human experience could not be explained by biblical commentary and rabbinical jurisprudence alone. For the kabbalist, creation (and consequently human history, galut, etc.) was not simply the story of the relationship between God and humankind. There was a hidden narrative available to only the most learned and disciplined among Jewish scholars, a narrative that spoke of the relationship between the Shekhinah (God's feminine aspect according to kabbalistic doctrine) and the Jewish people. According to this narrative, the Shekhinah is sent by God to accompany the Jews in their exile and to protect them until the redemption.[93]

While Ibn Verga confronts the forces of history embodied in the form of Christian kings and clerics, Karo comes face to face with the embodiment of mystical eschatology. Karo recorded a series of visions in which the Shekhinah spoke through him. One night, as Karo was staying up late with his study companions on the eve of the Shavuot festival, the voice of the Shekhinah spoke through Karo in the guise of a preacher, urging him and his fellow Talmudists to help redeem her from exile. This would be accomplished both through study of Torah and kabbalistic meditative practice and through actual repatriation to the land of Israel:

> My friends, my beloved [...] blessed are you [...] that you have undertaken to crown me tonight, for it is now many years since the crown fell from my head, I have no one to comfort me and I am cast into the dust,

embracing dunghills. But now you have restored the crown to its former glory through your studies. [...] Therefore my sons, be strong, resolute, and joyful in my love, my torah, and my reverence; and if you could surmise the minutest part of the grief that is my lot [...] Therefore be strong and resolute and desist not from study. [...] Therefore, stand on your feet and exalt me [...] and she repeated, blessed are you, resume your studies and desist not one instant and go to the Land of Israel instantly [...] and through you I have been exalted tonight.[94]

What is fairly shocking about Karo's proposition is not that a leading rabbi might have mystical visions, but rather, that God, or the Shekhinah, would require the *assistance*—and not simple obedience—from the faithful. That is, instead of humans being completely dependent upon God to bring about the ge'ulah (redemption), the kabbalists suggested that God was in fact dependent upon humans to prepare the way for the coming of the Messiah, who would not appear until humanity reached a higher level of spiritual development.[95]

Until the sixteenth century, the study of the Kabbalah, and the *Zohar* in particular, was restricted to the most learned of male Jews. The ideas it contained were considered dangerous to those who lacked a solid grounding in the study of Torah and rabbinics. This tendency to protect the Kabbalah, or perhaps to protect the majority of Jews from the Kabbalah, gave way to a new messianic urgency after the expulsion from Spain. In the sixteenth century, leading rabbis reversed their position, instead condoning and encouraging the diffusion of messianic Kabbalah in hopes that it might hasten the arrival of the Messiah and deliver the Jews from oppression.[96]

Karo's visions of the angel/Shekhinah's sermons promote an extreme asceticism virtually unknown in prior Jewish tradition.[97] Karo summarized its tenets in the introduction to his *Magid Meisharim* (Preacher of Righteousness):

Be careful to avoid taking pleasure while eating meat and drinking, or while partaking of any other kind of enjoyment. Act as if a demon were forcing you to eat this food or indulge in the enjoyable activity. You should very much prefer it were possible to exist without food and drink altogether, or were it possible to fulfill the obligation of procreation without enjoyment.[98]

The particular flavor of mystic asceticism practiced by Karo and his associates in Safed was a novelty in the Jewish context, bringing to a head a tendency that had been percolating in Sephardic religious practice at least since the anti-Jewish violence of 1391 in Spain.[99] The expulsion had kicked off a messianic fervor that led some, most notably Isaac Abravanel (leader of Castilian Jewry and father of Leone Ebreo, the author of the *Dialogues of Love*), to predict the arrival of the Messiah in 1503.[100] This movement died out after the 1540 arrival predicted by the self-fashioned Messiah Solomon Molkho did not come to pass. In the Ottoman Palestinian context, messianic hopes increased when Suleyman the Magnificent rebuilt the walls of Jerusalem between 1536 and 1542.[101] Afterward, kabbalists such as those gathered at Safed changed course, urging a general purification of Judaism and of Jews worldwide in order to *hasten* the arrival of the Messiah. And while their messianism was not as urgent as that of the previous century, they introduced an important innovation in Jewish messianism: Karo himself was the first to suggest that it was human action, and not divine action, that would bring about the coming of the Messiah and the redemption of the Jews.[102] They took on personal responsibility for what they perceived as the moral failings of the exiled Sepharadim and strove for a spiritual perfection that would pave the way for the coming of the Messiah through the mystical work of reuniting the Shekhinah with her lover.

This line of thought begun by Karo would come to represent the most important innovation in kabbalistic thinking: human agency. Karo did not leave behind many writings on the subject of Kabbalah, but his student Moses Cordovero did. Cordovero likewise taught that redemption—allegorized in the reunion of the King (God's masculine aspect) with his Queen (God's feminine aspect)—depends upon human actions. When we do good, we draw them together; when we sin, we drive them apart.[103] He wrote a guide to making this happen called *The Palm Tree of Deborah*. According to Cordovero, when we do good, we do good not just to ourselves but also to God, who *benefits* from our actions: "In the acts of benevolence man carries out in the lower world he should have the intention of perfecting the upper worlds after the same pattern and this is what is meant by doing lovingkindness to the creator."[104] Likewise, bad deeds do *harm* to the Shekhinah, God's feminine aspect in kabbalistic thinking: "The flaw of his deeds pushes away the Shekhinah from above. He should fear to cause this great evil of separating the love of the King from the Queen."[105] When we imitate a given divine trait (as revealed in scripture), we act not only on this world but also upon the divine world. The good deed of healing the sick heals not only the sick person on Earth, but also helps to cure the sickness of the Shekhinah in heaven, who is lovesick due to her separation from the King (God). Cordovero therefore instructs us to "visit the sick and heal them. For it is known that the Shekhinah is love-sick for the Union, as it is written: 'For I am love-sick.' Her cure is in the hands of man who can bring her the good medicine she requires, as it is written: 'Stay me with dainties, support me with apples' [Song of Songs 2:5]."[106]

This mystical messianism was not in the least political—on the contrary, Jewish messianic doctrine had long held that Jewish sovereignty would not return to Zion until the Messiah had already arrived. But the introduction of human agency into the messianic idea would have its impact on political matters. Although it is not a call to sovereignty per se, it suggests that Jews have a certain measure of control over their history; and following traditional messianic ideas, it suggests also that the redemption will result in a renewal of Jewish sovereignty. The key difference is that the Jews themselves have the capacity to make it happen in accordance with divine will. Such a turn in the way Karo and other kabbalists imagined the path to redemption is not so far out of step with Ibn Verga's focus on human agency and his study of the effects of sovereignty and lack of sovereignty on Jewish history.

TWO VIEWS OF HUMAN AGENCY

How, then, to explain these diverse reactions to the experience of expulsion in the work of Karo and Ibn Verga? Both introduce, in very different modes, an element of human agency into a traditionally providential worldview. There are at least three ways to interpret this gesture. On the one hand it may simply have been a sign of the times. There is yet some truth in the shopworn idea of the Renaissance as a time of renewed emphasis on human agency in worldly matters, and Ibn Verga's and Karo's affirmations of the power of human action in the cosmic drama may simply be part of this movement. From a psychological perspective, one reaction to the trauma and overwhelming sense of the futility of human action on the historic stage would be to extend a bit of rationalism to one's theology. That is, we can read the affirmation of the power of human agency in Karo and Ibn Verga as a way to restore faith in a just God who rewards *good* behavior. For Karo in particular, if the chosen people are offered a clear connection between the works of humanity and the rewards of redemption, the same God who allowed the expulsion and the Inquisition to happen is ultimately a just God and one deserving of our faith. Finally, it is possible that the experience of belonging to the majoritarian culture as a converso may have given the generation of Karo and Ibn Verga a taste of life on the other side, a taste for agency, for power, that finds expression in their writing inflected variously in theosophic and historiographic discourses.[107] The converso experience is therefore key to understanding the diverse reactions of Karo and Ibn Verga to the experience of expulsion and re-diaspora. Both authors appear to have taken something of the majoritarian culture and transformed it into ideas of the value of human agency in the context of their diasporic tradition and experience.

As we have seen, these ideas are inflected differently in the works of Ibn Verga and his contemporary Joseph Karo. Karo and his companions turned inward, while Ibn Verga looked out to history. Like the Peninsular authors we have studied, Ibn Verga's own words pay lip service to traditional prophetic understandings of Jewish history, while his prose and literary technique tell a far more nuanced, complex story, one of a doubly diasporic culture assessing itself in an imperial moment whose structural similarities to imperial Rome fuel both messianic and humanistic historiographical impulses. Like authors such as Ben Elazar and Benvenist, who advocate for a kind of Jewish protonationalism while making good use of all the literary resources available to them from the literatures of the majority-Christian vernacular community, Ibn Verga hews to traditional ideas about *history* while making a series of bold experiments in *historiography*, most of which were made in direct imitation of Christian historiographers, who in turn worked under the influence of classical models.

Reading Amadís in Constantinople:
Spanish Fiction in the Key of Diaspora

> In exile, facing the painful reality of being Jews and no longer being
> Spaniards, the Sepharadim chose to continue to be Jews and Spaniards at
> the same time.
>
> Samuel Armistead and Joseph Silverman, *En torno al Romancero sefardí*

Sephardic authors in the generation following the expulsion gave
voice to a new layer of diasporic consciousness, of being in diaspora
from Spain. Ibn Verga's work couches this consciousness in a Sephardic
humanist voice, building on and reacting to the humanist historiography
of Spain and Italy, creating a diasporic counterhistory to that of the official
chronicler of the Spanish royalty. Joseph Karo's project, while patently
spiritual and not concerned with temporal history, still demonstrates a
familiarity with the current belief that human agency was now a factor one
must take into account when discussing the sweep of human history, even
when the parameters of that history are determined by God. Both adapted
the intellectual practices of the dominant culture into specifically Jewish
intellectual traditions. Ibn Verga, more than Karo, deliberately repackages
Spanish culture as Sephardic culture, writing as he does from outside the
Spanish imperium and in a literary language that had a rapidly shrinking
audience on the Iberian Peninsula itself.

Jacob Algaba's translation of the iconic chivalric romance *Amadís de
Gaula* (Constantinople, 1554) is a very different diasporic project, but one

that likewise refashions the literary tastes of the dominant culture of the Sephardic homeland, performing this cultural identity for the other diasporic Jewish communities of the Ottoman Empire. Like Jacob Ben Elazar's thirteenth-century recasting of courtly romance in the tale of Sahar and Kima, Algaba's translation remixes the chivalric ideal for a Jewish audience. However, unlike Ben Elazar, whose Iberian audience was well familiar with the world of knights and ladies that populated the chivalric imagination, Algaba aims more to perform his Sephardic identity for the wider Jewish communities of the Ottoman Empire and beyond. His translation of *Amadís* into Hebrew is a diasporic reappropriation of the values of the chivalric novel in a Sephardic setting. It is a simultaneous deployment of Spanish culture as an engine of Sephardic prestige and a rejection of the imperial culture, substituting in its place a reading that reflects the values of a diasporic minority. In the face of the Sepharadim's rejection from and abjection by the Spanish imperium, Algaba's *Amadís* duplicates aspects of Spanish cultural imperialism within Jewish communities of the Ottoman Empire. We can therefore read Algaba's *Amadís* as a product of what I will call Sephardic humanism, a response to the imperial culture of letters practiced by the intellectuals active at the courts of the Catholic Monarchs and later of Carlos V.

As in the case of writers associated with the court of Ferdinand and Isabella, Sephardic humanists worked across and between historiography and fiction. The translator Jacob Algaba is a proponent of a counterhumanism that flourished in Sephardic communities during the sixteenth century. Sephardic humanism is not often studied in relation to configurations of Spanish imperial power, but more frequently as a precursor to a modern Jewish national history rather than as the obscure counterhistory of an emergent Spanish nation state.

AMADÍS DE GAULA AS IMPERIAL HERO

Every culture has its knight in shining armor, its Superman. In sixteenth-century Spain this was the tradition of literary knights-errant inaugurated in print by *Amadís de Gaula,* protagonist of a wildly successful franchise of chivalric novels. Along with the Arthurian legends that arrived in the Iberian Peninsula from France during the late twelfth and early thirteenth centuries, tales of Amadís had been circulating in Iberia for over a century when Garcí Rodríguez de Montalvo published his authorized, updated recension of the deeds of Amadís de Gaula in Zaragoza in 1508. Juan Bautista Avalle-Arce dates the first mention of the story of Amadís to the mid-fourteenth century.[1] Entwistle's preliminary comments suggest that the hispanization of Arthurian legend was conditioned by the desire to appropriate the symbolic capital of the Arthurian narratives by casting them as rooted in local political history. Entwistle's study establishes, among other things, that Arthurian romances were known in the Peninsula since the mid-twelfth century, when Catalan troubadours began to make mention of Tristan and Lancelot. In the following century, Alfonso X mentions Tristan, Arthur, and Merlin in the *Cantigas de Santa Maria*.[2] By the fourteenth century, Arthurian knights-errant were already firmly established as the heroic ideal in courtly circles in Portugal, Castile, and Aragon. Children were named after Lancelot and Tristan, and writers such as Pero López de Ayala were able to confess to their addiction to chivalric romances.[3] The popularity of Arthurian romances in Iberia may have been reinforced during the fourteenth century by numbers of English knights and ladies who came to participate in the campaigns against Granada and in the pilgrimage to Santiago de Compostela.[4]

In any event, Rodríguez de Montalvo's *Amadís* was a huge success, and Montalvo and his successors capitalized on it by bringing out first some ten sequels chronicling the adventures of Esplandián, son of Amadís, and then a series of related sequels.[5]

One need go no further than Miguel de Cervantes's *Don Quixote* to find evidence of the tremendous hold *Amadís* had on the popular imagination. In a scene where the town barber and the priest are preparing to burn protagonist Alonso Quijano's library, they debate the fate of *Amadís*:

> "This one seems to be a mystery, because I have heard that this was the first book of chivalry printed in Spain, and all the rest found their origin and inspiration here, and so it seems to me that as the proponent of the doctrine of so harmful a sect, we should, without any excuses, condemn it to the flames."
>
> "No, Señor," said the barber, "for I've also heard that it is the best of all the books of this kind ever written, and as a unique example of the art, it should be pardoned."

"That's true," said the priest, "and so we'll spare its life for now. Let's see the one next to it."[6]

This cult of the hero that sprang up around Amadís and his successors was a product of the times. In the sixteenth century, the struggle with the Ottoman Empire was the symbolic stage on which Amadís made his entry. The Spanish knight-errant became, in the popular imagination, a hero for the times, one who, like Captain America during World War II, would serve as a fictional bulwark against popular fears of military defeat and invasion. In the second half of the book, Cervantes lampoons this very notion of the Spanish knight-errant as Christian imperial soldier. When Don Quixote is discussing an impending Turkish attack on Spain with the barber and the priest, he suggests that King Philip assemble a crack unit of super soldiers to defend Spain against the Ottomans:

> "What else can His Majesty do but command by public proclamation that on a specific day all the knights-errant wandering through Spain are to gather at court, and even if no more than half a dozen were to come, there might be one among them who could, by himself, destroy all the power of the Turk. Your graces should listen carefully and follow what I say. Is it by any chance surprising for a single knight-errant to vanquish an army of two hundred thousand men, as if all of them together had but one throat or were made of sugar candy? Tell me, then: how many histories are filled with such marvels? If only—to my misfortune, if not to anyone else's—the famous Don Belianís were alive today, or any one of the countless descendants of Amadís of Gaul! If any of them were here today and confronted the Turk, it would not be to his advantage!"[7]

Heroes embody the values that are important to a given society, and Amadís and his successors were avatars of Spanish imperial desire.[8] Accordingly, Montalvo's introduction to *Amadís* paints the knight hero as a man who, had he been born a real knight and not a fictional character, might have fought alongside the Catholic Monarchs as they claimed the last redoubts of Islamic sovereignty on the Iberian Peninsula, before setting their sights on Constantinople.

In this propagandistic turn, Montalvo was following the lead of humanists working at the court of the Catholic Monarchs who actively promoted a program of imperial imagery. They very deliberately deployed tropes from imperial Rome, mixing these with specifically Iberian and Catholic

elements to create a narrative of temporal and spiritual imperial renova-
tion. Antonio de Nebrija, for example, writes of the Spain of the Catholic
Monarchs as the last stage of Roman *imperium*.[9] Martin Biersack explains
that the cultivation of a Roman imperial legacy by the Catholic Monarchs
was meant to shore up their position before the nobles of Castile and
Aragon.[10] According to this narrative, the Spanish crown is a renewal of
the Holy Roman Empire, itself a renewal of Classical Rome.[11] Just as the
Holy Roman Empire was renewed through Christian salvation, the Spanish Empire is renewed through a spiritual discipline that transcends the
Roman example in that Christianity is to be the guiding force not only of
government, but of the souls of all imperial subjects as well.

Like the humanist historians of the court of the Reyes Católicos, Montalvo in his introduction stresses that the value of history is to study the
deeds of great men.[12] He legitimates his work by placing *Amadís* on the
same stage as his king, Fernando of Aragón, suggesting that the orators
of classical antiquity would be equally inspired by Fernando's deeds as
by those of Caesar. Here Montalvo turns the conventional justification
of fictional exemplarity on its head: while Cligès was a model for twelfth-
century knights, Amadís is a model for *writers* to celebrate the deeds of
kings. This is the humanist turn: the story is an exemplar of a *story*, not of
a propagandistic retelling, nor is it an example of excellent conduct. The
Hebrew introduction restores the classical Romance claim to exemplarity, which makes sense: Hebrew is at an earlier stage of its development
in its fictional consciousness. It had developed strategies for dealing with
fictionality in the thirteenth century, but here is dealing with a new sort of
fiction. In any event, the translator of the Hebrew Arthur legitimates the
reading of historical romance in the introduction: "It is possible to learn
wisdom and ethics from these fables concerning a man's conduct toward
himself and toward his fellow man. Therefore they are neither idle nor
profane talk."[13]

Cervantes performs a similar mimetic sleight of hand, in offering up
Amadís and his successors as champions in the struggle of his own king,
Philip III, with the Turks. Don Quixote's logic is simple: if Amadís is the
avatar of the (successful) Christian struggle against Granada, it stands
to reason he might be at least as successful against the Turks. And while
Quixote admits the anachronism of such a scenario, he ignores the prob-

lem, true to character, of a fictional hero facing off against a flesh-and-blood foe. He frames the deeds of Amadís within a discussion of those of the great [historical/mythical] heroes of antiquity, next to those of Fernando in the present day. What connects fictional Amadís, mythical Achilles, historical Caesar, and contemporary Fernando? The rhetorical excellence with which their deeds are celebrated, the "flowers" and "roses" planted in their honor by great orators in the tradition of courtly, martial rhetoric:

> So then, if in the time of these [classical] orators, who more in matters of reputation than in personal gain applied their intelligence and wearied their spirits, should have taken place that holy conquest that our very brave King made of the kingdom of Granada, what flowers, what roses might they have planted on its occasion, as concerns the bravery of the knights in the battles, skirmishes, and dangerous duels and all the other cases of confrontations and travails that were performed in the course of that war, as well as of the compelling speeches made by the great King to his nobles gathered in the royal campaign tents, the obedient replies made by them, and above all, the great praises, the lofty admirations that he deserves for having taken on and accomplished such a divinely inspired task![14]

Montalvo projects upon the fictional Amadís the very real desires to continue the trajectory of imperial holy war begun by the elimination of Islamic political power on the Iberian Peninsula. If the Christian conquest of al-Andalus had long been framed as a domestic crusade, and the pope himself gave the title "Catholic Monarchs" to Fernando and Isabella, it follows that what made them "Catholic" was their military commitment to expand Christendom and diminish Dar al-Islam.[15] Constantinople, still rather recently conquered by the Ottomans, would replace Granada as the object of imperial desire.[16] The former Byzantine capital emerges in the novel as a site of Christian imperial fantasy, an alternate past in which the Byzantine Christians successfully fight off the Ottomans.[17]

In Montalvo's sequel, Esplandían, son of Amadís, falls in love with the daughter of the Byzantine emperor of Constantinople, then successfully leads the Byzantines in their routing of an attempted Muslim invasion. After the great victory, the emperor abdicates in favor of Esplandían, who ascends to the throne himself.[18] Subsequent Amadís sequels feature protagonists, descendants of Amadís, who likewise rule over or defend a Christian Constantinople.[19]

Amadís, and to an even greater extent his son Esplandían, are imagined by Montalvo and his readers as Christian heroes in service of a Christian imperial project. In *Amadís* the imperial fantasy takes the shape of moralizing digressions and the mostly discursive (but not narrative, as is the case in *Sergas de Esplandían*) expression of an imperial Catholic ideology. In the *Sergas*, however, this ideology drives not only Montalvo's characterization of the hero and the tone of the narrator, but also the plot and settings themselves. The drama of *Amadís* is powered mostly by the classically Arthurian quest of the hero to prove himself in the name of his lady, but in *Sergas* the quest is far more universal: to unite Christendom against the threat of Islam, here represented by the pagan Persians who threaten the Byzantine Empire. It is not just the Arthurian hero's efforts that are redirected, but rather the modes of heroic effort themselves. The scenes of single combat so characteristic of French chivalric romance give way to massive battles between huge armies that are more reminiscent of the epic struggles between Christians and pagans in the *Chanson de Roland* or the battles waged by Rodrigo Díaz de Vivar in the *Cantar de Mio Cid*.[20] In this way Montalvo maps the values of a new kind of Catholicism, one yoked to imperial aspirations (as in the Constantinian past, *pace* court humanists) and mapped onto the figure of the Arthurian knight-errant as a means of redemption, precisely at the time when the mode of combat the knight-errant represents—individual combat in the name of one's lady—is passing into a ceremonial, symbolic practice that no longer has pride of place in real warfare and that has been surpassed by mass warfare carried out by professional armies on a grand scale.

As we have seen in Montalvo's introduction to *Amadís*, the author frames the exploits of his fictional hero in terms of the military victories of Fernando over the Muslim enemy Granada. Once the boundaries of the Peninsula are secure against the infidel, and the North African coast pacified, the next logical grand imperial gesture would be to recuperate Constantinople for Christendom. The Ottoman Turks had, after all, conquered Constantinople in the not-so-distant past, and their looming presence on the Mediterranean was seen as a serious threat to Spanish political power in the region and even on the Iberian Peninsula itself.[21]

Contemporary chroniclers confirm that the loss of Christian Constantinople was, during the reign of the Catholic Monarchs, still a fresh wound.
Diego Enríquez del Castillo, writing before 1503, says that "the pain of the
loss of Constantinople, that the Turk had conquered, was very recent in
the hearts of all."[22]

It is a natural move for the chivalric hero to be cast in a crusading role.
According to some theories of chivalric romance, the very figure of the
knight-errant is based in part on the itinerant crusader knights either
making their way to or returning from the East.[23] Crusade chronicles,
a well represented genre, were an important influence in determining
the shapes of chivalric romance, and vice versa.[24] Both genres (including many texts that combined elements of both chronicle and romance)
were marketed by printers under the same rubric, and a cursory review
of author and translator introductions to works of "real" history and romance bear this out. Chronicle and romance were two sides of a coin, two
ways of approaching the truth(s) about war, politics, and power. Marina
Brownlee writes that romance is a reaction to historical events and trends,
"a continuous and sophisticated reinvention of itself as a response to an
ever-changing historico-political configuration."[25] Barbara Fuchs likewise registers the complementarity of romance and chronicle, holding
that "romances simply have a different purchase on the truth" that has
"little to do with empiricism; it connotes instead a moral stance towards
political and historical events."[26]

This sort of conflation of history and courtly narrative runs parallel in
peninsular literature of the late fifteenth and early sixteenth centuries.
Chivalric novels such as *Amadís de Gaula* and its successors represented
themselves as a kind of history, or at best as offering some of the same
benefits to be had from reading "real" histories of kings who actually lived
and acted. In his introduction to *Amadís,* Montalvo compares his work
"chronicling" the deeds of the fictional Amadís to that of the classical
writers who chronicled the great deeds of Hector, Achilles, and Ajax, and
to those works of fiction that likewise describe great feats of arms and
strength of character. These, he explains, can be equally beneficial to the
reader on a spiritual level despite having no basis in historical reality.
What we can glean from these (fictional) stories of chivalric adventures
are "good examples and guidelines that bring us that much closer to our

salvation. . . . We use them as wings upon which our souls might fly up to the height of Glory whither they are destined."[27]

In understanding this tendency we should bear in mind that humanist historians were very focused on the value of rhetoric and on the effect generated by narrating great deeds in elevated language. Their obsession with the great orators and rhetors of classical antiquity carried over into their actuality. Putting aside the question of how fifteenth-century historiographers understood the concept of *history*, we can be sure that they understood and valued excellence in rhetoric in both fictional and historical narratives.

Montalvo's mapping of the fictional knight-errant onto the political concerns of the day was very much in keeping with the history of chivalric romance.[28] His innovation is his deliberate and explicit application of the fictional exploits of Amadís and Esplandián to the specific exploits of the rulers of an emergent nation state.[29] In this, Montalvo was continuing a long tradition of fantasizing about Iberian expansion in the Mediterranean, as Castilian and Aragonese monarchs had been doing for hundreds of years before the reign of the Catholic Monarchs. The sorties of Castilian forces into North Africa during the reign of Alfonso X in the mid-thirteenth century (Salé 1260), for example, go hand in hand with his designs on the Holy Roman imperial throne, and we should remember that the flag of the crown of Aragon flew over the Duchy of Athens from 1311 to 1388. In fact, there had been a continuous presence of Western Christian forces, including Aragonese, in parts of Byzantium going back to the Crusades.[30]

The fantasy of recuperating Constantinople is played out with abandon in the fictional literature of the time of the Catholic Monarchs, even if it is minimized in the royal chronicles of the time. Even if documents emanating from the royal chancery did not voice specific imperial designs on Istanbul, there was an undeniable artistic trend fantasizing a Christian Constantinople.[31]

Given this trend, and with the historic precedent of Iberian conquest of Byzantine territories, it should not surprise that Montalvo locates the origin of his *Amadís* in Constantinople itself. In his introduction to *Amadís de Gaula* he explains that his book is a revised version of the first three books that have long been circulating in manuscript form, together with books four and five that he edited from a manuscript that was found in Constantinople, in the tomb of Esplandían himself, and thence found its way to Spain:[32] "By great fortune [this book] appeared in a stone tomb that was found below ground in a hermitage near Constantinople, and brought to these parts of Spain by a Hungarian merchant, in a hand and on a parchment so antique, that only with great effort could be read by those who understood the language."[33]

This bit of mimetic rapprochement between historical author and fictional text adds to the sense of Amadís and Esplandían's role as avatars of imperial desire. The manuscript's origin in a hermitage, what would be a minority religious outpost in (by Montalvo's day) an officially Muslim state, and the poor condition in which it was found, both point up Montalvo's role as conservator and rejuvenator of a Christian chivalric tradition precisely at a moment when the Spanish Empire is gaining momentum and beginning to fantasize about expansion into the East. This goal is more evident in the symbolic and artistic spheres than in the political, and though the Catholic Monarchs sent a number of flotillas against the Ottoman Turks, they were never in a position to consider a full-on invasion of Constantinople. Nonetheless, the dream of the "Reconquest" of Constantinople was a powerful idea, one that was conveniently suited to the articulation of an imperial identity. This is the *Amadís* that Jacob Algaba set his pen to translate in the very Constantinople that many readers of *Amadís* imagined the knight might one day conquer in the name of Spain. What follows is the story of Algaba's Sephardic *Amadís,* whom he creates, as it were, in the eye of the storm, the center of the metropolis of Spain's enemy.

THE SEPHARADIM IN THE IMPERIAL SPANISH CONTEXT

The publication of Jacob Algaba's Hebrew translation of *Amadís* is a sort of ironic restoration of *Amadís* to Constantinople, but hardly in the ways imagined by Montalvo. The publication of this Ottoman Hebrew *Amadís* will serve as a focal point for my discussion of the Sephardic role in the Hispanic cultural imaginary of the sixteenth century, precisely during Spain's emergence as a global imperial power. We have mentioned the chroniclers and authors working at the court of Ferdinand and Isabella

and their task to construct an imperial identity. What role do the Sepharadim play in this imperial idea? Why are they worth mentioning, since they
had been fairly decisively cut out of the picture by the Edict of Expulsion?

In light of recent calls for more global approaches to early modern
Hispanic studies, critics have been studying traditional topics in broader
contexts, using approaches that de-center the idea of an author representing a single national culture or ethos. Carroll Johnson, a distinguished
Cervantes scholar, held that the future of his field lay in the study of Cervantes's works in the context of Spanish imperialism in the New World
and in Islam.[34] This sentiment has been echoed and carried out by younger
scholars who argue for more transnational, transterritorial approaches to
Spanish literature and history.[35]

Early modern Sephardic culture is very much a product of imperial
Spain and reproduces aspects of it in its own way. We can think of it as
a kind of parallel shadow imperialism that the Sepharadim brought to
bear on the existing Jewish communities of the Ottoman Empire where
many of them settled. The idea that the Sepharadim were deterritorialized
Spaniards was common among Spanish liberals in the late nineteenth and
twentieth centuries.[36] The Spanish Hebraist Federico Pérez Castro made
the following observation about the Sepharadim in a paper he delivered
in 1964:

> The roots of Spanishness took hold so deeply in the souls of our Jews that
> the Hispano-Hebrews, upon leaving Spain, although they physically left
> her behind, carried her with them inside their hearts, and in distant lands
> not only continued to live according to our ways, but even imposed these
> ways upon others wherever they established themselves; a sociospiritual
> phenomenon so perfectly Spanish that it may most clearly define their
> deep identification with Spain.[37]

When I first read this passage, I dismissed it as rhetoric typical of a Franco-
era academic anxious to demonstrate that history did indeed validate
the ideology of the current regime. Pérez Castro seemed to be saying
that what qualified Sepharadim as *authentic* Spaniards was their gift for
cultural imperialism. And this was probably true to a certain extent. However, I have come to believe that there is something to Pérez Castro's argument: the Sepharadim were performing their Spanishness in what could
be argued was a form of colonization of the Ottoman Jewish world.

Significant numbers of Sepharadim had been emigrating to the Otto-man Empire since the fourteenth century, with a spike after the anti-Jew-ish violence of 1391 and a larger one following the 1492 expulsion. Sepha-radim and conversos continued to arrive over the course of the sixteenth century as well, some coming directly from Spain and Portugal, others from North Africa, Western Europe, and other points.[38] The Ottoman Empire was a popular destination for Spanish and Portuguese conversos who, although well situated materially in Spain and Portugal, sought to practice Judaism openly. By the mid-sixteenth century the Sepharadim had largely overwhelmed the native Greek-speaking Romaniote and other Jewish groups living in the Ottoman Empire. Judeo-Castilian came to dominate the Romance languages spoken by Ottoman Jews of Proven-çal, Portuguese, Catalan, and Italian origin, and Sephardic customs and liturgical rite dominated those of other groups as well.[39]

Contemporary sources bear out this characterization of the Sepha-radim as the socially and culturally dominant group within Ottoman Jewry, imposing their liturgy, rabbinic jurisprudence, cuisine, language, and social customs on the wider community. Writing in 1509, Rabbi Moses Aroquis of Salonika bears witness to this phenomenon:

> It is well known that the Sepharadim and their scholars in this empire,
> together with the other communities that have joined them, make up
> the majority, may the Lord be praised. To them alone the land was given,
> and they are its glory and its splendor and its magnificence, enlighten-
> ing the land and its inhabitants. Who deserves to order them about? All
> these places too should be considered as ours, and it is fitting that the
> small number of early inhabitants of the empire observe all our religious
> customs.[40]

The Ottoman embrace of the Sepharadim only underscores this point. They effect a massive *translatio studii* from Spain to the Ottoman Empire that spans commercial, industrial, military, and intellectual spheres.[41] The Sultans incentivized the Sepharadim to settle in secondary and tertiary commercial centers with generous concessions and tax relief. This policy was designed to stimulate economic development of provincial centers throughout the Ottoman Empire. They were also key players in promoting international trade.[42] Just as Ottoman policy enabled Sephardic elites to reproduce the favorable economic conditions they had enjoyed in Spain,

Sephardic intellectuals and printers saw it as their duty to reproduce the intellectual ferment of Spain in their new Ottoman context.[43]

This fact was certainly not lost on Sultan Bayazid II, who is famously rumored to have marveled at the foolishness of the Catholic Monarchs for impoverishing their own kingdom while enriching his own.[44] Neither was it lost on outside observers such as Nicholas de Nicolay, a French traveler and diplomat who marveled at the extent of the Sephardic economic domination of the Ottoman scene:

> [The Jews] have amongst them workmen of all artes and handicraftes moste excellent, and specially of the Maranes [Marranos] of late banished and driven out of Spaine and Portugale, who to the great detriment and damage of the Christianitie, have taught the Turkes divers inventions, craftes and engines of warre, as to make artillerie, harquebuses, gunne powder, shot, and other munitions: they have also there set up printing, not before seen in those countries, by the which in faire characters they put in light divers bookes in divers languages, as Greek, Latin, Italian, Spanish, and the Hebrew tongue, beeing too them naturall, but are not permitted to print the Turkie or Arabic tongue.[45]

Such reports of the overwhelming successes of the Sepharadim were couched in messianic terms. The increased proximity of the exiled Sepharadim (who were said to descend from Jerusalemite Hebrews) to the Holy Land was seen as a harbinger of the Messiah. This went back at least to the Ottoman conquest of Constantinople, which Jewish writers understood in a messianic sense.[46] This gathering messianism was accelerated by the expulsion of the Jews from Spain and the subsequent annexation of the Holy Land, *Eretz Yisrael,* to the Ottoman Empire in 1516.[47]

The popular historical imagination has been flooded as of late with various versions of the Golden Age of al-Andalus as a place where Jewish culture flourished side by side with Muslim and Christian cultures. This is not the place to go into a full deconstruction of this fantasy, and scholars such as Brian Catlos, Jonathan Ray and others have already done a fine job of nuancing the dream of the so-called convivencia that emanates from medieval Iberia into present day discussions.[48] Specialists in medieval Spanish literature, in questioning the legacy of national philologies and literary histories, have begun to address the role of the Sepharadim in medieval Spanish literary history. In the 2004 *Cambridge History of Spanish Literature,* John Dagenais calls for a Spanish literary history that includes the contributions of medieval Sephardic authors:

> The remarkable flourishing of Sephardic culture, including numerous publications in Ladino, often using the Hebrew alphabet, in the centuries following the expulsion, as well as the survival today of hundreds of ballads whose origins can be traced back to late medieval Spain among the Jewish communities of North Africa, the eastern Mediterranean, the Near East, and the New World, give a shape to "medieval" Iberian literature which defies not only the national and ethnic boundaries but also the temporal ones we might place upon it. It requires a rethinking, especially, of what such temporal boundaries mean.[49]

Dagenais here nuances Pulido's notion that the Sepharadim were bearers of a Spanish tradition despite their political and geographic rupture with the government and land of origin. Non-academic, official pronouncements of the importance of Sephardic culture in the Spanish context likewise seem to view 1492 as a *terminus ad quem* past which there is no Sephardic role in Spanish imperial history until King Juan Carlos II officially invites the Jews back into the country in 1989 and again in 1992 as part of the many celebrations and condemnations taking place during the *quinentario* (five-hundred-year anniversary) of the Christian conquest of Granada, the expulsion of Spanish Jewry, and the first voyage of Columbus.[50]

However, when academics write on Hispano-Jewish or Sephardic topics, they rarely do so with a critical consciousness of configurations of Spanish imperial power going beyond canonical understandings of the relationships between Christian sovereigns and Jewish courtiers. When a Hispanist does consider a Jewish topic, it is typically that of the Iberian conversos, who are still constituted as subjects of Spanish imperial authority. The Sepharadim, ethnically Spanish, religiously Jewish, and politically Ottoman, have largely eluded the Hispanist gaze in the current discussion.

As we pointed out in the previous chapter, Barbara Fuchs's idea of "imperium studies" works well as a framework for approaching Sephardic culture in that it emphasizes the transnational and transterritorial aspects of cultural production within the context of an imperial society. She proposes

> the category of *imperium studies* as a way to address the links between met-
> ropolitan sovereignty and expansion abroad, and the cultural productions
> that sustain them both. Imperium studies enables the critical recognition
> of the centrality of empire in Old World texts that are not explicitly en-
> gaged with colonial ventures, and reveals the transatlantic or international
> dimension of texts previously read within narrow national traditions.[51]

The Sepharadim, as representatives of the cultural moment that produced a massive Spanish Empire, are involved in Spanish imperial culture, but not as imperial subjects or objects. They are scarcely on the radar in the imperial view, yet they are themselves repositories of Spanish culture and actors in what we might call Spanish imperial culture, broadly writ. As Ottoman subjects, they are politically legitimate under the Ottoman *sürgün* system, an adaptation of the Islamic Qur'anic doctrine of *ahl al-dhimma*, the tolerated monotheistic religious minorities allowed to practice their own religion in an Islamic state.[52] They enact Spanish culture on the Ottoman stage in a kind of Sephardic counternationalism that mimics and distorts Spanish imperial culture.

This counterformation of Spanishness is quite different than it might have been in the context of a modern nation state, one functioning with a political structure that enforces a homogeneous national cultural iden-tity.[53] That is, it is not as if the price of admission to the Ottoman arena were to renounce one's Sephardicness. The *sürgün* system allowed for ethnic and religious diversity within the Islamic state. Significant num-bers of Greek and Armenian Christians, Sephardic, Romaniote, and Ash-kenazic Jews, and a host of other ethnic and religious minorities lived and often (but not always) thrived in Ottoman lands in the fifteenth and sixteenth centuries. Nonetheless, I think it particularly interesting that Sephardic ethnic identity in this context was largely based on the Sepha-radim's "Spanishness," given both the circumstances of their separation from Spain and the political antipathy between Spain and the Ottoman Empire. Unlike the Armenians, Ashkenazi Jews, and other minorities, the Sepharadim were a product of the culture of the Spanish crown, the enemy of the Sultan, and spoke the language of the court of the rival superpower of the Mediterranean basin.

THE HEBREW *AMADÍS:* REVENGE OF THE ABJECT

What is the role of a Hebrew *Amadís* in this context? As with the case of Ibn Verga's history book (*Shevet Yehudah*), the project of the Sephardic intellectuals was twofold: on the one hand, they sought to legitimize their work by drawing on the prestige of Spanish humanism; on the other, they reshaped this humanism into one that reflected the values of the community in a diasporic, transimperial context. Jacob Algaba's Hebrew *Amadís* recasts the heroic values of Montalvo's book to bring them more fully in line with Sephardic tastes.

Both versions were of course shaped by market considerations. Montalvo, in order to maximize his version's appeal, tailored the story to fulfill popular expectations of Christian, chivalric behavior. This he accomplished without a doubt. But Algaba's challenge was different. He was assured of the popularity of the narrative franchise—this was never in question. The figure of Amadís was so compelling in the Sephardic imagination that he achieved a certain symbolic universality. There is a series of popular ballads in the Sephardic tradition that, although they have nothing to do with the story of Montalvo's *Amadís,* still call their heroic protagonist by his name. None of these versions, however, relates material taken from Montalvo's narrative. Rather, the name Amadís becomes emblematic of any "knight in shining armor."[54] To the Sepharadim, as to the Spanish, Amadís was the archetypical hero, and therefore every hero was Amadís.

Even well before Algaba's Hebrew translation appeared, Ottoman Sepharadim were avid readers of Spanish editions of *Amadís* and other chivalric novels. In the early sixteenth century, Jerusalem Rabbi Menahem di Lunzano chastised his community for reading *Amadís* and *Palmerín* on Shabbat (the Sabbath), when they should have been reading religious books.[55] Unlike the bootleg Spanish copies of *Amadís* and *Palmerín* mentioned by Lunzano, a Hebrew *Amadís* would need to bear the imprimatur of the rabbis of Constantinople in order to see the light of day, and that would require some revisions. The social values of the Spanish Christian nobility associated with the heroes of chivalric novels were incompatible with Sephardic mores and tastes, and this discrepancy was responsible for the acculturation of the chivalric hero to the Sephardic context.[56] Sephardic authors and translators therefore had to recast chivalric heroes in values that were consonant with those of the community. At the very least, they had to *say* that's what they were doing.

Some of Algaba's emendations to the text are superficial and "de-Christianizing." For example, he corrects *obispo* (bishop) and *clérigo* (cleric) to Hebrew *hakhamim* (wise men, often with religious connotation).[57] However, more numerous and more significant are those changes where he inserts examples of obscene, improper, or nonchivalric behavior.[58] These changes are in my opinion more significant for understanding Algaba's translation in its transimperial Sephardic context. In one example, Algaba includes an episode omitted by Montalvo where Amadís tricks his opponent into looking away in order to hit him: he asks the knight "to whom does that beautiful maiden behind you belong?" When the knight looks away, Amadís sticks him in the groin with his lance, spilling his guts.[59] In another example, Montalvo omits a reference to a character farting that is included by Algaba.[60] These are scenes that do not pass muster with the chivalric imaginary of the Spain of the Catholic Monarchs. Others are explanations of chivalric expectations or behavior that might not have been comprehensible to Jewish audiences not familiar with Christian courtly culture.

These examples are not very significant for thinking about the text's Sephardicness. If we suppose that Algaba *did not have access to* Montalvo's edition, then he is not really exercising any editorial power or making artistic decisions that shed light on his personality as a translator or on the Sephardic literary culture of his times. However, it is safe to assume that Algaba would have had access to Montalvo's book, which had been published some thirty years earlier. If Algaba indeed had access to both a pre-Montalvo manuscript version *as well as* Montalvo's edition, then his editorial choices are more significant. He is *choosing* the manuscript over Montalvo's version. When he chooses to write about farts where Montalvo elides them, or when he shows us an Amadís who fights dirty ("Hey, whose girlfriend is *that*? Gotcha!"), then he is consciously rejecting the authorized *Amadís* in favor of an earthier, more wily protagonist whose motives and actions (at least as far as Algaba is concerned) better resonate with his imagined public. The culture of Montalvo's *Amadís*, with its exaggerated religious rhetoric and rarefied standards of courtliness, has rejected Algaba (who was born in Spain), and Algaba is happy to return the favor, refashioning Amadís as a Sephardic hero, one who springs from Iberian tradition but who is free of the restraints of official Spanish culture as propagated at court. Here I would like to talk more directly about the text of the translation itself, in order to show what Algaba's translation achieves as a translation made by and for members of a culture in diaspora.

Amadís was a natural favorite for Sephardic Jews who, while living in Constantinople, Salonika, or elsewhere, spoke Spanish and still identified strongly with the vernacular culture of their land of origin. Its reception by Sephardic Jews and its translation into Hebrew offers us a glimpse into the literary practices of the Sephardic diaspora. The Hebrew Amadís can help us to better understand the diasporic cultural production of the Sepharadim.

DOUBLE DIASPORA AND THE CHIVALRIC IMAGINATION

Why does this repackaging of popular chivalric romance matter when we are studying the cultural significance of a translation? It matters because in doing so we are expanding the discussion of Jewish diaspora. First-wave modern theorists of diaspora writing in the 1970s and 1980s argued that the cultural imagination of diasporic populations vacillates between two geographical territories, constantly mediating between the symbolic value of their homeland and the lived reality of their current hostland. Later theorists of more recent diasporas have criticized this dual-territorial model. Sudesh Mishra, one of the harshest critics of this approach, argues that it cannot address the complexities of the modern diasporas of Indian, African, Chinese, and other populations.[61]

Before examining the text of the translation itself, it is worth considering Algaba's Hebrew Amadís in the context of the Hebrew print culture and of the Ottoman Jewish society of the times. The Hebrew print industry was active in Spain from the late fifteenth century, and presses in Spain produced a great number of religious works (Bibles, Talmuds, biblical commentaries, liturgical and moralistic texts) but also volumes of philosophy, science, and what we might call secular prose such as histories and fiction. In the early sixteenth century Hebrew printing continued to flourish, first in Italy, and then in Ottoman cities such as Salonika, Adrianopole, and Constantinople.[62]

For most of the sixteenth century nearly all titles with any discernible Jewish content were published in Hebrew. In Salonika printers brought out a few titles in Judeo-Spanish, and Italian printers published some in Italian or in both Italian and Hebrew, but for the most part Hebrew had pride of place as the prestige language of the Jewish press.[63] However, Jewish printers in Italy and the Ottoman Empire learned languages of their non-Jewish neighbors and were not culturally isolated or closed to the vernacular. On the contrary, the itinerant printer Gershon Soncino (who moved his press a number of times to various locations in Italy and the Ottoman Empire) published several titles for Christian patrons in Italian, Greek, and Latin.[64]

In Ottoman Jewish society, Hebrew was the academic and religious lingua franca of a number of different ethnic groups who had settled in Ottoman cities. While Salonika in the sixteenth century was overwhelmingly Sephardic, the indigenous Greek-speaking Romaniote Jews had significant communities in the cities and were joined by Ashkenazi Jews from Western and Eastern Europe as well as some Mizrahi (Eastern) Jews from the Arabic-, Persian-, and Turkic-speaking areas of the Ottoman Empire and beyond. But by their numbers, their superior cultural level, and their considerable network of commercial and diplomatic contacts, the Sepharadim quickly emerged as the prestige subculture of Ottoman Jewry. This, along with the fact that Sepharadim conversant in Spanish would have no need of a Hebrew translation in order to read *Amadís*, suggests that the translation was made either for Greek-speaking (but Hebrew-reading) Romaniote Jews in Ottoman lands or perhaps for non-Spanish-speaking Jewish readers in any country that Algaba's edition might eventually reach. At this time Jewish merchants, diplomats, and scholars traveled widely throughout the Mediterranean and beyond. While we have no documentary evidence of the reception of Algaba's translation, it is not unreasonable to think that copies may have ended up in the hands of readers in Cairo, Tunis, Venice, Troyes, or Cochin, for that matter.

Sephardic culture (in the broad sense) had a long history of prestige in the East, going back to Maimonides, who retained the sobriquet "Ha-

Sefardí" long after leaving his native Cordoba. The Ottoman Sepharadim likewise represented this prestige, expressed both in their Spanish vernacular culture and in the wealth and influence they wielded. Accordingly, the Sephardic community attracted and assimilated members from the other groups and soon was the dominant ethnic culture in Ottoman Jewish society.[65] As we read Algaba's text we should keep two things in mind: he was in all likelihood writing for non-Sephardic Jews, and he was consciously representing Sephardic culture to them in choosing to translate a Spanish (European) novel, a genre that had yet to be introduced to Hebrew.[66]

As is often the case with translations into Hebrew, a certain amount of adaptation is necessary in order to predispose the text for Jewish religious and cultural sensibilities. The Ibn Tibbon translations, followed by those of Judah al-Harizi and others, developed differing approaches toward the translation of Arabic texts from a Muslim milieu.[67] While Jewish translators brought over numerous scientific and medical texts from Latin into Hebrew during the Middle Ages, translations into Hebrew of literary fiction were scarce. Apart from the thirteenth-century *Melekh Artus* (King Arthur), there were very few, if any, models to follow.[68]

Algaba worked with Montalvo's version to appeal to Jewish audiences and (it must be said) to *sell* copies of his translation. He de-Christianized the text, removing references that might offend Jewish sensibilities. It is noteworthy that in most of these cases he avoids substituting specifically Jewish terms or concepts. Algaba's *Amadís* is the first major narrative work in a register of Hebrew that is largely free of the dense weave of shibbutzim, clever biblical and rabbinical allusions characteristic of nearly every other work of Hebrew prose being published at the time, and only the histories of Joseph Hakohen and Solomon ibn Verga, roughly contemporary original works composed in Hebrew, shared Algaba's plain prose style.

In Algaba's translation, priests become laymen, oaths are secularized, and moralizing digressions (to which Montalvo was famously inclined) are simply omitted.[69] Most of these examples are superficial and predictable. When Amadís exclaims "¡Sancta María!" Algaba substitutes "Long live my Lord the King!"[70] Montalvo has the Queen lead Amadís into her *capilla* (chapel), which Algaba renders—in Castilian—as *cámara* (chamber).[71] Elsewhere, Amadís comes upon a wounded knight in the road who asks to be taken to an *hermitaño* (Anchorite) who might "tend to his soul," which Algaba renders as "someone who might heal me."[72]

Occasionally Algaba changes the moral valence of a term that is not specifically Christian but that might have been unseemly to Montalvo's target readership. Montalvo describes the inaugural sexual encounter between Amadís and Oriana, for example, as *vicio y plazer* (vice and pleasure), which Algaba renders as "delight and happiness." When Amadís comes upon a damsel who has been sexually assaulted, in Montalvo's version she relates that she was "escarnecida" ('dishonored') by her attacker, while Algaba's damsel simply says: "He lay with me."[73]

Most of the examples of Algaba's de-Christianization of the text are similarly pro forma, but some merit interpretation. When King Languines orders a traitorous woman burned to death, Algaba instead has her thrown to her death from a high tower. His reluctance to depict her being burned may be out of respect to victims of the Spanish Inquisition. Instead he supplies a ready-made phrase from the Hebrew Bible describing the fate Jezebel meets as punishment for her sins.[74]

Despite his secularizing tendency, there are some moments in which he (for lack of a better, less historically charged term) "Judaizes" the text, inserting references to Jewish texts, cultural concepts, and observances. A few of these replace Christian references, but many appear to be spontaneous, whether out of a desire to appeal to his audience or, occasionally, for ironic effect. In one particularly playful rabbinical allusion, Amadís deals his enemy a crippling blow to the thigh. In addition to the direct translation for thigh (*yareakh*) Algaba adds a technical term drawn from the rabbinic discourse on koshering animal carcasses: *maqom tsomet hagidin*, "the place where the tendons come together."[75] This is Algaba's ironic response to the episode in Genesis where the angel, tired of wrestling with Jacob all night long, finally "wrenched Jacob's hip at the socket" (32:26). The biblical text then explains, "that is why the children of Israel to this day do not eat the thigh muscle that is on the socket of the hip [i.e. sirloin, top loin, etc.], since Jacob's hip socket was wrenched at the thigh muscle" (32:33). Where the biblical text derives its dietary ruling from the battle between Jacob and the angel, Algaba playfully writes the language of dietary restriction back into the battle between Amadís and his opponent. Here Algaba inserts a rabbinic sensibility into a chivalric text, in a move that parallels and challenges Montalvo's Christian moralizing tendency, substituting a jurisprudential mode for a moralistic one.

An important part of the appeal of Montalvo's Amadís was its representation of Arthurian chivalric manners and speech. Part of the fantasy that Montalvo was selling to his readers was to clothe the fictional chivalric hero in the courtly mores of Montalvo's time, to blend in his protagonist the imagined courtly world of the knights-errant of Arthurian imagination with the speech and courtly culture of the Spanish elite.[76] This presented a particular problem for Algaba's readers, who were likely unfamiliar with the European traditions of chivalric behavior common to both chivalric fiction and to the social life of the Western European upper classes. His challenge was to render Montalvo's frequent representations of the chivalric imaginary intelligible to non-Sephardic Ottoman Jews while still retaining the cultural cachet and novelty of the world it represented to his readers. It stands to reason that non-Sephardic Jews, who had never lived in Christian Europe, would be unfamiliar with the institutions and practices of chivalry that form the fabric of the social world of *Amadís*. You cannot, of course, trade on foreign cachet that is totally incomprehensible to your audience. To this end Algaba tailors Montalvo's references to the institutions of chivalry, social conventions, and courtly practices that may have fallen outside the experience of his non-Sephardic readers. As with de-Christianization, some such examples are superficial, but telling of what *courtly* or *chivalric* might mean to non-Sephardic, Jewish audiences.

A character named *la doncella de la guirnalda* (the damsel of the garland), so named because she always wore a garland of flowers to accentuate her beautiful hair, becomes in Algaba's version "the damsel of the crown," an accessory that ostensibly made more sense to the Ottoman readers to whom a garland of flowers might have seemed more rustic than idyllic.[77] Algaba often renders declarations couched in elevated courtly language (which abound), in biblical Hebrew, which better emphasizes their high register. When Amadís declares *"¡muerto soy de corazón!"* (I shall die of heartbreak!), Algaba renders this *"mah anokhi, she-nitraf libi!"* (What will become of me, for my heart is torn asunder!), deploying the rarer first-person pronoun *anokhi* found in the Hebrew Bible. When a rival knight mocks Amadís as unworthy to love Oriana and challenges Amadís to "tell me who she is, so that *I* may love her,"[78] Algaba puts into his mouth the instantly recognizable words of the Song of Songs (6:10): *haged na li mi ha-nishkafa-kemo shahar* (please tell me who is she that shines through like the dawn).[79] Again Algaba shows a bit of playfulness in his ironic deployment of biblical language, emphasizing the intensity of the discussion between Amadís and his rival in a way that makes sense to his audience.

Algaba translates some of the specific conventions and practices of Spain's chivalric culture into more familiar, general terms. When Amadís swears an oath of service to Helisenda, he does so "upon this cross and sword which I received with the Order of Chivalry," referencing a specifically Christian, chivalric practice of swearing upon a sword planted point down so that the handle and guard resemble a cross.[80] The reference to the Order of Chivalry would most likely be opaque and swearing on the cross unacceptable to a Jewish audience. Algaba has him swear simply upon his sword as a kind of shorthand. When Helisena appeals to the honor of King Perión's squire, she asks him if he is an *hidalgo* (nobleman of low rank); by this she means "Are you an honorable individual with whom I can trust my secret?" Algaba preserves the equation of high birth and good moral conduct implied by the word *hidalgo*, but his Helisena asks the squire, "Who are you and your family? Are they high-born?" (*me'olah*, literally superior or fine).[81]

Very occasionally, Algaba demonstrates his familiarity with courtly and chivalric discourses by introducing elements of them into the Hebrew when they are absent from the Spanish. In one such example, Amadís is complaining to Oriana about the difficulty of deferring his sexual desire for her. His complaint is couched in standard language of the courtly lover. He claims it is an impossible task, because his "better judgment cannot resist those mortal desires by which it is cruelly tormented."[82] What is interesting is that Algaba's Hebrew rendering introduces a different trope of the courtly lover, one that is also characteristic of Montalvo's day but that is absent from prior Hebrew tradition. He writes: "My heart is bound and tied in iron chains," an image very much consistent with the late medieval Western European poetic convention of love as a form of slavery or imprisonment (Spanish books on amorous topics of the late fifteenth century included *Siervo libre de amor* [Free Slave of Love] and *Cárcel de amor* [Prison of Love]). Here Algaba proves himself a knowledgeable reader of Spanish tradition who actively seeks to reconcile, integrate, and mediate between Hebrew and Spanish literary traditions. His insertion of this courtly trope speaks to his bi-culturality and more importantly to his role of translator mediating between diasporic communities, the Sepharadim, who represented the prestige of European courtly culture, and the Greek- and Arabic-speaking Jews, who were his target audience.

Algaba's translation project was likely a commercial failure. His translation of the first book of Montalvo's *Amadís* was of very low quality and for whatever reason did not appear to have stimulated demand for subsequent installments. We have no concrete data to explain this fact, but we may speculate. Perhaps the time had not yet come for light literature in Hebrew. Algaba's *Amadís* was certainly alone in that respect: it is the only Hebrew edition of its time of a popular novel. The other secular works that were published in the sixteenth century were more serious literature: difficult rhyming prose narratives that were showy displays of erudition and arcana, histories of Jewish persecutions or of the regimes that persecuted them, and a smattering of philosophical and scientific works. Algaba's test balloon novel was an aberration, and the European novel would not make a significant debut in Hebrew until the eighteenth century. Nonetheless, Algaba's *Amadís* does tell us a great deal about how he sought to represent Sephardic popular culture to the other communities of the Jewish diaspora in the Ottoman Empire of his day. His adaptation of Montalvo's iconic work for a non-Sephardic Jewish audience is an illuminating example of how Sepharadim chose to articulate their relationship with the land from which they found themselves in a second, Sephardic diaspora.

Conclusion

In this book I have attempted to demonstrate how Sephardic authors gave voice to a doubly diasporic consciousness in secular literary texts. As I have mentioned, this study is not intended to be an exhaustive literary history of Sephardic culture from the thirteenth through the sixteenth centuries. Rather, I have selected a series of diasporic moments in medieval and early modern Sephardic literature that illustrate this one particular phenomenon. It would be irresponsible to broadly characterize all Sephardic literature from this period as "diasporic" or to argue that diasporicity is the most salient, most important, or even most interesting characteristic of Sephardic literature from this period. Indeed, it might even be problematic to speak of "Sephardic" literature from the medieval period, given that, according to some authors (but not according to me), there was no cohesive Sephardic identity until after the expulsion.[1]

When I first began this study I focused on the question of language and of the problem of language use in Sephardic literary practice. I was interested in questions of who used which language for what purpose. I wanted to better understand how vernacular culture influenced Sephardic writers writing in Hebrew. Originally, as I watched coverage of the wars in Iraq and Afghanistan, I imagined these authors as "embedded" within the dominant literary culture, as journalists were "embedded" within combat units in the field. But this metaphor was wanting. More than mere observers (and according to the observer principle, we know that even the most cautious observers are also participants), Sepharadim were (and continue to be) a part of the dominant cultures in which they live. Eventually I found that this approach did not distinguish Sephardic authors from other diasporic Jewish populations: they all worked with materials common to their counterparts in dominant groups.

The Sephardic difference was in the doubly diasporic consciousness after 1492. While other Jewish populations suffered expulsions during the middle ages, the best-known literary record of Jewish expulsions documented the Spanish case. Some of the ideas on diasporic cultures that I have used here (Tölölyan, Boyarins, Mishras, etc.) have helped me to broaden and nuance my thinking about Sephardic literary practice, and to avoid thinking about these texts as either "Jewish" or "Spanish," but instead to develop a third critical space in which to work. The fact that I trained as a Hispanist and work in a Spanish section of a Department of Romance Languages also has a lot to do with how I focused this study. And while I realize that it can be problematic to study medieval Sephardic texts in the framework of modern Hispanism (for example, you run the risk of anachronistically imposing modern national linguistic categories on a texts and authors that did not have a modern national experience), ultimately I believe—and hope you have likewise found—that the readings in this study are more productive than they are problematic.

As we have seen, the discussion of diaspora and diasporic cultures is well-trodden territory. The bibliography is enormous. What could I hope to contribute to this vast discussion? As I hoped I have shown, I wanted to demonstrate that the authors and texts that appear here each approached the question of diaspora in their own way, on their own terms. They were all guided by similar basic principles and circumstances: the Jewish doctrine of galut and ge'ulah, the Jews' minority status, vernacular–Hebrew diglossia, etc. However, the results are different and are a product of each individual author's training, tastes, originality, and circumstances of production. These results support the ideas of Tölölyan, S. Mishra, and others on the complexity and dynamism of the diasporic experience.

There is no monolithic diasporic experience, and these studies have borne out this idea. Disaporic consciousness grows, adapts, and changes according to historical circumstances. This is what we learn from Ben Elazar's adaptation of chivalric romance and allegorization of the political life of the Castilian Jewish community, or from Todros Abulafia's inventive response to troubadour poetry. Likewise, Shem Tov's navigation of vernacular and Hebrew literary production speaks more directly to the pragmatics of the diasporic condition and to the fate of the community before royal power. Vidal Benvenist also takes up the problem of assimilation to the dominant culture, rallying his audience to stand firm in Jewish values during a time of increasing conversion and crisis. He is facing, in a very immediate fashion, the concerns about which Ben Elazar only theorizes in his debate between the pen and the sword: how to preserve the traditions of the pen when the sword threatens? In the work of the post-expulsion authors, this question is writ large. The sword has not merely threatened, it has severed the community from its homeland Sepharad. The question facing Ibn Verga, Karo, and Algaba is not *what if,* but *what now?* The doubly diasporic consciousness to which their work gives voice is the product of a trauma, but one that also serves as the forge of a new phase of Sephardic cultural identity: the fusing of Hispanic and Jewish cultural identity, of which Jacob Algaba's Hebrew translation of *Amadís de Gaula* is an excellent example. Algaba de-Christianizes and "Judaizes" the chivalric novel at the same time when Hispanic culture is being reworked in a global, imperial framework. Just as new Hispanic identities are resulting from Spanish conquest in the New World, the projection of Sephardic culture onto the greater Mediterranean (and beyond) represents another product (or by-product) of the Spanish imperial project.

Many of these conclusions lead to new questions. As we have mentioned, there is a great deal of premodern Sephardic literature that has not been studied, or that could really benefit from a second look. There are scores of medieval texts that are unedited, and many texts that exist in modern editions have been overlooked by literary scholars. The vast corpus of early editions of texts from the Western Sephardic communities, particularly that of Amsterdam, is almost entirely unedited, despite having been recently published on microfiche, and very recently made available in online facsimiles.[2] Moving forward into modernity, there is a substantial corpus of Ladino journalism from both the Ottoman Empire and the United States that has been studied by historians but that has not yet received attention from literary scholars.

NOTES

INTRODUCTION

1. By *Sephardic* I mean the Jews whose vernacular cultural home is the Iberian Peninsula. This includes Jews living in al-Andalus, in the Christian Iberian kingdoms, and in the Sephardic diaspora. In this study I use *Zion* to refer to the idea or symbolic construct of the Jewish homeland as opposed to the current political boundaries of Israel/Palestine or the Hebrew *Eretz Yisrael* (Land of Israel).

2. I will use the Sephardic pronunciation of the Hebrew plural *Sepharadim* (sing. *Sephardí*) instead of the anglicized Ashkenazi pronunciation, "Sephardim."

3. Personal correspondence with Jonathan Boyarin cited in Clifford, "Diasporas," 305.

4. See Decter, *Iberian*; Balbuena, "Identities."

1. DIASPORA STUDIES FOR SEPHARDIC CULTURE

1. But like all metaphors, it has its limit. John Szwed has argued that biological metaphors apply overly restrictive biological terms to cultural processes that are less mathematically defined and more emergent. See Szwed, "Metaphors."

2. Safran, "Deconstructing," 9, and "Myths"; S. Mishra, *Diaspora criticism*, 48; Baumann, "Diaspora."

3. D. Boyarin, "Purim," 3. On the Jewish diaspora, see Waxman, *Exile*; Baer, *Galut*; Yerushalmi, *Zakhor*; Funkenstein, *Perceptions*; Spero, *Holocaust*; Eisen, *Galut*; Boyarin and Boyarin, "Diaspora" and *Powers*. On non-Jewish diasporas, see Gilroy *The Black Atlantic*; V. Mishra, *Theorizing*; R. Cohen, *Global*; Hall and Rutherford, "Cultural Identity"; Clifford, "Diasporas." See also Sudesh Mishra's lively typology of the development of diaspora studies. S. Mishra, *Diaspora Criticism*, 14–17.

4. See, for example, Brubaker, "The 'Diaspora' Diaspora"; S. Mishra, *Diaspora Criticism*; Dufoix, *Diasporas*.

5. See, for example, Braziel, *Diaspora: An Introduction*, and Braziel and Mannur, *Theorizing Diaspora: A Reader*.

6. Martin Baumann, for example, complains of the term's "semantic dissolution" at the hands of successive critics. See M. Baumann, "Diaspora," 315. James Clifford is more generous, conceding that "for better or worse, diaspora discourse is being widely appropriated." Clifford, "Diasporas," 306.

7. Connor, "Impact," 16, cited in Tölölyan, "Contemporary."

8. Tölölyan, "Contemporary"; Dufoix, *Diasporas*, 107.

9. S. Mishra, *Diaspora Criticism*, 55.

10. B. Edwards, *Practice*, 12. Elsewhere, he writes that "the scholarship that began to critique the presupposition of an 'English' national frame . . . moves to a diasporic register as a remedy to the constitutive links between racism and nationalism." See B. Edwards, "Uses," 57.

11. This is Sudesh Mishra's somewhat disparaging term for theorists who focus too heavily on the relationship between a single homeland and a single hostland, as opposed to the "resolutely multilocal and polycentric" nature of diasporas proposed by Tölölyan and others. See Tölölyan, "Contemporary." S. Mishra, *Diaspora Criticism*, 41.

12. See Tölölyan, "Contemporary."

13. Ibid.

14. Tölölyan, "Rethinking," 7–8.

15. Baer, *Galut*, 10.

16. Baron, *Social* 1:3.

17. Eisen, *Galut*, 4. In this work Eisen puts forth a series of studies of Genesis, Deuteronomy, and Mishnaic tractate Avodah Zarah that trace the development of the theme of exile in forming Jewish identity and habits of thought. For a full accounting of the concept in biblical and rabbinic literature, see Waxman, *Exile*.

18. Eisen, *Galut*, 19.

19. Avodah Zarah is key in establishing a diasporic system of homeland/hostlands at a time when "Jewish life was geographically scattered as never before." Eisen, *Galut*, 36.

20. Funkenstein, *Perceptions*, 2.

21. Ibid., 36.

22. Raphael Patai sums up this idea nicely; for him, Jewish history is "the record of Israel's enduring chosenness, its continuous search for the will of God, and its ceaseless reassertion of the special relationship between it and its Father in Heaven." Patai, *Jewish Mind*, 35–36.

23. Yosef Yerushalmi argues that such "ritualized public readings [of biblical narratives] . . . endowed [the] past with the inevitably cyclical quality of liturgical time." Yerushalmi, *Zakhor*, 42.

24. We will deal with this question in more detail in our study of Solomon ibn Verga's *Shevet Yehudah* (chapter 6).

25. Yerushalmi, *Zakhor*, 33. While this may be technically accurate, Eric Lawee reminds us that many Jewish thinkers demonstrated what he calls "historical thinking" centuries before the appearance of works of Jewish historiography per se. Lawee, "Threshold," 291.

26. Yerushalmi, *Zakhor*, 36.

27. For an overview of the responsa genre, see Peter Haas's literary history (*Responsa*), Solomon Freehof's anthology of translated texts (*Responsa*), and Matt Goldish's anthology (with substantial historical introduction) of Early Modern Sephardic responsa (*Jewish Questions*).

28. See, for example, Epstein, *Responsa*; Morell, "Rabbinic."

29. See Baron, "Ghetto," and Chazan, *Reassessing*, xviii. On Baron's conception of the "lachrymose" school of Jewish history, see Engel, "Crisis."

30. Funkenstein, *Perceptions*, 19.

31. Biale, "Confessions," 40.

32. Ibid., 40.

33. Ibid., 45.

34. Sáenz-Badillos, "Estudio," 139 and 39.

35. Biale, "Confessions," 43.

36. Boyarin and Boyarin, "Diaspora," 711.

37. Ibid., 718.

38. Ibid.

39. Ibid.

40. Ibid., 722.

41. We will deal with the question of Jewish messianism in greater detail in the chapter on Solomon ibn Verga and Joseph Karo (chapter 7).

42. Chazan, *Reassessing*.

43. Ketuvot 11a, Shabbat 41a, Berachot 24b, cited in Serotta, "Galut," 113.

44. Serotta, *Galut,* 123.

45. Neusner, *History,* 107–108.

46. Serotta, "Galut," 120. Later rabbis write that the shekhinah went into exile with the Jews in order to protect them in galut. Interestingly, Maimonides disputes the essential purity of *Eretz Yisrael* (the Land of Israel) that is outlined in the Talmud, arguing instead that its holiness derives from consensus and from historical conditions, but is not inherent in the land. See Kellner, *Confrontation,* 107–115.

47. For a full accounting of the concept in biblical and rabbinic literature, see Waxman, *Exile.*

48. Alfonso, *Islamic,* 143n45. English translation found in Kobler, *Letters* 1:98. On the concept of exile and domicile in Andalusi Jewish letters and thought, see Alfonso, *Islamic,* 51–82.

49. Alfonso points out that such positive portrayals are rare and cites another by Bahya ibn Paquda, who in Spain wrote in the century after Ibn Shaprut. Ibn Paquda notes that Andalusi Jews' quality of life approached that of Andalusi Muslims. Alfonso, *Islamic,* 62, citing Mansoor's English translation found in Ibn Paquda, *Direction,* 117.

50. Kobler, *Letters* 1:98.

51. Ibid. 1:104.

52. Spero, *Holocaust,* 129.

53. Ibn Daud, *Sefer ha-Qabbalah,* 63–66, Hebrew text on page 46, ll.2–48, l.41. See also G. Cohen, "Story."

54. On the Noahic origins of racial diversity, see Braude, "Sons of Noah."

55. The undercover scholar in Ibn Daud's narrative also recalls the shabby yet rhetorically brilliant rogue characters in medieval Hebrew and Arabic *maqamat* (rhyming prose narratives). See Allen, *Introduction,* 163–166; Drory, "Maqama," 195; Wacks, *Framing,* 42, 65.

56. Serotta, *Galut,* 126.

57. For example, Boyarin and Boyarin similarly claim that many narratives of Jewish history privilege an eventual return to Zion, while repressing "memories of coming from somewhere else." Boyarin and Boyarin, "Diaspora," 714.

58. Judah Halevi is considered one of the most important Hebrew poets of the medieval period and consequently one of the founders of literary Hebrew. On Halevi's biography see Goitein, *Mediterranean* 5:448–468. His *Divan* (collected poems) has been edited by Brody and Habermann; there are also selections of his poetry edited in Schirmann, *Hebrew* 2:425–536. See also the selected English translations by Cole (*Dream,* 143–170), as well as those of Halkin's poetic biography (*Yehudah Halevi*). For Spanish translations of selected poems, see Millás Vallicrosa, *Yehudá Ha-Leví;* Pérez Castro (*Poesía secular,* 325–399), and Sáenz-Badillos (*Poetas hebreos,* 175–204).

59. *Kitab al-Khazari* or *Sefer ha-Kuzari* was first translated into Hebrew by Judah ibn Tibbon. There is also a fifteenth-century Ladino translation edited by Lazar, an English translation (from the Arabic) by Hirschfeld, and a seventeenth-century Spanish translation by Abendana. See also Silman, *Philosopher;* Shear, *Kuzari;* Lasker, "Proselyte"; Berger, "Understanding"; Szpiech, *Conversion,* 102–107.

60. Spero, *Holocaust,* 143, citing Halevi, *Kuzari,* 226.

61. Halevi, *Kuzari,* 227.

62. Spero, *Holocaust,* 144.

63. Spero writes that the Kuzari kingdom meant that "the messianic vision of 'and they all shall accept the yoke of Thy kingdom' was quite realistic." See Spero, *Holocaust,* 145.

64. Halevi's apocryphal death legend is by now widely known thanks to its popularization by German poet and translator Heinrich Heine. See Heine, *Melodien.*

65. Scheindlin, *Song,* 156.

66. See Silman, *Philosopher,* 154–155.

67. On the medieval literature of the Camino de Santiago, see Rudolph, *Pilgrimage;* Bango Torviso, *Camino;* Atienza and Sánchez, *Leyendas.*

68. Rudolph, *Pilgrimage,* 1.

69. Díaz y Diáz, *Escritos;* Regalado, "Santos," 114; Bango Torviso, *Camino,* 55 and 104.

70. On Maimonides' life and times, see H. Davidson, *Moses Maimonides* 3–74. See also the popular studies by Kraemer (*Maimonides*) and Nuland (*Maimonides*).

71. According to Yochanan Silman, while Halevi in his youth espoused the Aristotelianism that was in vogue in Spain, in his maturity he came to assert that while Aristotelian philosophy was useful, it alone could not explain such problems as human mortality. See Silman, *Philosopher,* 4–5. On the subject of Maimonides and the incipient kabbalistic tradition, see Kellner, *Confrontation.* It should be noted that Maimonides' father, Maimon ben Yosef, also wrote a treatise on the subject of exile, *Iggeret ha-Nehama* (The Epistle of Consolation) after the family was forced to flee Cordova when the intolerant Almohad dynasty came to power in al-Andalus. See Maimon ben Yosef, *Consolation.*

72. Spero, *Holocaust,* 153, citing Isaiah 11:9.

73. Maimonides, *Letter,* iii.

74. Elior, "Exile," 12.

75. For a general introduction to kabbalistic thought, see Dan, *Introduction;* Scholem, *Kabbalah;* Matt, *Essential.*

76. On the doctrine of *galut ha-shekhinah* (the exile of the shekhinah), Scholem (*Major Trends,* 404n89) cites De León, *Zohar* 2:41b, 216b, and 3:77b. See also De León, *Zohar* 2:216b–217a.

77. Joseph Karo is better known as the author of the *Shulkhan Arukh,* the most influential Talmudic index to halakha, or Jewish law governing daily life. He was also an accomplished kabbalist. See Werblowsky, *Karo.* For a more complete discussion

of Karo's work and its meaning for diasporic culture, see chapter 6.

78. Elior, "Exile," 16. One wonders if this turn in the human-divine relationship concerning prophecy and revelation might have been developed under the influence of Christian theology. In a parallel example, Arthur Green has suggested that the Jewish doctrine of the divine feminine represented by the shekhinah was a response to Marian devotion. See Green, "Shekhinah."

79. See, for example, the laments for the violence of 1391 (Pagis, "Dirges"; van Bekkum, "O Seville!"; Targarona Borrás, "Dirges"), and the various accounts of the expulsions of 1492 and 1497 studied in the context of Solomon ibn Verga's *Shevet Yehudah* in chapter 7.

80. There are, naturally, some exceptions. Rastafarian doctrine, for example, very deliberately adapts Jewish doctrines of galut and ge'ulah in the modern African experience of captivity, slavery, and African diaspora. See Erskine, *Garvey,* 47–48.

81. V. Mishra, *Literature,* 5–6.

2. ALLEGORY AND ROMANCE IN DIASPORA

1. Brann, "The Moors?," 309; Márquez Villanueva, *Concepto,* 161. See also Hoerder, "Revising," 4, and the examples brought together by Szpiech, "Convivencia Wars."

2. On the question of *convivencia,* see Ray, "Beyond"; Soifer, "Beyond"; Novikoff, "Between"; Szpiech, "Convivencia Wars." For alternatives to Américo Castro's concept of convivencia see Catlos, "Contexto" and Wacks, *Framing,* 5. Spanish authors have made a virtual cottage industry of debunking convivencia in a series of mass-market works whose titles belie their ideological pedigrees: Serafín Fanjul, *Al-Andalus contra España;* Rosa María Rodríguez Magda, *Inexistente Al Ándalus;* César Vidal Manzanares, *España frente al Islam: de Mahoma a Ben Laden.*

3. On the maqama see Arié, "Notes"; Blachère, "Étude"; Drory, "Maqama"; Hämeen-Anttila, *Maqama*. On the transition between al-Andalus and Christian Iberia and its impact on Sephardic writers see Decter, *Jewish Iberian*.

4. Schirmann, "Contes," 295.

5. Pagis, *Innovation*, 220–221.

6. For Nehemiah Allony's modern edition of Ben Elazar's text see Ben Elazar, *Kitab al-Kamil*. On medieval and early modern references to the text see Delgado, "Nuevas alusiones." Excerpts of Ben Elazar's translation of *Kalila wa-Dimna* are in Schirmann, *Hebrew Poetry*, 2:233–237. There is a complete edition of the manuscript in Derenbourg, *Deux versions*, 312–388. See also the relevant studies of the Hebrew translation: Navarro Peiro, "Versiones" and "Versión."

7. Sáenz-Badillos, "Estudio," 159. This trend in the academic world also obtains in Israeli secondary education. In the 2004 Israeli high school exit exam, the *bagrut,* the section on the short story skips the Middle Ages and Early Modernity altogether, beginning with the twentieth-century author S. Y. Agnon. Medieval verse is well represented, and students are examined on poems by Solomon ibn Gabirol and Samuel Naghrela Hanagid.

8. On the literary culture of the court of Alfonso X, see the following chapter on Todros Abulafia, who enjoyed the patronage of the "Learned King."

9. The first four chapters are literary debates between body and soul, poetry and prose, this poet and that one, and the pen and the sword. The next six are tales narrating various configurations of love interests, whether a boy and a man, a woman and two men, a man and two women, an old man, a man and a woman, or in the final chapter, a boy raised by a wolf. Jonathan Decter has written studies of individual chapters. Decter, *Jewish Iberian*, 164–174, "'Sodomite,'" "Landscapes."

10. The maqama is a form of prose narrative fiction that relates the misadventures of a foolish narrator who is repeatedly duped by a wily street orator whose shabby appearance belies his rhetorical mastery. It was invented in Baghdad by the Arabic writer Badi' al-Zaman al-Hamadhani in the tenth century (Abbasid era). Its most important practitioner was Muhammad al-Qasim ibn Ali al-Hariri, who lived in Basra (present-day Iraq) at the end of the eleventh and beginning of the twelfth centuries. Al-Hariri's maqamat came to define the genre. For a comprehensive history of the genre, see Hämeen-Anttila, *Maqama*. For a history of the genre in the Arabic East and in al-Andalus, see Drory, "Maqama." James Monroe also provides an overview of the genre in the introduction to his translation of al-Saraqusti's *Maqamat al-luzumiyya*. See Monroe, "Preliminary Study," 1–18.

11. Hayim Schirmann included excerpts of Ben Elazar's *Love Stories* (2:207–233), together with selections of his Hebrew translation of *Kalila wa-Dimna* (2:233–237), in his landmark anthology *Hebrew Poetry in Spain and Provence*, published in Israel in the fifties. Schirmann, incidentally, perhaps due to his European education, was very sensitive to the tendency of medieval Hebrew authors to incorporate features of Latin and vernacular literatures in their compositions. There is no complete edition before that of Yonah David appears in 1992. Another fifteen years pass before Jonathan Decter dedicates a chapter to Ben Elazar in 2007. Since then we have signs of renewed interest in Ben Elazar in the studies by Decter and Alba Cecilia. See Schirmann, *Hebrew Poetry* 2:207–237; Schirmann and Fleischer, *History* 222–240; Ben Elazar, *Love Stories;* Decter, *Jewish Iberian*, 138–156, "'Sodomite'"; Alba Cecilia, "Debate."

12. In the nineteenth century, Abraham Geiger complained about its macaronic language. Geiger, "History," 161, cited in Alba Cecilia, "Debate," 294n11.

13. Goldziher, *Muslim Studies*, 150–152; Kahle, "Arabic." For an introduction to pre-Islamic poetry in English, see Sells, *Tracings*. On the expansion of Arabic as a poetic language see Nicholson, *History*, xxiv and 276–278.

14. During the Abbasid period, lexicographers from cities such as Baghdad, Basra, and Kufa undertook fieldwork among Bedouin tribes to document rare forms occuring in the Qur'an. See Carter, "Lexicography." For an overview of the science of Arabic grammar during this period, see Carter, "Grammar." Individual biographies of key Arab philologists from the Umayyad and Abbasid periods can be found in Cooperson and Toorawa, *Literary*. A comprehensive history of Arab philology in English is lacking; in Arabic see Tanukhi, *History*.

15. Al-Farra' was a native of Kufa (in present-day Iraq) and a major grammarian of his generation. He was author of over a dozen treatises on grammar, lexicography, and Qur'anic exegesis. See *Encyclopedia of Islam*, "al-Farra'."; Carter, "Grammar," 123–124.

16. Kahle, "Arabic," 69, and *Geniza*, 144; original Arabic text of al-Farra' edited in Kahle, *Geniza*, 345.

17. Goldziher, *Muslim Studies*, 150. Arabic in al-Tha'alibi, *Yatimat* 3:272.

18. Norris, "Shu'ubiyyah," 31.

19. Monroe, *Shu'ubiyya*, 24. Arabic text in Abbadi, *Eslavos*, 34.

20. Monroe, *Shu'ubiyya*, 25–26. Arabic text in Abbadi, *Eslavos*, 35.

21. See Allony, "Reaction"; N. Roth, "Reactions."

22. Brann, *Compunctious*, 23.

23. M. Ibn Ezra, *Poems* 1:29, l. 15. English translation in Allony, "Reaction," 35. I have corrected Allony's citations of Brody's edition.

24. M. Ibn Ezra, *Poems* 1:243, l. 132. English translation in Allony, "Reaction," 35.

25. M. Ibn Ezra, *Poems* 1:34, l. 1. English translation in Allony, "Reaction," 35.

26. Judah al-Harizi (1165–1225) was born in Castile and traveled widely throughout the Mediterranean. He was a prolific translator of Arabic literature into Hebrew as well as a poet and author in his own right. He translated Maimonides' *Guide for the Perplexed* as well as the maqamat of al-Hariri into Hebrew and was author of his own maqamat, titled *Tahkemoni*. See *Encyclopedia Judaica*, "al-Harizi, Judah ben Solomon." For studies of al-Harizi as a multicultural figure, see Sadan, "Crossroads" and "Intellectuel." See also the edition of Yahalom and Blau of the Judeo-Arabic travelogues attributed to al-Harizi; al-Harizi, *Travels*.

27. al-Harizi, *Tahkemoni*, trans. Reichert, 1:32. Hebrew text in al-Harizi, ed. Zamora and Toporovsky, 9–10.

28. Ben Elazar, *Love Stories*, 14–15.

29. S. Harvey, *Epistle*, 97 and 97n44.

30. Malter, "Palquera," 170.

31. On the Ibn Tibbon family of translators, see J. Robinson, "Dynasty."

32. On the scientific works of Abraham ibn Ezra, see Sela, *Ibn Ezra*.

33. Brann, *Compunctious*, 123. On the 'arabiyya/'ibraniyya phenomenon, see Allony, "Reaction"; N. Roth, "Reactions"; Brann, *Compunctious*, 23–24, 69, 88–89.

34. On medieval poets' use of shibbutzim (direct borrowing of biblical language), see Yellin and Pagis, *Theory*, 118–149; Pagis, *Innovation*, 70–79; Kozodoy, "Reading"; Cole, *Dream*, 253. The humorous exploitation of shibbutzim was pioneered by Joseph ibn Zabara in *Sefer Sha'ashu'im* (The Book of Delights) but elevated to virtuosic levels in Judah al-Harizi's *Tahkemoni*. Schirmann and Fleischer, *History*, 252n12.

35. See Brann, *Compunctious*, 14 and 23.

36. Cole, *Dream*, 253. Cole is a prominent translator of medieval Hebrew poetry into English. For his translation of excerpts

of Ben Elazar's text see Cole, *Dream,* 218–220.

37. Kozodoy, "Reading," 117. See also Brann, *Compunctious,* 25.

38. Kozodoy, "Reading," 116.

39. Even-Zohar, "Translated," 47.

40. Al-Hariri's *Maqamat* have drawn massive critical attention, second only to the Qur'an. Prendergast, *Maqamat, 24.* See also Essa and Ali, *Studies,* 152.

41. Even-Zohar, "Translated," 46.

42. Alba Cecilia provides an overview of these debates in Arabic, Hebrew, and Castilian. Alba Cecilia, "Espada."

43. On the arms vs. letters trope in Spain, see G. Menéndez Pidal, "Armas." For France, see Supple, *Arms and Letters.* For Italy, see E. Haywood, "*Querelle,*" and Quint, "Debate." Miguel de Cervantes has Don Quijote argue vigorously for the superiority of arms over letters in the first part of *Don Quixote.* Perhaps not surprisingly, given that Cervantes was in the end far better served by letters than by arms (he lost the use of his hand in the Battle of Lepanto), Don Quijote comes down on the side of letters, concluding that "*aunque es mayor el trabajo del soldado, es mucho menor el premio*" (even though the hardship of a soldier is greater, his reward is much smaller). Cervantes Saavedra, *Don Quijote,* 420–424; Cervantes Saavedra, *Don Quixote,* trans. Grossman, 331.

44. Israel Levin brings together representative examples of descriptions of pens and swords in medieval Arabic and Hebrew poetry. Levin, "Pen."

45. Ahmad ibn Burd al-Asghar (the Younger) was a native of Cordova who lived during the first half of the tenth century. In addition to the *Risalat al-sayf wa-l-qalam,* he composed an elegy for the noted Andalusi poet Abu Amir ibn Shuhaid. *Encyclopedia of Islam,* "Ibn Burd." For the Arabic text, see the edition of Ibn Bassam, *Dhakhira I,* 2:523–545. See also the Spanish translation in de la Granja, *Maqamas,* 32–44.

46. Abu-l Jaysh al-Muwaffaq bin Abdallah al-Amiri "al-Mujahid" ruled Denia and the Balearic Islands from 1014 to 1044 or 1045. *Encyclopedia of Islam,* "Mudjahid."

47. The sense of the phrase "to let one's garment drag" is of extreme luxury. One who can afford to drag the hem of his mantle on the ground is perforce rich enough to replace it frequently. See de la Granja, *Maqamas,* 42; Ibn Bassam, *Dhakhira,* I, 2:527. On the motif of sleep being banished or restored on one's eyelids, compare with the verse cited by Ibn Hazm in his section on "The Signs of Love": "If the darkness had not dissipated [in the morning],/Would my eyelids not have been closed by slumber?" Ibn Hazm, *Ring,* 20. Arabic text in Ibn Hazm, *Tawq,* 32.

48. Text of al-Harizi's debate between the pen and the sword in al-Harizi, *Tahkemoni,* 312–316. English translation in al-Harizi, *Tahkemoni,* trans. Reichert, 247–254. See also Segal's "Analysis of Gate Forty," in which he argues that the "presentation of pen as conqueror-slayer and sword as metaphorizer, rhymer, rhetor, and debater" echo the narrator's own roguish playfulness and unpredictability. Al-Harizi, *Book,* trans. Segal, 601–603.

49. Monroe, "Preliminary," 12. See my discussion of Abulafia's poetry vis-à-vis his Christian troubadour counterparts in the following chapter.

50. Abrahams, *Jewish Life,* 378. Ray, *Sephardic,* 21n15. See also Baron, *Social* 4:36, 251n43.

51. Ibn Verga, *Shevet,* 47, ll. 27–29. Spanish translation in Ibn Verga, *La vara,* 75.

52. Baer, *History,* 1:81.

53. Baron, *Social* 10:355n4.

54. Ray, *Sephardic* 21n15. See also Baron, *Social* 4:36, and 251n43.

55. There exists a corpus of poetry commemorating those who lost their lives in such violence. On the martyrological poetry written by French Jews about the violence of 1066, see Einbinder, *Beautiful*

Death. On the *kinot* (laments) written in the wake of the pogroms of 1391, 1412, and 1492 see Bernstein, *Rivers;* van Bekkum, "O Seville!"; C. Roth, "Elegy"; Targarona Borrás, "Dirges."

56. The clerks consistently prevail. At the end of the *Concile de Remiremont,* the council of women end up excommunicating the lovers of the knights from their company. Oulmont, *Débats* 106–107. The narrators of both the *Jugement d'amours* and "Melior et Ydoine" declare the clerk's superiority. Oulmont, *Débats,* 141, vv. 401–404, and 196, vv. 403–404. One notable exception is the Castilian *Elena y María* (ca. 1280) in which the knight's lover makes the clerk's lover swear an oath of fealty to the former. The knight is likewise victorious in the Anglo-Norman *Florence et Blancheflour.* See R. Menéndez Pidal, *Tres Poetas,* 16, 29–30.

57. David Biale writes that "just as the rabbis were substitute kings, so the institutions of the Diaspora became surrogates for full political sovereignty." Biale, *Power,* 45.

58. al-Harizi, trans. Reichert, 2:253. Hebrew text in al-Harizi, *Tahkemoni,* 316.

59. al-Harizi, trans. Reichert, 2:254. Hebrew text in al-Harizi, *Tahkemoni,* 316.

60. al-Harizi, trans. Reichert, 2:253. Hebrew text in al-Harizi, *Tahkemoni,* 316.

61. Nirenberg, *Communities,* 20.

62. Baer, *History,* 1:85.

63. Biale, *Power,* 43. Daniel and Jonathan Boyarin argue something like the converse: that, historically, the Jewish nation (however you choose to understand the concept) is more authentically and essentially diasporic than sovereign, and that the foundational biblical narratives belie subsequent attempts to constitute or reconstitute Jewish national sovereignty. See Boyarin and Boyarin, "Diaspora."

64. Ben Elazar, *Love Stories,* 32, l. 1.

65. Ibid., 36, ll. 115–116.

66. Ibid., 32, ll. 130–131.

67. For "mouth" we should read "the split opening of my quill from where the ink flows."

68. Ben Elazar, *Love Stories,* 32, ll. 141–145.

69. This was the Maimonidean controversy, the debate that mirrored the reception of the work of Ibn Rushd in the Muslim world and of Thomas Aquinas in the Christian. On this topic, see Septimus, *Hispano-Jewish,* 61–74; Dobbs-Weinstein, "Maimonidean"; D. Silver, *Maimonidean.* In broad strokes, this is a debate that should be familiar to those of us living in the United States (and other countries) in the twenty-first century. Many communities are similarly torn today by debates between believers of creationism and evolution, and more generally between various bands of fundamentalists and rationalists.

70. Maimonides wrote of nine such principles in his *Nine Chapters on the Unity of God.* See Rosner, *Existence,* 183–233. Alba Cecilia ("Debate," 309n222) suggests Aristotle and Ibn Paquda as direct referents. See also Ben Elazar, *Love Stories,* 38, ll. 169–171. Compare with Maimonides' *Treatise on the Unity of God:* "He is detached from all that is implied, or follows, from corporeality. Just as one cannot conceive of Him as a compound [consisting of separate 'parts'], nor separation, nor as occupying space, having neither quantity nor quality, neither height nor depth, nor right and left, nor front and back, nor as standing and sitting. He is not confined by time and He has no beginning or end." Rosner, *Existence,* 39. Hebrew text in Maimonides, *Maamar,* 2.

71. In a characteristically diasporic move, Ben Elazar here deploys the sword vs. pen framework in addressing a debate internal to the Jewish community, that of the Maimonidean controversy.

72. Such excommunications were enacted by partisans on both sides of the debate. Baer mentions one enacted in 1232 by members of the Aragonese *aljamas* (Jewish

communities) of Zaragoza, Huesca, Mon-
zon, Calatayud, and Lerida against Rabbi
Solomon of Montpellier in retaliation for
the latter's excommunication of those who
studied Maimonidean texts. Baer, *History*,
1:105. This localized "culture war" was parodied by Judah ibn Shabbetay in *The Writ of
Excommunication*, in which five members
of the Zaragoza *aljama* burn the protagonist's book (which, if the representation is
historical, is Ibn Shabbetay's own history of
famous members of the Jewish community)
and ban him from the community. I. Davidson, *Parody*, 12–13.

73. Baer, *History*, 1:100. In a recent biography of Maimonides, Joel Kraemer argues
that the *Mishneh Torah* "[freed] the individual from having to study Talmud." Kraemer, *Maimonides*, 324. For a general introduction to Maimonides' *Mishneh Torah* see
Twersky, *Introduction*. For an authoritative
discussion of the halakhic (jurisprudential)
dimensions of the *Mishneh Torah* see also
H. Davidson, *Moses Maimonides*, 189–262.

74. Ben Elazar, *Love Stories*, 38, ll. 181–
183. Maimonides also notes that the "unity"
of God is not the same as the "unity" of
earthly things or concepts: Maimonides,
Mishneh Torah, 1.4.34b; *Guide* 1.3, cited in
Rudavsky, *Maimonides*, 38. Elsewhere he
writes that "there exists no unity similar to
His in this world." Maimonides, *Hilkhot*,
144 (1:7). See also Maimonides, *Guide*, 2,
7–8, cited in Wolfson, "Maimonides," 451.

75. "This is like the saying of the Christians: God is one but also three and the
three are one." Maimonides, *Guide*, 2. 8–9,
cited in Wolfson, "Maimonides," 451.

76. On the flourishing of the religious
polemic and public dispute in thirteenth-
century Iberia (and their relationship to
the mendicant orders), see Chazan, *Daggers*
and *Barcelona*; J. Cohen, *Friars*; Hames,
"Language" and "Tango"; Vose, *Dominicans*; Szpiech, *Conversion*.

77. Decter, *Jewish Iberian*, 100 and 106.

78. Thus Virgil's Aeneas is recast as the
founder of the French dynasty in Frege-
darius' figure of Franco, and Geoffrey of
Monmouth connects the British dynasty to
antiquity by positing Brutus as another descendant of Aeneas. Fogelquist, *Amadís*, 30.
In Castile, Jiménez de Rada writes Hercu-
les into the early history of Castilian Kings.
Jiménez de Rada, *Estoria*, 57–58.

79. One striking example of this tendency to localize Arthurian, French, or Roman legend is found in the novelization of
the story of Flores and Blancaflor inserted
into the *Estoria de España* of Alfonso X. In
Alfonso's version, Flores and Blancaflor are
cast as the ancestors of the Umayyad Dynasty of Cordova and of Charlemagne. See
Arbesú, "Introduction," 31–33.

80. Hans Ulrich Gumbrecht and Helga
Bennett claim that in Spain "courtly subjects do not begin to appear until 1300
in the genre of the *Libros de caballería*."
Gumbrecht and Bennett, "Literary Translation," 208.

81. Entwistle, *Arthurian*, 12; Thomas,
Romances, 21.

82. Thomas, *Romances*, 22–23.

83. Entwistle, *Arthurian*, 12.

84. Pere Bohigas explains that *Çifar*
combines "all of the genres and tendencies
of the Spanish literature of the end of the
thirteenth and beginning of the fourteenth
centuries, from the Oriental tale to the
narrative of the Britannic cycle." Bohigas,
"Orígenes," 532.

85. Bohigas, "Orígenes," 528.

86. Thomas, *Romances*, 28.

87. Entwistle, *Arthurian*, 31.

88. O'Callaghan, *Reconquest*, 26, 37,
58–59, and 70.

89. Entwistle, *Arthurian*, 15.

90. Thomas, *Romances*, 26. On cancionero poetry in general, see Whinnom, *Poesía*;
Dutton, *Cancionero*; Gerli and Weiss, *Poetry*; Alonso, *Poesía*.

91. Decter, *Jewish Iberian*, 156.

92. Oettinger, "Criticism," 91.

93. Fuchs, *Romance*, 47. See also Gaunt, "Romance," 47.

94. Michelle Hamilton argues that Zerah's chastity is in imitation of Muslim asceticism as adapted in Ibn Paquda's *Duties of the Heart*. Hamilton, *Representing*, 60. But it may also be a mockery of clerical celibacy, following Oettinger's assertion that al-Harizi's satire of the priest is in imitation of Latin estates satires. Oettinger, "Criticism," 91. Tova Rosen writes that Zerah's celibacy may well have reflected Christian debates, but that in any event "a fascination with celibacy, created by the contradictory commitments to marriage and to the study of Torah, was already present in Talmudic culture." Rosen, *Unveiling*, 121.

95. Segre, "Bakhtin," 28.

96. Brownlee and Brownlee, "Introduction," 14.

97. Hermes, "Author," 6.

98. Gaunt, "Romance," 52–53.

99. See C. Robinson, *Medieval Andalusian*, 187.

100. Thus it is the exception when Judah al-Harizi criticizes the Jewish *nedivim* (courtiers) in his *Tahkemoni*, precisely because he relied on their patronage. Oettinger, "Criticism," 91. On the motif of the Hebrew poet lamenting the absence of good patrons, see Brener, *Isaac ibn Khalfun*, 65–66.

101. The shipwreck motif also appears in the *Libro del cavallero Cífar*. Thomas, *Romances*, 16. It is a characteristic feature of the Byzantine novel. In her discussion of Achilles Tatius's *Kleitophon and Leukippé*, Margaret Doody refers to the "usual shipwreck." Doody, *True*, 54. Margaret Mullett writes that shipwrecks were "essential . . . to the world view of Byzantium." Mullett, "Peril," 259. For an overview of the shipwreck in the Byzantine novel (both ancient and medieval), see Mullett, "Peril" 269–272.

102. See also Decter, *Jewish Iberian*, 150–152.

103. Ben Elazar, *Love Stories*, 90, ll. 100–105. We find similar such examples of love-before-first-sight in Ibn Hazm's *The Dove's Neck Ring*, where he discusses those who fall in love by dreaming of their beloveds or by hearing others talk about them. Ibn Hazm, *Ring* 26–30, *Tawq*, 28–29.

104. Ben Elazar, *Love Stories*, 94, ll. 214–217.

105. Ben Elazar, *Love Stories*, 89–90, ll. 90–91. I have not been able to find any other examples of courtly hand-kissing between lovers in Hebrew or Arabic texts. There are, however, a number of instances of servants kissing the hands of their superiors in *Qissat Bayad wa-Riyad* (late twelfth or early thirteenth century, Granada or North Africa). Nykl, *Historia*, 20, 45, 48.

106. Ben Elazar, *Love Stories*, 98, ll. 330–331.

107. Ibid., 92, ll. 155–158. On courtly love as a game, see Duby, *Love*, 57. As we will see in the following chapter, Todros Abulafia similarly adapts troubadouresque ideas about spiritual love and the nobility of the beloved in his verse.

108. On the 'Udhri poets, see *Encyclopedia of Islam*, "'Udhri."

109. Allen, *Introduction*, 105.

110. Schirmann, "Contes," 295.

111. Segre, "Bakhtin," 35, cited in Fuchs, *Romance*, 42.

112. Mastery of poets and rhetoric was professional currency among Jewish functionaries at court. Consider the well-known anecdote about Yehuda Halevi in which the teenage poet sends some verses to Moshe ibn Ezra in Granada, who is so impressed he invites Halevi to join him there. For a literary docu-dramatization of Halevi's youthful aspirations and his début in the Andalusi Hebrew poetic circles, see Halkin, *Yehuda Halevi*, 9–18. We have a later, fictional example in Ibn Sahula's *Meshal ha-Qadmoni*, in which a young man impresses the local scribal community with his extemporaneous verse and is immedi-

ately brought to court, where he is offered a high position by the king. Ibn Sahula, *Meshal,* 2:467–469.

113. Cynthia Robinson writes of "the conversion of the female beloved into a poetic symbol" and of "striking parallels in plot and themes" between *Bayad wa-Riyad* and *Floire et Blancheflor.* C. Robinson, *Medieval Andalusian,* 134 and 172.

114. We have a parallel in the thirteenth century Arabic romance *Bayad wa-Riyad* (Granada or North Africa), which is also a site of convergence of Arabic and Romance traditions. Nykl, *Historia,* 1. Cynthia Robinson has described *Bayad wa-Riyad* as a "grafting of topoi from the classic Arabic love lyric onto a structure almost certainly borrowed from the *roman idyllique;* the resulting product was then topped off by a garnish of courtly *adab.*" C. Robinson, *Medieval Andalusian,* 187. Responding to Nykl's comparisons of the work with *Aucassin et Nicolette,* she argues that a closer match is to be found in *Floire et Blancheflor.* Ibid., 172.

3. POETRY IN DIASPORA

1. Although this study focuses on the Jewish literary production of the Iberian Peninsula, it is worth noting that Hebrew poetry likewise flourished during the period in question in other Romance-speaking areas, such as Provence, Occitania, and especially Italy. On Provence and Occitania, see Schippers, "Poètes," and Kfir, "Center and Periphery" and *Geography.* On Italy, see Genot-Bismuth, "Révolution," and Schippers, "Questions."

2. See the complete edition of Yellin (Abulafia, *Garden*); the selections edited by Schirmann (*Hebrew Poetry* 2:414–438); the English translations of selected poems by Carmi (*Hebrew Verse,* 410–416); and Cole (*Dream,* 256–269).

3. See the comments of Targarona Borrás on poems dedicated to Alfonso X. Targarona Borrás, "Todros," 208–210. On

Todros ben Yehuda Abulafia's poems in praise of his older relative, the influential Rabbi Todros ben Yosef Abulafia, see also Sáenz-Badillos, "Todros."

4. Procter, *Alfonso X,* 130–132.

5. N. Roth, "Translators," 440.

6. O'Callaghan, *Learned,* 144–146.

7. Salvador Martínez, *Alfonso X,* 446n44.

8. Schirmann and Fleischer, *History,* 390.

9. Sáenz-Badillos, "Todros," 512.

10. Johnson, "Phantom," 181.

11. On the situation of the Jewish elites during the rule of Alfonso X, see Baer, *History* 2:118–123.

12. Denise Filios has written on how modern scholars and novelists project their own desires for lost homelands onto al-Andalus. Filios, "Expulsion."

13. According to Aloysius Nykl, "the term 'origins' is not appropriate" to describe the early Romance lyric." Nykl, *Hispano-Arabic,* 372–373. Roger Boase, however, has no such reservations, as the title of his study indicates: *The Origin and Meaning of Courtly Love.*

14. This claim, already under fire by scholars such as Nykl in 1946, became more difficult to defend after Samuel M. Stern established in 1948 that many Andalusi Arab and Hebrew poets wove bits of vernacular lyric into their courtly compositions. Stern, "Vers finaux." This account is a condensation of the narratives treated in far greater depth by other scholars. On the Siege of Barbastro and its implications for the transfer of Andalusi courtly lyric to Provence, see Nykl, *Hispano-Arabic,* 371–411; Boase, *Origin,* 62–75; Menocal, *Arabic,* 28–33; C. Robinson, *Praise,* 295–299.

15. We have an interesting (modern) analogue in the case of African musical styles that traveled to Cuba with African slaves brought there by the Spaniards and then repatriated to Africa to be transformed into such modern styles as the Congolese rum-

ba, a reinterpretation of musical styles that, much like Andalusi courtly lyric, were exported, transformed, and reintroduced into the region where they were first developed. On the Afro-Cuban influence on Congolese rumba see B. White, "Congolese."

16. Fanon's concept of mimicry is more productive than "imitation" for thinking about Sephardic culture vis-à-vis that of the Christian majority, because it takes power into account. Nadia Altschul writes that "mimicry offers a more flexible and complex frame of interpretation." Altschul, "Future," 12.

17. Yellin, *Research,* 7.

18. Pagis, *Middle Ages,* 6.

19. Scheindlin, *Wine,* 5.

20. Brann, *Compunctious,* 7. On the adaptation of specific Arabic themes in Sephardic poetry see Schippers, *Spanish Hebrew.*

21. The one notorious exception is of course that of the Arabic and Hebrew *muwashshahat* (strophic poems), which end in final couplets (*kharjat*) taken from (or perhaps composed in imitation of) popular Andalusi lyric tradition. I will not attempt a complete bibliography of *kharja* scholarship here. See Armistead, "Brief," "Kharjas," and "Problema." There is a thorough overview of the debate in Heijkoop and Zwartjes, *Muwaššah.*

22. For an in-depth discussion of this transition and its implications for Hebrew poetics, see Decter, *Iberian.*

23. The argument with which Julián Ribera (*Music*) enthusiastically tied the music of the *Cantigas* to classical Arabic compositions was refuted by Higinio Anglés (*Música*). Manuel Pedro Ferreira, after weighing the evidence from Andalusi and Romance musical traditions, concludes that both are correct and that the music of the *Cantigas* "juxtaposes and combines a number of musical styles which we are just beginning to identify." Ferreira, "Andalusian," 16.

24. Joseph Snow tears down the received wisdom that Alfonso's invective was the product of his youth, while the devotional *Cantigas de Santa Maria* were the product of a more mature and spiritual mind. Snow's argument makes more sense when thinking about Alfonso as a troubadour, for whom it was standard practice to write amorous verse along with invective. See Snow, "Satirical," 111.

25. Abulafia was also active during the early part of the reign of Sancho IV, but since he lived most of his intriguing life during Alfonso's reign and dedicated a number of poems to him, we will focus on that period in this study and think of Abulafia as an Alfonsine writer. Other Hebrew writers likewise enjoyed the patronage of important courtiers and functionaries at the courts of Christian kings. During the twelfth century, the Barcelonan writer Joseph ibn Zabara (author of the *Book of Delights* or *Sefer Shaashuim*) enjoyed the patronage of the wealthy and influential Sheshet Benveniste. See Ibn Zabara, *Shaashuim,* 2, l. 5. Davidson brings together the scant available biographical information on Ibn Zabara. I. Davidson, "Introduction," xxv–xxviii. Baer notes that the most highly placed Jewish courtiers, such as members of the Sheshet and Benveniste families in the early thirteenth century, were "removed from the jurisdiction of local administrative and judicial authorities, which, in effect, conferred upon them the legal status of the highest nobility of the realm." Baer, *History* 1:91.

26. On Alfonso's translation activity, see Burnett, "Institutional"; Jacquart, "L'école"; Gil, *Escuela;* Sáenz-Badillos, "Participación." Anthony Cárdenas argues that Alfonso's motives in making both scriptorium and chancery vernacular was to more tightly bind "translatio imperii" with "translatio potestatis," or to cement the bonds between government and culture, rather than any democratizing im-

pulse to reach a broader audience within his own country. Cárdenas, "Scriptorium." This is in line with David Rojinsky's assertion that vernacularization is both patriotric and imperial. Rojinsky, *Companion*, 60.

27. Alfonso X, *Primera crónica general de España*. See the edition of Ramón Menéndez Pidal for the history of the Iberian Peninsula through the death of Alfonso X's father, Fernando III. See Alfonso X, *Primera crónica*, 2.

28. Selections from the *Cantigas* are commonly anthologized alongside classic texts of medieval Castilian and even (in at least one case) in an anthology of Spanish literature directed at North American university students. See Rodríguez, *Momentos*, 27–32.

29. Menocal, "Create," 195.

30. Francisco López Estrada argues that Alfonso's target audience was his court, consisting mostly of nobles who lacked Latin education. His massive vernacularization project, meant to elevate the level of learning at court, prefigures the courtly literary culture that Castiglione prescribes in *Il Corteggiano*. López Estrada, *Prosa*, 19.

31. See Lacarra and López Estrada, *Orígenes*, 124. In a similar vein, Fernando Gómez Redondo speaks of a "clerecía cortesana," a curriculum patterned after those of the ecclesisastic *studii* intended to elevate the general level of learning at court. Gómez Redondo, *Prosa* 1:403. See also Gómez Redondo, "Building."

32. O'Callaghan, *History*, 356, original Castilian in Alfonso X, *Primera crónica general* 2:1132.

33. On Frederick II's patronage of letters, see Mallette, *Sicily*, 47–64 and "Poetries"; on that of Alfonso X see Cárdenas, "Scriptorium," and Rodríguez Llopis and Estepa Díez, *Legado*, 29.

34. On the Alfonsine vernacularization project in an imperial key, see Rojinksy, *Companion*, 59–91.

35. On Galician Portuguese see Snow, *Bibliography*, 7, and Cabo Aseguinolaza et al., *Comparative*, 398.

36. C. Alvar, "Poesía" 7. Fernando III did, however, institute the use of Castilian in his chancery and is responsible for laying the groundwork for the institutionalization of Castilian as an official language. This significant fact is often overshadowed (especially in literary criticism) by the comparatively hulking Alfonsine literary project. See González Ollé, "Establecimiento," 234. Anthony Cárdenas reminds us that Alfonso "inherited not only his father's chancery but also the use of the vernacular in chancery documents," which dates to at least 1214. Cárdenas, "Scriptorium," 95.

37. "Amon dinz lur maizos/ mais bos vis e bos morseus/ c'ab afan penre casteus." C. Alvar, *Trovadorescos*, 53, ll. 36–28.

38. "Enque cab sai chanz e solatz/ por los mante lo reis N'Anfos." C. Alvar, *Trovadorescos*, 54, ll. 102.

39. "On fadiar/ n·s pot nulhs hom bos en son do,/ e cort ses tolr'e ses forsar,/ e cort on escot'om razo;/ cort ses erguelh e cort ses vilania,/ e cort on a cent donadors que fan/ d'aitan ricx dons mantas vetz ses deman." C. Alvar, *Trovadorescos*, 81, ll. 9–15.

40. "On es atendutz / sabers e car tengutz." C. Alvar, *Trovadorescos*, 123, ll. 56–57.

41. "Pus cabal . . . tan fay sos faitz grazer." C. Alvar, *Trovadorescos*, 230.

42. Nykl argues that it was very likely that troubadours such as William IX would have learned the meanings of Hispano-Arabic poems from secretaries and courtiers familiar with Arabic. Nykl, *Hispano-Arabic*, 380. Elsewhere he argues that Petrus Alfonsi (who worked precisely during the time that the first generation of troubadours were porting Andalusi poetic culture into Provençal) drew on Arabic verse in compiling his *Disciplina Clericalis*. In fact, in the introduction to *Disciplina*, Alfonsi states that he "compiled" (*compegi*) the work. Petrus Alfonsi, *Disciplina*, 2. The role

of anthologizer or compiler was already
a recognized literary-artistic category in
tenth-century al-Andalus, when Ibn Abd
al-Rabbihi writes, "The selection of wise
sayings is more difficult than their composition, for they have said: 'Man's freedom
of decision is the ambassador of his intelligence.'" Ibn Abd al-Rabbihi, *Iqd al-farid*
1:2. Malcolm Parkes writes that it was not
until the thirteenth century that Latin (and
then vernacular) authors began to theorize
compilatio as a category of literary production, one that then informed the emerging
vernacular literatures of the thirteenth
and fourteenth centuries. Parkes, "Influence," 127–130. See also Reynolds, *Reading,*
130–134; Minnis, *Theory,* 94–102.

43. Even if one makes the argument that
there was, after the Christian conquests, no
appreciable culture of courtly Arabic poetry in Castile, it would have been a simple
matter for Alfonso to send for poets from
Granada or elsewhere to serve at court. We
have ample documentation that Andalusi
(or mudéjar) musicians worked at his court,
if we read the miniatures in the *Cantigas* as
representative.

44. Elezar Gutwirth notes that while the
manuscript record of Judeo-Spanish poetic
texts is very sparse, there is a good deal of
documentary evidence (if one knows how
to find it) of a vibrant Judeo-Spanish *song*
tradition. Gutwirth, "Archival."

45. For English language introductory
studies of the Provençal troubadour tradition, one might begin with Gaunt and Kay,
Troubadours, and Akehurst and Davis,
Handbook. For an English-language anthology of troubadour poems, see Bonner,
Songs.

46. See Sáenz-Badillos, "Invective."

47. On the spread of Provençal troubadour poetry to Catalonia and elsewhere
south of the Pyrenees, see Milá Fontanals,
Trovadores, 53–65; Martín de Riquer's section on Catalan troubadours provides a
good overview of the flourishing of Proven-

çal poetry in Catalonia, but distinguishes
Provençal poets *working* in Catalonia from
truly Catalan troubadours. Riquer, *Història*
1:21–39.

48. Milá Fontanals, *Trovadores,* 179–199;
C. Alvar, *Poesía,* 181; O'Callaghan, *Learned,*
144. Several troubadours make mention of
Alfonso X in their verse. C. Alvar, *Textos,*
35–38, 54, 81, 123, 230.

49. C. Alvar, *Trovadorescos;*
O'Callaghan, *Learned,* 144.

50. Beltrán, "Trovadores," 165–166.

51. In the following chapter on Shem
Tov ben Isaac Ardutiel, we will deal with
the question of Sephardic writers' relationship to the literary vernacular in the context of fourteenth-century Castile.

52. See Schirmann, *Hebrew Poetry*
2:416; Brann, *Compunctious,* 149; Cole,
Dream, 257.

53. Doron, *Poet,* 42.

54. Sáenz-Badillos, "Invective," 67.

55. To give you some idea of how marginalized this material is, as of 2011 there
was a *single* copy of Doron's book available
to the Interlibrary Loan System, housed
at Karl Ebershard University in Germany.
Checking the entry on WorldCat one year
later, I found the record had since disappeared. The author provided me with pho-
tocopies of the relevant chapters.

56. On Alfonso X's intellectual activi-
ties, the general reader may consult Keller,
Alfonso X. For for specialized studies, see
Procter, *Alfonso X,* Ballesteros Beretta and
Llopis, *Alfonso X,* and Salvador Martínez,
Alfonso X. For Alfonso X as a patron of arts
and sciences see Burns, *Emperor.*

57. Wacks, *Framing,* 94–103.

58. *Mester de clerecía* (the priestly style)
refers to (usually) religious vernacular narrative poetry written in Alexandrine verse
during the twelfth and thirteenth centuries
in Castile-León. These works are often
cited as literary compositions in Castilian.
Works of *clerecía* included novels of antiquity (*Libro de Alexandre, Libro de Apolonio*),

many saints' lives (Gonzalo de Berceo's *Vida de San Millán de Cogolla* and *Vida de Santa Oria*), gnomic literature such as we will see in the following chapter (Shem Tov ben Isaac Ardutiel's *Proverbios morales*), and other original compositions such as Juan Ruiz's *Libro de buen amor*. On the *mester de clerecía* genre see Barcia, *Mester*, and Weiss, *Intellectuals*.

59. On the decline of Arabic as vernacular language of the Mozarab community of Toledo in the twelfth and thirteenth centuries, see Ferrando Frutos, *Dialecto*, 8; Beale-Rivaya, "Written," 41; Olstein, *Era*, 134.

60. This would not come to pass until the late nineteenth century, when European Zionists reconstituted Hebrew as a natural language. See Stavans, *Resurrecting*; Harshav, *Language*; Sáenz-Badillos, *History*, 271. It is interesting to note that Eliezer Ben Yehuda, who is considered the father of Modern Hebrew, reports that he found inspiration for his Zionist linguistic project after reading a Russian translation of George Eliot's novel *Daniel Deronda*. Ben-Yehuda, *Dream*, 27.

61. On Alfonso's participation in translating prose works from Arabic into Castilian, and for works of Castilian prose in general emanating from his court, see Gómez Redondo, *Prosa*, 180–240 and 423–852.

62. Menocal, "Create"; Cárdenas, "Scriptorium"; Rodríguez Llopis and Estepa Díez, *Legado*, 29.

63. On the Tibbonid translations, see J. Robinson, "Dynasty."

64. Wacks, "Vernacular Commonality," 424n53.

65. On the larger significance of the Alfonsine translation project, see Menocal, "Create."

66. On preaching and the vernacular in the Middle Ages, see Bataillon, *Prédication*; H. Martin, *Métier*; Zink, *Prédication*.

67. On this question see also Wacks, "Vernacular Anxiety."

68. The question of the Sephardic relationship to the Romance vernacular is key to understanding the diasporicity of their literary culture. As Tölölyan and other theorists stress, this diasporicity is dynamic, and each case study will reveal a different engagement with the vernacular culture, responding to political climate, social change, individual experience and artistic sensibility. By the time of Solomon ibn Verga in the sixteenth century (see chapter 6) we will see a much different response to the linguistic challenges posed by diaspora.

69. Such inscribed drinking cups were common in medieval European courtly settings. The so-called Cup of Charlemagne, for example, is Syrian glass with a French mount, dating to the fourteenth century. It bears an Arabic inscription. Whitehouse, *Medieval Glass*, 230–231. See also the examples of inscribed drinking cups in Homeric sources discussed in R. Fox, *Travelling*, 148, 159, and 172.

70. English translation in Cole, *Dream*, 262. See also the Spanish translation in Targarona, "Todros," 208; original Hebrew in Abulafia, *Garden*, no. 636, 2a, 96 s. Yellin says the cup is metaphorical (Abulafia, *Garden*, 101n1) and Schirmann says it is real (*Hebrew Poetry* 2:413).

71. Deleuze and Guattari's idea of a "minor literature" is helpful, but some adjustment may be made. Their example of Kafka as a Czech Jew writing in German is that of an artist of a linguistic and religious minority writing in the dominant language (and therefore writing *across* the power divide). See Deleuze and Guattari, *Minor*.

72. On the linguistic influence of the biblical Hebrew originals on the Castilian translations, see Viejo Sánchez, "Influjo"; Pérez Alonso, "Contribución"; Del Barco, "Subyacente"; Arbesú-Fernández, "Fazienda."

73. María Rosa Menocal speaks in similar terms about Norman Sicilian appreciation for the indigenous Siculo-Arabic

culture they encountered there. Menocal, *Ornament*, 189–193. Karla Mallette
likewise describes Frederick II as one who
"displayed a genuine admiration for the scientific and political culture of the Arabic-
speaking world." Mallette, "Poetries," 381.

74. Salvador Martínez's suggestion that
Alfonso himself "certainly possessed good
command of all Peninsular languages,
including Galician-Portuguese, Catalan,
Arabic, Hebrew, and some foreign ones"
is probably wishful thinking with regard
to Hebrew and possibly Arabic as well. He
bases this comment on a passage from Alfonso's prologue to part six of the *General
estoria* where he states that he "ordered
the composition [*compilegi*] of this book
after gathering all the ancient books and
chronicles and all the histories in Latin, in
Hebrew, and in Arabic that had been or had
fallen into oblivion." Salvador Martínez,
Alfonso X, 73, and 73n63.

75. Nykl assures us that "these rough
warriors [i.e. the troubadours] could appreciate the beauty of the singing slave-girls
and their art even if they understood nothing of the meaning of the words. . . ." Nykl,
Hispano-Arabic, 381.

76. Cynthia Robinson explores the idea
of simultaneous translation of courtly poetry in her discussion of Arabic courtly lyric
in Christian courts of Provence, Aragon,
and Castile. C. Robinson, *Praise*, 280.

77. Ibn Shabbetay, *Offering of Judah*
2:33, ll. 779–793. The Alfonso in question
is most likely Alfonso VIII of Castile, who
reigned from 1158–1214. O'Callaghan, *History*, 679. Ibn Shabbetay lived from approxi-
mately 1168 (or 1188) until after 1225. Cole,
Dream, 205.

78. Judit Targarona Borrás's observations about the Jewish patrons named in
Abulafia's *diwan* sheds some light on this
question. She mentions that all of the 438
poems in the first volume edited by Yellin
are dedicated to the most important Jewish personalities at Alfonso's court: no.

2–48 and 349–406 to Ishaq ben Sadoq,
182–388 and 407–418 to Shemuel ben Sadoq
(Ishaq's father). Numbers 49–181 and 419–
431 are dedicated to his relative, Todros ben
Yosef Abulafia, and the balance to his son,
Yosef ben Todros Abulafia. This pattern
clearly establishes that his base consists of
the Jewish notables, even when he is writing in praise of King Alfonso. Targarona
Borrás, "Todros," 197–198.

79. As we will see in the chapter on Vidal Benvenist's *Efer and Dina*, this becomes
increasingly true as the situation of Iberian
Jewry deteriorates in the late fourteenth
and early fifteenth centuries.

80. Schirmann, "Isaac Gorni," 178–179.

81. Pagis, *Innovation*, 189.

82. Sáenz-Badillos, "Invective."

83. See Doron, "Dios" and *Poet*. She later
refines this argument somewhat further in
"Poesía."

84. Brann, *Compunctious*, 145.

85. Cole, *Dream*, 275.

86. The notable exceptions to this rule
are the monograph of Doron and the article
of Sáenz-Badillos on Abulafia's invective
poetry. Doron, *Poet*; Sáenz-Badillos, "Invective." Abulafia's prolific output and the
relative scarcity of comparative studies of
his work make him an excellent subject for
further critical studies, particularly as regards his participation in literary practices
in vogue at the court of Alfonso X.

87. Abulafia, *Garden*, 2, l. 13. Targarona
Borrás rightly points out that this line is
the "first case of which we know in which a
poet describes his adaptation of elements of
popular Romance literature in Hebrew in a
positive light." Targarona Borrás, "Todros,"
200–201.

88. Baer, *History* 1:119.

89. Doron, *Poet*, 45.

90. Ibid., 123.

91. Ibid. However, Doron limits her
inquiry to comparisons between Abulafia
and canonical troubadours who did not live
and work in Castile, missing the oppor-

tunity to examine the work of those troubadours who were known to have worked at Alfonso's court, and makes no mention of the Galician-Portuguese troubadours whose presence was perhaps even more important to Alfonsine poetry.

92. The classic study of Denomy is also useful in providing an overview of the central concepts and sociohistorical context of the courtly love phenomenon, particularly as regards the Christian religious context. Denomy, *Heresy*.

93. For a cogent overview of the game of courtly love in the context of the social values of the nobility, see Duby, *Love*, 56–63.

94. The two poems of Abulafia I study here have most recently been anthologized by Israel Levin and figure prominently as poems no. 1 and 2 of his collection. Abulafia, *Shirim*, 5–7 and 8–10.

95. Hispano-Arabic poets, most notably Ibn Hazm in his own formulation of courtly love *The Dove's Neck Ring*, speak of falling in love at first sight, at the sound of the beloved's voice, or by listening to a third party describe the beloved. Ibn Hazm, *Ring*, 26–30, *Tawq* 28–29. However, they do not celebrate or exalt the anxiety and suffering that results.

96. Andreas Capellanus stresses nobility of character over high birth. He writes that "love can endow a man even of the humblest birth with nobility of character" and that it is "excellence of character alone which first made a distinction of nobility among men and led to the difference of class." Capellanus, *Art*, 31, 35.

97. "Desirat ai, enquer desir / voil ades mais desirar/ Que tener ma dona e baisar." Cardenal, *Poésies*, 24, no. 5, vv. 1–3.

98. "Que, ja plazer no-m fezés / Eu fora sos homs adès." Cardenal, *Poésies*, 16:3, vv. 12–13.

99. Abulafia, *Garden*, no. 714, 124, v. 15

100. In other compositions Abulafia takes a different tack and dispenses altogether with the spiritual side of love. See, for

example, his altogether lascivious composition comparing the sexual prowess of Christian and Arab women. Abulafia, *Garden*, no. 731, 130. English translation in Cole, *Dream*, 260.

101. Abulafia, *Garden*, 125, no. 714, v. 21

102. One recalls the words of Melibea to Calisto in *Celestina* when, upon his arrival, Calisto asks Melibea why she has stopped singing: "¿Cómo cantaré, que tu desseo era el que regía mi son y hazía sonar mi canto? Pues conseguida tu venida, desaparecióse el deseo; destémplase el tono de mi boz" (How shall I sing, for it was desire for you that ruled my voice and caused me to sing? Now that you are here, the desire has gone and my voice is out of tune). Rojas, *Celestina*, 323.

103. Abulafia, *Garden*, 125, no. 714, vv. 17–18.

104. Ibid., 126, no. 715, v. 8.

105. "Mas s'ieu pogues veser soen, / D'aisso non dissera nïent / Car del veser o del solatz / Mi tengra per pagatz assatz." Bernardet, *Flamenca*, 168–169, vv. 2824–2830, English translation in Bernardet, *Flamenca*, 170–171.

106. "Que si plagues amar a dieu / Dompna del mon, avinen plai /Auri' en leis, que chausid ai." Calvo, *Poems*, 34, no. 5, vv. 30–32; English translation in ibid., 36.

107. Abulafia, *Garden*, no. 715, vv. 9–10.

108. Ibid., 126, no. 715, v. 18. This problematic turn of phrase is probably meant (again) in the Neoplatonic sense, that God has exalted the beloved by granting her with a beauty unsurpassed by that of all other women. Bernardet, author of *Flamenca*, more than once characterizes Guillem as a "pilgrim of love" whose arduous travels are motivated not by piety but by love. See Covarsí Carbonero, *Roman*, 32, n. 21.

109. "E·l sieus hontraz chapteners / Es tant genzer dels gensors." Calvo, *Poems*, 24, no. 1, vv. 36–37, English translation in Calvo, *Poems*, 25.

110. My italics. The allusion is to Song of Songs 6:4 and 6:10. Abulafia, *Garden,* 124, no. 714, v. 4.

111. Abulafia, *Garden* 124, no. 714, v. 7

112. "Qual dona Deus fez melhor parecer / e que fezo de quantas outras son / *falar melhor, e en melhor razon*" (my italics). Jensen, *Galician-Portuguese,* 308, no. 45, cantiga 1, vv. 1–3, English translation in ibid., 309.

113. Calvo, *Poems* 25, vv. 36–37, English translation on page 25.

114. Abulafia, *Garden,* 125, no. 714, v. 20. The liturgical reference is to the *'amidah* prayer from the morning service (*shaharit*). See *Sidur Bene Romi,* 31.

115. "Quando a vejo, que per ren non sei / que lhi dizer: e el assi fará! / Se per ventura lhi dizer quiser / algũa ren, ali u estever / ant' ela, todo lh'escaecerá!" Jensen, *Galician-Portuguese,* 308, no. 45, cantiga 1, vv. 22–28. English translation ibid., 309.

116. On *mu'arada* in the Andalusi context, see Elinson, "Contrapuntal."

117. The words I have italicized are taken directly from Jonah 1:6. Jonah is traveling from Jaffa to Nineveh when his ship runs afoul of a very intense storm. As the storm worsens, Jonah is enjoying a nap. The frantic captain wakes him, saying, "How can you be sleeping so soundly! Up, call upon your god! Perhaps the god will be kind to us and we will not perish!"

118. Abulafia, *Garden,* 126, no. 715.

119. In her analysis of Abulafia's poem number 714, Doron argues that the difference between the love expressed here and that of the Andalusi Hebrew tradition is that the poet is ultimately unable to possess the beloved, a stance that according to Doron is characteristic of troubadour poetry. Doron, *Poet,* 124.

120. We do find images of captivity in Andalusi Hebrew poetry, most commonly calques of the Arabic trope of the lover wanting to give himself as a ransom for the beloved (or, alternatively, the patron).

There are even cases of the lover being enslaved and in chains (sometimes represented by the tresses of the beloved's hair), but the prison image is, I believe, unique to the Romance tradition of courtly love lyric.

121. Doron compares the use of the Provençal *senhal* to Abulafia's use of the Hebrew *plonit* to indicate his beloved in Abulafia's poem no. 714, v. 25. Doron, *Poet,* 125.

122. Capellanus has the King of Love formulate the twelve precepts of love as if rendering a legal document. Capellanus, *Art,* 116–117.

123. Holmes, *Assembling,* 1. Stephen Nichols argues (against what he perceives as Paul Zumthor's "neoromantic celebration of orality") that the troubadours push back against scholastic textualization of the authorial voice as a book-originating and textually resident phenomenon. Nichols, "Voice," 151 and 139.

124. *Encyclopedia of Islam,* "Sha'ir."

125. Cole, *Dream,* 371.

126. Targarona Borrás, "Todros," 197.

127. I would not go so far as to say that the idea to compile all of his own works in a single volume occurred to Cardenal because he saw Hebrew and Arabic poets doing the same in Castile, but the coincidence certainly is suggestive. Alfonso's court was the site of much technology transfer. His collection of translations of astronomical texts, the so-called *Tablas alfonsíes,* provided the basis for navigational techniques that were not surpassed until Copernicus. By contrast, the single-author codex seems a relatively minor borrowing.

128. Baer, *History* 1:237–238.

129. Schirmann and Fleischer, *History,* 389–390.

130. Cole, *Dream,* 257.

131. Bakhtin defines polyphony (in the novels of Dostoevsky) as "a plurality of independent and unmerged voices and consciousness, a genuine polyphony of fully valid voices." Bakhtin, *Problems,* 6.

132. Louise Vasvári has written that the "novelness" of Juan Ruiz's *Libro de buen amor* manifests in a sort of Bakhtinian polyphony or multiplicity of discourses." Vasvári, "Novelness," 166.

133. Bernardet is thought to have been a cleric, but like the Castilian Juan Ruiz, who flourished in the mid-fourteenth century, a particularly sophisticated and well-read cleric who, in the eyes of his modern editor Merton Hubert, displayed a "decidedly un-Christian" element in his work. Bernardet, *Flamenca,* 7.

134. Kay, *Subjectivity,* 10.

135. Ibid., 69.

136. One such poet, Ibn Quzman (1078–1160), lived from the late eleventh to mid-twelfth century and is particularly interesting for the present study for two reasons. One, he wrote in the vernacular as opposed to Classical Arabic, something that was not entirely unprecedented in Arabic but was certainly an innovation. Like the troubadours, he was an educated poet who wrote sometimes scurrilous verse in a register of the vernacular that bore the earmarks of a classical education. Like the later troubadours, his work also trends heavily toward the autobiographical and the narrative, and his best-known poems narrate his own amorous and Dionysian misadventures, often in ways that are clearly parodic of classical models. James Monroe writes that he was participating in a very well-established tradition of *zajal* poets, some of whom left written texts and some of whom did not, but none of whom "deemed it necessary to declare themselves independent members of a distinctively *literate* as opposed to an *oral* tradition." Monroe, "Juglaría," 56. Federico Corriente, by contrast, maintains that although there are examples of Ibn Quzman using high or low register for purposes of indicating class differences (*coloración social*) between speakers, for the most part these variations are due to formal, prosodic exigencies. Corriente, *Léxico,* 11. For a com-

parative study of the erotic poetry of the "first troubadour," William IX of Aquitaine, alongside that of Ibn Quzman, see García Peinado and Monferrer Sala, "Pornografía."

137. Cole, *Dream,* 257.

138. Critics of Hebrew poetry have pointed up this difference in Abulafia's profile. According to Peter Cole, where his predecessors innovated by presenting stock tropes in new ways, Abulafia turned these tropes on their heads or invented altogether new ones. Cole, *Dream,* 257. Hayim Schirmann praises him for his "unique personality" and links him to later European literature, writing that Abulafia created what Goethe would call "fragments of a great confession." Schirmann and Fleischer, *History* 389–390, cited in Cole, *Dream,* 493. Yitzhak Baer likewise finds Abulafia far more autobiographical than any other Hebrew poet, taking his verses at face value as a historical source. Baer, *History* 1:123, cited in Cole, *Dream,* 494.

139. Zink argues that authorial consciousness in the French romance was a product of the "intellectual adventure" of translating and romanizing Latin narratives for courtly audiences. Authors would insert themselves into the narratives as entextualized narrator-minstrels, a sort of educated and (demi-)fictionalized version of the real-life *jongleurs* who performed *chansons de gestes.* Zink, *Invention,* 26–33.

140. See de Looze, *Pseudo-Autobiography.*

141. Brann, *Compunctious* 145.

142. About Abulafia's protorealism, Ross Brann writes, "Whereas the alluring 'gazelles' of Andalusian love poetry are typically nameless and faceless archetypes of loveliness, the maidens and wenches flirting about in Todros's poetry are more tangible embodiments of beauty who are occasionally singled out as either Arab, Spanish (*edomit*), or Slavic (*bat kena'an*)." Brann, *Compunctious,* 145. Laurence de Looze distinguishes between autobiography and autobiographical fiction and

points out that the absence of recognizable
conventions of literary autobiographical
fiction makes it more likely that readers will
read a text as *real* autobiography. De Looze,
Pseudo-autobiography, 27–28. Therefore,
Abulafia's departure from the conventions
of the Andalusi poetic voice may be what
fuels the perception that his verses are
more authentically autobiographical.

143. The important exception in the time
of Abulafia are the sections of Alfonso
X's *Siete Partidas* dedicated to governing
relations among Christians, Muslims, and
Jews. See Carpenter, *Alfonso X*.

144. As we will see in the following chapters, the anti-*converso* backlash of the late
fourteenth and fifteenth centuries and the
promulgation of the *estatutos de limpieza de
sangre* (statutes of blood purity) meant that
even conversion to Christianity did not
guarantee full acceptance into Christian
society.

4. THE ANXIETY OF VERNACULARIZATION

1. See Rodrigue Schwarzwald, "Language Choice," 403; Fudeman, *Vernacular*.

2. Lawrence Besserman locates the
origins of the modern concept of *secular*
in the circulation of Aristotelian thought
in the Latin West during the twelfth and
thirteenth centuries. According to him,
this period saw "a new Christian attitude
toward the place of humanity in the secular
world that was largely shaped by a rediscov-
ered and Christianized Aristotelian philosophy." Besserman, "Introduction," 11. By
secular here we mean a public domain and
a literary discourse not characterized first
and foremost by the adherence to a particular religious doctrine (in literature) or, in
government, the court of a monarch whose
policies are influenced by church interests
to a far lesser degree than was historically
the case.

3. Here secularity does not mean
"irreligious or hostile to religion," but

rather that the Castilian monarchy did not
depend on ecclesiastical authorization to
the same extent as the French or English
monarchies at the same time. O'Callaghan,
Cantigas, 72.

4. The obvious exception would be,
of course, the Mozarabic community of
Toledo, which retained Arabic as a notarial
language well into the late Middle Ages.
For González Palencia this community was
"bilingual," but he does not distinguish
between written and oral communication
nor between Classical and Andalusi Arabic.
González Palencia, *Mozárabes* 1:129–130.
See also Beale-Rivaya, "Written," 41; Olstein, *Era*, 34; Hitchcock, *Mozarabs*, 97.

5. There is very little concrete information available about literacy, lay or otherwise, in the Iberian Peninsula during the
Middle Ages. Thompson does not include
a chapter on Spain and in fact makes no
mention of the Peninsula anywhere in his
book. Thompson, *Literacy*. In medieval
Castile, lay literacy was generally linked to
Christian indoctrination, and elementary
education was carried out by sacristans for
this purpose. Still, the clergy overall was
characterized by very low levels of Latin
(and perhaps vernacular) literacy. By the
fifteenth century, private schools began to
appear in the larger cities that would challenge this model. Martín Martín, "Alfabetización," 96–100.

6. See, for example, Lacarra and Cacho
Blecua, *Oralidad*, 142–169.

7. Though there were still, especially
in Aragon and Valencia, a great number of
primary Andalusi Arabic speakers in the
Muslim communities of those regions. See
L. Harvey, *Islamic*, 7; Catlos, *Victors*, 239;
Meyerson, *Muslims*, 228.

8. A dialect of this Aramaic was still
spoken by Kurdistani Jews until just after
the Israeli War of Independence, when
nearly the entire community was removed
to Israel and other destinations. The lin-
guist Yona Sabar, who is himself a speaker

of Judeo-Aramaic, has documented the language and its folkloric forms. See Sabar, *Kurdistani.*

9. Nirenberg, "Enmity," 153–154; Meyerson, *Muslims,* 11–12.

10. For a concise overview of the evolution of the *estatutos de limpieza de sangre,* see G. Kaplan, "Inception." See also the full study by Sicroff, *Estatutos.* Jonathan Edwards makes a convincing argument for the *Estatutos* as a major contributor to modern ideas of race. J. Edwards, "Beginnings." David Nirenberg points out that "race" was already a term applied to discussions of Jewish lineage in fifteenth-century Spain, some three hundred years before it would emerge as such elsewhere in Europe. Nirenberg, "Was There Race?" 249–253.

11. Shem Tov ibn Isaac Ardutiel de Carrión, known also as Santob de Carrión, is the only known Jewish author of a major surviving original work in medieval Castilian. His Hebrew works include the *Milhemet ha-'Et ve-ha-Misparayim* (Debate between the Pen and the Scissors), also known as *Ma'ase ha-Rav* (The Rabbi's Tale); the gnomic poem *Yam Qohelet* (Sea of Ecclesiastes); and the *Vidui gadol* (Great Confession), known in Sephardic congregations, where it is still sung as part of the Yom Kippur liturgy, as *Ribbono shel 'olam* (Lord of the Universe). In addition, Shem Tov wrote four *pizmonim,* or penitential hymns and translated Israel Israeli's commentary on the liturgy, *Mitsvot Zemaniyot* (Seasonal Duties), from Arabic to Hebrew. Zemke, *Approaches,* 25–32.

12. During Ardutiel's lifetime many Jews were at court serving as physicians, financiers, tax farmers, and so forth. See Shatzmiller, *Medicine,* 59–61; Baer, *History* 1:326–327; Assis, *Spain,* 25. Ardutiel's contemporary, the powerful nobleman Juan Manuel, held his court physician in such high regard that he lamented (in writing) not being able to name him executor of his

estate because he was not a Christian. Giménez Soler, *Don Juan Manuel,* 699.

13. Wacks, *Framing,* 160–165.

14. Ye'or, *Dhimmi.*

15. O'Callaghan, *History,* 466; Valdeón Baruque et al., *Feudalismo,* 54–81; Macpherson and Tate, "Introduction," xxx.

16. Juan Manuel, *Obras* 1:208.

17. Valdeón Baruque, *Conflictos,* 34.

18. O'Callaghan, *History,* 466; Ben-Shalom, "Medieval," 175.

19. Baer, *History* 1:354–357.

20. Ibid. 1:357. Shepard argues that Ardutiel was targeting Abner personally in both the *Debate* and the *Proverbios.* Shepard, *Shem Tov,* 22–38.

21. Márquez Villanueva, *Concepto,* 43.

22. Mary Louise Pratt defines *contact zone* as "the space in which peoples geographically and historically separated come into contact with each other and establish ongoing relations, usually involving conditions of coercion, radical inequality, and intractable conflict." Pratt, *Imperial,* 6.

23. Faulhaber counts 143 extant translations from Arabic and Hebrew into Hispano-Romance vernaculars, of which we may safely assume the lion's share were translated by Jews. Faulhaber, "*Semitica,*" 875. There is no original profane composition in the literary vernacular that is not a translation of a prior work. For example, the Catalan *Llibre paraules e dits de savis e filosofs* by Jafudà Bonsenyor, compiled at the end of the thirteenth century and presented to Jaume II, while compiled in the vernacular, is not an original literary composition. Bonsenyor, *Llibre;* Lacarra and López Estrada, *Orígenes,* 32.

24. Brann, *Compunctious,* 123.

25. Isaac ibn Sahula, best known for his encyclopedic narrative, *Meshal Haqadmoni,* was a late thirteenth-century Castilian Kabbalist and writer, a contemporary of Alfonso X and of *Zohar*'s author, Moses of León. Loewe includes a bibliography of Ibn Sahula in his edition of that work. Loewe,

"Introduction," xv–xxi. For an edition of Ibn Sahula's commentary on the Song of Songs, see Green, "Commentary." See also the excerpts of *Meshal* edited by Schirmann (*Hebrew Poetry* 2:349–412), the excerpts translated into Spanish in Navarro Peiro, *Narrativa*, 147–168, the (faulty) edition by Zamora (Ibn Sahula, *Meshal Haqadmoni*), the English translation of Loewe (Ibn Sahula, *Fables*), and the English translations of the tale of the sorceror by Scheindlin ("Sorceror") and Wacks ("Tale") as well as the study of the same tale compared with Don Juan Manuel's *Conde Lucanor,* no. 11, in Wacks, "Vernacular Commonality."

26. Loewe, "Introduction," lxx.

27. Ibid., lxix. See also Wacks, "Vernacular Commonality."

28. Loewe, "Introduction," lxx and c.

29. Loewe, "Introduction," lxxxvi–ci.

30. Wacks, "Tale," 432n78.

31. Ibn Sahula, *Fables,* ed. Loewe, 5, vv. 6–7.

32. Ibid., vv. 50–51a.

33. Ardutiel, *Proverbios,* ed. Díaz Mas and Mota, 137, st. 65. English translation in T. Perry, *Moral,* 20, v. 193.

34. On evidence of Jewish preaching in Hispano-Romance during the Middle Ages and Early Modernity, see Saperstein, *Jewish Preaching,* 39–40 and 408; and Gross, *Iberian,* 63n36.

35. Ribera, *Disertaciones,* 12; Stern, *Hispano-Arabic,* 151.

36. Ibn Gabirol, *Secular* 1:376, v. 8.

37. Monroe, "Maimonides," 20.

38. Brann et al., "Poetic" 81; Díaz Esteban, "*Debate,*" 69; Ibn Sasson, *Avnei hashoham,* 76, no. 44.

39. De Piera, *Diwan,* 89, no. 92, vv. 47–50.

40. Zwiep, *Mother,* 14; De Piera, *Diwan,* 89, vv. 47–50.

41. Paloma Díaz Mas writes that while some of the formal characteristics of the *Proverbios* have led critics to link it to the thirteenth-century works of *mester de*

clerecía (such as the *Libro de Alexandre* or the *Milagros de Nuestra Señora* and saints' lives of Gonzalo de Berceo), his sources point up his Andalusi Jewish formation. These include Talmudic material, especially of the Tractate *Avot,* and adaptations of biblical material, as well as some material that seems to have been adapted from known Andalusi Sephardic authors such as Solomon ibn Gabirol. Díaz Mas, "Perdido," 330. See also Theodore Perry's notes in his edition of manuscript M of the *Proverbios,* as well as his notes to his English translation. Ardutiel, *Proverbios,* ed. Perry; T. Perry, *Moral.*

42. Nepaulsingh, *Composition,* 205.

43. In texts drawn from popular tradition it is not uncommon to represent Islam as though it were a perversion of Christianity. For example, the Christian troops in the *Cantar de Mio Cid,* when they hear the Muslim forces' battle cry of "Mafomet!" (Muhammad), respond "Santi Yague!" (Santiago!). See R. Menéndez Pidal, *Cantar* 3:931, v. 731. This does not reflect any historical practice and, in fact, would be considered heretical from an Islamic perspective, but the example is instructive in characterizing how Christians who were ignorant of Islamic doctrine imagined Islam. For in-depth studies on medieval Christian attitudes toward and representations of Islam, see Tolan, *Saracens* and *Sons of Ishmael.*

44. "Si mi razón es Buena, non sea despreçiada / porque la diz persona rafez, que mucha espada / de fin azero sano sab de rota vaína / salir, e del gusano se faz la seda fina, / e astroso garrote faze muy çiertos trechos, / e algunt roto pellote encubre blancos pechos, / e muy sotil trotero aduze buenas nuevas, / e muy vil vocero presenta çiertas pruevas. / por nasçer en el espino non val la rosa, çierto / menos, nin el buen vino por salir del sarmiento; / non val el açor menos, por nasçer de mal nido, / nin los exemplos Buenos por los dezir judío."

Ardutiel, *Proverbios,* ed. Díaz Mas and Mota, 135–137, st. 59–64; English translation in T. Perry, *Moral,* 19–20, vv. 169–189.

45. Weiss, *Intellectuals,* 1.

46. Ibid., 7.

47. Ibid., 16.

48. Díaz Mas and Mota write that the dialectical features of Ardutiel's *Proverbios* are obscured by the long delay (about a century on average) between composition and manuscript transmission, so that it is difficult to come to any meaningful conclusions about the *language* of the original text. What they do argue, following Emilio Alarcos Llorach and Pedro Barcia, is that Ardutiel "casi obsesiva[mente]" (almost obsessively) populates his text with rhetorical figures and strategies (parallelism, homonymy, synonymy, etc.) that are valued far more highly in Hebrew and Arabic than in Greco-Roman tradition. Díaz Mas and Mota, "Introducción," 60; Alarcos Llorach, "Lengua"; Barcia, "Recursos."

49. "Lo que uno denuesta, veo a otro loallo; / Lo que este apuesta, veo a otro afeallo; / La vara que menguada la diz el comprador, / Esta mesma, sobrada diz el vendedor; / El que lança la lança seméjal vagarosa, / Pero al que alcança, seméjal presurosa." Ardutiel, *Proverbios,* ed. Díaz Mas and Mota, 138, st. 72–74. English translation in T. Perry, *Moral,* 20, vv. 221–229.

50. Zemke lists a number of fifteenth- and sixteenth-century Spanish authors who make reference to Shem Tov's writings. Zemke, *Approaches,* 34–46.

51. Díaz Mas and Mota, "Introducción," 23.

52. "Yo estando con cueita por miedo de pecados / muchos que fiz, sin cuenta, menudos e granados, / teníame por muerto, mas vínom al talante / un conorte muy çierto que·m fizo bienandante: / omre torpe, sin seso, sería a Dios baldón / la tu maldat en peso poner con su perdón / Él te fizo naçer, bibes en merçed suya: / ¿cómo podrá vençer a su obra la tuya?" Ardutiel, *Prover-*

bios, ed. Díaz Mas and Mota 124, st. 17–20. English translation in T. Perry, *Moral,* 17, vv. 29–41.

53. T. Perry, *Moral,* 156.

54. By contrast, Juan Ruiz's *Libro de buen amor* is in the end (and despite its relentless parody) a Christian book that is ultimately reverent of Christian doctrine, despite its many moments of anticlericalism and other adventures in ecclesiastical satire.

55. Díaz Mas, "Perdido," 330.

56. Scheindlin, "Secular," 34.

57. de la Granja, "Fiesta."

58. It is tempting to suggest that it was the maqama and the diwan, two textual genres with a long history in Spain and Sicily, that provided the model for development of this textual- and book-based authorial persona. However, in the absence of sufficient evidence I will limit my claim to the observation that there is such a movement that is begun in Europe by Arabic and Hebrew authors and continued by authors working in Romance vernaculars.

59. Sylvia Huot writes (*pace* Cerquiglini, "Clerc") that "the 'I' of the *dit* in turn is a voice projected into writing." Huot, *Song,* 213; Cerquiglini, "Clerc," 159–160.

60. See also my comments on the textual encoding of storytelling performance in medieval maqamat and frametales. Wacks, *Framing,* 41–85.

61. T. Perry, *Moral,* 164.

62. Finnegan, *Literacy,* 146.

63. Ancos argues that the audience for works of mester de clerecía was itself primarily clerical. Ancos, "Audience." Bailey suggests that the frequent shifts of perspective and high level of formulaic diction in works of clerecía owe more to the fact of their oral composition than of conscious imitation of such by authors who composed in writing. Bailey, "Oral Composition," 87–89. Deyermond, writing specifically on the *Mocedades de Rodrigo,* concludes that the evidence cited by critics to establish

popular authorship is insufficient. He argues for a learned author but adds that the existence of many popular features in the poem "does not exclude either the recasting in this form of a non-learned original or the diffusion of the learned product by [non-learned] *juglares* (minstrels)." Deyermond, *Epic*, 81. Grande Quejigo argues for a mixed popular/clerical textuality that is ultimately "una actividad más escolar que juglaresca" (is more scholarly than minstrelesque). Grande Quejigo, "Quiero leer," 104. See also the sources brought together in Zemke, *Approaches*, 119.

64. On textual encoding (or perhaps "entextualization") of storytelling performance in medieval Iberian narrative, see Wacks, *Framing*, 41–44.

65. Richard Bauman writes that verbal performance draws attention to itself by "highlight[ing] the social, cultural, and aesthetic dimensions of the communicative process." Bauman, "Performance," 41.

66. Michael Solomon writes that Juan Ruiz "presents a pre-established idea of the book as a functional apparatus which will constitute a diversity of textual entities." Solomon, "Idea," 138.

67. "La mejoría del callar non podemos / Negar, mas toda vía convién que la contemos. / Porque la miatad de cuant oyermos fablemos / Una lengua, por ende, e dos orejas avemos. / Quien mucho quier fablar sin grand sabiduría, / Çierto en se callar major baratería / El sabio que loar el callar bien quería / E fablar afear, está razón dezía: /—Si fuse el fablar de plata figurado, / figurarién callar de oro apurado." Ardutiel, *Proverbios*, ed. Díaz Mas and Mota, 217, st. 567–571. English translation in T. Perry, *Moral*, 50, vv. 2117–2137. The entire section on the value of silence is found in Ardutiel, ed. Díaz Mas and Mota, 216–225, st. 566–618.

68. Perry, *Moral*, 4–5; Díaz Mas and Mota, "Introducción," 78.

69. Theodore Perry points out that "while moderns may not consider this a very original form of literary activity, originality held less interest for medieval authors than for us." T. Perry, *Moral*, 164.

70. "Çierto es, y non fallesçe, proverbio todavía: / El huésped y el peçe fieden al terçer día." Ardutiel, *Proverbios*, ed. Díaz Mas and Mota, 213, st. 542. The *refrán* persists in oral tradition: "El huésped y el pece a los tres días hiede." Campos and Barella, *Diccionario*, 246, no. 1680. There are a number of variants recorded in Martínez Kleiser, *Refranero*, 358, nos. 31 and 586–591. See also the Hebrew analog: "On the first day, a guest (*oreah*); on the second, a nuisance (*toreah*); on the third, a pest (*soreah*)!" Alcalay, *Basic*, 197, no. 1871. Perry notes that the inclusion of this proverb is exemplary of Ardutiel's authorial intervention in the traditional wisdom material of which he makes use: "One should also note his mild disagreement with the adage, since his context claims that they stink even on the first!" T. Perry, *Moral*, 163.

71. On the wide range of sources upon which Ibn Zabara drew, see Abrahams, *Delight*, 18; I. Davidson, "Introduction," xxxviii–lxxvi.

72. "Non ha lança que false todas las armaduras / nin que tanto trespase como las escribturas" (To pierce and pass through all kinds of armor, there is no lance so effective as writing). Ardutiel, *Proverbios*, ed. Díaz Mas and Mota, 201, st. 465; T. Perry, *Moral*, 45, st. 1793. The comparison between arms and letters continues for several more stanzas through Ardutiel, *Proverbios*, ed. Díaz Mas and Mota, 201, st. 469; T. Perry, *Moral*, 45, st. 1809.

73. Schirmann, *Hebrew Poetry* 4:529, cited in Einbinder, "Pen," 264; Cole, *Dream*, 289. For a Spanish translation of the excerpts edited in Schirmann, *Poetry* 2:529–540, see Díaz Esteban, "Debate," as well the (deficient) English translation in Shepard, *Shem Tov*, 79–97, and that in

Colahan, "Santob's Debate." Complete and rigorous Spanish and English translations of the *Debate* are still wanting.

74. The Hebrew maqama had, by Ardutiel's time, been cultivated by a great many authors for centuries. A sampler of Hebrew maqamat would include those of Ibn Saqbel, al-Harizi, Ibn Shabbetay, Ibn Zabara, and Isaac ibn Sahula, among others.

75. Spanish Hispanists are divided on the question of Ardutiel's relationship to "Castilianness" or "Spanishness." These divisions tend to break along political lines. Those on the left tend to argue for the national or regional nature of his work, but there are some interesting exceptions. Marcelino Menéndez y Pelayo writes that the poem has "un color oriental tan marcado" (an oriental shading so pronounced) that it seems to have been written in Hebrew and then translated into Castilian. Menéndez y Pelayo, *Antología*, 3 cxxv. Américo Castro, in contrast, describes his folkloric tone as "sancho-pancezco" (Sancho Panza-esque), but elsewhere describes him as a foreign aggressor who "invade con su lírica hebraica la lengua literaria de Castilla" (invades the literary language of Castile with his Hebrew lyric). Castro, *Aspectos*, 163, *España*, 252. For a full discussion of the political conditioning of modern critical reactions to the *Proverbios*, see Wacks, "Vernacular Anxiety."

76. On the *Proverbios*, there are major critical editions by González-Llubera, Shepard, Perry, and Díaz Mas and Mota; see also the following major studies: Shepard, *Shem Tov*; T. Perry, *Moral*; Zackin, "Jew."

77. Shepard, *Shem Tov*, 31–38. For an introduction to the biography and works of Abner/Alfonso, see Carpenter, "Alfonso de Valladolid." Szpiech discusses the possible relationship between Abner/Alfonso and Shem Tov. Szpiech, *Conversion*, 143–173.

78. Nini and Fruchtman, "Introduction," 36, cited in Einbinder, "Pen," 266.

This lament echoes that of Jacob Ben Elazar in the introduction to his debate between the pen and the sword.

79. Einbinder, "Pen," 270. Readers of the Castilian *Libro de buen amor* will recognize this trope from Juan Ruiz's debate between the Greeks and the Romans, which emphasizes dual perspectivism and how two different parties will draw different conclusions from the same data set. See Parker, "Parable." Shem Tov also includes a discourse on this question in the *Proverbios morales*. Ardutiel, *Proverbios*, ed. Díaz Mas and Mota, 138–142, st. 70–95; T. Perry, *Moral*, 20–22, st. 213–313.

80. Zackin, "Jew," 201–203.

81. Einbinder, "Pen," 274.

82. Cole, *Dream*, 290.

83. van Gelder, "Conceit"; Alba Cecilia, "Espada," "Debate."

84. Julian Weiss notes that the Spanish *Elena y María* is unique in that it presents *both* knight and cleric in a poor light and goes into great detail in linking the debate to the particulars of the current economic and political factors influencing the relative prestige of church and court in Castile. Weiss, *Intellectuals*, 180–196.

85. According to Spain's national weather service, the average low temperature in Soria during the month of January is -1.6 Celsius, or 29 Farenheit. *Agencia Estatal de Metereología*. Web. 14 Mar. 2012. Dorothy Severin points out in the introduction to her study of *Celestina* that the work, like the nineteenth-century novel, takes place primarily indoors. Severin, *Tragicomedy*, 1.

86. See Moner's "Cobles de les tisores" in Moner, *Obres*, 167–178.

87. The topos of false modesty was a well-worn convention in authors' prologues in Ardutiel's time. Juan Manuel, author of the *Conde Lucanor* (ca. 1335), describes himself as a man "de non muy grand saber" (not of very great learning). Juan Manuel, *Conde Lucanor*, 70. Juan Ruiz, another contemporary of Ardutiel, likewise paints himself

as a man "de poquilla çiençia e de mucha e grand rudeza" (of little knowledge and of much and great coarseness). Ruiz, *Libro de buen amor*, 9, l. 90–91. One is reminded of Winnie the Pooh's self-characterization as a "bear of very little brain."

88. "Cuand viento se levanta—ya apelo, ya aviengo—, / la candela amata, ençiende el grant fuego; / dó luego por sentençia que es bien del cresçer e tomar grant acuçia por ir bollesçer, / que por la su flaqueza la candela murió/ e por su Fortaleza el grant fuego bivió; / mas apelo a poco rato d'este juïzio, / que vi escapar el flaco e peresçer el rezio, / que ese mesmo viento que estas dos fazía / fizo çoçobra d'esto en ete mesmo día: / él mesmo menuzó el árbol muy granado / e non se espeluzó d'él la yerba del prado. / Quien sus casas se·l queman grant pesar ha del viento, / cuando sus eras toman con él gran pagamiento. / Por end, non sé jamás tenerme a una estaca, / nin sé cuál me val más: si prieta o si blanca." Ardutiel, *Proverbios*, ed. Díaz Mas and Mota, 140–141, st. 83–90. English translation in T. Perry, *Moral*, 21, vv. 265–293.

89. Einbinder, "Pen," 271; T. Perry, *Moral*, 3. See also Nini and Fruchtman, "Introduction," 36, cited in Zackin, "Jew," 195n103.

90. And one could, I suppose, press the metaphor of the inkwell a bit farther: the freezing represents the unfavorable conditions for the Jewish community, the sociopolitical freeze (think "cold war" for an analogue in modern rhetoric).

91. Ardutiel, *Maase*, 61, vv. 319. Nini and Fruchtman explain that the opposition *form/matter* is derived from philosophy and cite the Arabic cognate *surah* to the Hebrew *tsurah* (form). See Nini and Fruchtman, "Introduction," 61n310. Shem Tov ben Joseph ibn Falaquera (d. 1290), the great synthesizer of Aristotelian philosophy and Jewish tradition, in the introductory poem to his *Sefer Hamevakesh* (Book of the Seeker), writes: "Man should learn to recognize

the efficient cause in every object, its final cause, form, and substance." Falaquera, *Seeker*, trans. Levine, 97; original Hebrew in Falaquera, *Epistle*, 8. Cf. Maimonides, *Guide*, trans. Friedländer 3:8, 261.

92. Ardutiel, *Maase*, 61, vv. 315–316.

93. Even original Hebrew compositions by medieval authors are redolent of biblical authority, as they are a sort of *bricolage* made from modules of biblical utterances. Brann, *Compunctious*, 23–25.

94. Ardutiel, *Maase*, 67, v. 398.

95. Einbinder notes that the narrator claims the freezing of the inkwell (the cessation of Hebrew poetic practice) has made him a laughing stock among "the members of my household" (l. 257), which seems to anticipate the critique of Ibn Sasson. Einbinder, "Pen," 273.

96. David Rojinsky makes the convincing argument (*contra* Márquez Villanueva and others) that Castilian vernacularization was at once a patriotic and Christian gesture by which Castilian, in becoming the new vehicle for higher-order thinking and writing, comes to be a new, local Latin. See Rojinksy, *Companion*, 60. At the same time, Castilianization (particularly of learned texts) was a way to assert Castilian intellectual independence from the French Cluniac order, which had dominated the monasteries of northern Castile and León for over a century. The conquest of the Andalusi cities of Seville and Córdoba opened up new territory where Cluny might never assert their influence and created the possibility of a major intellectual project relatively free of Cluniac influence.

97. Ardutiel, *Maase*, 73, vv. 497–498. On the figure of the shabby yet eloquent rogue see Drory, "Maqama," 190.

98. The reference is to Deuteronomy 14:14, from a list of birds that are considered unclean and not fit for consumption by the Israelites.

99. The Hebrew word for spy (*meragel*) derives from the root meaning foot or leg

(*regel*), so that in Hebrew a spy is one who walks or runs around (i.e., explores; cf. English *gumshoe*). Shem Tov is here engaging in a bit of wordplay, suggesting that the scribe is using his eyes as spies to "run around the house" as a spy "legs around" enemy territory in order to report back.

100. Although the Hebrew *yeraqraq* (lit. greenish) would seem to suggest a green tone (Heb. *yaroq*, green), its usage in Psalms 68:14 compares the iridescence of a dove's feathers to the shimmering of gold.

101. The allusion is to Deuteronomy 28:29, which compares those who do not follow God's law to blind men, who must grope their way around even in full daylight.

102. Ardutiel, *Maase*, 74, vv. 505–519.

103. See Wacks, *Framing*, 177–181.

104. Ardutiel, *Maase*, 80, v. 611. Nini and Fruchtman's note clarifies that Shem Tov meant that "all of it was written with scissors." Nini and Fruchtman, "Introduction," 80n611.

105. On the intrusion of the author into the narrative of the maqama, see Wacks, *Framing*, 185.

106. Cole, *Dream*, 289.

107. Between the twelfth and fourteenth century, a number of Peninsular writers experimented with putting into narrative practice some of the teachings of the *kalaam*, or rationalist theology, of Ibn Rushd (Averroes) and Maimonides (the Rambam). In particular, the figure of the unreliable narrator in the rhymed prose narrative fiction (maqamat) of Muhammad al-Saraqusti and Judah al-Harizi, as well as Juan Ruiz's *Libro de buen amor* (1334) can be read as a sort of a workbook for rationalist thought. Wacks, *Framing*, 177–193.

108. "Un astroso cuidava, y, por mostrar que era / Sotil, yo le enviaba escripto de tijera. / El nesçio non sabía que lo fiz por infinta, / Porque yo non quería perder en él la tinta; / Ca, por non le deñar, fize vazia la llena / Y no·l quise donar la carta

sana, buena: / Como el que tomava meollos d'avellanas / Para sí y donava al otro caxcas vanas, / Yo del papel saqué la razón que dezía; / Con ella me finqué, díle carta vazía." Ardutiel, *Proverbios,* ed. Díaz Mas and Mota, 130–131, st. 40–44.

109. The nut/shell metaphor is a popular one in late medieval literature and goes back at least as far as Augustine. Ardutiel's contemporary Juan Manuel includes an exemplum in the *Conde Lucanor* about a rich man who, fallen on hard times, finds himself with nothing to eat but a handful of lupini beans (Sp. *altramuces*, O.Sp. *atramuzes*). As he sits crying over his misfortune and eating his lupini beans, "sintió que estava otro omne en pos dél e bolbió la cabeça e vio un omne cabo dél, que estava comiendo las cortezas de los atramizes que él echava en pos de sí" (he heard someone behind him, and turned his head and saw a man following him, who was eating the shells of the lupini beans that he had been throwing behind him). Juan Manuel, *Conde Lucanor,* 116. On the question of the nut/shell metaphor in medieval Castilian literature see Urbina, "Antithesis." On the Arabic origins of the tale, see de la Granja, "Origen."

110. Einbinder, "Pen," 265. On protonationalism in medieval Hebrew poetry, see Brann, *Compunctious,* 16, 24.

111. Einbinder, "Pen," 267, cf. Ardutiel, *Maase,* l. 575, ll. 581–582; Targarona Borrás, "Lengua."

112. As we have observed in the previous chapter, most examples of Hebrew texts written to or for Christian kings were actually rhetorical ploys meant to emphasize the author's privileged position at court or to exalt the Christian monarch in the eyes of the Jewish community.

113. On the problematics of adapting postcolonial criticism to the study of medieval culture, see Altschul, "Postcolonialism," 590.

114. To be fair to previous Christian Iberian monarchs (and I have made this argument elsewhere), the Christian conquest of al-Andalus was itself a kind of colonialist, expansionist project. See Wacks, "Reconquest" and *Framing*, 133–136. In any event, as discussed in the previous chapter, the time of Alfonso X was one of imperial designs, protonationalist linguistic policy, and territorial expansion and could well serve as a kind of a testing grounds for postcolonial approaches to medieval literary culture.

115. Raden, "Writing," 1. While I find the postcolonial framework a laudable effort to expand the discussion of these works, I think that the difference in discursive strategies between Juan Manuel and Ardutiel is more a function of their theologies. Catholic theology is codified in canon law and in councils that are ratified by the pope, who is the final terrestrial authority on theological matters. This provides a hierarchical structure for Catholic theological discourse. Judaism lacks such a central authority; consequently practice is determined by individual rabbinical decisions, not by reference to a fixed code. Although by Ardutiel's time Maimonides' *Mishneh Torah* had provided a very powerful tool for rabbinic jurisprudence, any given rabbi might differ with Maimonides, and rule against him without fear of censure.

116. This period includes the massive Western Sephardic corpus of editions printed in Amsterdam and in Italy, many of which were written by conversos who had left Portugal and Spain to live openly as Jews. See Y. Kaplan, *Judíos*, and den Boer, *Literatura*. If we exclude them on the basis of their having been educated as Christians, and therefore far more likely to view the vernacular as an appropriate literary language, then we must wait until the second half of the eighteenth century before we see any significant literary production in Judeo-Spanish, and even later

for a significant body of *secular* literature in Judeo-Spanish. The lively debate over the correct application of the terms *Judeo-Spanish, aljamiado,* and *Ladino* falls outside of the scope of this study, but one might begin with the sources brought together in Hamilton, "Text," 161n2: Blasco Orellana and Magdalena Nom de Déu, *Aljamías;* Díaz Mas and Mota, "Introducción"; Pascual Recuero, "Aljamiado," 851–876.

117. In 1263, the Catalan rabbi Nahmanides was invited by King Jaime I ("the Conqueror") of Aragon to debate the relative truths of Judaism and Christianity with the converso Pablo Cristiani. Despite royal assurances of freedom of expression in the debate, Nahmanides was later persecuted by the Dominican order, who objected to certain details of Nahmanides' written account of the proceedings. Jewish delegates to the 1413–1414 Disputation of Tortosa, presided over by Pedro IV of Aragon, likewise feared for their lives. Maccoby, *Judaism*, 39, 83; Baer, *History* 2:210–211.

118. This has driven Sanford Shepard's interpretation of the *Debate* as a representation of the conflict between the apostate Abner of Burgos (Alfonso de Valladolid) and the Castilian Jewish community. Yitzhak Baer was the first to advance this thesis relative to selections of the *Proverbios*, which he suggests in *History* 1:285 and 2:730n53. Shepard extends this interpretation to include the *Debate* in Shepard, *Shem Tov*, 22–38. I concur with John Zemke that Shem Tov is not engaging in an *ad hominem* attack on Abner. Zemke, *Approaches*, 161.

5. DIASPORA AS TRAGICOMEDY

1. On the Disputation, see the critical edition and study the source texts by Antonio Pacios López. Pacios López, *Disputa*. For English translations of the Hebrew and Christian accounts of the Disputation, see Maccoby, *Judaism*, 168–215. The Hebrew account is reproduced in Ibn Verga, *Shevet Yehudah*, 94–107. On the disastrous results

for the Jewish communities of Castile and Aragon, see Baer, *History* 2:170–234.

2. Eugene Dorfman defines *narremes* as a "chain of functionally central incidents, linked to each other in organic relationship." Dorfman, *Narreme,* 5.

3. See M. Jacobs, "Love."

4. Michael Fox suggests that the Esther story comes from a period of Jewish communal life in diaspora before rabbinical culture had developed sufficient jurisprudence to guide Jews through life in diaspora. M. Fox, *Character,* 147–148.

5. On Esther as a model for diaspora, see Humphreys, "Life-Style"; Levenson, "Ecumenical." Sidnie Ann White describes Esther as "a model for the successful conduct of life in the often uncertain world of the Diaspora." S. White, "Esther," 173.

6. Nonetheless Dina's story also recognizes the temptation to mix culturally. Dina leaves her father's home "to go out to see the daughters of the land," a phrase that exegetes have interpreted variously but that recognizes the impulse to assimilate and acculturate. The biblical commentary *Midrash Rabbah* explains that Dina's behavior proves both her own and her mother's immodesty: "A woman is not immoral until her daughter is immoral." *Midrash Rabbah,* 736.

7. Allegory was, for medievals, a way to imbue the earthly with heavenly significance. Eco, *Art,* 53–54. In Jewish tradition, Kabbalists took this idea quite literally (pun intended); the Hebrew alphabet itself was the medium through which God was understood to have created the world. This idea is systematically developed in the *Sefer Yetzirah* (Book of Creation), which laid the foundation for the ideas about the alphabet's role in creation found in the thirteenth-century *Zohar.* On the *Sefer Yetzirah,* see the introduction, translated excerpt, and extensive bibliography in Cole, *Kabbalah,* 37–47 and 290–299. For an English translation, see *Sefer Yetzirah,*

trans. Kaplan. For Isidor Kalisch's edition of the Hebrew text accompanied by a Spanish translation by Manuel Algora, see *Sefer Yetzirah: El libro de formación.*

8. Schirmann, *Hebrew Poetry* 2:564; Huss, "Introduction," 5–12; Targarona Borrás and Scheindlin, "Literary"; Scheindlin, "Secular," 26; Cole, *Dream,* 305.

9. Peretz, "Introduction," xv. See also Jonathan Decter's comments about the *Sefer Ha-meshalim* (The Book of Parables) of Jacob ben Elazar vis-à-vis the European romance narrative. Decter, *Iberian,* 149–156.

10. On the term *melitsah* as representative of a literary genre, see Genot-Bismuth, "Contribution."

11. "Huss, "Introduction," 3n1. The fact that print editions introduced the eponymous lovers title convention favored by authors of the chivalric romances so popular among Sephardic readers suggests that even if Benvenist himself did not consciously envision *Efer and Dina* as a kind of parodic romance, the printers certainly did.

12. See Yassif, *Folktale,* 345. On the novella in Europe, see Clements and Gibaldi, *Anatomy.*

13. Grieve, *Floire,* 22; Infantes and Baranda, *Narrativa,* 85–127. David Arbesú-Fernández points out that the earliest reference to the *Flores and Blancaflor* narrative is in the *Ensenhamen* of Catalan trouabadour Guerau de Cabrera (ca. 1170). Arbesú-Fernández, "Introduction," 14. Arbesú-Fernández has edited the more fully novelized version found in the *Primera crónica general* of Alfonso X. See *Crónica de Flores y Blancaflor,* ed. Arbesú-Fernández. On *Bayad wa-Riyad,* see the Arabic edition and Spanish translation in Nykl, *Historia,* and the English translation and study in C. Robinson, *Medieval Andalusian.*

14. Huss, "Introduction," 141, vv. 1–3.

15. Schirmann and Fleischer, *History,* 610.

16. Baer, *History* 2:95–116; N. Roth, *Conversos,* 34; Marcó i Dachs, *Judíos,* 172–188;

Hinojosa Montalvo, *Jews,* 21–66; Doñate Sebastià and Magdalena Nom de Deu, *Three,* 41–44.

17. N. Roth, *Conversos,* 55–61.

18. Maccoby, *Trial,* 83; Schirmann, *Hebrew* 2:566; Baer, *History* 2:211; Targarona Borrás and Scheindlin, "Literary," 68–69.

19. Baer, *History* 2:105. On Crescas's exaggeration, see N. Roth, *Conversos,* 34.

20. Targarona Borrás, "Últimos," 249.

21. De Piera, *Diwan,* 89, no. 92, vv. 47–50.

22. Allony, "Reaction"; Brann, *Compunctious,* 23–58; Drory, "Words."

23. Brann et al., "Poetic," 81; Díaz Esteban, "Debate," 69.

24. Ibn Sasson, *Hashoham,* 76, no. 44, vv. 1–2. Emphasis mine.

25. Brann et al., "Poetic," 77. This shift in literary sensibility meant that Shem Tov ben Isaac Ardutiel (in the previous century) was able to write about scissors instead of swords, and Benvenist about a more realistically unhappy marriage (when compared with the wild grotesqueries such as are found in the marriage parodies of Judah al-Harizi and Judah Ibn Shabbetay). This is not to say that the courtly ideals disappeared entirely, for the quintessential chivalric romance, *Amadís de Gaula,* was a best-seller alongside works that parodied traditional values (de Rojas's *Celestina* and the anonymous *Lazarillo*).

26. On the parody of the conventions of the chivalric novel in *Lazarillo de Tormes,* see Rico, *Picaresque,* 1, and Deyermond, *Guide,* 52.

27. Baer, *History* 2:134.

28. Barbour, "Nationalism," 2.

29. Armstrong, *Nations,* 3. See also Ross Brann's discussion of the "cultural nationalism" in Andalusi Hebrew poetry. Brann, *Compunctious,* 26–58.

30. J. Fishman, *Nationalism,* 9. James Monroe has noted a similar siege-mentality effect in the poetry of Nasrid Granada in the fifteenth century. The response of Granadan poets and artists to Christian political superiority and imminent annexation was to vigorously eschew Christian influences and turn to African and Eastern models that recalled the heyday of the Caliphate. Monroe, *Hispano-Arabic,* 62–63.

31. Targarona Borrás, "Últimos," 263.

32. This is not to say that regimes cannot and have not pressed folkloric texts into political service; one could raise many such examples in the modern period of national, official folklores. My point here is that a given person's experience of the folkloric traditions with which they were raised transcends the political realities in which they lived, precisely because folklore (at least in the fourteenth century) is not generated, promulgated, or mediated by the state but rather from below, by individuals and social networks of families and neighbors.

33. Raymond Scheindlin notes that "if there had been an impulse to imitate the new vernacular literature of Spain, there was still no Jewish vernacular to be molded into a language of high culture." Scheindlin, "Secular," 37.

34. For example, in the *Conde Lucanor* Juan Manuel sets many of the *exempla* in known locations in Castile or other regions. Others (many drawn from Aesopic or other fable traditions) are free of specific geographic or historical markers. Known historical figures protagonize a number of *exempla.* The same can be said of Bocaccio's *Decameron.* By contrast, *Amadís de Gaula* travels through a variety of historical and fantastic locations. In one example, on his way to Constantinople (historical enough) he stops off at "Devil's Island," where he defeats a dragon-like monster (the Endriago) before continuing his journey. Rodríguez de Montalvo, *Amadís de Gaula,* ed. Cacho Blecua 2:1129–1151.

35. "A rhyming prose tale for the wise scholar, both enjoyable and intelligent. A respectable man comes forth as a *bon vivant;* [these are] tales fit for the season of

love; enjoy the amorous yarns and the light entertainments for Purim time." Benvenist, *Efer and Dina,* 201.

36. The figure of Esther as a heroine obliged to conceal her true faith yet loyal to her Jewish roots naturally resonated with the situation of the conversos. According to Inquisition records, the Fast of Esther was the most significant observance in the Marrano liturgical calendar (such as it was). See C. Roth, *Marranos,* 186–188; Yerushalmi, *Court,* 38; Gitlitz, *Secrecy,* 377–379.

37. D. Boyarin, "Purim," 5.

38. Modern critics have dismissed the book of Esther as a "fairy tale" narrative, comparable in (lack of) sophistication to the Cinderella story. Carruthers, *Esther,* 2. The Esther story shares traits that the European fairy tale has in common with the Hellenistic romance, such as "attention to the King's love life (such as it is) and a delight in depictions of royal luxury." M. Fox, *Character,* 145. Sephardic Jews were familiar with many such tales that circulated in Iberia, a number of which are preserved in modern oral tradition. For example, several of the ballads collected and published by Yacob Abraham Yoná (1847–1922) in Salonika deal with similar issues of problematic romances between kings and women of lower station, and other related themes that find their analogues in the book of Esther. See, for example, the ballads of Melisenda and El Conde Alemán in Armistead and Silverman, *Folk,* 100–115.

39. Abrahams, *Life,* 261.

40. Perfet, *Responsa* 2:551, sec. 388.

41. Silberstein, *Esther;* Einbinder, "Proper" and *Place,* 85; I. Davidson, *Parody,* 32–34.

42. Silberstein, *Esther,* 34–36; I. Davidson, *Parody,* 32–34.

43. Benvenist, *Efer and Dina,* 158, ll. 89–90; I italicize literal biblical allusions.

44. "Wine and new wine destroy / The mind of / My people: / It consults its stick, / Its rod directs it!" (Hosea 4:12).

45. Benvenist, *Efer and Dina,* 172, ll. 252–255.

46. See Huss's note in Benvenist, *Efer and Dina,* 172n254. One might also argue that the synesthesia of the crowd of Israelites *seeing (ro'im)* rather than *hearing (shom'im)* the voices heightens the sense of the thunder's supernatural character.

47. On the Rodrigo/La Cava narrative, see Grieve, *Eve.*

48. David Nirenberg notes that since the fourteenth century, some Iberians adduced to Judaism a biological aspect, which then translated into heightened anxiety over "contamination" and "purity of blood." This is a logical basis for an increased focus on sexual mixing and miscegenation as a threat to the community's integrity, be it Jewish or Christian. Nirenberg, "Race." Américo Castro earlier had argued that the Christian preoccupation with *limpieza de sangre* (purity of blood) was actually a Jewish concept (matrilineal transmission of religion; the idea that every Jew is a direct descendant of the biblical Israelites) that had taken hold in the Christian community. See Castro, *España,* 512–515; his ideas are further explained and critiqued in Pérez, *Isabel,* 253–260.

49. This mapping of social concerns onto the body of individuals is consistent with Mary Douglas's idea that "the powers and dangers credited to [the] social structure [are] reproduced in small on the human body." Women in particular, being the "gates of entry to the caste," are metonymically responsible for the purity of the larger social group. Douglas, *Purity,* 142 and 155.

50. Yerushalmi, *Zakhor,* 47; Horowitz, *Reckless,* 279–316.

51. Gitlitz, *Secrecy,* 439n29. New Mexican informants report having celebrated the *Fiesta de Santa Ester* in New Mexico until the late twentieth century, when a local priest made a point of eliminating all observances thought to have been of Jewish origin. Janet Jacobs, *Hidden,* 62–63.

52. Compare to Ibn Shabbetay's parody of the traditional reading of the ketubah in *Minhat Yehudah*. Schirmann, *Hebrew Poetry* 2:79–80; Ibn Shabbetay, *Offering* 2:24–25, *La ofrenda*, 185; I. Davidson, *Parody*, 11.

53. N. Roth, *Daily*, 44.

54. Benvenist, *Efer and Dina*, 173, ll. 259–264. For "horns and whistles" we should understand something along the lines of rim shots and catcalls from the crowd, meaning the dowry that she brings is her own nubile self. Here the Aramaic *karnah* denotes the horn blown as an instrument, but also connotes (following Hispanic convention) the horns Efer will wear as the impotent old husband to a beautiful young wife. Benvenist, *Efer and Dina*, 174n264.

55. The explanation of the allegory is found in Benvenist, *Efer and Dina*, 186–200, ll. 410–568. On the tradition of allegory in Jewish literature and in particular in Hebrew maqamat, see Drory, "Maqama," 202–203.

56. Benvenist, *Efer and Dina*, 187–188, ll. 410–424.

57. Schirmann and Fleischer, *History*, 612–613; Huss, "Introduction," 68–69.

58. Benvenist, *Efer and Dina*, 187, l. 420. On the nut/meat allegory in medieval literature, see Laird, *Figures*, 151–152. The allegory also appears in Juan Ruiz's *Libro de buen amor* (Book of Good Love). Ruiz, *Libro de buen amor*, 14–15, st. 17–18. In the *Libro de buen amor*, however, the tenor of Ruiz's moral message is much more ambivalent, whereas Benvenist is explicit about his sincere moral agenda.

59. Bernstein, *Rivers*; C. Roth, "Elegy"; Pagis, "Dirges"; van Bekkum, "O Seville!"

60. Baer, *History* 2:134–137. Targarona Borrás discusses specific examples of Hebrew poets who denounce the apostates in verse. Targarona Borrás, "Últimos," 261–262. On literary correspondence between Jews and apostates in the fifteenth century, see also Sáenz-Badillos, "Intelectuales."

61. Baer, *Juden* 2:150; N. Roth, *Conversos*, 47.

62. "*Que pudia subir estando judio de rabi en suso? Agora so jurado en cap, y por un enforcadillo ahora me fazen tanta honra, y mando y viedo toda la ciudat de Çaragoça...*" Baer, *Juden* 2:463; English translation in Baer, *History* 2:277.

63. Marcó i Dachs, *Judíos*, 209.

64. Schirmann and Fleischer, *History* 613–614; Huss, "Introduction," 48.

65. See Cole, *Dream*, 300 and 314.

66. Scheindlin "Secular," 35.

67. Gerli, "Estudio," 14.

68. Boase, *Troubadour*, 7–8, 72, and 81.

69. Hillgarth, *Kingdoms* 2:68–69.

70. Eisenberg, "Heterosexual," 252; Deyermond, "Parody," 69–70. Ruiz also anticipates Benvenist's critique of bourgeois culture's threat to conjugal responsibility in the episode of the painter Pitas Payas, who is cuckolded when he leaves his wife alone during an extended business trip. Ruiz, *Libro de buen amor*, 477b.

71. Wacks, *Framing*, 196–200.

72. C. Robinson, *Mediterranean*, 2.

73. Severin, *Tragicomedy*, 23–24. See also Gregory Kaplan's chapter "*Celestina* and *Cárcel de amor* as *Converso* Laments" in Kaplan, *Evolution*, 106–129.

74. Juan Ruiz parodies a number of courtly genres and types in the *Libro de buen amor*, including, for example, the *pastourelle* in which the traveling courtier has an amorous encounter with a beautiful country girl (famously and grotesquely parodied in the *serrana* episodes). Alan Deyermond brings together previous scholarship and explains a number of examples of parody in the text. Deyermond, "Parody." On satire in the *LBA*, see also L. Haywood, *Sex*, 114; Casillas, "Serranas"; Gerli, *Celestina*, 34. For a full study of Calisto's problematic relationship with the courtly love tradition, see J. Martin, *Fools*, 71–124.

75. Biale, *Eros*, 92–95; Rosen, *Unveiling*, 122.

76. *Holy Letter,* 66–67.

77. *Ibid.,* 140 and 143–145. Compare with the Christian discussion of the Pauline "debt" in which the husband's conjugal duties are viewed as a concession (to nature) rather than as a commandment, as in Judaism. Feldman, *Birth,* 64 and 62. Even the relatively enlightened Aquinas viewed marital sex as "a source of moral and spiritual impurity." Brundage, *Law,* 448. In Benvenist's day most Catholic theologians held that "sexual pleasure in marriage should be feared and shunned." Brundage, *Law,* 503.

78. Dorothy Severin argues that the *alcahuetas* ('go-betweens') in both *Libro de buen amor* and *Celestina* use love potions in order to win the hearts of their respective clients' love objects. Severin, "Relationship." Recipes for several such potions can be found in the pages of the Hebrew *Sefer Ahavat Nashim* (Book of the Love of Women, thirteenth century, circulated in fifteenth-century Spain). See Caballero-Navas, *Book,* 35–39; Schirmann and Fleischer, *History,* 6.

79. Hermes, "Author," 6.

80. Wacks, *Framing,* 231–235.

81. Pagis, "Poetic"; T. Fishman, "Parody"; Rosen, *Unveiling,* 103–123; Jill Jacobs, "Defense"; Matulka, *Novels,* 5–37; Muriel Tapia, *Antifeminismo;* Archer, *Misoginía* and *Problem.*

82. Hamilton, *Representing,* 64.

83. Ibn Shabbetay, *Offering* 2:25, ll. 583–598.

84. Septimus, *Hispano-Jewish,* 61–74; Dobbs-Weinstein, "Maimonidean"; Hamilton, *Representing,* 72.

85. Marie de France, *Lais,* 109–112; Doss-Quinby et al., *Songs,* 151–164; Bruckner Tomaryn et al., *Songs,* 130–133.

86. Frenk Alatorre, *Corpus,* 103–113, nos. 223–244; Rodríguez Puértolas, *Poesía,* 345–346.

87. Sepúlveda, *Romances,* fol. 258.

88. M. Alvar, *Tradicional,* 167, no. 213.

89. Cervantes Saavedra, *Ejemplares,* 97–135.

90. *"Al tehal·lel* passà qui primer donà / sa filla al *zaqén,* qui la·n féu *zoná.* / El *zaqén* se'n va a colgar al *roš ha-mità* / La *ne'arà* lo desperta am gran *geburà* / Lo *zaqén* li·n diu: "Que n'ès tu *sotà*?/ *Šéer we-kesut* n'hauras, mas no pas *'onà*." Riera i Sans, *Cants,* 17. Italicized words are Hebrew as opposed to Catalan. *"Do not profane"* is a reference to Leviticus 19:29: "Do not profane thy daughter, to cause her to be a whore."

91. Benvenist, *Efer and Dina,* 173n264.

92. See Eli Yassif's comments on the assimilation of gender folk novellas into Jewish religious and literary culture. Yassif, *Folktale,* 346.

93. Armistead and Silverman, *Judeo-Spanish,* 12.

6. EMPIRE AND DIASPORA

1. Baer, *Galut,* 64.

2. Ryan Szpiech notes that in medieval narratives of Christian conversion there is a tendency for the personal narratives to "[reflect] the transformation of society." Szpiech, *Conversion,* 32.

3. N. Roth, *Conversos,* 212 and 272. Kamen explains that although the Inquisition technically had no power over unconverted Jews, it was nonetheless instrumental in bringing about their expulsion from Castile and Aragon. Kamen, *Inquisition,* 16–22.

4. *"El gran daño que a los christianos se a seguido e sigue de la participaçion, conbersaçion, comunicaçion que han tenido e tienen con los judios."* Suárez Fernández, *Documentos,* 392, no. 177. Expulsion was, therefore, the result of a fear of the conversos undermining Christianity from within. See Suárez Fernández, *España,* 307.

5. The literature on conversos is vast, and I will not attempt to address all of it here. For general studies, see C. Roth, *Marranos;* Netanyahu, *Toward;* Faur, *Shadow;* Melammed, *Question* and *Heretics;* N. Roth, *Conversos;* Rosenstock, *New Men;*

Márquez Villanueva, *España*; Belmonte Díaz, *Judeoconversos*; Alcalá, *Judeoconversos*. On the Inquisition and the statutes of *limpieza de sangre* see C. Roth, *Spanish*; Netanyahu, *Origins*; Kamen, *Inquisition*; Sicroff, *Limpieza*; Perry and Cruz, *Cultural*.

6. Faur, *Shadow*, 41.

7. Geraldine Brooks does an excellent job of novelizing this problem in the sections of her novel *People of the Book* that are set in fifteenth-century Spain. Brooks, *People*, 217–258; 276–316.

8. Fuchs, "Imperium," 71.

9. Young, *Postcolonialism*, 4.

10. On Ibn Verga's biography, see Neuman, "Historiography"; Cantera Burgos, "Introducción," 5–6; Baer, "Introduction," 8–9; Cano, "Introducción," 9–12. *Shevet Yehudah* has gone through numerous Hebrew editions and has been translated into a number of languages, which attests to its appeal outside of specifically Sephardic readerships. In fact, Matthias Lehmann has argued that it was, before its (partial) translation into Ladino in the nineteenth century, virtually unknown among Ottoman Sepharadim. It has never been translated into English in its entirety. Haim Maccoby has translated Ibn Verga's account of the Disputation of Tortosa; Maccoby, *Trial*, 168–186. Michael Meyer includes two short excerpts in his anthology of Jewish historical writing. Meyer's titles tell us much about how the book has been read by modern Jewish historians: "Why the Jews are Hated" and "The Causes of Jewish Suffering." Meyer, *Ideas*, 110–114. In Spanish, there are two modern translations by Francisco Cantera Burgos (1927) and María José Cano (1987), and despite these and the existence of an Early Modern Spanish translation (Amsterdam 1744), it has for the most part evaded the Hispanist gaze. See also Matthias Lehmann's comments on the excerpts of *Shevet Yehudah* included in Ladino works of historiography in the 1840s. Lehmann, *Ladino*, 177–180.

11. The major studies on *Shevet Yehudah* are Baer, *Untersuchungen*; Cantera Burgos, "Introducción"; Yerushalmi, *Lisbon*; Neuman, "Historiography"; and Gutwirth, "Expulsion." See also Cantera Montenegro's study of the image of the Jew in *Shevet Yehudah*. Cantera Montenegro, "Negación."

12. Yerushalmi focuses on the relationship between crown and Jews and how this relationship is reflected in the Ibn Verga's portrayal of the 1506 massacre of conversos in Lisbon. He argues that the Jewish archetype of the Just King was so powerful and so crucial to Jewish identity in diaspora that it colors Ibn Verga's representation of events. For example, he essentially absolves Ferdinand of any responsibility for the edict of expulsion, instead shifting the blame onto Isabella. Yerushalmi, *Lisbon*, 50 and 53–54. This transformation is picked up by subsequent Jewish historiographers such as Elijah Capsali, who portrays Isabella as a kind of royal fishwife, browbeating her husband on a daily basis to get rid of the Jews. Yerushalmi, *Lisbon*, 55; Capsali, *Seder*, 63.

13. David, "Exiles," 86.

14. Sáenz-Badillos, "Intelectuales," 273.

15. Faur, *Shadow*, 177.

16. Yerushalmi, *Lisbon*, 39.

17. Ibid., 49.

18. Gutwirth, "Expulsion," 156.

19. Gutwirth, "Duran," 72–74.

20. On Spanish historiographers' imitation of imperial Roman models, Brian Tate writes that the "the *Pax Augusta* becomes, in this way, the *Pax Hispanica*." Tate, *Ensayos*, 292.

21. Abraham Neuman notes that the *Yosippon* is the only work of medieval Hebrew historiography that resembles royal histories, in that its purpose is not to arouse sympathy for Jewish suffering but rather to track historical events. Ibn Verga's reliance on the *Yosippon* suggests that his goals are similarly exceptional among Jewish historiographers. Martin Cohen adds that

until Samuel Usque's *Consolaçam ás tribulaçoens de Israel* (Ferrara, 1553), Ibn Verga
is the first Jewish author to "recuperate"
the original Josephus as a historiographical
source. M. Cohen, "Appendix B," 272. On
the *Yosippon* as historiography, see Reiner,
"Original"; Bowman, "Yosippon"; Dönitz,
"Historiography."

22. Gutwirth, "Expulsion," 148. Robert
Bonfil confirms this tendency in his study
of Italian Jewry in the sixteenth century.
Bonfil, *Life,* 110.

23. Du Bois, *Souls,* 3.

24. Gilroy, *Atlantic,* 127.

25. Mignolo, "Rethinking," 174.

26. Altschul, "Future," 12. Elsewhere
Altschul defends the use of postcolonial
and other cultural critical theories to ana-
lyze medieval cultural production. She
argues that medieval Europe looks more
like the postcolonial world than the ideal
nation state proposed by modern national
philologies, and that medievalists' use of
postcolonial theoretical language is a quite
valid effort to "communicate the relevance
of the Middle Ages in the language of current intellectual capital." Altschul, "Postcolonialism," 590 and 594.

27. D. Boyarin, "Purim," 3.

28. G. Kaplan, *Evolution,* 58.

29. Gerli, "Condition," 3–4.

30. Rosenstock, "Nation," 187.

31. Fraker, *Scope,* 157–161.

32. For a discussion of incipient nationalism in the Spain of the Catholic Monarchs, see Marx, *Faith,* 107–110.

33. Pagden, *Lords,* 29. Pagden further
notes that Augustine had already begun
the conflation of Roman *virtus* (including
a willingness to subordinate one's own
welfare for that of the common good) with
Christian *pietas,* and that it was a simple
matter to apply this concept to a medieval
European framework. Pagden, *Lords,* 30.

34. Pagden, *Lords,* 32.

35. Biersack, "Tradición," 35. This work
had already begun in earnest in Aragon

in the previous century and earlier in the
fifteenth. See Tate, *Ensayos,* 125; Conde
Salazar, "Julio César."

36. *"Pues si Apolonio así se dolía que de los
griegos por yndustria de Tulio la eloqüencia
fuese a los rromanos leuada, quanto más con
rrazón oy los de Ytalia se deuen doler e quexar
que por lumbre y ynjenio deste señor a ellos
sea quitada e trayda a nuestra Castilla . . ."*
Schiff, *Bibliothèque,* 462, cited in Gómez
Moreno, *Humanistas,* 141. Other writers,
including Antonio de Nebrija, echoed de
Burgos's lionization of Santillana as the
orchestrator of the "modern" *translatio
imperii.* See Gómez Moreno, *Humanistas,*
143–145.

37. Biersack, "Tradición," 37.

38. Anthony Marx argues that the Catholic Monarchs were successful in building
national symbolic capital through administrative centralization and in the creation
of state religion, but stopped short at using
print technology to stimulate national
feeling at the popular level. In his opinion,
the Spain of the Catholic Monarchs was a
sort of laboratory for nationalism but did
not achieve full-fledged nationalism in
the modern sense. Marx, *Faith,* 4, 41–42,
107–110.

39. *"Porque en nuestra súbdita lengua se
leyese lo que vuestro súbdito en los tiempos
antiguos compuso."* Seneca, *Providentia,* 4r,
cited in Gómez Moreno, *Humanistas,* 134.

40. Gómez Moreno, *Humanistas,* 134.

41. Ibid., *Humanistas,* 278–279.

42. Biersack, "Tradición," 34.

43. Ibid., 35.

44. Bonfil critiques Yosef Yerushalmi's
argument that Jews did not write historiography before the sixteenth century,
suggesting that in the first place, neither
Jews *nor* Christians wrote what would be
considered historiography by modern standards, and in the second, many of the texts
that Yerushalmi holds forth as examples
of Jewish historiography likewise do not

fit modern definitions of historiographical writing. Bonfil, "Golden."

45. There is a certain logic at work here. In discussing Ben Elazar we looked at David Biale's theory that national sovereignty is sublimated into rabbinical authority. In the absence of a Jewish government, the rabbinical courts were the highest Jewish authority and, as such, were a sort of royalty without portfolio, awaiting the day when they might serve as royalty for a renewed Jewish polity following redemption. Biale, *Power*, 45 and 57.

46. León Tello, "Introducción," 25–35.

47. Yerushalmi's thesis is that the shock of the expulsion was responsible for the birth of Jewish historiography in the sixteenth century. Yerushalmi, *Zakhor*, 33–36; Ray argues counter to this trend, asserting that Sephardic intellectuals flourished *despite* the trauma of expulsion, not *because* of it. Ray, "Iberian Jewry," 60–61. Robert Bonfil argues against Yerushalmi, noting that much of what Yerushalmi calls "historiography" does not fit most conventional definitions of the genre and that without a sovereign state there cannot be any historiography in the sense of *narratio rerum gestarum*, the narration of great deeds of princes and kings. Bonfil, "Golden," 84.

48. Gutwirth, "Don Ishaq," 650–652.

49. Gutwirth, "Expulsion," 149–150.

50. Castilian humanist Alfonso de Palencia translated the Greek Josephus into Castilian, which makes one wonder if Ibn Verga's citations of the Hebrew Josephus (*Sefer Yosippon*) might actually be from Palencia. Tate and Lawrance, "Introducción," liv. While I think Ibn Verga would have been more likely to consult the Hebrew *Yosippon*, the fact that both Christian and Jewish historians consulted Josephus is emblematic of the moment during which Ibn Verga worked and reinforces the idea of a Sephardic humanism that flourished alongside the Christian humanism of the court of the Catholic Monarchs.

51. Elazar Gutwirth notes Ibn Verga's tendency to mimic the Christian perspective. Gutwirth, "Expulsion," 148.

52. There are a few exceptional cases of (unconverted) Jews in imperial service living in newly acquired territories. The Cansino family, originally from Seville, served as translators in Spanish Oran from its conquest in 1509 until the expulsion of Jews from that territory in 1669. Jacob Cansino even lived openly as a Jew for several years in Madrid, a fact that did not pass unnoticed by a literary figure such as Quevedo. Hillgarth, *Mirror*, 198. On the Jews of Spanish Oran see also Alonso Acero, "Aceptación," and Hirschberg, *History* 1:58–68.

53. Kamen opens his study with the notion that the formation of a Spanish national identity was a reaction to French occupation under Napoleon. Kamen, *Imagining*, 1.

54. Ibid., 22. Martin Biersack notes that the Catholic Monarchs increasingly sought to project an image of imperial power after 1509 through frequent royal processions and references to classical imperial precedents in official communication. According to Biersack, this symbolic campaign was designed to shore up their position vis-à-vis the Castilian nobility. Biersack, "Tradición," 37–42.

55. According to Julia Kristeva, the subject is formed by establishing its relationship with the object and by excluding that which is neither subject nor object: the abject. The abject is a sort of by-product of the process of subjectivity, of the construction of self-awareness in relation to others. If we can map individual subjectivity onto the body politic, and think of a Spanish imperial identity in terms of individual subjectivity, then the imperial subject is formed by abjecting parts of its self that do not serve the imperial agenda. In Kristeva's words, the abject is that which "does not respect borders, positions, rules" and "disrupts identity, system, order." It is "radically

excluded" in the process of subject formation. Kristeva, *Powers*, 2.

56. Ibid., 1.

57. Ibid., 2.

58. My favorite (though admittedly logically flawed) allegory of the abject came from a student in colleague Leah Middlebrook's graduate seminar, "The Subject of the Subject": the dog walker is the subject, the dog is the object, and the dog's feces are the abject.

59. My understanding of "Sephardic humanism" differs somewhat from that of David Shasha, for whom it is the counterpoint to what he views as the anti-intellectualism of the Ashkenazi majority during medieval and early modern periods. See Shasha, "Sephardic Literature."

60. Graetz, *History*, 6:557.

61. Neuman, *Historiography*, 260.

62. Yerushalmi, *Lisbon*, 50.

63. Gutwirth, "Expulsion," 144.

64. Graetz, *History*, 6:557.

65. For an overview of messianism in rabbinical thought, see Alexander, "Rabbis." On mystical messianism in Spain and in the Sephardic diaspora during the fifteenth and sixteenth centuries, see Goldish, "Patterns" and "Mystical"; Scholem, *Major Trends*, 245–247 and *Messianic* 38–50. For an interesting case study of converso messianism in fifteenth-century Valencia, see Meyerson, "Seeking." Américo Castro argued that this popular Jewish messianism was absorbed by Christian Spaniards, for whom it became an "*importante ingrediente en el ánimo del pueblo hispánico*" (important ingredient in the psyche of the Hispanic people). Castro, *Aspectos*, 23.

66. See Alexander, "Rabbis"; Biale, *Power*, 216; Urbach, *Sages*, 649–690; A. Silver, *Messianic*. On Sephardic immigration to Ottoman Palestine, see David, *Come*.

67. Ibn Verga, *Shevet*, 121, ll. 30–33.

68. Ibid., 122, ll. 6–11.

69. Eleazar Gutwirth has noted Ibn Verga's "attempt to mimic in Hebrew a Spanish Christian mentality and its image of the Jew." Gutwirth, "Expulsion," 148.

70. Ibn Verga, *Shevet*, 30, ll. 22–27.

71. Ibid., *Shevet*, 48, ll. 18–24.

72. In fact, Neuman points out that Ibn Verga selects his materials according to the themes he wishes to emphasize (the political process behind persecution) rather than by any effort to reconstruct history in its entirety. Neuman, *Historiography*, 272.

73. In a note, Cano observes that the description of the Temple Ibn Verga cites from Versoris's letter to Alfonso corresponds to that found in *Yosippon*, chapters 55–58. See also Josephus, *Antiquities*, chapter XV, lines 391–427.

74. Ibn Verga, *Shevet*, 128, ll. 8–10.

75. Ibid., 128, ll. 23–26.

76. The letters to Alfonso attributed to Nicolas Versoris in *Shevet Yehudah* are not extant in the Latin original. Rivet de la Grange et al., *Histoire*, 789.

77. Stinger, *Renaissance*, 238–246.

78. Ibid., 222–223.

79. Gutmann, "Messianic," 129. For messianic references to the Temple in Jerusalem in Jewish liturgy, see Alexander, "Rabbis," 228.

80. The Sicilian humanist Lucio Marineo Siculo, one of the most important proponents of Latin humanism in Spain during the reign of the Catholic Monarchs, brought this tradition to Iberia in his *De Hispaniae Laudibus*, modeled after Leonardo Bruni's *Laus Florentinae urbis*. According to Teresa Jiménez Calvente, these humanist studies equate the glories of current states with that of the ancient states that preceded them. Jiménez Calvente, "Teoría," 203. In 1530 *De Hispaniae Laudibus* was translated into Castilian with the title *De las cosas memorabiles de España*.

81. "*Vestigios admirables de un pasado clásico que se elevaba a categoría de mito cultural para el presente.*" Gómez Moreno, *Humanistas*, 256.

82. Goldhill, *Temple*, 59.

83. Chyutin, *Architecture,* 169–180.

84. Ezra deals with the question of the restoration of the Temple as a political issue in the context of how the returned exiles to Judea navigate life under a colonial administration. When the local governor, Tattenai, attempts to block construction of the Temple and intimidate the returned exiles who are managing the project, Ezra relates that they were able to secure a letter from King Darius himself authorizing the completion of the Temple. Darius adds (in Ezra 6:11) that any who would threaten the project would be tied to one of the beams used to build the Temple and publicly flogged in addition to losing his own property. Coggins, *Ezra,* 32–37.

85. For example, Isaac Abravanel relies on Josephus in his historical writing. Gutwirth, "Humanism," 644. Samuel Usque's *Consolaçam ás tribulaçoens de Israel* (Consolation for the Tribulations of Israel) draws on both Josephus and *Yosippon* without appearing to distinguish between the two. M. Cohen, "Appendix B," 271.

86. Alexander, "Rabbis," 237.

87. Melammed dedicates chapters of her study to the communities of conversos in Portugal and in Italy. Melammed, *Question,* 51–69 and 109–133.

88. See, for example the following entries: Parashat Shemot, Friday, 18 Tevet, "Then I will favor you with being burned to sanctify my Name." Karo, *Magid,* 48; trans. Skaist, 123. Parashat Beshalach, Eve of the Sabbath day, 11 Shevat: "Afterward you will be burned to sanctify my name and you will depart like pure wool and go to rest as your lot at the end of days." Karo, *Magid,* 61; trans. Skaist, 154.

89. Werblowsky, *Karo,* 98.

90. Dunn, *Picaresque,* 163.

91. Ray, "Iberian," 60.

92. Werblowsky, *Karo,* 87–88. On the Safed mystics, see also Schechter, "Safed"; Fine, *Safed* and "New Approaches."

93. On the doctrine of *galut ha-shekhinah,* see chapter 1, note 76.

94. Karo, *Magid,* 19, cited and translated by Elior, "Exile," 16. The account is related by Karo's teacher of Kabbalah, Solomon Alkabetz, in a letter published as an introduction to the 1645 Lublin edition of the *Magid.* See also the English translation of K. Skaist in Karo, *Preacher* (unpaginated preface).

95. Elior, "Exile," 16. One wonders if this turn in the human-divine relationship concerning prophecy and revelation might have been developed under the influence of Christian theology. In a parallel example, Arthur Green has suggested that the Jewish doctrine of the divine feminine represented by the Shekhinah was a response to Marian devotion. See Green, "Shekhinah." Harvey Hames has also written on the connections between Franciscan Joachimite millenarianism and the Kabbalah of Abraham Abulafia. Hames, *Angels.*

96. Elior notes that the messianic formulations of the great kabbalist Isaac Luria (transmitted by his student Haim Vital) represented a "comprehensive breach of restraint which was motivated by eschatological speculation." Elior, "Exile," 22.

97. It is possible that an influx of conversos who had returned to Judaism in the Ottoman Empire had introduced some ascetic practices from Spanish Catholicism. Goldish, "Patterns."

98. Karo, *Magid,* 2; trans. Fine, *Safed,* 56.

99. Goldish, "Patterns," 50–51.

100. Netanyahu, *Abravanel,* 216–226.

101. Levy, *Sephardim,* 20–21.

102. Rachel Elior writes that "Karo broke the boundaries of divine–human relations by reversing the traditional order of the subject of redemption." Elior, "Exile," 22. In the following century Isaac Luria and his followers would develop this doctrine and place it at the center of their theosophy. Subsequent movements such as the Lubavitcher Hasidim have further

developed the idea and made it a central part of their spiritual practice. Modern mainstream Judaism has tended to minimize messianic thinking and Kabbalah in general. On messianism in the context of modern Zionism see Ravitzky, *Messianism*.

103. L. Jacobs, "Introduction," 37.

104. Cordovero, *Palm Tree*, 91–92; Hebrew in Cordovero, *Tomer*, 22.

105. Cordovero, *Palm Tree*, 117; Hebrew in Cordovero, *Tomer*, 28.

106. Cordovero, *Palm Tree*, 94, Hebrew in Cordovero, *Tomer*, 24.

107. That is, if the people of Israel suffer exile for not keeping the *mitzvot* (commandments), they should be able to work toward redemption by keeping them. This is the basic premise of Maimonidean (and Averroist) rationalism, what the Mu'tazilite rationalists called the *wa'd wa-l wa'īd* (the threat and the promise). God grants us freedom of decision ("free will") to enable us to *choose* the correct path, for which we are rewarded. If we were not free to choose between right and wrong, then it would be unjust of God to punish us for our misdeeds and reward our good deeds. On the Mu'tazilite doctrine, see Peters, *Created*.

7. READING *AMADÍS* IN CONSTANTINOPLE

1. Avalle-Arce, *Amadís*, 94–98.

2. Entwistle, *Arthurian*, 12, 119.

3. Ibid., 15.

4. Ibid., 31

5. Avalle Arce dates the primitive, manuscript version of Amadís, which circulated in three books, to ca. 1290. Avalle Arce, *Amadís*, 101. Montalvo's *Amadís de Gaula* (books 1–4) came out in no fewer than twenty editions between 1508 and 1588. This makes it the most published Spanish chivalric novel in the sixteenth century, leaving aside for the moment the very many translations into languages other than Spanish. Book 5 of Montalvo's cycle, *Las sergas de Esplandían*, went

through ten editions between 1510 and 1588, and *Palmerín* (part 1) went through thirteen editions between 1511 and 1581. Lucía Megías, *Imprenta*, 259–262 and 597–598; Wilkinson, *Iberian*, 641–644. On the reception of Rodríguez Montalvo's *Amadís* see Cacho Blecua, "Introducción," 197–206.

6. "—*Parece cosa de misterio ésta, porque, según he oído decir, este libro fue el primero de caballerías que se imprimió en España, y todos los demás han tomado principio y origen de éste, y así, me parece que, como a dogmatizador de una secta tan mala, le debemos sin excusa alguna condenar al fuego.*

—*No señor,—dijo el barbero—, que también he oído decir que es el mejor de todos los libros que de este género se han compuesto; y así, como a único en su arte, se debe perdonar.*

—*Así es verdad—dijo el cura—, y por esa razón se le otorga la vida por ahora. Veamos estotro que está junto a él.*" Cervantes Saavedra, *Don Quijote*, 61; trans. Cervantes Saavedra, *Don Quixote*, Grossman, 46.

7. "*¿Hay más sino mandar Su Majestad por público pregón que se junten en la corte para un día señalado todos los caballeros andantes que vagan por España, que aunque no viniesen sino media docena, tal podría venir entre ellos, que solo bastase a destruir toda la potestad del Turco? Estenme vuestras mercedes atentos y vayan conmigo. ¿Por ventura es cosa nueva deshacer un solo caballero andante un ejército de doscientos mil hombres, como si todos juntos tuvieran una sola garganta o fueran hechos de alfenique? Si no, díganme cuántas historias están llenas de estas maravillas. ¡Había, en hora mala para mí, que no quiero decir para otro, de vivir hoy el famoso don Belianís o alguno de los del innumerable linaje de Amadís de Gaula! Que si algunos de éstos hoy viviera y con el Turco se afrontara, a fe que no le arrendara la ganancia.*" Cervantes Saavedra, *Don Quijote*, 552; Cervantes Saavedra, *Don Quixote*, trans. Grossman 461.

8. To give you an idea as to the symbolic weight of the Amadís franchise, it is worth noting that California is named for Montalvo's fictional Kingdom of Amazon Warriors ruled by the Queen Calafia, which features in the first sequel, the *Adventures of the Very Brave Knight Esplandián, Son of Amadís*. See Ruth Putnam's exhaustive study of the history of the toponym "California," which includes a section on the sixteenth-century Spanish context. Putnam, *California*.

9. Tate, *Ensayos*, 292.

10. Biersack, "Tradición," 41–42.

11. Rojinksy, *Companion*, 119–120. The Donation of Constantine (proved in the mid-fifteenth century to be a forgery by the Italian humanist Lorenzo Valla) was a letter from Emperor Constantine that conferred spiritual authority over his imperial subjects to the church, thereby fusing to a certain degree the powers of state and church by which the state might become an instrument of salvation. Pagden argues that one of the aims of the Catholic Monarchs' historiographers was to replicate this model of political and spiritual legitimacy. See Pagden, *Lords*, 32.

12. Fifteenth-century humanists in Italy and Spain had produced several editions and translations of classical inventories of the deeds of great men, and historiographers took this material "seriously" as source material. Burke, "Exemplarity," 51. Historians such as Fernán Pérez de Guzmán (*Generaciones y semblanzas*) and Fernando del Pulgar (*Claros varones de Castilla*) were its most important innovators, introducing the discourse and the biographical portrait to the new style of chronicle. Domínguez Bordona, "Introducción," xvii-xviii. According to Deyermond, medieval authors inflected classical models of literary exemplarity in a broad spectrum of genres and approaches. Deyermond, "Ejemplaridad." Pontón adds that authors often pressed their historical *exempla* into the service of a given regime. Pontón, "Ejemplaridad." This trend is reflected in the prologue to the Venice edition of *Amadís*, where the protagonists' deeds are framed in terms of historical exemplarity. Binotti, "Humanistic," 87.

13. Leviant, *Artus*, 11; Hebrew text on page 10. On fictionality in medieval Hebrew prose, see Drory, *Models*, 22–27.

14. "*Pues si en el tiempo destos oradores, que más en las cosas de la fama que de interesse ocupavan sus juizios y fatigavan sus spíritus, acaesciera aquella santa conquista que el nuestro muy esforçado Rey hizo del reino de Granada, ¡cuántas flores, cuántas rosas en ella por ellos fueran sembradas, assí en lo tocante al esfuerço de los cavalleros, en las rebueltas, escaramuças y peligrosos combates y en todas las otras cosas de afruentas y trabajos, que para la tal Guerra se aparejaron, como en los esforçados razonamientos del gran Rey a los sus altos hombres en las reales tiendas ayuntados, y las obedientes respuestas por ellos dadas, y sobre todo, las grandes alabanças, los crescidos loores que meresce por haver emprendido y acabado jornada tan cathólica!*" Rodríguez de Montalvo, *Amadís*, 219–220.

15. The Catholic Monarchs were hardly the first Iberian Christian rulers to benefit from papal support of domestic crusades. Even before the First Crusade, Pope Alexander II (1062–1073) established the Christian campaigns in al-Andalus as holy wars, in which participation might be repaid by remission of sins and relief from penance. O'Callaghan, *Reconquest*, 24–26. As in the case of the campaigns in the Eastern Mediterranean, such indulgences sweetened the deal for knights from abroad (England, France, etc.) who came to the aid of Navarre, Aragon, and Castile. Christian knights from as far away as Denmark came to assist Sancho I in the siege of Silves in 1189, and this was by no means the exception in the major battles of the Christian

conquest of al-Andalus. O'Callaghan, *Reconquest*, 58–59.

16. This idea of a city as object of desire is best exemplified by the Spanish ballad "Abenámar," in which King Juan II is portrayed as being in love with Granada, which he wishes to conquer. Díaz Roig, *Romancero*, 93–94.

17. Díaz Mas notes that many of the official chroniclers of the Catholic Monarchs gloss over the Ottoman question and that some ignore it completely. However, literary sources of the times give voice to Iberian memories and anxieties of struggle with the Turks and the desire to recuperate Constantinople, notably in the fifteenth-century Catalan romance *Curial e Güelfa*, and most pointedly in *Tirant lo Blanc*. Díaz Mas, "Eco," 343–344. For a thorough study of how Aragonese concerns (as expressed in royal chronicles of the thirteenth and fourteenth centuries) in the Eastern Mediterranean are mapped onto *Tirant* and *Curial*, see Piera, "Tirant."

18. Rodríguez de Montalvo, *Sergas*, 696–698. The narrator of *Sergas* makes frequent exhortations in favor of Christian unity before the Turkish menace. Giráldez, *Sergas*, 24–25. According to Susan Giráldez, this reflects contemporary concerns of an Ottoman invasion in Iberia (the Ottomans had successfully taken the Italian city of Taranto in 1471) and the belief that the Great Schism had weakened Christianity. Consequently, it fell to Latin Christendom to reverse the trend by conquering now-Ottoman Byzantium. Giráldez, *Sergas*, 23–24.

19. María José Rodilla León lists at least six protagonists of medieval and early modern chivalric romances who were crowned emperor of Constantinople: "*Partinoples, Tirante, Esplandían, Palmerín de Olivia, Primaleón y Claribalte.*" Rodilla León, "Troya," 307–308.

20. Susan Giráldez has argued that these innovations were inspired by changes in the relationship between the Catholic Monarchs and the church and in the increased focus at court on the question of Turkish domination of the Eastern Mediterranean. Giráldez, *Sergas*, 19–27.

21. Susan Giráldez points out that ever since 1481, Aragonese writers were preoccupied by the possibility of a Turkish invasion of the Peninsula. Giráldez, *Sergas*, 24.

22. "*El dolor de la perdición de Constantinopla, que el turco avya tomado, estava muy rreçiente en los coraçones de todos.*" Enríquez del Castillo, *Crónica*, 156. The author is also identified as the poet known as Diego del Castillo in the *Cancionero general*. See Perea Rodríguez, *Estudio*, 53–60.

23. Authors of some thirteenth-century French romances included representations of crusading activities, to cater to the tastes of patrons who had themselves participated in the Fourth Crusade as well as for propagandistic reasons. Trotter, *Crusades*, 169. Bloch notes that chivalry was a product of crusading culture. Bloch, *Law*, 196.

24. In his biography of French crusader Robert Curthose, William Aird points out that successive waves of crusade chronicles demonstrate increasing influence of chivalric romance. Aird, *Robert*, 156. Sharon Kinoshita argues, with more intensity, that historicity and fictionality are difficult to separate in Robert de Clari's *Conquête de Constaninople*. Kinoshita, *Boundaries*, 139.

25. M. Brownlee, "Iconicity," 119.

26. Fuchs, *Romance*, 103.

27. "*Los Buenos enxemplos y doctrinas que más a la salvación nuestra se allegaren. . . . tomemos por alas con que nuestras animas suban a la alteza de la Gloria para donde fueron criadas.*" Rodríguez de Montalvo, *Amadís*, 223.

28. Trotter has studied the propagandistic uses of chivalric romances in promoting upcoming crusades or in backing the claims of authors' patrons to territories in the Eastern Mediterranean. See Trotter, *Crusades*, 127–169.

29. Susan Giráldez describes book 5 of *Amadís,* the *Sergas de Esplandían,* as a work of propaganda. Giráldez, *Sergas,* 4. Imagine if George Lucas introduced the Skywalker dynasty as supersoldiers in service of U.S. interests in the Middle East or elsewhere. The English translator of *Esplandían,* William Little, first coined the Star Wars analogy in 1992, calling Luke Skywalker "a kind of Esplandían redivivus." Little, "Introduction," 21. A more direct analogy might be the deployment of comic book heroes such as Captain America in anti-Nazi propaganda during World War II and then as an anti-Communist crusader during the 1950s. See Saemann, *Comics,* 71–72; Dittmer, "Retconning." Recently the creators of *Team America World Police* have made much fun of the idea of a crack team of super soldiers patrolling the world in the name of U.S. interests. See Stone and Parker, *Team America.*

30. Zurita, *Anales,* 736–746. Since the Fourth Crusade of 1204 there had been a constant presence of Aragonese in the Eastern Mediterranean. In a sense this was the first transposition of Iberian holy war beyond the Peninsula. The storied Catalan *almogàvers,* fierce footsoldiers whose military culture developed to serve the needs of Christian campaigns in al-Andalus, were effectively surplused after the frontier between Aragon and al-Andalus was cut off by Castilian expansion. Subsequently they found employment in Sicily, supporting Frederick II, and eventually in Byzantium, where Andronikos II was threatened by the Ottoman Turks. They were the first Europeans to call themselves *conquistadors* (sic. in Catalan). Housley, *Crusades,* 161. On the *almogàvers* see also Hillgarth, *Problem,* 11; Lowe, *Vengeance;* Soldevila, *Almogàvers.*

31. Given the Crown of Aragon's Mediterranean disposition and extensive colonial history in the Eastern Mediterranean, it is logical that the question of Constantinople appears more frequently in Catalan

texts of the fifteenth century. See Díaz Mas, "Eco," 343–344.

32. Even the Hungarian merchant fits the Spanish-Ottoman context as a go-between. Because Hungary had resisted the Mongol invasion and because it actively supported the Pope in fighting the Orthodox Christian heresy, Hungary was considered the Eastern Front of Catholic Europe. This would not have gone unnoticed in Montalvo's time, when Hungary resisted Ottoman incursions. Finkel, *Dream,* 25.

33. "*Por gran dicha paresció en una tumba de piedra, que debaxo de la tierra en una hermita, cerca de Constantinopla fue hallada, y traído por un úngaro mercadero a estas partes de España, en letra y pergamino tan antiguo, que con mucho trabajo se pudo leer por aquellos que la lengua sabían.*" Rodríguez de Montalvo, *Amadís,* 224–225.

34. See, for example, Johnson's posthumous monograph, *Transliterating a Culture: Cervantes and the Moriscos.* In it Johnson goes as far as to say that the binary of the Morisco narrator, Cidi Hamete Benengeli, and the Christian narrator, the fictional Cervantes, serves as the "work's organizing principle." Johnson, *Transliterating,* 203.

35. Fuchs, for example, proposes readings that emphasize "the transatlantic or international dimension of texts previously read within narrow national traditions." Fuchs, "Imperium," 71. Kinoshita questions the usefulness of modern categories of "nationalism, Orientalism, and postcolonialism," calling for "alternate genealogies of a medieval West." Kinoshita, *Boundaries,* 12.

36. Early twentieth-century Spanish Sephardist Ángel Pulido titled his book on Sepharadim *Españoles sin patria* (Spaniards Without a Fatherland). On this tendency, see also Bush, "Beginnings," 14; Wacks, "Spanish?" 324–326. Beckwith notes that Pulido's pro-Sephardism was "superficial" and was predicated on Sepharadim's linguistic assimilation to modern Castilian. Beckwith, "Facing," 186–187. The idea of

Sepharadim as displaced Spaniards justified the use of Sephardic Jews as colonial
administrators in North Africa in the early
twentieth century. See Rohr, "Spaniards."

37. *"Tan profundamente calaron en el
alma de nuestros judíos las raíces de lo español, que los hispano-hebreos, al salir de
España, si bien físicamente la dejaron atrás,
se la llevaron consigo dentro de sus corazones,
y en lejanas tierras, no sólo siguieron viviendo
según nuestros modos, sino que los impusieron
allí donde fueron a establecerse; fenómeno
espiritual y social éste tan perfectamente
español, que acaso sea el que más netamente
defina su honda indentificación con España."*
Pérez Castro, *Aspectos,* 83–84.

38. Ray, "Iberian," 45–47. Avigdor Levy
points out that relatively few Spanish Jews
settled in the Ottoman Empire in 1492.
Most migrated first to Portugal and Italy
and thence to Ottoman lands, once conditions in their first refuge proved intolerable.
Levy, *Sephardim,* 4–6.

39. Levy, *Sephardim,* 23–27, 60–63.

40. Hacker, "Sephardim," 111.

41. Hacker, "Sürgün," 3.

42. Shmuelevitz, *Jews,* 129.

43. Schmelzer, "Hebrew," 261–262
and 264.

44. Seventeenth-century Sephardic
author Immanuel Aboab relates the famous
yet likely apocryphal anecdote. Aboab, *No-
mologia,* 304–305.

45. Nicolay, *Navigations,* 93a, cited in
Levy, "Introduction," 26.

46. Levy, *Sephardim,* 19–20. The imperial discourse of the Catholic Monarchs
was likewise couched in millenarian and
prophetic terms. See Liss, "Isabel," 65.

47. As we have seen in the previous
chapter on Solomon Ibn Verga and Joseph
Karo, converso messianism (and early
modern Jewish messianism in general)
often displayed a curious mix of Christian,
traditional Jewish, and innovative elements. See Goldish, "Patterns," 41–42 and
50–51; Meyerson, "Seeking."

48. Catlos, *Victors;* Ray, "Beyond";
Novikoff, "Between."

49. Dagenais, "Medieval," 55. See also
Menocal, "Beginnings," 71.

50. It is less known that Franco's regime
officially repealed the Edict of Expulsion in
1968. Avni, *Franco,* 202. The Spanish author
Juan Goytisolo famously pointed out that
these acts of contrition did not extend to
the descendants of the Moriscos expelled
from Spain in the early seventeenth century. Goytisolo, "Legado." Daniela Flesler
argues that this unwillingness to "welcome
back" descendants of Andalusis and Moriscos is due to a deeply rooted historical
resentment by which contemporary North
African Muslims are "identified with Arab
and Berber Muslims who colonized the
Iberian Peninsula in A D 711 and were responsible for its Arabization and Islamiza-
tion in the Middle Ages." Flesler, *Return,* 3.

51. Fuchs, "Imperium," 71.

52. On the *sürgün* (cf. *dhimma*) system in the sixteenth century, see Hacker,
"Sürgün."

53. For example, if the Sepharadim
had arrived in Istanbul in 1933, things
would have been different. As it happens,
a group of German Jews did in fact spend
the thirties and forties in Istanbul working as academics. Their presence there was
often heralded as a kind of reenactment of
the storied arrival of the Sepharadim after
the 1492 expulsion. What was similar was
that the Jewish academics were seen as a
valuable resource in bringing Turkish universities up to date. See Kader Konuk's fascinating study of Erich Auerbach's years in
Istanbul, precisely when he was developing
his influential theory of *mimesis.* Konuk,
Auerbach.

54. Some of these ballads are sung
well into the twentieth century. Samuel
Armistead and the late Joseph Silverman
record a robust tradition of ballads featur-
ing the exploits of *Don Amadí, Amalvi,* and

other variants. Armistead and Silverman, "Amadís," 29–30.

55. *Palmerín de Olivia* (Salamanca 1511). See the modern edition of María Marín Piña. Malachi, *Loving,* 39. Di Lonzano's text, the moralistic poem *Tovah Tokhehat* (The Best of Remonstrations) found in his *Shete yadot* (Two Hands), a modern facsimile of the 1618 Venice edition. Lonzano, *Shete yadot,* f. 135v. Minna Rozen points out that Lonzano likely took the reference from the scene in *Don Quijote* where the barber and the priest discuss which is the superior knight, Palmerín of England or Amadís of Gaul. Rozen, *History,* 268–269; Cervantes Saavedra, *Don Quijote,* 64–65.

56. Markova, "Fragmento," 160.

57. Piccus, "Corrections," 210n4.

58. Based on a painstaking comparison of passages from both versions, Jules Piccus concludes that Algaba's translation of *Amadís* is based on a received manuscript rather than on Montalvo's edition. Piccus provides a lengthy series of examples where the Hebrew translation differs from Montalvo's text and, in at least one case, where Algaba's translation is correct where Montalvo errs. However, I find Piccus's argument ultimately unconvincing. Many of the suppressions and corrections of the missing manuscript from which he argues Algaba worked could just as well have been additions and innovations introduced by Algaba, whose audience was less likely to favor Rodríguez de Montalvo's prim, moralizing narrative voice. See Piccus, "Corrections."

59. Ibid., 187–188.

60. Ibid., 201. One wonders whether this elocution of Algaba's *motsi' ruhot me-lematah* (I brought forth winds from below) is one of the first farts represented in the Hebrew language. One precedent was brought to my attention by Shamma Boyarin and is found in the medieval Alphabet of Ben Sira (eleventh century). The tale explaining the letter *het* includes a princess who suffers from a case of chronic flatulence. Although

the Hebrew verb for flatulence is somewhat ambiguous and can refer to sneezing or passing gas, Gili Orr explains that at least one of the manuscripts makes it clear that the princess suffers from the latter. See Yassif, *Tales,* 234–245, and Orr, "Alpha Beta," 7n6.

61. S. Mishra, *Diaspora Criticism,* 41. See also chapter 1, n14.

62. The Hebrew press at Constantinople attracted printers and writers from the surrounding region, and its books were destined not just for the Jews of the Ottoman Empire but for the entire community beyond Turkey. Ya'iri, *Printing,* 12.

63. Other than Moshe Almosnino's *Regimiento de la Vida* and *Tratado de los suenyos* (Salonika 1564) and *Extremos y grandezas de Constantinopla* (actually an excerpt of Almosnino's inedited *Crónicas otomanas* published only in a transliteration by Jacob Cansino in Oran in 1638), very few (if any) secular volumes in Ladino were published during the sixteenth century.

64. On the Hebrew book in Italy, see Hacker and Shear, *Hebrew Book.* On the Hebrew press in Constantinople, see Ya'iri, *Printing.* Wilkinson also lists a number of titles printed in Judeo-Spanish in Salonika, all of which are later than Algaba's translation. Wilkinson, *Iberian,* 817.

65. For example, within some twenty years of their arrival in Istanbul, Sephardic Jews came to dominate the local financial and mercantile sectors. Levy, *Sephardim,* 23.

66. Joseph Dan argues very forcefully that it was Algaba's translation of *Amadís de Gaula,* and not the novels of the eighteenth- and nineteenth-century *maskilim* (proponents of the *Haskalah* or Hebrew Enlightenment), that was "the first European novel to see light in Hebrew clothes in print." Dan, "First," 188. As such arguments often do, Dan's takes on a political cast in which he accuses the Ashkenazi- (Eastern European Jewish) dominated Israeli liter-

ary establishment of revisionism: "There is no truth in the claim that it was the Jews of Ashkenaz that brought European culture to the tents of Israel." Dan, "First," 181.

67. On the Ibn Tibbon family, see J. Robinson, "Ibn Tibbon."

68. The anonymous translator of *Melekh Artus* felt it necessary to write a lengthy apology for his work of secular fiction, despite the fact that (as the editor of the text points out) Sephardic authors had cultivated secular fiction for over a century by the time the Hebrew Arthur appeared in Italy in 1279. Like Algaba, he was careful to de-Christianize the text and to insert numerous biblical and Talmudic allusions in order to make the romance more palatable to Jewish literary sensibilities. See Leviant, *King Artus*, 61–72. See also Drukker, "Arthurian."

69. Piccus, "Corrections," 187.

70. Rodríguez de Montalvo, *Amadís*, 235; *'Alilot ha-abir*, trans. Algaba, 7. This change follows the trend we have observed in Ben Elazar and elsewhere of Jewish authors modifying the conventions of chivalric discourse to reflect their own political values.

71. Rodríguez de Montalvo, *Amadís*, 276; *'Alilot ha-abir*, trans. Algaba, 28.

72. On de-Christianization in the Sephardic romancero, see Armistead and Silverman, "Christian." They note elsewhere that by contrast, "Judaization," or the substitution of Jewish terminology and concepts for specifically Christian terms, is relatively rare. Armistead and Silverman, *En torno*, 138.

73. Compare to the original biblical language in Genesis 34:2: *vayikah otah vayishkav otah vaya'neha* (he took her and lay with her by force), and its more euphemistic gloss in the Sephardic ballad, "El Robo de Dina": *Ayegóse más a eya, hizo lo que non es razón* (he came closer to her, and did that which is not right). Armistead and Silverman, *New York*, 31 v. 11.

74. Montalvo writes simply *mandóla quemar* (he ordered that she be burned), while Algaba moralizes a bit, drawing on the context of the biblical allusion to the death of Jezebel (1 Kings 9:30–37, especially 33): "'Drop this accursed woman!' And so they dropped her from a high tower and she died in all of her wickedness (*b'rov rasha'tah*)." Rodríguez de Montalvo, *Amadís*, 301; *'Alilot ha-abir*, trans. Algaba, 42.

75. This language is drawn from Joseph Karo's discussion of kosher butchery in the *Shulhan Arukh*. Karo, *Shulhan 'Arukh, Yoreh de'ah*, 55:1.

76. Eisenberg notes that Carlos V promoted the popularity of the chivalric novel through his personal interest in it as well as his enthusiastic support for tournaments and "chivalric spectacle." Eisenberg, *Romances*, 95.

77. Rodríguez de Montalvo, *Amadís*, 227; *'Alilot ha-abir*, trans. Algaba, 1.

78. Rodríguez de Montalvo, *Amadís*, 307.

79. Rodríguez de Montalvo, *Amadís* 306; *'Alilot ha-abir*, trans. Algaba, 46.

80. *"En esta cruz y espada con que la orden de cavallería recebí."* Rodríguez de Montalvo, *Amadís*, 234; *'Alilot ha-abir*, trans. Algaba, 6.

81. Rodríguez de Montalvo, *Amadís*, 235; *'Alilot ha-abir*, trans. Algaba, 7. Compare to Todros Abulafia's rendering of the concept of noble or high-born above, chapter 3, pages 158–161.

82. "Mi juizio no puede resistir aquellos mortales deseos de quien cruelmente es atormentado." Rodríguez de Montalvo, *Amadís*, 384; *'Alilot ha-abir*, trans. Algaba, 89.

CONCLUSION

1. Norman Roth discusses the problem of 'Sephardic literature,' paying special attention to the lack of studies on medieval Hebrew literature by Sephardim. Roth, "Sephardic literature." The title of Jonathan Ray's recent book, *After Expulsion: The*

Making of Sephardic Jewry, suggests that
Sephardic Jewry was as-yet unmade before
1492.

2. See den Boer, *Sephardic Editions* and
Literatura.

BIBLIOGRAPHY

'Abbadi, Ahmad Mukhtar 'Abd al-Fattah. *Los eslavos en espana.* Trans. Francisco de la Granja Santamaría. Madrid: Instituto Egipcio de Estudios Islamicos, 1953.

Aboab, Imanuel. *Nomología, o, discursos legales.* Ed. Moisés Orfali Levi. Salamanca: Ediciones Universidad de Salamanca, 2007.

Abrahams, Israel. *The Book of Delight, and Other Papers.* New York: Arno Press, 1980. First published 1899 by America, 1899.

———. *Jewish Life in the Middle Ages.* College edition. New York: Atheneum, 1981.

Abulafia, Todros Ha-Levi ben Yehudah. *The Garden of Parables and Saws: A Collection of Poems* [Hebrew]. Ed. David Yellin. Jerusalem, 1932.

———. *Shirim* [Hebrew]. Ed. Israel Levin. Tel-Aviv: Tel Aviv University, 2009.

Aird, William. *Robert Curthose, Duke of Normandy.* Woodbridge, UK: Boydell and Brewer, 2007.

Akehurst, F. R. P., and Judith M. Davis. *A Handbook of the Troubadours.* Berkeley: University of California Press, 1995.

al-Harizi, Judah. *The Book of Tahkemoni: Jewish Tales From Medieval Spain.* Trans. David Simha Segal. London: Littman Library of Jewish Civilization, 2001.

———. *Judah's Travels: Five Chapters from Al-Harizi's Egyptian Travels* [Hebrew]. Ed. Joseph Yahalom and Joshua Blau. Jerusalem: Hebrew University, 2002.

———. *Tahkemoni.* Ed. Israel Zamora and Israel Toporovsky. Tel Aviv: Mehaberot Lesifrut, 1952.

———. *The Takhkemoni.* Trans. Victor Reichert. Jerusalem: Raphael Haim Cohen, 1965.

al-Tha'alibi, 'Abd al-Malik ibn Muhammad. *Yatimat al-dahr, fi mahasin ahl al-'asr.* 5 vols. Ed. Mufid Muhammad Qumayhah. Beirut: Dar al-Kutub al-'Ilmiyah, 1983.

Alarcos Llorach, Emilio. "La lengua de los *Proverbios morales* de don Sem Tob." *Revista de Filología Española* 35 (1951): 249–309.

Alba Cecilia, Amparo. "El debate del cálamo y la espada, de Jacob ben Eleazar de Toledo." *Sefarad* 68.2 (2008): 291–314.

———. "Espada vs. cálamo: debates medievales hispánicos." In *Homenaje al Prof. J. Cantera.* Madrid, 47–56: Universidad Computense, 1997.

Alcalá, Angel. *Los judeoconversos en la cultura y sociedad españolas.* Madrid: Trotta, 2011.

Alcalay, Reuben. *A Basic Encyclopedia of Jewish Proverbs, Quotations, and Folk*

Wisdom. New York: Hartimore House, 1973.

Alexander, Philip S. "The Rabbis and Messianism." In *Redemption and Resistance: The Messianic Hopes of Jews and Christians in Antiquity,* ed. Markus N. A Bockmuehl and James Carleton Paget, 227–244. London: T&T Clark, 2009.

Alfonso X. *Primera crónica general de España.* 2 vols. Ed. Ramón Menéndez Pidal. Madrid: Editorial Gredos, 1977.

Alfonso, Esperanza. *Islamic Culture through Jewish Eyes: Al-Andalus from the Tenth to Twelfth Century.* London: Routledge, 2007.

Allen, Roger. *An Introduction to Arabic Literature.* New York: Cambridge University Press, 2000.

Allony, Nehemiah. "The Reaction of Moses Ibn Ezra to 'arabiyya." *Bulletin of the Institute of Jewish Studies* 3 (1975): 19–40.

Almosnino, Moses. *Crónica de los reyes Otomanos.* Trans. Pilar Romeu Ferré. Barcelona: Tirocinio, 1998.

———. *Extremos y grandezas de Constantinopla.* Ed. Jacob Cansino. Madrid: Francisco Martínez, 1638.

———. *Regimiento de la vida; Tratado de los suenyos: (Salonika, 1564).* Ed. John Zemke. Tempe: Arizona Center for Medieval and Renaissance Studies, 2004.

Alonso Acero, Beatriz. "Entre la aceptación y el rechazo: La presencia judía en Orán, 1589–1639." In *Jewish Studies at the Turn of the Twentieth Century: Proceedings of the 6th EAJS Congress,* ed. Judit Targarona Borrás and Ángel Sáenz-Badillos, 430–439. Leiden: Brill, 1999.

Alonso, Alvaro, ed. *Poesía de Cancionero.* Madrid: Cátedra, 1995.

Altschul, Nadia R. "The Future of Postcolonial Approaches to Medieval Iberian Studies." *Journal of Medieval Iberian Studies* 1.1 (2009): 5–17.

———. "Postcolonialism and the Study of the Middle Ages." *History Compass* 6.2 (2008): 588–606.

Alvar, Carlos. *La poesía trovadoresca en España y Portugal.* Madrid: Editorial Planeta; Real Academia de Buenas Letras, 1977.

———. "Poesía y política en la corte alfonsí." *Cuadernos Hispanoamericanos* 410 (1984): 4–21.

———. *Textos trovadorescos sobre España y Portugal.* Madrid: Cupsa, 1978.

Alvar, Manuel, ed. *Poesía tradicional de los judíos españoles.* Mexico City: Porrúa, 1966.

Ancos, Pablo. "The Primary Audience and Contexts of Reception of Thirteenth-Century Castilian *Cuaderna Vía* Poetry." In *Al-Andalus, Sepharad and Medieval Iberia: Cultural Contact and Diffusion,* ed. Ivy A. Corfis and Ray Harris-Northall, 120–135. Leiden: Brill, 2009.

Anglés, Higinio. *La música de las* Cantigas de Santa Maria *del Rey Alfonso el Sabio.* Barcelona: Diputación provincial de Barcelona, 1943.

Arbesú-Fernández, David. "Introduction." *Crónica de Flores y Blancaflor.* 1–47.

———, ed. "La Fazienda de Ultramar." *La Fazienda de Ultramar.* Miami: University of South Florida, 2009–2013. 20 Dec. 2013.

Archer, Robert. *Misoginía y defensa de mujeres: Antología de textos medievales.* Madrid: Cátedra, 2001.

———. *The Problem of Woman in Late-Medieval Hispanic Literature.* London: Tamesis, 2004.

Ardutiel, Shem Tov ben Isaac. *Maase Ha-Rav.* Tel Aviv: Tel Aviv University, 1980.

———. *Proverbios morales.* Ed. Ignacio Gonzalez Llubera. Cambridge: Cambridge University Press, 1947.

———. *Proverbios morales.* Ed. Paloma Díaz Mas and Carlos Mota. Madrid: Cátedra, 1998.

———. *Proverbios Morales.* Ed. Theodore Perry. Madison: Hispanic Seminary of Medieval Studies, 1986.

Arié, Rachel. "Notes sur la maqama andalouse." *Hesperis-Tamuda* 9.2 (1968): 204–205.

Armistead, Samuel G. "A Brief History of Kharja Studies." *Hispania* 70 (1987): 8–15.

———. "Kharjas and Villancicos." *Journal of Arabic Literature* 34.1–2 (2003): 3–19.

———. "El problema de las jarchas." In *Dejar hablar a los textos: Homenaje a Francisco Márquez Villanueva*, ed. Pedro M. Piñero Ramírez, 57–64. Seville: Universidad de Sevilla, 2005.

Armistead, Samuel G., and Joseph H. Silverman. "*Amadís de Gaula* en la literatura oral de los sefardíes." In *La pluma es lengua del alma: Ensayos en honor del E. Michael Gerli*, ed. José Manuel Hidalgo, 27–32. Newark, DE: Juan de la Cuesta Hispanic Monographs, 2011.

———. "Christian Elements and De-Christianization in the Sephardic Romancero." In *Collected Studies in Honor of Américo Castro's Eightieth Year*, ed. Marcel Hornik, 21–38. Oxford: Lincombe Lodge Resarch Library, 1965.

———. *En torno al romancero sefardí: Hispanismo y balcanismo de la tradición judeo-española*. Madrid: Seminario Menéndez Pidal, 1982.

———. *Folk Literature of the Sephardic Jews*. Berkeley: University of California Press, 1971.

———, eds. *Judeo-Spanish Ballads from New York*. Berkeley: University of California Press, 1981.

Armstrong, John Alexander. *Nations before Nationalism*. Chapel Hill: University of North Carolina Press, 1982.

Assis, Yom Tov. *The Jews of Spain: From Settlement to Expulsion*. Jerusalem: Hebrew University Press, 1988.

Atienza, Juan G., and Ricardo Sánchez. *Leyendas del Camino de Santiago: La ruta jacobea a través de sus ritos, mitos y leyendas*. Madrid: Editorial EDAF, 1998.

Avalle-Arce, Juan. Amadís de Gaula: *El primitivo y el de Montalvo*. México: Fondo de Cultura Económica, 1990.

Avni, Haim. *Spain, the Jews, and Franco*. Philadelphia: Jewish Publication Society, 1982.

Baer, Yitzhak. *Galut*. New York: Schocken Books, 1947.

———. *A History of the Jews in Christian Spain*. 2 vols. Trans. Louis Schoffman. Philadelphia: Jewish Publication Society, 1978.

———. "Introduction." In Solomon ibn Verga, *Sefer Shevet Yehudah*, ed. Azriel Shohet, 1–15. Jerusalem: Mossad Bialik, 1946.

———. *Die Juden im christlichen Spanien: Urkunden und Regesten*. 2 vols. Berlin: Akademie-Verlag, 1929.

———. *Untersuchungen über quellen und komposition des Schebet Jehuda*. Berlin: C. A. Schwetschke and Sohn, 1923.

Bailey, Matthew. "A Case for Oral Composition in the *Mester De Clerecía*." *Romance Quarterly* 53.2 (2006): 82–91.

Bakhtin, Mikhail. *Problems of Dostoevsky's Poetics*. Trans. Caryl Emerson. Minneapolis: University of Minnesota Press, 1984.

Balbuena, Monique Rodrigues. "Diasporic Sephardic Identities: A Transnational Poetics of Jewish Languages." Doctoral dissertation. University of California at Berkeley, 2003.

Ballesteros Beretta, Antonio, and Miguel Rodríguez Llopis. *Alfonso X El Sabio*. Barcelona: El Albir, 1984.

Bango Torviso, Isidro Gonzalo. *El Camino de Santiago*. Madrid: Espasa-Calpe, 1993.

Barbour, Stephen. "Nationalism, Language, Europe." In *Language and Nationalism in Europe*, ed. Stephen Barbour and Cathie Carmichael, 1–17. Oxford: Oxford University Press, 2000.

Barcia, Pedro Luis. "Los recursos literarios en los *Proverbios morales* de Sem Tob." *Románica* 9 (1980): 57–92.

———. *El mester de clerecía*. Buenos Aires: Centro Editor de América Latina, 1967.

Baron, Salo Wittmayer. "Ghetto and Emancipation: Shall We Revise the Traditional View?" *Menorah Journal* 14 (1928): 515–526.

———. *A Social and Religious History of the Jews*. 18 vols. New York: Columbia University Press, 1952–1983.

Bataillon, Louis J. *La prédication au XIIIe siècle en France et Italie*. Aldershot-Brookfield, VT: Variorum, 1993.

Bauman, Richard. "Performance." In *Folklore, Cultural Performances, and Popular Entertainments*, ed. Richard Bauman, 41–49. New York: Oxford University Press, 1992.

Baumann, Martin. "Diaspora: Genealogies of Semantics and Transcultural Comparison." *Numen* 47.3 (2000): 313–337.

Beale-Rivaya, Yasmine. "The Written Record as Witness: Language Shift from Arabic to Romance in the Documents of the Mozarabs of Toledo in the Twelfth and Thirteenth Centuries." *La corónica* 40.2 (2012): 27–50.

Beckwith, Stacy N. "Facing Sepharad, Facing Israel and Spain: Yehuda Burla and Antonio Gala's Janus Profiles of National Reconstitution." In *Sephardism: Spanish Jewish History and the Modern Literary Imagination*, ed. Yael Halevi-Wise, 169–188. Palo Alto: Stanford University Press, 2012.

Belmonte Díaz, José. *Judeoconversos hispanos: La cultura*. Bilbao: Ediciones Beta III Milenio, 2010.

Beltrán, Vicenç. "Trovadores en la corte de Alfonso X." *Alcanate: Revista de estudios Alfonsíes* 5 (2006): 163–190.

Ben Elazar, Jacob. *The Love Stories of Jacob Ben Eleazar (1170–1233?)* [Hebrew]. Ed. Yonah David. Tel Aviv: Ramot Publishing, 1992.

———. *Ya'akov ben El'azar, Kitab al-kamil*. Ed. Nehemiah Allony. Jerusalem: American Society for Jewish Research, 1977.

Ben-Shalom, Ram. "Medieval Jewry in Christendom." In *Oxford Handbook of Jewish Studies*, ed. Martin Goodman, Jeremy Cohen, and David Sorkin, 153–192. Oxford: Oxford University Press, 2002.

Ben-Yehuda, Eliezer. *A Dream Come True*. Ed. George Mandel. Trans. T. Muraoka. Boulder: Westview Press, 1993.

Benvenist, Vidal. *The Tale of Efer and Dina* [Hebrew]. Ed. Matti Huss. Jerusalem: Magnes, 2003.

Berger, Michael S. "Toward a New Understanding of Judah Halevi's 'Kuzari.'" *The Journal of Religion* 72.2 (1992): 210–228.

Bernardet. *The Romance of Flamenca: A Provençal Poem of the Thirteenth Century*. Ed. Marion Porter. Trans. Merton Hubert. Princeton: University of Cincinnati, 1962.

Bernstein, Simon. *By the Rivers of Sefarad* [Hebrew]. Tel Aviv: Hotsaat Mahberot le-Sifrut, 1956.

Besserman, Lawrence. "Introduction." In *Sacred and Secular in Medieval and Early Modern Cultures: New Essays*, ed. Lawrence Besserman, 1–16. New York: Palgrave Macmillan, 2006.

Biale, David. "Confessions of an Historian of Jewish Culture." *Jewish Social Studies* 1.1 (1994): 40–51.

———. *Eros and the Jews*. New York: Basic Books, 1992.

———. *Gershom Scholem: Kabbalah and Counter-history*. Cambridge, MA: Harvard University Press, 1979.

———. *Power and Powerlessness in Jewish History*. New York: Schocken Books, 1986.

Biersack, Martin. "Los Reyes Católicos y la tradición imperial romana." *eHumanista* 12 (2009): 33–47.

Bin Gorion, Joseph. *Sefer Yosippon*. Ed. David Gustav Flusser. Jerusalem: Zalman Shazar Center, 1978.

Binotti, Lucia. "Humanistic Audiences: *Novela sentimental* and *Libros de ca-*

ballerías in Cinquecento Italy." *La coróni-ca* 39.1 (2010): 67–113.

Blachère, Régis. "Étude sémantique sur le nom maqama." *Al-Mashriq* 47 (1953): 646–652.

Blasco Orellana, Meritxell, and José Ramón Magdalena Nom de Déu. *Aljamías hebraicorromances en los Responsa de rabí Yishaq bar Séset (RYba"S) de Barcelona.* Barcelona: PPU, 2005.

Bloch, Howard R. *Medieval French Literature and Law.* Berkeley: University of California Press, 1977.

Boase, Roger. *The Origin and Meaning of Courtly Love.* Manchester: Manchester University Press, 1977.

———. *The Troubadour Revival: A Study of Social Change and Traditionalism in Late Medieval Spain.* London: Routledge and Keegan Paul, 1978.

Bohigas Balaguer, Pedro. "Orígenes de la novela caballeresca." In *Historia general de las literaturas hispánicas,* ed. Guillermo Díaz Plaja, 521–537. 5 vols. Barcelona: Barna, 1949. 2:

Bonfil, Robert. "How Golden Was the Age of the Renaissance in Jewish Historiography?" *History and Theory* 27.4 (1988): 78–102.

———. *Jewish Life in Renaissance Italy.* Trans. Anthony Oldcorn. Berkeley: University of California Press, 1994.

Bonner, Anthony. *Songs of the Troubadours.* New York: Schocken Books, 1972.

Bonsenyor, Jafudà. *Llibre de paraules e dits de savis e filosofs.* Ed. Gabriel Llabrés. Palma de Mallorca: Joan Colomar y Salas, 1889.

Bowman, Steven. "*Sefer Yosippon:* History and Midrash." In *The Midrashic Imagination Jewish Exegesis, Thought, and History,* ed. Michael Fishbane, 280–294. Albany: State University of New York Press, 1993.

Boyarin, Daniel. "Purim and the Cultural Poetics of Judaism." *Poetics Today* 15.1 (1994): 1–8.

Boyarin, Daniel, and Jonathan Boyarin. "Diaspora: Generation and the Ground of Jewish Identity." *Critical Inquiry* 19.4 (1993): 693–725.

Boyarin, Jonathan, and Daniel Boyarin. *Powers of Diaspora: Two Essays on the Relevance of Jewish Culture.* Minneapolis: University of Minnesota Press, 2002.

Brann, Ross. *The Compunctious Poet: Cultural Ambiguity and Hebrew Poetry in Medieval Spain.* Baltimore: Johns Hopkins University, 1991.

———. "The Moors?" *Medieval Encounters* 15.2/4 (2009): 307–318.

Brann, Ross, Ángel Sáenz-Badillos, and Judit Targarona Borrás. "The Poetic Universe of Samuel ibn Sasson, Hebrew Poet of Fourteenth-Century Castile." *Prooftexts* 16 (1996): 75–103.

Braude, Benjamin. "The Sons of Noah and the Construction of Ethnic and Geographical Identities in the Medieval and Early Modern Periods." *William and Mary Quarterly* 54.1 (1997): 103.

Braziel, Jana. *Diaspora: An Introduction.* Malden, MA: Blackwell Pub., 2008.

Braziel, Jana, and Anita Mannur. *Theorizing Diaspora: A Reader.* Malden, MA: Blackwell, 2003.

Brener, Ann. *Isaac ibn Khalfun: A Wandering Hebrew Poet of the Eleventh Century.* Leiden; Boston: Brill, 2003.

Brooks, Geraldine. *People of the Book: A Novel.* New York: Viking, 2008.

Brownlee, Kevin, and Marina Scordilis Brownlee. "Introduction." In *Romance: Generic Transformation from Chrétien de Troyes to Cervantes,* ed. Kevin Brownlee and Marina Scordilis Brownlee, 1–22. Hanover: University Press of New England, 1985.

Brownlee, Marina. "Iconicity, Romance and History in the *Crónica Sarracina.*" *diacritics* 36.3–4 (2006): 119–130.

Brubaker, Rogers. "The 'Diaspora' Diaspora." *Ethnic and Racial Studies* 28.1 (2005): 1–19.

Bruckner Tomaryn, Matilda, Laurie
Shepard, and Sarah White, eds. *Songs
of the Women Troubadours.* New York:
Garland, 1995.

Brundage, James A. *Law, Sex, and Christian
Society in Medieval Europe.* Chicago: University of Chicago Press, 1987.

Burke, Peter. "Exemplarity and Anti-
exemplarity in Early Modern Europe." In
*The Western Time of Ancient History His-
toriographical Encounters with the Greek
and Roman Pasts,* ed. Alexandra Lianeri,
48–59. Leiden: Cambridge University
Press, 2011.

Burnett, Charles. "The Institutional Con-
text of Arabic–Latin Translations of the
Middle Ages: A Reassessment of the
'School of Toledo.'" In *Vocabulary of
Teaching and Research between the Middle
Ages and Renaissance,* ed. O. Weijers,
214–235. Turnhout, BE: Brepols, 1995.

Burnett, Charles. "The Translating Activity in Medieval Spain." In *The Legacy
of Muslim Spain,* ed. Salma K. Jayyusi,
1036–1058. Leiden: Brill, 1994.

Burns, Robert I., ed. *Emperor of Culture:
Alfonso X the Learned of Castile and His
Thirteenth-Century Renaissance.* Philadel-
phia: University of Pennsylvannia, 1990.

Bush, Andrew. "Amador de los Ríos and the
Beginnings of Modern Jewish Studies in
Spain." *Journal of Spanish Cultural Stud-
ies* 12.1 (2011): 13–34.

Caballero-Navas, Carmen. The Book of
Women's Love *and Jewish Medieval Lit-
erature on Women,* Sefer Ahavat Nashim.
London: Kegan Paul, 2004.

———, ed. *El libro de amor de mujeres.*
Granada: Universidad de Granada, 2003.

Cabo Aseguinolaza, Fernando, Anxo
Abuín González, and César Domínguez,
eds. *A Comparative History of Literatures
in the Iberian Peninsula.* Amsterdam:
John Benjamins, 2010.

Cacho Blecua, Juan Manuel. "Introducción." In *Amadís de Gaula,* ed. Juan

Manuel Cacho Blecua, 19–225. Madrid:
Cátedra, 1996.

Calvo, Bonifacio. *The Poems of Bonifacio
Calvo.* Ed. and trans. William D. Horan.
The Hague: Mouton, 1966.

Campos, Juana G., and Ana Barella. *Diccionario de Refranes.* Madrid: Real Academia Española, 1975.

Cano, María José. "Introducción." In Solomon ibn Verga, *La vara de Yehudah* (Sefer
Shebet Yehudah), ed. María José Cano,
9–17. Barcelona: Riodpiedras, 1991.

Cantera Montenegro, Enrique. "Negación
de la 'imagen del judío' en la intelectuali-
dad hispanohebrea medieval: el ejemplo
del *Shebet Yehudah.*" *Aragón en la Edad
Media* 14–15.1 (1999): 263–274.

Capellanus, Andreas. *The Art of Courtly
Love.* Trans. John Jay Parry. New York:
Columbia University Press, 1990.

Capsali, Elijah. *El judaísmo hispano según
la crónica hebrea de Rabí Eliyahu Capsali:
Traducción y estudio del "Seder Eliyahu
Zutá," capítulos 40–70.* Trans. Yolanda
Moreno Koch. Granada: Universidad de
Granada, 2005.

———. *Seder Eliyahu Zuṭa.* Ed. Aryeh
Shmuelevitz, Shlomo Simonsohn, and
Meir Benayahu. Jerusalem: Hebrew Uni-
versity, 1975.

Cardenal, Peire. *Poésies complètes du troubadour Peire Cardenal (1180–1278).* Ed. René
Lavaud. Toulouse: É. Privat, 1957.

Cárdenas, Anthony. "Alfonso's Scriptorium
and Chancery: Role of the Prologue
in Bonding the *Translatio Studii* to the
Translatio Potestatis." In *Emperor of
Culture: Alfonso X the Learned and His
Thirteenth-Century Renaissance,* ed. Rob-
ert Ignatius Burns, 90–108. Philadelphia:
University of Pennsylvania Press, 1990.

Carmi, T. *The Penguin Book of Hebrew Verse.*
New York: Viking Press, 1981.

Carpenter, Dwayne. "Alfonso de Valladolid." In *Diccionario filológico de literatura
medieval española: Textos y transmisión,*

ed. Carlos Alvar and José Manuel Lucía Megías, 140–152. Madrid: Castalia, 2002.

———. *Alfonso X and the Jews: An Edition of and Commentary on Siete Partidas 7.24 "De los judíos."* Berkeley: University of California Press, 1986.

Carruthers, Jo. *Esther through the Centuries.* Malden, MA: Blackwell, 2008.

Carter, M. G. "Arabic Grammar." In *Religion, Learning and Science in the Abbasid Period,* ed. M. J. L. Young, J. D. Latham, and R. B. Serjeant, 118–138. Cambridge: Cambridge University Press, 1990.

———. "Lexicography." In *Religion, Learning and Science in the Abbasid Period,* ed. Young, Latham, and Serjeant, 106–118.

Casillas, Wendi. "El significado arquetípico de las serranas en el *Libro del buen amor.*" *La corónica* 27.1 (1998): 81–98.

Castro, Américo. *Aspectos del vivir hispánico: Espiritualismo, mesianismo, actitud personal en los siglos xiv al xvi.* Santiago: Cruz del Sur, 1949.

———. *España en su historia cristianos, moros y judíos.* Buenos Aires: Editorial Losada, 1948.

Catlos, Brian A. "Contexto y conveniencia en la Corona de Aragón: Propuesta de un modelo de interacción entre grupos etno-religiosos minoritarios y mayoritarios." *Revista d'Història Medieval* 12 (2001): 259–268.

———. *The Victors and the Vanquished: Christians and Muslims of Catalonia and Aragon, 1050–1300.* Cambridge: Cambridge University Press, 2004.

Cerquiglini, Jacqueline. "Le clerc et l'écriture: Le 'voir dit' de Guillaume de Machaut et la définition du 'dit.'" *Literatur in der Gesellschaft des Spätmittelalters Recueil d'articles* 1 (1980): 151–168.

Cervantes Saavedra, Miguel. *Don Quixote.* Trans. Edith Grossman. New York: Ecco, 2003.

———. *Don Quijote de la Mancha.* Ed. Francisco Rico. Madrid: Punto de Lectura, 2007.

———. *Novelas ejemplares.* Ed. Harry Sieber. Madrid: Cátedra, 1998.

Chazan, Robert. *Barcelona and Beyond: The Disputation of 1263 and Its Aftermath.* Berkeley: University of California, 1992.

———. *Daggers of Faith: Thirteenth-Century Christian Missionizing and Jewish Response.* Berkeley: University of California, 1989.

———. *Reassessing Jewish Life in Medieval Europe.* New York: Cambridge University Press, 2010.

Chyutin, Michael. *Architecture and Utopia in the Temple Era.* New York: T&T Clark, 2006.

Clements, Robert John, and Joseph Gibaldi. *Anatomy of the Novella: The European Tale Collection from Boccaccio and Chaucer to Cervantes.* New York: New York University Press, 1977.

Clifford, James. "Diasporas." *Cultural Anthropology* 9.3 (1994): 302–338.

Coggins, R. J. *The Books of Ezra and Nehemiah.* Cambridge: Cambridge University Press, 1976.

Cohen, Gerson D. "The Story of the Four Captives." *Proceedings of the American Academy for Jewish Research* 29 (1961): 55–131.

Cohen, Jeremy. *The Friars and the Jews: The Evolution of Medieval Anti-Semitism.* Ithaca: Cornell University Press, 1982.

Cohen, Martin. "Appendix B." *Samuel Usque's Consolation for the Tribulations of Israel (Consolaçam ás tribulaçoens de Israel).* 2nd ed. 269–287. Philadelphia: Jewish Publication Society of America, 1977.

Cohen, Robin. *Global Diasporas: An Introduction.* London: University Collge of London Press, 1997.

Colahan, Clark. "Santob's Debate between the Pen and the Scissors." Doctoral dissertation. University of Washington, 1977.

Cole, Peter. *The Dream of the Poem: Hebrew Poetry from Muslim and Christian Spain,*

950–1492. Princeton: Princeton University Press, 2007.

———. *The Poetry of Kabbalah: Mystical Verse from the Jewish Tradition.* New Haven: Yale University Press, 2012.

Conde Salazar, Matilda. "La obra y la biografía de Julio César en los *Paralipomenon Hispaniae Libri X* de Joan Margarit." *eHumanista* 13 (2009): 14–37.

Connor, Walker. "The Impact of Homelands Upon Diasporas." In *Modern Diasporas in International Politics,* 16–46. New York: St. Martin's Press, 1986.

Cooperson, Michael, and Shawkat M. Toorawa. *Arabic Literary Culture, 500–925.* Detroit: Thomson Gale, 2005.

Cordovero, Moses ben Jacob. *Sefer Tomer Devorah.* Ed. Bentsiyon Vainshtok. Jerusalem: Ahuzat Yisrael, 1969.

———. *The Palm Tree of Deborah.* London: Vallentine Mitchell, 1960.

Corriente, Federico. *Léxico estándar y andalusí del Diwan de Ibn Quzman.* Zaragoza: Universidad de Zaragoza, 1993.

Covarsí Carbonero, Jaime. *Roman de Flamenca.* Murcia: Editum, 2010.

Crónica de Flores y Blancaflor. Ed. David Arbesú-Fernández. Tempe: Arizona Center for Medieval and Renaissance Studies, 2011.

Dagenais, John. "Medieval Spanish literature in the twenty-first century." In *The Cambridge History of Spanish Literature,* ed. David Gies, 39–57. Cambridge: Cambridge University Press, 2004.

Dan, Joseph. *Kabbalah: A Very Short Introduction.* Oxford: Oxford University Press, 2006.

———. "The First Hebrew Novel: Jacob Algabe's *Amadis of Gaul* [Hebrew]." *Moznayim* 45 (1977): 181–188.

David, Abraham. "The Spanish Exiles in the Holy Land." In *The Sephardi Legacy,* ed. Haim Beinart, vol. 2, 77–108. Jerusalem: Magnes Press, Hebrew University, 1992.

———. *To Come to the Land: Immigration and Settlement in Sixteenth-Century Eretz-Israel.* Tuscaloosa: University of Alabama Press, 1999.

Davidson, Herbert A. *Moses Maimonides: The Man and His Works.* New York: Oxford University Press, 2005.

Davidson, Israel. "Introduction." In *Sefer Shaashuim: A Book of Mediaeval Lore,* xv–ci. New York: Jewish Theological Seminary, 1914.

———. *Parody in Jewish Literature,* 1907. Reprint, New York: AMS Press, 1966.

de la Granja, Francisco. "La maqama de la fiesta de Ibn al-Murabi al-Azdi." *Etudes d'orientalisme dedieés a la mémoire de Lévi-Provencal.* Paris: Maisonneuve et Larose, 1962. 591–603.

———. *Maqāmas y risālas andaluzas.* Madrid: Instituto Hispano-Árabe de Cultura, 1976.

———. "Origen árabe de un famoso cuento español." *al-Andalus* 24 (1959): 319–332.

De León, Moses. *The Zohar (Sefer ha-Zohar).* 6 vols. Ed. Daniel C. Matt. Pritzker. Stanford: Stanford University Press, 2004–2010.

———. *Sefer ha-Zohar; 'al hamishah humshe Torah.* Ed. Moses Cordovero. Jerusalem: Ahuzat Yisrael, 1962.

De Looze, Laurence. *Pseudo-autobiography in the fourteenth century: Juan Ruiz, Guillaume de Machaut, Jean Froissart, and Geoffrey Chaucer.* Gainesville: University Press of Florida, 1997.

De Piera, Shlomo ben Meshullam. *Diwan.* Ed. Simon Bernstein. New York: Alim, 1941.

Decter, Jonathan. "A Hebrew 'Sodomite' Tale from Thirteenth-century Toledo: Jacob Ben El'azar's Story of Sapir, Shapir, and Birsha." *Journal of Medieval Iberian Studies* 3 (2011): 187–202.

———. "Changing Landscapes of the Hebrew Rhymed Prose Narrative." In *Studies in Medieval Jewish Poetry: A Message Upon the Garden,* ed. Alessandro Guetta and Masha Itzhaki, 55–67. Leiden: Brill, 2011.

———. *Jewish Iberian Literature: From al-Andalus to Christian Spain*. Bloomington: Indiana University Press, 2007.

Del Barco, Francisco Javier. "Texto hebreo subyacente y variación morfosintáctica en algunas biblias romanceadas." In *Maestra en mucho: Estudios filológicos en honor de Carmen Isasi Fernández*, ed. Sara Gómez Seibane and José Luis Ramírez Luengo, 17–27. Buenos Aires: Voces del Sur, 2010.

Deleuze, Gilles, and Félix Guattari. *Kafka: Toward a Minor Literature*. Minneapolis: University of Minnesota Press, 1986.

Delgado, J. "Nuevas alusiones al *Kitāb al-Kāmil* de Ya'āqob Ben El'azar (edición, traducción y estudio)." *Sefarad* 69.2 (2009): 315–360.

den Boer, Harm. *La literatura sefardí de Amsterdam*. Alcalá de Henares: Universidad de Alcalá, 1995.

———. *Sephardic Editions, 1550–1820: Primary Sources*. Leiden: Brill, 2013.

Denomy, Alexander Joseph. *The Heresy of Courtly Love*. New York: D. X. McMullen, 1947.

Derenbourg, Joseph, ed. *Deux versions hébraïques du livre Kalîlâh et Dimnâh, la première accompagnée d'une traduction française*. Paris: F. Vieweg, 1881.

Deyermond, Alan D. *Epic Poetry and the Clergy: Studies on the* Mocedades De Rodrigo. London: Támesis, 1968.

———. "Ejemplaridad e historia: unas palabras finales." *Diablotexto: Revista de crítica literaria* 3 (1996): 245–260.

———. *Lazarillo de Tormes: A Critical Guide*. London: Grant and Cutler, 1975.

———. "Some Aspects of Parody in the *Libro de buen amor*." Libro de buen amor *Studies*. Ed. G. B. Gybbon-Monypenny, 53–78. London: Tamesis, 1970.

Díaz Esteban, Fernando. "El *Debate del cálamo y las tijeras*, de Sem Tob Ardutiel,

don Santo de Carrión." *Revista de la Universidad de Madrid* 18 (1969): 61–102.

Díaz Mas, Paloma. "El eco de la caída de Constantinopla en las literaturas hispánicas." In *Constaninopla 1453: Mitos y realidades*, ed. Pedro Bádenas de la Peña and Inmaculada Pérez Martín, 318–349. Madrid: Consejo Superior de Investigaciones Cientificas, 2003.

———. "Un género casi perdido de la poesía castellana medieval: la clerecía rabínica." *Boletín de la Real Academia Española* 73.259 (1993): 329–346.

Díaz Mas, Paloma, and Carlos Mota. "Introducción." In *Proverbios Morales,* ed. Díaz Mas, Paloma and Carlos Mota, 9–102. Madrid: Cátedra, 1998.

Díaz Roig, Mercedes, ed. *El Romancero Viejo*. Madrid: Cátedra, 1992.

Díaz y Díaz, Manuel C. *Escritos jacobeos*. Santiago de Compostela: Consorcio de Santiago; Universidad de Santiago de Compostela, 2010.

Dittmer, Jason. "Retconning America: Captain America in the Wake of World War II and the McCarthy Hearings." In *The Amazing Transforming Superhero! Essays on the Revision of Characters in Comic Books, Film and Television*, ed. Terrence R. Wandtke, 33–51. Jefferson, NC: McFarland, 2007.

Dobbs-Weinstein, Idit. "The Maimonidean Controversy." In *History of Jewish Philosophy*, ed. Daniel H. Frank and Oliver Leaman, 331–349. London: Routledge, 1997.

Domínguez Bordona, Jesús. "Introducción." In Fernando del Pulgar, *Claros varones de Castilla*, ed. Jesús Domínguez Bordona, i–xxxii. Madrid: Espasa-Calpe, 1954.

Doñate Sebastià, José María, and José Ramón Magdalena Nom de Déu. *Three Jewish Communities in Medieval Valencia*. Jerusalem: Magnes, 1990.

Dönitz, Saskia. "Historiography among Byzantine Jews: The Case of *Sefer Yosip-*

pon." In *Jews in Byzantium: Dialectics of Minority and Majority Cultures*, ed. Robert Bonfil, 953–970. Leiden: Brill, 2012.

Doody, Margaret. *The True Story of the Novel*. New Brunswick, NJ: Rutgers University Press, 1996.

Dorfman, Eugene. *The Narreme in the Medieval Romance Epic: An Introduction to Narrative Structures*. Toronto: University of Toronto Press, 1969.

Doron, Aviva. "'Dios, haz que el rey se apiade de mí'. Entrelazamiento de lo sacro y lo profano en la poesía hebrea-toledana en el transfondo de la poesía cristiana-española." *Sefarad* 46.1–2 (1986): 151–160.

———. "La poesía de Todros Ha-Levi Abulafia como reflejo del encuentro de las culturas: la hebrea y la española en la Toledo de Alfonso X el Sabio." In *Actas del X congreso de la Asociación Internacional de Hispanistas*, ed. Antonio Vilanova. Barcelona: PPU, 1992. 171–178.

———. *A Poet in the King's Court: Todros Halevi Abulafia, Hebrew Poetry in Christian Spain* [Hebrew]. Tel Aviv: Dvir, 1989.

Doss-Quinby, Eglal, et al. *Songs of the Women Trouvères*. New Haven: Yale University Press, 2001.

Douglas, Mary. *Purity and Danger: An Analysis of Concept of Pollution and Taboo*. London: Routledge, 2005 [1966].

Drory, Rina. "The Maqama." In *The Literature of Al-Andalus*, ed. Maria Rosa Menocal, Michael Sells, and Raymond P. Scheindlin, 190–210. Cambridge: Cambridge University, 2000.

———. *Models and Contacts: Arabic Literature and Its Impact on Medieval Jewish Culture*. Leiden: Brill, 2000.

———. "Words Beautifully Put: Hebrew vs. Arabic in Tenth-Century Jewish Literature." In *Genizah Research after 90 Years: The Case for Judeo-Arabic*, ed. Joshua Blau and Stefan Reif, 53–66. Cambridge: Cambridge University Press, 1992.

Drukker, Tamar. "A Thirteenth-Century Arthurian Tale in Hebrew: A Unique Literary Exchange." *Medieval Encounters* 15.1 (2009): 114–129.

Du Bois, W. E. B. *The Souls of Black Folk*. New York: Bantam Books, 1989.

Duby, Georges. *Love and Marriage in the Middle Ages*. Chicago: University of Chicago Press, 1994.

Dufoix, Stéphane. *Diasporas*. Trans. William Rodarmor. Berkeley: University of California Press, 2008.

Dunn, Peter N. *Spanish Picaresque Fiction: A New Literary History*. Ithaca: Cornell University Press, 1993.

Dutton, Brian. *El Cancionero del siglo XV: c. 1360–1520*. Salamanca: Universidad de Salamanca, 1990.

Eco, Umberto. *Art and Beauty in the Middle Ages*. New Haven: Yale University Press, 1986.

Edwards, Brent. *The Practice of Diaspora: Literature, Translation, and the Rise of Black Internationalism*. Cambridge: Harvard University Press, 2003.

———. "The Uses of Diaspora." *Social Text* 19.1 (2001): 45–73.

Edwards, John. "The Beginnings of a Scientific Theory of Race? Spain, 1450–1600." In *From Iberia to Diaspora: Studies in Sephardic History and Culture*, ed. Yedida K. Stillman and Norman A. Stillman, 179–196. Leiden: Brill, 1999.

Einbinder, Susan L. *Beautiful Death: Jewish Poetry and Martyrdom in Medieval France*. Princeton, NJ: Princeton University Press, 2002.

———. *No Place of Rest: Jewish Literature, Expulsion, and the Memory of Medieval France*. Philadelphia: University of Pennsylvania Press, 2009.

———. "Pen and Scissors: A Medieval Debate." *Hebrew Union College Annual* 65 (1994): 261–276.

———. "A Proper Diet: Medicine and History in Crecas Caslari's *Esther*." *Speculum* 80.2 (2005): 437–463.

Eisen, Arnold. *Galut: Modern Jewish Reflection on Homelessness and Homecoming.* Bloomington: Indiana University Press, 1986.

Eisenberg, Daniel. "Juan Ruiz's Heterosexual 'Good Love.'" In *Queer Iberia: Sexualities, Cultures, and Crossings from the Middle Ages to the Renaissance,* ed. Josiah Blackmore and Gregory S. Hutcheson, 250–274. Durham: Duke University Press, 1999.

———. *Romances of Chivalry in the Spanish Golden Age.* Newark, DE: Juan de la Cuesta, 1982.

Elinson, Alexander. "Contrapuntal Composition in a *Muwashshah* Family, or Variations On a Panegyric Theme." *Medieval Encounters* 7.2/3 (2001): 174–196.

Elior, Rachel. "Exile and Redemption in Jewish Mystical Thought." *Journal of the Interdisciplinary Study of Monotheistic Religions (JISMOR)* 4 (2008): 11–24.

Encyclopedia Judaica CD-ROM Edition (Version 1.0). Jerusalem: Keter; Judaica Multimedia, 1997.

Encyclopedia of Islam CD-ROM Edition. Leiden: Brill, 2004.

Engel, David. "Crisis and Lachrymosity: On Salo Baron, Neobaronianism, and the Study of Modern European Jewish History." *Jewish History* 20.3–4 (2006): 243–264.

Enríquez del Castillo, Diego. *Crónica de Enrique IV de Diego Enríquez del Castillo.* Ed. Aureliano Sánchez Martín. Valladolid: Secretariado de Publicaciones Universidad de Valldolid, 1994.

Entwistle, William. *The Arthurian Legend in the Literatures of the Spanish Peninsula.* New York: Phaeton Press, 1975.

Epstein, Isidore. *The "Responsa" of Rabbi Solomon Ben Adreth of Barcelona (1235–1310) as a Source of the History of Spain.* London, 1925.

Erskine, Noel. *From Garvey to Marley: Rastafari Theology.* Gainesville: University Press of Florida, 2005.

Essa, Ahmed, and Othman Ali. *Studies in Islamic Civilization: The Muslim Contribution to the Renaissance.* Herndon, VA: International Institute of Islamic Thought, 2010.

Even-Zohar, Itamar. "The Position of Translated Literature Within the Literary Polysystem." *Poetics Today* 11.1 (1990): 45–51.

Falaquera, Shem Tov ben Joseph. *The Book of the Seeker.* Trans. Herschel Levine. New York: Yeshiva University Press, 1976.

———. *Epistle of the Debate: Between a Pious Man and a Philosopher, Being Between the Torah and Science* [Hebrew]. Ed. Adolph Jellinek. Jerusalem: Sifriyat Meḳorot, 1969.

Fanjul, Serafín. *Al-Andalus contra España: La forja del mito.* Madrid: Siglo XXI de España Editores, 2000.

Faulhaber, Charles. "*Semitica Iberica:* Translations from Hebrew and Arabic into the Medieval Romance Vernaculars of the Iberian Peninsula." *Bulletin of Spanish Studies* 81 (2004): 873–896.

Faur, José. *In the Shadow of History: Jews and Conversos at the Dawn of Modernity.* Albany: State University of New York Press, 1992.

Feldman, David M. *Birth Control in Jewish Law.* New York: New York University Press, 1968.

Ferrando Frutos, Ignacio. *El dialecto andalusí de la Marca Media: Los documentos mozárabes toledanos de los siglos XII y XIII.* Zaragoza, ES: Universidad de Zaragoza, 1995.

Ferreira, Manuel Pedro. "Andalusian Music and the *Cantigas de Santa Maria.*" In *Cobras e son: Papers on the Text, Music and Manuscripts of the* Cantigas de Santa Maria, ed. Stephen Parkinson, 7–19. Oxford: Legenda, 2000.

Filios, Denise. "Expulsion from Paradise: Exiled Intellectuals and Andalusian Tolerance." In *In the Light of Medieval Spain:*

Islam, the West, and the Relevance of the Past, ed. Simon Doubleday and David Coleman, 91–113. New York: Palgrave Macmillan, 2008.

Fine, Lawrence. "New Approaches to the Study of Kabbalistic Life in 16th-Century Safed." In *Jewish Mysticism and Kabbalah: New Insights and Scholarship,* ed. Frederick Greenspahn, 91–111. New York: New York University Press, 2011.

———. *Safed Spirituality.* New York: Paulist Press, 1984.

Finkel, Caroline. *Osman's Dream: The Story of the Ottoman Empire, 1300–1923.* New York: Basic Books, 2006.

Finnegan, Ruth. *Literacy and Orality: Studies in the Technology of Communication.* Oxford: Blackwell, 1988.

Fishman, Joshua A. *Language and Nationalism: Two Integrative Essays.* Rowley, MA: Newbury House, 1973.

Fishman, Talya. "A Medieval Parody of Misogyny: Judah Ibn Shabbetai's *Minhat Yehudah, Soneh Hanashim.*" *Prooftexts: A Journal of Jewish Literary History* 8.1 (1988): 89–111.

Flesler, Daniela. *The Return of the Moor: Spanish Responses to Contemporary Moroccan Immigration.* West Lafayette, IN: Purdue University Press, 2008.

Fogelquist, James Donald. *El Amadís y el género de la historia fingida.* Madrid: José Porrúa Turanzas, 1982.

Fox, Michael. *Character and Ideology in the Book of Esther.* Columbia: University of South Carolina Press, 1991.

Fox, Robin Lane. *Travelling Heroes: Greeks and Their Myths in the Epic Age of Homer.* London: Allen Lane, 2008.

Fraker, Charles. *The Scope of History: Studies in the Historiography of Alfonso El Sabio.* Ann Arbor: University of Michigan Press, 1996.

Freehof, Solomon. *The Responsa Literature and a Treasury of Responsa.* New York: Ktav, 1973.

Frenk Alatorre, Margit, ed. *Corpus de la antigua lírica popular hispánica (siglos XV a XVII).* Madrid: Castalia, 1987.

Fuchs, Barbara. "Imperium Studies: Theorizing Early Modern Expansion." In *Postcolonial Moves: Medieval Through Modern,* ed. Patricia Clare Ingham and Michelle R. Warren, 71–90. New York: Palgrave Macmillian, 2003.

———. *Romance.* New York: Routledge, 2004.

Fudeman, Kirsten Anne. *Vernacular voices: Language and Identity in Medieval French Jewish Communities.* Philadelphia: University of Pennsylvania Press, 2010.

Funkenstein, Amos. *Perceptions of Jewish History.* Berkeley: University of California Press, 1993.

García Peinado, Miguel Ángel, and Juan Pedro Monferrer Sala. "De poesía y pornografía medievales: Dos muestras, dos ejemplos: Guillermo de Aquitania e Ibn Quzman." *Thélème: Revista complutense de estudios franceses* 13 (1998): 71–86.

Gaunt, Simon. "Romance and Other Genres." In *The Cambridge Companion to Medieval Romance,* ed. Roberta L. Krueger, 45–59. Cambridge: Cambridge University Press, 2000.

Gaunt, Simon, and Sarah Kay, eds. *The Troubadours: An Introduction.* Cambridge: Cambridge University Press, 1999.

Geiger, Abraham. "History of the Radak." *Otsar Nehmad* 2 (1857): 159–173.

Genot-Bismuth, Jacqueline. "Contribution a une recherche sur l'élaboration d'un métalangage de la poétique dans la pratique hébraïque médiévale: L'exploitation du terme meliza." *Sefarad* 41 (1981): 231–271.

———. "La révolution prosodique d'Immanuel de Rome." *Israel Oriental Studies* 9 (1991): 161–186.

Gerli, E. Michael. *Celestina and the Ends of Desire.* Toronto: University of Toronto Press, 2011.

———. "The *Converso* Condition: New Approaches to an Old Question." In *Medieval Iberia: Changing Societies and Cultures in Contact and Transition,* ed. Ivy A. Corfis and Ray Harris-Northall. London: Tamesis, 2007. 3–15.

———. "Estudio preliminar." In *Poesía cancioneril castellana,* ed. E. Michael Gerli, 5–28. Madrid: Akal, 1994.

Gerli, E. Michael, and Julian Weiss, eds. *Poetry at Court in Trastamaran Spain: From the* Cancionero de Baena *to the* Cancionero General. Tempe, AZ: Medieval and Renaissance Texts and Studies, 1998.

Gil, José S. *La escuela de traductores de Toledo y los colaboradores judíos.* Toledo: Diputación Provincial de Toledo, 1985.

Gilroy, Paul. *The Black Atlantic: Modernity and Double Consciousness.* Cambridge, MA: Harvard University Press, 1993.

Giménez Soler, Andrés. *Don Juan Manuel. Biografía y estudio crítico.* Zaragoza, ES: F. Martínez, 1932.

Giráldez, Susan. *Las sergas de Esplandián y la España de los Reyes Católicos.* New York: P. Lang, 2003.

Gitlitz, David M. *Secrecy and Deceit: The Religion of the Crypto-Jews.* Albuquerque: University of New Mexico Press, 2002.

Goitein, S. D., ed. *A Mediterranean Society; The Jewish Communities of the Arab World as Portrayed in the Documents of the Cairo Geniza.* Berkeley: University of California Press, 1967–1993.

Goldhill, Simon. *The Temple of Jerusalem.* Cambridge, MA: Harvard University Press, 2005.

Goldish, Matt. *Jewish Questions: Responsa on Sephardic Life in the Early Modern Period.* Princeton: Princeton University Press, 2008.

———. "Mystical Messianism from the Renaissance to the Enlightenment." In *Jewish Mysticism and Kabbalah: New Insights and Scholarship,* ed. Frederick Greenspahn, 115–138. New York: New York University Press, 2011.

———. "Patterns in Converso Messianism." In *Jewish Messianism in the Early Modern World,* ed. Matt Goldish and Richard Popkin, vol. 1, 41–63. Dordrecht: Kluwer, 2001.

Goldziher, Ignác. *Muslim Studies.* Trans. C. K. Barber and S. M. Stern. Chicago: Aldine, 1968.

Gómez Moreno, Angel. *España y la Italia de los humanistas: Primeros ecos.* Madrid: Editorial Gredos, 1994.

Gómez Redondo, Fernando. "Building a Literary Model: Prose in the Court of Alfonso X (1252–84)." In *A Comparative History of Literatures in the Iberian Peninsula.* ed. Fernando Cabo Aseguinolaza et al, 582–594. Vol. 1. Amsterdam: Benjamins, 2010.

———. *Historia de la prosa medieval castellana.* 3 vols. Madrid: Cátedra, 1998.

González Ollé, Fernando. "El establecimiento del castellano como lengua oficial." *Boletín de la Real Academia Española* 58.214 (1978): 231–282.

González Palencia, Ángel. *El Arzobispo Don Raimundo de Toledo.* Barcelona: Editorial Labor, 1942.

———. *Los mozárabes de Toledo en los siglos XII y XIII.* 3 vols. Madrid: Instituto de Valencia de Don Juan, 1926–1930.

González-Llubera, Ignacio. "Introduction." In Antonio de Nebrija, *Gramática de la lengua castellana,* ed. Ignacio González-Llubera, xiii–lxii. London: Oxford University Press, 1926.

Goytisolo, Juan. "El Legado Andalusí: Una Perspectiva Occidental." In *Ensayos Escogidos,* ed. Adolfo Castañón, 17–22. Mexico City: Fondo de Cultura Económica, 2007.

Graetz, Heinrich. *History of the Jews.* 6 vols. Trans. Bella Löwy. Philadelphia: Jewish Publication Society of America, 1891.

Grande Quejigo, Francisco Javier. "'Quiero leer un libro': Oralidad y escritura en el mester de clerecía." In *La memoria de los libros: Estudios sobre la historia del escrito y de la lectura en Europa y América,* ed. Pedro Manuel Cátedra García, María Isabel Páiz Hernández, and María Luisa López-Vidriero Abello, 101–112. La Rioja: CiLengua, 2004.

Green, Arthur. "Isaac Ibn Sahula's Commentary on the Song of Songs [Hebrew]." In *The Beginnings of Jewish Mysticism in Medieval Thought,* ed. Joseph Dan, 393–491. Jerusalem: Hebrew University, 1987.

———. "The Shekhinah, the Virgin Mary, and the Song of Songs: Reflections on a Kabbalistic Symbol in Its Historical Context." *AJS Review* 26.1 (2002): 2–52.

Grieve, Patricia. *The Eve of Spain: Myths of Origins in the History of Christian, Muslim, and Jewish Conflict.* Baltimore: Johns Hopkins University Press, 2009.

———. Floire and Blancheflor *and the European Romance.* Cambridge: Cambridge University Press, 1997.

Gross, Abraham. *Iberian Jewry from Twilight to Dawn: The World of Rabbi Abraham Saba.* Leiden: Brill, 1995.

Gumbrecht, Hans Ulrich, and Helga Bennett. "Literary Translation and Its Social Conditioning in the Middle Ages: Four Spanish Romance Texts of the 13th Century." *Yale French Studies* 51 (1974): 205–222.

Gutmann, Joseph. "The Messianic Temple in Spanish Medieval Manuscripts." In *The Temple of Solomon: Archaeological Fact and Medieval Tradition in Christian, Islamic, and Jewish Art,* ed. Joseph Gutmann, 125–145. Missoula: Scholars Press, 1976.

Gutwirth, Eleazar. "Archival Poetics: Questions of Evidence in Reconstructions of Judeo-Spanish Culture." *Bulletin of Spanish Studies* 88.5 (2011): 631–654.

———. "Don Ishaq Abravanel and Vernacular Humanism in Fifteenth-Century Iberia." *Bibliothèque d'Humanisme et Renaissance* 60.3 (1998): 641–671.

———. "Duran on Ahitophel: The Practice of Jewish History in Late Medieval Spain." *Jewish History* 4.1 (1989): 59–74.

———. "The Expulsion from Spain and Jewish Historiography." In *Jewish History: Essays in Honour of Chimen Abramsky,* ed. Ada Rapoport-Albert and Steven Zipperstein, 141–161. London: Peter Halban, 1988.

Haas, Peter. *Responsa: Literary History of a Rabbinic Genre.* Atlanta: Scholars Press, 1996.

Hacker, Joseph. "The Sephardim in the Ottoman Empire in the Sixteenth Century." In *The Sephardi Legacy,* ed. Haim Beinart, vol. 2 of 2, 108–133. Jerusalem: Magnes Press, 1992.

———. "The Sürgün System and Jewish Society in the Ottoman Empire." In *Ottoman and Jewish Turkey: Community and Leadership,* ed. Aron Rodrigue, 1–65. Bloomington: Indiana University Press, 1992.

Hacker, Joseph, and Adam Shear. *The Hebrew Book in Early Modern Italy.* Philadelphia: University of Pennsylvania Press, 2011.

Hakohen, Joseph. *The Chronicles of Rabbi Joseph Ben Joshua Ben Meir, the Sphardi.* Trans. Christoph Heinrich Friedrich Bialloblotzky. London: Published for the Oriental Translation Fund of Great Britain and Ireland by R. Bentley, 1835.

———. *Sefer Divre ha-yamim: Le-malkhe Tsarefat u-malkhe Bet Oṭoman ha-Tugar.* Ed. David Arie Gros. Jerusalem: Mossad Bialik, 1955.

———. *Sefer 'Emeq ha-bakha (The Vale of Tears: With the Chronicle of the Anonymous Corrector).* 2nd ed. Ed. Karin Almbladh. Uppsala: Uppsala University, 1981.

———. *The Vale of Tears. (Emek Habacha).* Ed. Samuel David Luzzato. Trans. Harry S. May. The Hague: Nijhoff, 1971.

———. *El Valle del Llanto.* Trans. Pilar León Tello. Barcelona: Riodpiedras, 1989.

Halevi, Judah. *Book of the Kuzari: A Book of Proof and Argument in Defense of a Despised Faith: A 15th-Century Ladino Translation (Ms. 17812, B.N. Madrid).* Ed. Moshe Lazar. Culver City, CA: Labyrinthos, 1990.

——. *Cuzari.* Ed. Jesús Imirizaldu. Trans. Jacob Abendana. Madrid: Editora Nacional, 1979.

——. *Divan: Ve-hu Sefer Kolel Kol Shire Abir Ha-meshorerim, Yehudah ha-Levi (1901).* Ed. Hayyim Brody and Abraham Meir Habermann. Farnborough: Gregg International, 1971.

——. *Book of Kuzari (Kitab Al Khazari).* Trans. Hartwig Hirschfeld. Brooklyn: P. Shalom, 1969.

Halkin, Hillel. *Yehuda Halevi.* New York: Nextbook/Schocken, 2010.

Hall, Stuart, and Jonathan Rutherford. "Cultural Identity and Diaspora." In *Identity: Community, Culture, Difference,* ed. Jonathan Rutherford, 222–237. London: Lawrence and Wishart, 1990.

Hämeen-Anttila, Jaakko. *Maqama: A History of a Genre.* Weisbaden: Harrassovitz, 2002.

Hames, Harvey. "It Takes Three to Tango: Ramon Llull, Solomon Ibn Adret and Alfonso of Valladolid Debate the Trinity." *Medieval Encounters* 15.2/4 (2009): 199–224.

——. "The Language of Conversion: Ramon Llull's Art as a Vernacular." In *The Vulgar Tongue: Medieval and Postmedieval Vernacularity,* ed. Fiona Somerset and Nicholas Watson, 43–56. University Park: Pennsylvania State University Press, 2003.

——. *Like Angels on Jacob's Ladder: Abraham Abulafia, the Franciscans and Joachimism.* Albany: State University of New York Press, 2007.

Hamilton, Michelle M. *Representing Others in Medieval Iberia.* New York: Palgrave Macmillan, 2007.

——. "Text and Context: A Judeo-Spanish Version of the *Danza de la muerte.*" In *Marginal Voices: Studies in Converso Literature of Medieval and Golden Age Spain,* ed. Gregory Kaplan and Amy Aronson-Friedman, 161–181. Leiden: Brill, 2012.

Harshav, Benjamin. *Language in Time of Revolution.* Stanford: Stanford University Press, 1999.

Harvey, L. P. *Islamic Spain, 1250 to 1500.* Chicago: University of Chicago Press, 1990.

Harvey, Steven. *Falaquera's Epistle of the Debate: An Introduction to Jewish Philosophy.* Cambridge: Harvard University Center for Jewish Studies, 1987.

Haywood, Eric. "The *Querelle* of Arms and Letters During the Renaissance in Italy." Doctoral dissertation. University of Edinburgh, 1981.

Haywood, Louise M. *Sex, Scandal and Sermon in Fourteenth-century Spain: Juan Ruiz's Libro de buen amor.* New York: Palgrave Macmillan, 2008.

Heijkoop, Henk, and Otto Zwartjes. *Muwaššaḥ, Zajal, Kharja: Bibliography of Strophic Poetry and Music from al-Andalus and Their Influence in East and West.* Leiden: Brill, 2004.

Heine, Heinrich. *Hebraeische melodien.* München: Hyperionverlag, 1923.

Hermes, Eberhard. "The Author and His Times." In *The* Disciplina Clericalis *of Petrus Alfonsi,* trans. Eberhard Hermes, 3–102. Berkeley: University of California Press, 1977.

Hillgarth, Jocelyn N. *The Mirror of Spain, 1500–1700: The Formation of a Myth.* Ann Arbor: University of Michigan Press, 2000.

——. *The Problem of a Catalan Mediterranean Empire, 1229–1327.* London: Longman, 1975.

——. *The Spanish Kingdoms, 1250–1516.* 2 vols. Oxford: Clarendon Press, 1976.

Hinojosa Montalvo, José. *The Jews of the Kingdom of Valencia: From Persecution to*

Expulsion, 1391–1492. Jerusalem: Magnes Press, 1993.

Hirschberg, H. Z. *A History of the Jews in North Africa.* 2 vols. Leiden: Brill, 1974.

Hitchcock, Richard. *Mozarabs in Medieval and Early Modern Spain: Identities and Influences.* Aldershot, UK: Ashgate, 2008.

Hoerder, Dirk. "Revising the Monocultural Nation-State Paradigm: An Introduction to Transcultural Perspectives." In *The Historical Practice of Diversity: Transcultural Interactions from the Early Modern Mediterranean to the Postcolonial World,* ed. Dirk Hoerder, Christiane Harzig, and Adrian Shubert, 1–12. New York: Berghahn Books, 2003.

Holmes, Olivia. *Assembling the Lyric Self.* Minneapolis: University of Minnesota Press, 2000.

The Holy Letter: A Study in Jewish Sexual Morality. Ed. Seymour Cohen. Northvale, NJ: Jason Aronson, 1993.

Horowitz, Elliott. *Reckless Rites: Purim and the Legacy of Jewish Violence.* Princeton: Princeton University Press, 2006.

Housley, Norman. *The Later Crusades, 1274–1580: From Lyons to Alcazar.* New York: Oxford University Press, 1992.

Humphreys, W. Lee. "A Life-Style for Diaspora: A Study of the Tales of Esther and Daniel." *Journal of Biblical Literature* 92.2 (1973): 211–223.

Huot, Sylvia. *From Song to Book: The Poetics of Writing in Old French Lyric and Lyrical Narrative Poetry.* Ithaca: Cornell University Press, 1987.

Huss, Matti. "Introduction." In Vidal Benvenist, *Don Vidal Benveniste's Tale of Efer and Dina* [Hebrew], ed. Matti Huss, 3–146. Jerusalem: Hebrew University, 2003.

Ibn 'Abd al-Rabbihi, Ibn 'Umar Ahmad ibn Muhammad. *al-'Iqd al-farīd.* Ed. Ahmad Amīn, Ahmad al-Zayn, and Ibrāhīm al-Ibyārī. 7 vols. Beirut: Dār al-Kitāb al-'Arabī, 1982.

Ibn Bassām al-Shantarīnī, 'Alī. *al-Dhakīrah fī maḥāsin ahl al-jazīrah.* 2 vols. al-Qāhirah: Maṭba'at Lajnat al-Ta'līf wa-al-Tarjamah wa-al-Nashr, 1939.

Ibn Daud, Abraham ben David. *A Critical Edition with a Translation and Notes of the Book of Tradition (Sefer ha-Qabbalah).* Ed. and trans. by Gerson D. Cohen. London: Routledge and Keegan Paul, 1969.

Ibn Ezra, Moses. *Secular Poems* [Hebrew]. Ed. Heinrich Brody. Berlin: Shocken, 1934. Vol 1.

Ibn Gabirol, Solomon. *The Secular Poetry of Shelomo ibn Gabirol* [Hebrew]. Ed. Hayyim Brody and Hayim Schirmann. 2 vols. Jerusalem: Shocken, 1974.

Ibn Ḥazm, 'Alī ibn Ahmad. *The Ring of the Dove: A Treatise on the Art and Practice of Arab Love.* Trans. A. J Arberry. London: Luzac, 1953.

———. *Ṭawq al-ḥamāmah fī al-ulfah wa-al-ullāf.* Ed. Muhammad Ibrahim Salim. al-Qāhirah: Maktabat Ibn Sīnā, 1993.

Ibn Paquda, Bahya ben Joseph. *The Book of Direction to the Duties of the Heart.* Trans. Menahem Mansoor. London: Routledge and Keegan Paul, 1973.

Ibn Sahula, Isaac ben Solomon. *Meshal ha-Qadmoni.* Ed. Israel Zamora. Tel Aviv: Mahberot Lesifrut, 1953.

———. *Meshal Haqadmoni: Fables from the Distant Past.* Ed. and trans. Raphael Loewe. Portland: Littman Library of Jewish Civilization, 2004.

Ibn Sasson, Samuel. *Sefer avnei hashoham.* Ed. Hayim Chamiel. Jersusalem: Mahbarot Lesifrut, 1962.

Ibn Shabbetay, Judah ben Isaac. *The Offering of Judah, Succour of Women,* and *Wellspring of Justice* [Hebrew]. 2 vols. Ed. Matti Huss. Jerusalem: Hebrew University, 1991.

———. *La Ofrenda de Judá.* Trans. Ángeles Navarro Peiro. Granada: Editorial Universidad de Granada, 2006.

Ibn Verga, Solomon. *Chébet Jehuda (La Vara De Judá,* "Introducción"). Trans.

Francisco Cantera Burgos, 3–43. Granada: López Guevara, 1927.

———. *La vara de Yehudah (Sefer Sebet Yehudah)*. Trans. María José Cano. Barcelona: Riopiedras Ediciones, 1991.

———. *Sefer Shevet Yehudah*. Ed. Azriel Shohet. Jerusalem: Mossad Bialik, 1946.

Ibn Zabara, Joseph ben Meir. *Sepher Sha'ashu'im, a Book of Mediaeval Lore*. Ed. Israel Davidson. New York: Jewish Theological Seminary of America, 1914.

Infantes, Victor, and Nieves Baranda, eds. *Narrativa popular de la Edad Media: Doncella Teodor, Flores y Blancaflor, París y Viana*. Torrejón de Ardoz: AKAL, 1995.

Jacobs, Janet Liebman. *Hidden Heritage: The Legacy of the Crypto-Jews*. Berkeley: University of California Press, 2002.

Jacobs, Jill. "'The Defense Has Become the Prosecution:' *Ezrat HaNashim*, a Thirteenth-century Response to Misogyny." *Women in Judaism: A Multidisciplinary Journal* 3.2 (2003): 1–9.

Jacobs, Louis. "Introduction." In *The Palm Tree of Deborah,* trans. Louis Jacobs. 9–38. London: Valentine Mitchell, 1960.

Jacobs, Mignon. "Love, Honor, and Violence: Socioconceptual Matrix in Genesis 34." In *Pregnant Passion: Gender, Sex,and Violence in the Bible,* ed. Cheryl Kirk-Duggan, 11–35. Atlanta: Society of Biblical Literature, 2003.

Jacquart, D. "L'école des traducteurs." *Tolède, XIIe–XIIIe siècles*. Ed. Louis Cardaillac. Paris: Editions Autrement, 1991. 177–191.

Jensen, Frede, ed. *Medieval Galician-Portuguese Poetry: An Anthology*. Trans. Frede Jensen. New York: Garland, 1992.

Jiménez Calvente, Teresa. "Teoría historiográfica a comienzos del siglo XVI." In *Imágenes históricas de Felipe II,* ed. Alfredo Alvar Ezquerra, 197–216. Alcalá de Henares: Centro de Estudios Cervantinos, 2000.

Jiménez de Rada, Rodrigo. *Estoria de Los Godos*. Ed. Aengus Ward. Oxford: Society for the Study of Mediaeval Languages and Literature, 2006.

Johnson, Carroll B. "Phantom Pre-texts and Fictional Authors: Sidi Hamid Benengeli, Don Quijote and the Metafictional Conventions of Chivalric Romances." *Cervantes: Bulletin of the Cervantes Society of America* 27.1 (2007): 179–200.

———. *Transliterating a Culture: Cervantes and the Moriscos*. Ed. Mark Groundland. Newark, DE: Juan de la Cuesta Hispanic Monographs, 2010.

Josephus, Flavius. *Jewish Antiquities*. Ed. H. St. John Thackeray. Cambridge, MA: Harvard University Press, 1998.

Juan Manuel. *El Conde Lucanor*. Ed. Alfonso I. Sotelo. Madrid: Cátedra, 1988.

———. *Obras completas*. 2 vols. Ed. José Manuel Blecua. Madrid: Gredos, 1982.

Kahle, Paul. "The Arabic Readers of the Koran." *Journal of Near Eastern Studies* 8.2 (1949): 65–71.

———. *The Cairo Geniza*. Oxford: Blackwell, 1959.

Kamen, Henry. *Imagining Spain: Historical Myth and National Identity*. New Haven: Yale University Press, 2008.

———. *Inquisition and Society in Spain in the Sixteenth and Seventeenth Centuries*. Bloomington: Indiana University Press, 1985.

Kaplan, Gregory. *The Evolution of Converso Literature: The Writings of the Converted Jews of Medieval Spain*. Gainesville: University Press of Florida, 2002.

———. "The Inception of *limpieza de sangre* (Purity of Blood) and its impact in Medieval and Golden Age Spain." In *Marginal Voices: Studies in Converso Literature of Medieval and Golden Age Spain,* ed. Gregory B. Kaplan and Amy Aronson-Friedman, 19–42. Leiden: Brill, 2012.

Kaplan, Yosef. *Judios nuevos en Amsterdam: Estudios sobre la historia social e intelectual del judaísmo sefardí en el siglo XVII*. Barcelona: Gedisa Editorial, 1996.

Karo, Joseph. *A Maggid [preacher] of Righteousness*. Trans. K. Skaist. Petach Tikva: Yechiel Bar Lev, 2009.

———. *Magid Meisharim*. Ed. Aharon Sorsky. Jerusalem: Orah, 1960.

———. *Shulhan 'arukh Yoreh de'ah*. Ed. Ya'akov Hayim Sofer. Jerusalem: M. Sofer, 1966.

Kay, Sarah. *Subjectivity in Troubadour Poetry*. Cambridge: Cambridge University Press, 1990.

Keller, John Esten. *Alfonso X, El Sabio*. New York: Twayne, 1967.

Kellner, Menahem. *Maimonides' Confrontation with Mysticism*. Portland: Littman Library of Jewish Civilization, 2006.

Kfir, Uriah. "Center and Periphery in Medieval Hebrew Poetry: Secular Poetry from the Provincial and Provençal Perspective" [Hebrew]. Doctoral dissertation. Tel Aviv University, 2011.

———. A Matter of Geography: A New Perspective on Medieval Hebrew Poetry. Leiden: Brill, forthcoming.

Kinoshita, Sharon. *Medieval Boundaries: Rethinking Difference in Old French Literature*. Philadelphia: University of Pennsylvania Press, 2006.

Kobler, Franz. *Letters of Jews through the Ages: From Biblical Times to the Middle of the Eighteenth Century*. 2 vols. New York: East and West Library, 1978.

Konuk, Kader. *East-West Mimesis: Auerbach in Turkey*. Stanford: Stanford University Press, 2010.

Kozodoy, Neal. "Reading Medieval Hebrew Love Poetry." *AJS Review* 2 (1977): 111–129.

Kraemer, Joel. *Maimonides: The Life and World of One of Civilization's Greatest Minds*. 1st ed. New York: Doubleday, 2008.

Kristeva, Julia. *Powers of Horror: An Essay on Abjection*. New York: Columbia University Press, 1982.

Lacarra, María Jesús, and Francisco López Estrada. *Orígenes de la prosa*. Madrid: Ediciones Júcar, 1993.

Lacarra, María Jesús, and Juan Manuel Cacho Blecua. *Entre la oralidad y escritura: La edad media*. Barcelona: Crítica, 2012.

Laird, Andrew. "Figures of Allegory from Homer to Latin Epic." In *Metaphor, Allegory, and the Classical Tradition*, ed. G. R. Boys-Stones, 151–176. Oxford: Oxford University Press, 2003.

Lasker, Daniel J. "Proselyte Judaism, Christianity, and Islam in the Thought of Judah Halevi." *The Jewish Quarterly Review* 81.1/2 (1990): 75–91.

Lawee, Eric. "On the Threshold of the Renaissance: New Methods and Sensibilities in the Biblical Commentaries of Isaac Abarbanel." *Viator* 26.1 (1995): 283–320.

Lehmann, Matthias. *Ladino Rabbinic Literature and Ottoman Sephardic Culture*. Bloomington: Indiana University Press, 2005.

León Tello, Pilar. "Introducción." In *El valle del llanto ('Emeq ha-Bakha)*, 9–35. Barcelona: Riodpiedras, 1989.

Levenson, Jon D. "Scroll of Esther in Ecumenical Perspective." *Journal of Ecumenical Studies* 13.3 (1976): 440–452.

Leviant, Curt. *King Artus: A Hebrew Arthurian Romance of 1279*. Assen: Van Gorcum, 1969.

Levin, Israel. "The Pen and the Rider." In *A. M. Habermann Jubilee Volume: Studies in Medieval Hebrew Literature*, ed. Zvi Malachi, 143–173. Jerusalem: Tel Aviv University Press, 1977.

Levy, Avigdor. "Introduction." In *The Jews of the Ottoman Empire*, 1–150. Princeton: Darwin Press, 1994.

———. *The Sephardim in the Ottoman Empire*. Princeton: Darwin, 1992.

Liss, Peggy. "Isabel, Myth, and History." In *Isabel la Católica, Queen of Castile,* ed. David A. Boruchoff, 57–78. New York: Palgrave, 2003.

Little, William. "Introduction." In Garci Rodríguez de Montalvo, *The Labors of the Very Brave Knight Esplandían,* trans. William Little, 1–61. Binghamton, NY: Medieval and Renaissance Texts and Studies, 1992.

Loewe, Raphael. "Introduction." Ibn Sahula, *Meshal Haqadmoni: Fables from the Distant Past,* ed. and trans. Raphael Loewe, xv–cxxxi. Portland: Littman Library of Jewish Civilization, 2004.

Lonzano, Menahem di. *Shete yadot.* Jerusalem: [s.n], 1969.

López de Gómara, Francisco. *Sefer ha-Indiah ha-hadashah.* Ed. Moshe Lazar. Trans. Joseph Hakohen. Lancaster, CA: Labirintos, 2002.

López Estrada, Francisco. *La prosa medieval: Orígenes-s. XIV.* Madrid: Editoral La Muralla, 1973.

Lowe, Alfonso. *The Catalan Vengeance.* London: Routledge and Keegan Paul, 1972.

Lucía Megías, José. *Imprenta y libros de caballerías.* Madrid: Ollero and Ramos, 2000.

Maccoby, Hyam. *Judaism on Trial: Jewish-Christian Disputations in the Middle Ages.* Portland, OR: Vallentine Mitchell, 1996.

Macpherson, Ian, and Robert Brian Tate. "Introduction." In *Libro de los Estados,* xv–xcii. Oxford: Clarendon Press, 1974.

Maimon ben Yosef. *The Letter of Consolation* [Hebrew]. Ed. Benjamin Klar and Yehudah Leyb Maimon. Jerusalem: Rav Kuk Institute, 2008.

Maimonides, Moses. *The Guide for the Perplexed.* Trans. Michael Friedländer. 2nd ed. New York: Dover, 1956.

———. *Hilkhot de'ot ve-hilkhot 'avodah zarah.* Bene Berak: Agudat netivot ha-Torah veha-hesed, 1979.

———. *Maamar ha-jichud: (Abhandlung Über Die Einheit).* Ed. Moritz Stein-schneider. Berlin: In Commission bei L. Weyl and Comp. Friedländersche Buchdruckerei, 1846.

———. *Maimonides' Letter to Yemen: The Arabic Original and the three Hebrew Versions.* Ed. and trans. Abraham S. Halkin. New York: American Society for Jewish Research, 1952.

———. *Mishneh Torah.* Ed. Moses Hyamson. Jerusalem: Feldheim, 1981.

———. *Moreh nevukhim (Dalalat al-hairin).* Ed. Yosef Kafah. Jerusalem: Rav Kuk Institute, 1972.

Malachi, Zvi. *The Loving Knight: The Romance: Amadis de Gaula and Its Hebrew Adaptation (Turkey, c.1541).* Trans. Phyllis Hackett. Lod: Haberman Institute for Literary Research, 1982.

Mallette, Karla. "Poetries of the Norman Courts." In Menocal et al., *Literature,* 377–387.

———. *The Kingdom of Sicily, 1100–1250: A Literary History.* Philadelphia: University of Pennsylvania Press, 2005.

Malter, Henry. "Shem Tob Ben Joseph Palquera: A Thinker and Poet of the Thirteenth Century: I." *Jewish Quarterly Review* 1.2 (1910): 151–181.

Marcó i Dachs, Lluís. *Los judíos en Cataluña.* Barcelona: Ediciones Destino, 1985.

Marie de France. *Les lais de Marie de France.* Ed. Jean Rychner. Paris: Honoré Champion, 1973.

Marín Piña, María, ed. *Palmerín de Olivia: (Salamanca, Juan de Porras, 1511).* Alcalá de Henares Madrid: Centro de Estudios Cervantinos, 2004.

Marineo Siculo, Lucio. *De Hispaniae Laudibus.* Burgos: Fridericus Biel de Basilea, 1497. Hathi Trust Digital Library.

Markova, Alla. "Un fragmento manuscrito de una novela de caballerias en judeo-español." *Sefarad* 69.1 (2009): 159–172.

Márquez Villanueva, Francisco. *El concepto cultural alfonsí.* Barcelona: Bellaterra, 2004.

———. *De la España judeoconversa.* Edicions Bellaterra, 2006.

Martin, Hervé. *Le métier de prédicateur à la fin du moyen age (1350–5320)*. Paris: Les Editions du Cerf, 1988.

Martin, June Hall. *Love's Fools: Aucassin, Troilus, Calisto and the Parody of the Courtly Lover*. London: Tamesis, 1972.

Martín Martín, José Luis. "Alfabetización y poder del clero secular en la Península Ibérica en la Edad Media." In *Educación y transmisión de conocimientos en la historia*, ed. Ángel Vaca Lorenzo, 95–132. Salamanca: Universidad de Salamanca, 2002.

Martínez Kleiser, Luis. *Refranero general ideológico español*. 2nd ed. Madrid: Hernando, 1982.

Marx, Anthony W. *Faith in Nation: Exclusionary Origins of Nationalism*. Oxford: Oxford University Press, 2003.

Matt, Daniel Chanan. *The Essential Kabbalah: The Heart of Jewish Mysticism*. San Francisco: HarperSanFrancisco, 1996.

Matulka, Barbara. *The Novels of Juan de Flores and Their European Diffusion*. New York, 1931.

Melammed, Renée Levine. *Heretics or Daughters of Israel?: The Crypto-Jewish Women of Castile*. New York: Oxford University Press, 1999.

———. *A Question of Identity: Iberian Conversos in Historical Perspective*. New York: Oxford University Press, 2004.

Menéndez Pidal, Gonzalo. "Las armas y las letras." *Escorial* 42 (1944): 227–244.

Menéndez Pidal, Ramón. *Tres poetas primitivos: Elena y María, "Roncesvalles," Historia Troyana Polimétrica*. 2nd ed. Buenos Aires: Espasa-Calpe Argentina, 1948.

———, ed. *Cantar de mío Cid*. Madrid: Espasa-Calpe, 1944.

Menéndez y Pelayo, Marcelino, ed. *Antología de poetas líricos castellanos desde la formación del idioma hasta nuestros días*. Vol. 3. Madrid: Librería de la Viuda de Hernando, 1892.

Menocal, Maria Rosa. *The Arabic Role in Medieval Literary History: A Forgotten Heritage*. Philadelphia: University of Pennsylvania Press, 1987.

———. "Beginnings." In *The Cambridge History of Spanish Literature*, ed. David Gies, 58–74. Cambridge: Cambridge University Press, 2004.

———. *The Ornament of the World*. Boston: Little Brown, 2002.

———. "To Create an Empire: *Adab* and the Invention of Castilian Culture." *Maghreb Review* 31.3–4 (2006): 194–202.

Meyer, Michael. *Ideas of Jewish history*. New York: Behrman House, 1974.

Meyerson, Mark D. *The Muslims of Valencia in the Age of Fernando and Isabel: Between Coexistence and Crusade*. Berkeley: University of California, 1991.

———. "Seeking the Messiah: Converso Messianism in Post-1453 Valencia." In *The Conversos and Moriscos in Late Medieval Spain and Beyond*, ed. Kevin Ingram, 51–82. Leiden: Brill, 2010.

Midrash Rabbah. Ed. H. Freedman and Maurice Simon. London: Soncino Press, 1983.

Mignolo, Walter D. "Rethinking the Colonial Model." In *Rethinking Literary History: A Dialogue on Theory*, 155–193. Oxford: Oxford University Press, 2002.

Milá Fontanals, Manuel. *De los trovadores en España*. Barcelona: Consejo Superior de Investigaciones Científicas, 1966.

Millás Vallicrosa, José María. *Yehudá Ha-Leví como poeta y apologista*. Madrid, Barcelona: Consejo Superior de Investigaciones Científicas, Instituto Arias Montano, 1947.

Minnis, A. *Medieval Theory of Authorship: Scholastic Literary Attitudes in the Later Middle Ages*. London: Scolar Press, 1984.

Mishra, Sudesh. *Diaspora Criticism*. Edinburgh: Edinburgh University Press, 2006.

Mishra, Vijay. *The Literature of the Indian Diaspora: Theorizing the Diasporic Imaginary*. London: Routledge, 2007.

Moner, Francesc. *Obres catalanes*. Ed. Peter Cocozzella. Barcelona: Barcino, 1970.

Monroe, James T. *Hispano-Arabic Poetry: A Student Anthology*. Berkeley: University of California Press, 1974.

———. "Ibn Quzman on I'rab: A zéjel de juglaría in Arab Spain?" *Hispanic Studies in Honor of Joseph H. Silverman*. Ed. Joseph Ricapito. 45–56. Newark, DE: Juan de la Cuesta, 1990.

———. "Maimonides on the Mozarabic Lyric." *La corónica* 17.2 (1988): 18–32.

———. "Preliminary Study." *al-Maqamat al-Luzumiyya*. 1–79. Leiden: Brill, 2002.

———. *The Shu'ubiyya in al-Andalus: The Risala of Ibn García and Five Refutations*. Berkeley: University of California Press, 1970.

Morell, Samuel. "Rabbinic Responsa as a Source for History: A Review Essay." *Modern Judaism* 7.2 (1987): 207–212.

Mullett, Margaret. "In Peril on the Sea: Travel Genres and the Unexpected." In *Travel in the Byzantine World*, ed. Ruth Macrides, 259–284. Aldershot, UK: Ashgate, 2002.

Muriel Tapia, María Cruz. *Antifeminismo y subestimación de la mujer en la literatura medieval castellana*. Cáceres: Editorial Guadiloba, 1991.

Naipaul, V. S. *Literary Occasions: Essays*. Ed. Pankaj Mishra. New York: Alfred A. Knopf, 2003.

Navarro Peiro, Ángeles. "La versión hebrea de *Calila y Dimna* de Ya'aqob ben El'azar." In *Jewish Studies at the Turn of the Twentieth Century*, ed. Judit Targarona Borrás and Ángel Sáenz-Badillos, 468–475. Boston: Brill, 1999.

———. "Las versiones hebreas de *Calila y Dimna*." *Revista de Filología Románica* 14.2 (1997): 325–333.

———. *Narrativa hispanohebrea (Siglos XII–XV)*. Cordoba: Ediciones el Amendro, 1988.

Nebrija, Antonio de. *Gramática de la llengua castellana*. Ed. Ignacio González-Lluberas. Oxford: Oxford University Press, 1926.

Nepaulsingh, Colbert. *Towards a History of Literary Composition in Medieval Spain*. Toronto: University of Toronto Press, 1986.

Netanyahu, Ben Zion. *Don Isaac Abravanel, Statesman and Philosopher*. 5th ed. Ithaca: Cornell University Press, 1998.

———. *The Origins of the Inquisition in Fifteenth-Century Spain*. New York: New York Review of Books, 2001.

———. *Toward the Inquisition: Essays on Jewish and Converso History in Late Medieval Spain*. Ithaca: Cornell University Press, 1997.

Neuman, Abraham. *The Shebet Yehudah and Sixteenth Century Historiography*. Reprinted from the Louis Ginzberg Jubilee Volume. New York: American Academy for Jewish Research, 1945.

Neusner, Jacob. *A History of the Jews in Babylonia*. Leiden: Brill, 1965.

Nichols, Stephen G. "Voice and Writing in Augustine and in the Troubadour Lyric." In Vox Intexta: *Orality and Textuality in the Middle Ages*, ed. A. N. Doane and Carol Braun Pasternak, 137–161. Madison: University of Wisconsin Press, 1991.

Nicholson, Reynold Alleyne. *A Literary History of the Arabs*. New York: C. Scribner's Sons T. Unwin, 1907.

Nicolay, Nicholas. *The Navigations, Peregrinatians and Voyages, Made into Turkie by Nicholas Nicolay*. Trans. T. Washington. London: [s.n.], 1585.

Nini, Yehudah, and Maya Fruchtman. "Introduction." In *Ma'ase ha-rav*, ed. Yehudah Nini and Maya Fruchtman, 11–37. Tel Aviv: Tel Aviv University, 1980.

Nirenberg, David. *Communities of Violence: Persecution of Minorities in the Middle Ages*. Princeton: Princeton University Press, 1996.

———. "Enmity and Assimilation: Jews, Christians, and Converts in Medieval Spain." *Common Knowledge* 9.1 (2003): 137–155.

———. "Race and the Middle Ages: The Case of Spain and the Jews." In *Reread-*

ing the Black Legend: The Discourses of Religious and Racial Difference in the Renaissance Empires, ed. Margaret R. Greer, Walter D. Mignolo, and Maureen Quilligan, 71–87. Chicago: University of Chicago Press, 2007.

———. "Was There Race Before Modernity? The Example of 'Jewish Blood' in Late Medieval Spain." In The Origins of Racism in the West, ed. Ben Isaac, Yossi Ziegler, and Miriam Eliav-Feldon, 232–264. Cambridge: Cambridge University Press, 2009.

Norris, H. T. "Shu'ubiyyah in Arabic Literature." In 'Abbasid Belles-Lettres, ed. Julia Ashtiany, 31–47. Cambridge: Cambridge University, 1990.

Novikoff, Alex. "Between Tolerance and Intolerance in Medieval Spain: An Historiographic Enigma." Medieval Encounters 11 (2005): 7–36.

Nuland, Sherwin. Maimonides. New York: Nextbook, 2005.

Nykl, A. R. Hispano-Arabic Poetry, and Its Relations with the Old Provençal Troubadours. Baltimore: J. H. Furst, 1946.

———, ed. and trans. Historia de los amores de Bayad y Riyad. New York: Hispanic Society of America, 1941.

O'Callaghan, Joseph F. Alfonso X and the Cantigas de Santa Maria: A Poetic Biography. Leiden: Brill, 1998.

———. A History of Medieval Spain. Ithaca: Cornell University Press, 1983.

———. The Learned King: The Reign of Alfonso X of Castile. Philadelphia: University of Pennsylvania Press, 1993.

———. Reconquest and Crusade in Medieval Spain. Philadelphia: University of Pennsylvania Press, 2003.

Oettinger, Ayelet. "Criticism of the Estates in Judah al-Harizi's Book of Tahkemoni and in European-Christian Literature of the Thirteenth Century: Affinity and Distinction." In A Message Upon the Garden—Studies in Medieval Jewish Poetry,

ed. A. Guetta and M. Itzhaki, 85–96. Leiden: Brill, 2009.

Olstein, Diego Adrian. La era mozárabe: Los mozárabes de Toledo (siglos XII y XIII) en la historiografía, las fuentes y la historia. Salamanca: Universidad de Salamanca, 2006.

Ong, Walter J. Orality and Literacy: The Technologizing of the Word. London: Methuen, 1982.

Orr, Gili. "The Medieval Alpha Beta deBen Sira I ('Rishona'): A Parody on Rabbinic Literature or a Midrashic Commentary on Ancient Proverbs?" Master's thesis. University of Amsterdam, 2009.

Oulmont, Charles. Les débats du clerc et du chevalier dans la littérature poétique du Moyen-Age. 1911. Genève: Slatkine Reprints, 1974.

Pacios López, Antonio, ed. La disputa de Tortosa. 2 vols. Madrid: Consejo Superior de Investigaciones Científicas, Instituto Arias Montano, 1957.

Pagden, Anthony. Lords of All the World: Ideologies of Empire in Spain, Britain and France c. 1500–c. 1800. New Haven: Yale University Press, 1995.

Pagis, Dan. "Dirges on the Persecutions of the Year 5151 in Spain [Hebrew]." Tarbiz 37 (1968): 355–373.

———. Hebrew Poetry of the Middle Ages and the Renaissance. Berkeley: University of California Press, 1991.

———. Innovation and Tradition in Secular Hebrew Poetry: Spain and Italy [Hebrew]. Jerusalem: Keter Israel, 1976.

———. "The Poetic Polemic on the Nature of Women [Hebrew]." Jerusalem Studies in Hebrew Literature 9 (1986): 259–300.

Parker, Alan A. "The Parable of the Greeks and the Romans in the Libro de buen amor." In Medieval Hispanic Studies Presented to Rita Hamilton, ed. Alan D. Deyermond, 139–147. London: Tamesis, 1976.

Parkes, Malcolm. "The Influence of the Concepts of Ordinatio and Compilatio on the Development of the Book." In

Medieval Learning and Literature: Essays Presented to Richard William Hunt, ed. Jonathan A. G. Alexander and Margaret T. Gibson, 115–141. Oxford: Clarendon, 1976.

Pascual Recuero, Pascual. "El aljamiado en la literatura sefardí y su transcripción." In *Miscelánea de estudios dedicados al profesor Antonio Marín Ocete,* 851–876. Granada: Universidad de Granada, 1974.

Patai, Raphael. *The Jewish Mind.* Detroit: Wayne State University Press, 1996.

Perea Rodríguez, Óscar. *Estudio biográfico sobre los poetas del* Cancionero general. Madrid: Consejo Superior de Investigaciones Científicas, 2007.

Peretz, Yitzhak. "Introduction." In Judah al-Harizi, *Mahberot I'ti'el,* ed. Yitzhak Peretz, iii–xl. Tel Aviv: Ha-Rav Kuk, 1950.

Pérez, Joseph. *Isabel y Fernando.* 2nd ed. Madrid: Nerea, 1997.

Pérez Alonso, María Isabel. "Contribución al estudio de los hebraísmos léxicos, semánticos y morfosintácticos en la Biblia Medieval Romanceada." *Miscelánea de Estudios Árabes y Hebraicos: Sección de hebreo* 46 (1997): 11–22.

Pérez Castro, Federico. *Aspectos de la cultura hebraicoespañola.* Santander, 1964.

———. *Poesía secular hispano-hebrea.* Madrid: Consejo Superior de Investigaciones Científicas (CSIC), 1989.

Perfet, Isaac ben Sheshet. *Responsa.* Ed. David Metzger. 2 vols. Jerusalem: Jerusalem Institute, 1992.

Perry, Mary Elizabeth, and Anne J. Cruz. *Cultural Encounters: The Impact of the Inquisition in Spain and the New World.* Berkeley: University of California Press, 1991.

Perry, T. Anthony. *The Moral Proverbs of Santob De Carrión: Jewish Wisdom in Christian Spain.* Princeton: Princeton University Press, 1987.

Peters, J.T.R.M. *God's Created Speech.* Leiden: Brill, 1976.

Petrus Alfonsi. *Disciplina clericalis.* Ed. Alfons Hilka and Werner Söderhjelm. Helsinki: Societatis Scientiarum Fennicæ, 1911.

Piccus, Jules. "Corrections, Suppressions, and Changes in Montalvo's *Amadís,* Book I." In *Textures and Meaning: Thirty Years of Judaic Studies at the University of Massachusetts Amherst,* ed. Leonard Ehrlich et al., 179–211. Amherst: Department of Judaic and Near Eastern Studies, University of Massachusetts Amherst, 2004.

Piera, Montserrat. "Tirant Lo Blanc: Re-historicizing the 'Other' Reconquista." In *Tirant Lo Blanc: New Approaches,* ed. Arthur Terry, 45–58. London: Tamesis, 1999.

Pontón, Gonzalo. "La ejemplaridad en la *Crónica* de Fernando de Pulgar." In *Actas del VI Congreso Internacional de la Asociación Hispánica de Literatura Medieval (Alcalá de Henares, 12–16 de septiembre de 1995),* ed. José Manuel Lucía Megías, 2:1207–1216. Alcalá de Henares: Universidad de Alcalá, 1997.

Pratt, Mary Louise. *Imperial Eyes: Travel Writing and Transculturation.* London: Routledge, 1992.

Prendergast, W. J. *The Maqamat of Badi 'Al-Zaman al-Hamadhani: Translated from the Arabic with an Introduction and Notes.* London: Curzon, 1915.

Procter, Evelyn. *Alfonso X of Castile: Patron of Literature and Learning.* Oxford: Oxford University Press, 1951.

Pulgar, Fernando del. *Claros varones de Castilla.* Ed. Jesús Domínguez Bordona. Espasa-Calpe: Madrid.

Pulido, Angel. *Españoles sin patria y la raza sefardí.* Ed. facsímil. Granada: Universidad de Granada, 1993.

Putnam, Ruth. *California: The Name.* Berkeley: University of California Press, 1917.

Quint, D. "The Debate Between Arms and Letters in the *Gerusalemme Liberata.*"

Medieval and Renaissance Texts and Studies 286 (2005): 363–388.

Raden, Matthew. "Writing from Margin to Center: The Case of Don Juan Manuel and Shem Tov." *Hispanófila* 135 (2002): 1–17.

Ravitzky, Aviezer. *Messianism, Zionism, and Jewish Religious Radicalism*. Chicago: University of Chicago Press, 1996.

Ray, Jonathan. "Beyond Tolerance and Persecution: Reassessing Our Approach to Medieval Convivencia." *Jewish Social Studies* 11.2 (2005): 1–18.

———. "Iberian Jewry Between West and East: Jewish Settlement in the Sixteenth-Century Mediterranean." *Mediterranean Studies* 18.1 (2009): 44–65.

———. *The Sephardic Frontier: The Reconquista and the Jewish Community in Medieval Iberia*. Ithaca: Cornell University Press, 2006.

Regalado, Antonio. "Santos, héroes, y peregrinos: Literatura y tradición oral en los orígenes del Camino de Santiago." In *El Camino de Santiago y la sociedad medieval*, ed. Javier García Turza, 111–134. Logroño, ES: Instituto de Estudios Riojanos.

Reiner, Jacob. "Original Hebrew *Yosippon* in the Chronicle of Jerahmeel." *Jewish Quarterly Review* 60.2 (1969): 128–146.

Reynolds, Suzanne. *Medieval Reading: Grammar, Rhetoric, and the Classical Text*. Cambridge: Cambridge University Press, 1996.

Ribera, Julián. *Disertaciones y opúsculos*. Madrid: E. Maestre, 1928.

———. *Music in Ancient Arabia and Spain*. Stanford: Stanford University Press, 1929.

Rico, Francisco. *The Spanish Picaresque Novel and the Point of View*. Trans. Charles Davis and Harry Sieber. Cambridge: Cambridge University Press, 1984.

Riera i Sans, Jaume, ed. *Cants de noces dels jueus catalans*. Barcelona: Curial, 1974.

Riquer, Martí de. *Història de la literatura catalana*. 10 vols. Barcelona: Edicions Ariel, 1964.

Rivet de la Grange, Antoine, et al. *Histoire littéraire de la France: XIVe siècle*. Paris: Imprimerie Nationale, 1893.

Robinson, Cynthia. *In Praise of Song: The Making of Courtly Culture in al-Andalus and Provence, 1005–1134 A.D.* Leiden: Brill, 2002.

———. *Medieval Andalusian Courtly Culture in the Mediterranean:* Hadith Bayad wa-Riyad. London: Routledge, 2007.

Robinson, James. "The Ibn Tibbon Family: a Dynasty of Translators in Medieval Provence." In *Be'erot Yitzhak: Studies in Memory of Isadore Twersky*, ed. Jay Michael Harris, 193–224. Cambridge: Harvard University Center for Jewish Studies, 2005.

Rodilla León, María José. "Troya, Roma, y Constantinopla en El Claribalte." In *Amadís y sus libros: 500 años*, ed. Aurelio González and Axayácatl Campos García Rojas, 303–311. Mexico City: El Colegio de México, 2009.

Rodrigue Schwarzwald, Ora. "Language Choice and Language Varieties Before and After the Expulsion." In *From Iberia to Diaspora: Studies in Sephardic History and Culture*, ed. Yedida K. Stillman and Norman A. Stillman, 399–415. Leiden: Brill, 1999.

Rodríguez, Rodney T. *Momentos cumbres de las literaturas hispánicas: Introducción al análisis literario*. Upper Saddle River, NJ: Pearson, Prentice Hall, 2004.

Rodríguez de Montalvo, Garci. *'Alilot ha-abir*. Ed. Tzvi Malachi. Trans. Jacob Algaba. Tel Aviv: Tel Aviv University Press, 1981.

———. *Amadís de Gaula*. Ed. Juan Manuel Cacho Blecua. Madrid: Cátedra, 1987.

———. *The Labors of the Very Brave Knight Esplandián*. Trans. William Little. Binghamton, NY: Center for Medieval and Early Renaissance Studies State University of New York at Binghamton, 1992.

———. *Sergas de Esplandían*. Ed. Carlos Sainz de la Maza. Madrid: Castalia, 2003.

Rodríguez Llopis, Miguel, and Carlos Estepa Díez. *El legado de Alfonso X*. Murcia: Editoral Regional de Murcia, 1998.

Rodríguez Magda, Rosa María. *Inexistente Al Ándalus: De cómo los intelectuales reinventan el islam*. Oviedo, ES: Ediciones Nobel, 2008.

Rodríguez Puértolas, Julio, ed. *Poesía crítica y satírica del siglo XV*. Madrid: Clásicos Castalia, 1989.

Rohr, Isabelle. "'Spaniards of the Jewish type': Philosephardism in the Service of Imperialism in Early Twentieth-century Spanish Morocco." *Journal of Spanish Cultural Studies* 12.1 (2011): 61–75.

Rojas, Fernando de. *La Celestina*. Ed. Dorothy S. Severin. Madrid: Cátedra, 2006.

Rojinsky, David. *Companion to Empire: A Genealogy of the Written Word in Spain and New Spain, c.550–1550*. Amsterdam: Rodopi, 2010.

Rosen, Tova. *Unveiling Eve: Reading Gender in Medieval Hebrew Literature*. Philadelphia: University of Pennsylvania Press, 2003.

Rosenstock, Bruce. "Alonso de Cartagena: Nation, Miscegenation, and the Jew in Late-Medieval Castile." *Exemplaria* 12.1 (2000): 185–204.

———. *New Men: Conversos, Christian Theology, and Society in Fifteenth-century Castile*. London: Department of Hispanic Studies, Queen Mary, University of London, 2002.

Rosner, Fred. *The Existence and Unity of God: Three Treatises Attributed to Moses Maimonides*. Northvale, NJ: J. Aronson, 1990.

Roth, Cecil. "A Hebrew Elegy on the Martyrs of Toledo, 1391." In *Gleanings: Essays in Jewish History, Letters, and Art*, 91–118. New York: Hermon Press, 1967.

———. *A History of the Marranos*. Philadelphia: Jewish Publication Society of America, 1932.

———. *The Spanish Inquisition*. New York: Norton, 1964.

Roth, Norman. *Conversos, Inquisition, and the Expulsion of the Jews from Spain*. Madison: University of Wisconsin Press, 2002.

———. *Daily Life of the Jews in the Middle Ages*. Westport, CT: Greenwood Press, 2005.

———. "Jewish Reactions to the *'Arabiyya* and the Hebrew Renaissance in Spain." *Journal of Semitic Studies* 28.1 (1983): 63–84.

———. "Jewish Translators at the Court of Alfonso X." *Thought* 60.239 (1985): 439–455.

———. "What Constitutes 'Sephardic Literature'?" In *From Iberia to Diaspora: Studies in Sephardic History and Culture*, ed. Yedida Stillman and Norman Stillman, 247–263. Leiden: Brill, 1999.

Rozen, Minna. *A History of the Jewish Community in Istanbul: The Formative Years, 1453–1566*. Leiden: Brill, 2002.

Rudavsky, Tamar. *Maimonides*. Chichester, UK: Wiley-Blackwell, 2010.

Rudolph, Conrad. *Pilgrimage to the End of the World: The Road to Santiago de Compostela*. Chicago: University of Chicago Press, 2004.

Ruiz, Juan. *Libro de buen amor*. Ed. Alberto Blecua. Madrid: Cátedra, 2006.

Sabar, Yona. *The Folk Literature of the Kurdistani Jews: An Anthology*. New Haven: Yale University Press, 1982.

Sadan, Joseph. "Un intellectuel juif au confluent de deux Cultures: Yehūda al-Ḥarīzī et sa biographie arabe." In *Judíos y musulmanes en al-Andalus y el Magreb. Contactos intelectuales*, 105–151. Madrid: Casa de Velázquez, 2002.

———. "Rabbi Judah al-Harizi as Cultural Crossroads: Arabic Biography of a Jewish Artist in the Eyes of an Orientalist [Hebrew]." *Pe'amim* 68 (1996): 18–67.

Saemann, Björn. *How Comics Reflect Society: The Development of American Superheroes*. Munich: GRIN Verlag, 2011.

Sáenz-Badillos, Ángel. "El estudio de la poesía y la prosa hispanohebrea en los últimos cincuenta años." *Miscelánea de Estudios Árabes y Hebraicos* 50 (2001): 133–161.

———. "Hebrew Invective Poetry: The Debate Between Todros Abulafia and Phinehas Halevi." *Prooftexts* 16 (1996): 49–73.

———. *A History of the Hebrew Language.* Cambridge: Cambridge University Press, 1993.

———. "Intelectuales judíos y conversos en el siglo XV." In *Dejar hablar a los textos: Homenaje a Francisco Márquez Villanueva,* ed. Pedro M. Piñero Ramírez, 261–277. Seville: Universidad de Sevilla, 2005.

———. "Participación de judíos en las traducciones de Toledo." In *La escuela de traductores de Toledo,* 65–70. Toledo: Diputación Provincial de Toledo, 1996.

———. *Poetas hebreos de al-Andalus: Siglos X–XII: Antología.* Córdoba: Ediciones El Almendro, 1988.

———. "Todros frente a Todros: Dos escritores hebreos de Toledo en el siglo XIII." In *Jewish Studies at the Turn of the Twentieth Century,* ed. Judit Targarona and Ángel Sáenz-Badillos, 504–512. Boston: Brill, 1999.

Safran, William. "Deconstructing and Comparing Diasporas." In *Diaspora, Identity, and Religion: New Directions in Theory and Research,* ed. Waltraud Kokot, Khachig Tölölyan, and Carolin Alfonso, 9–29. London: Routledge, 2004.

———. "Diasporas in Modern Societies: Myths of Homeland and Return." *Diasporas* 1.1 (1991): 83–99.

Salvador Martínez, H. *Alfonso X, El Sabio: Una biografía.* Madrid: Ediciones Polifemo, 2003.

Sánchez Sánchez, Manuel. *La primitiva predicación hispánica medieval: Tres estudios.* Salamanca: Seminario de Estudios Medievales y Renacentistas, 2000.

Saperstein, Marc. *Jewish Preaching, 1200–1800: An Anthology.* New Haven: Yale University Press, 1989.

Schechter, Salomon. "Safed in the Sixteenth Century: A City of Legists and Mystics." In *Studies in Judaism* [Second series], 202–285. Philadelphia, 1908.

Scheindlin, Raymond P. "Secular Hebrew Poetry in Fifteenth-Century Spain." In *Crisis and Creativity in the Sephardic World,* ed. Benjamin R. Gampel, 25–37. New York: Columbia University Press, 1997.

———. *The Song of the Distant Dove: Judah Halevi's Pilgrimage.* Oxford: Oxford University Press, 2008.

———. "The Sorceror." In *Rabbinic Fantasies,* ed. David Stern and Mark J. Mirsky, 295–311. New Haven: Yale University Press, 1990.

———. *Wine, Women, and Death: Medieval Hebrew Poems on the Good Life.* Philadelphia: Jewish Publication Society, 1986.

Schiff, Mario. *La bibliothèque du marquis de Santillane.* Paris: E. Bouillon, 1905.

Schippers, Arie. "Les poètes juifs en Occitanie au moyen age: le catalogue d'Abraham de Beziérs." *Revue des Langues Romanes* 103 (1999): 1–25.

———. "Some Questions of Italian Hebrew Poetics in the Light of the Spanish Hebrew Heritage." *Frankfurter Judaistische Beiträge* 36 (2010): 57–68.

———. *Spanish Hebrew Poetry and the Arabic Literary Tradition: Arabic Themes in Hebrew Andalusian Poetry.* Leiden: Brill, 1994.

Schirmann, Hayim. "Les Contes rimées de Jacob ben Eleazar de Toledo." In *Etudes d'orientalisme dédiées a la mémoire de Lévi-Provençal,* 285–297. Paris, 1962.

———. *Hebrew Poetry in Spain and Provence* [Hebrew]. 2 vols. Jerusalem; Tel Aviv: Mossad Bialik; Dvir, 1956.

———. "Isaac Gorni, poète hébreu de Provence." *Lettres Romanes* 3 (1949): 175–200.

Schirmann, Hayim, and E. Fleischer. *History of Hebrew Poetry in Christian Spain and Southern France* [Hebrew]. Jerusalem: Y. L. Magnes, 1997.

Schmelzer, Menahem. "Hebrew Manuscripts and Printed Books among the Sephardim Before and After the Expulsion." In *Crisis and Creativity in the Sephardic World*, ed. Benjamin R. Gampel, 257–266. New York: Columbia University Press, 1997.

Scholem, Gershom. *Kabbalah*. New York: New American Library, 1974.

———. *Major Trends in Jewish Mysticism*. New York: Schocken Books, 1961.

———. *The Messianic Idea in Judaism and Other Essays on Jewish Spirituality*. New York: Schocken Books, 1971.

Sefer Yetzirah: El libro de la formación. Ed. Isidor Kalisch. Trans. Manuel Algora. Madrid: EDAF, 1993.

Sefer Yetzirah. Trans. Aryeh Kaplan. York Beach, ME: Samuel Weiser, 1990.

Segre, Cesare. "What Bakhtin Left Unsaid." In *Romance: Generic Transformation from Chrétien de Troyes to Cervantes*, ed. Kevin Brownlee and Marina Scordilis Brownlee, 23–46. Hanover: University Press of New England, 1985.

Sela, Shlomo. *Abraham Ibn Ezra and the Rise of Medieval Hebrew Science*. Leiden: Brill, 2003.

Sells, Michael Anthony. *Desert Tracings: Six Classic Arabian Odes*. Middletown, CT: Wesleyan University Press, 1989.

Seneca. *De Providentia Dei*. Trans. Alonso de Cartagena. Seville: Meinardo Ungut et al., 1491.

Septimus, Bernard. *Hispano-Jewish Culture in Transition: The Career and Controversies of Ramah*. Cambridge: Harvard University, 1982.

Sepúlveda, Lorenzo de, ed. *Romances nuevamente sacados de historias antiguas de la crónica de España*. Antwerp, 1551.

Serotta, Gerald. *Galut in Rabbinic Literature*. New York: Hebrew Union College-Jewish Institute of Religion, 1974.

Severin, Dorothy Sherman. "The Relationship between the *Libro de buen amor* and *Celestina*: Does Trotaconventos Perform a *Philocaptio* Spell on Doña Endrina?" In *A Companion to the Libro de buen amor*, ed. Louise M. Haywood and Louise O. Vasvari, 123–127. London: Tamesis, 2004.

———. *Tragicomedy and Novelistic Discourse in Celestina*. Cambridge: Cambridge University Press, 1989.

Shasha, David. "Sephardic Literature: The Real Hidden Legacy." *Zeek* Sept. 2005.

Shatzmiller, Joseph. *Jews, Medicine, and Medieval Society*. Berkeley: University of California Press, 1994.

Shear, Adam. *The Kuzari and the Shaping of Jewish Identity, 1167–1900*. New York: Cambridge University Press, 2008.

Shepard, Sanford. *Shem Tov: His World and His Words*. Miami: Ediciones Universal, 1978.

Shmuelevitz, Aryeh. *The Jews of the Ottoman Empire in the Late Fifteenth and the Sixteenth Centuries: Administrative, Economic, Legal, and Social Relations as Reflected in the Responsa*. Leiden: Brill, 1984.

Sicroff, Albert A. *Los estatutos de limpieza de sangre: controversias entre los siglos XV y XVII*. Newark, DE: Juan de la Cuesta, 2010.

Sidur Bene Romi: Siddùr di rito italiano secondo l'uso delle Comunità di Roma e Milano. Rome: Rashi, 2004.

Silberstein, Susan Milner. "The Provençal Esther Poem Written in Hebrew Characters c. 1327 by Crescas de Caylar: Critical Edition." Doctoral dissertation. University of Pennsylvannia, 1973.

Silman, Yochanan. *Philosopher and Prophet: Judah Halevi, the Kuzari, and the Evolution of His Thought*. Albany: State University of New York Press, 1995.

Silver, Abba. *A History of Messianic Speculation in Israel from the First through the Seventeenth Centuries*. New York: Macmillan, 1927.

Silver, Daniel. *Maimonidean Criticism and the Maimonidean Controversy*. Leiden: Brill, 1965.

Snow, Joseph Thomas. "The Satirical Poetry of Alfonso X: A Look at Its Relationship to the *Cantigas De Santa Maria*." In *Alfonso X of Castile: The Learned King (1221–1284)*, ed. Francisco Márquez-Villanueva and Carlos Alberto Vega, 110–127. Cambridge: Department of Romance Langauges and Literatures, Harvard University, 1990.

———. *The Poetry of Alfonso X, el Sabio: A Critical Bibliography*. London: Grant and Cutler, 1977.

Soifer, Maya. "Beyond Convivencia: Critical Reflections on the Historiography of Interfaith Relations in Christian Spain." *Journal of Medieval Iberian Studies* 1 (2009): 19–35.

Soldevila, Ferran. *Els almogàvers*. Barcelona: R. Dalmau, 1994.

Solomon, Michael Ray. "'Yo, Libro': Juan Ruiz and the Idea of the Book." Doctoral dissertation. University of Wisconsin at Madison, 1987.

Spero, Shubert. *Holocaust and Return to Zion: A Study in Jewish Philosophy of History*. Hoboken: KTAV, 2000.

Stavans, Ilan. *Resurrecting Hebrew*. New York: Nextbook/Schocken, 2008.

Stern, Samuel M. *Hispano-Arabic Strophic Poetry: Studies*. Oxford: Clarendon Press, 1974.

———. "Les vers finaux en espagnol dans les *muwassahs* hispano-hébraïques: Une contribution à l'histoire du *muwassah* et à l'étude du vieux dialecte espagnol 'mozarabe.'" *Al-Andalus* 13 (1948): 299–348.

Stinger, Charles L. *The Renaissance in Rome*. Bloomington: Indiana University Press, 1985.

Stone, Matt, and Trey Parker. *Team America: World Police*. Paramount, 2005. Film.

Suárez Fernández, Luis. *La expulsión de los judíos de España*. Madrid: Editorial MAPFRE, 1991.

———, ed. *Documentos acerca de la expulsión de los judíos*. Valladolid: Consejo Superior de Investigaciones Científicas-Patronato Menéndez Pelayo, 1964.

Supple, James. *Arms and Letters: The Military and Literary Ideals in Renaissance France, with Special Reference to Montaigne*. Boston Spa: British Library Document Supply Centre, 1974.

Szpiech, Ryan. *Conversion and Narrative: Reading and Religious Authority in Medieval Polemic*. Philadelphia: University of Pennsylvania Press, 2013.

———. "The Convivencia Wars: Decoding Historiography's Polemic with Philology." In *A Sea of Languages: Literature and Culture in the Pre-modern Mediterranean*, ed. Suzanne Akbari and Karla Mallette, 135–161. Toronto: University of Toronto Press, 2013.

Szwed, John F. "Metaphors of Incommensurability." *Journal of American Folklore* 116.459 (2003): 9–18.

Tanūkhī al-Ma'arrī, Mufaḍḍal ibn Muḥammad ibn Mis'ar. *History of the Grammarians: From the Basrans to the Kufans and Others* [Arabic]. 2nd ed. Ed. 'Abd al-Fattāḥ Muḥammad Ḥulwa. Jīzah: Hajar, 1992.

Targarona Borrás, Judit. "The Dirges of Don Benvenist and Doña Tolosana de la Cavallería for Their Son Solomon's Death." In *Studies in Arabic and Hebrew Letters in Honor of Raymond P. Scheindlin*, ed. Jonathan P. Decter and Michael C. Rand, 213–226. Piscataway, NJ: Gorgias Press, 2007.

———. "La lengua con la que Dios creó el mundo: La poesía de Salamón ben Meshulam de Piera." In *Los quilates de su oriente, Homenaje a Francisco Márquez Villanueva*, ed. Mary Gaylord, Luis Girón Negrón, and Ángel Sáenz-Badillos. Newark, DE: Juan de la Cuesta Hispanic Monographs, forthcoming.

———. "Los últimos poetas hebreos de Sefarad: Poesía hebrea en el mundo románico." *Revista de Filología Románica* 19 (2002): 249–268.

———. "Todros Ben Yehuda ha-Leví Abulafia, un poeta hebreo en la corte de Alfonso X el Sabio." *Helmantica* 36.110 (1985): 195–210.

Targarona Borrás, Judit, and Raymond P. Scheindlin. "Literary Correspondence between Vidal Benvenist ben Lavi and Solomon ben Meshulam De Piera." *Révue des Études Juives* 160.1–2 (2001): 61–133.

Tate, Robert Brian. *Ensayos sobre la historiografía peninsular del siglo XV*. Madrid: Gredos, 1970.

Tate, Robert Brian, and Jeremy Lawrance. "Introducción." In Alfonso de Palencia, *Gesta Hispaniensia ex annalibus suorum dierum collecta*, ed. Brian Tate and Jeremy Lawrance, xxxv–lxix. Madrid: Real Academia de la Historia, 1998.

Thomas, Henry. *Spanish and Portuguese Romances of Chivalry: The Revival of the Romance of Chivalry in the Spanish Peninsula, and its Extension and Influence Abroad*. Cambridge: University Press, 1920.

Thompson, James. *The Literacy of the Laity in the Middle Ages*. Berkeley: University of California Press, 1939.

Tolan, John. *Saracens: Islam in the Medieval European Imagination*. New York: Columbia University Press, 2002.

———. *Sons of Ishmael: Muslims through European Eyes in the Middle Ages*. Gainesville: University Press of Florida, 2008.

Tölölyan, Khachig. "Rethinking Diaspora(s): Stateless Power in the Transnational Moment." *Diaspora* 5.1 3–36.

———. "The Contemporary Discourse of Diaspora Studies." *Comparative Studies of South Asia, Africa and the Middle East* 27.3 (2007): n. pag.

Trotter, D. *Medieval French Literature and the Crusades (1100–1300)*. Genève: Librairie Droz, 1988.

Twersky, Isadore. *Introduction to the Code of Maimonides* (Mishneh Torah). New Haven: Yale University Press, 1980.

Urbach, Efraim Elimelech. *The Sages, Their Concepts and Beliefs*. Jerusalem: Magnes Press, Hebrew University, 1979.

Urbina, Eduardo. "Now You See It, Now You Don't: The Antithesis *corteza/meollo* in the *Libro de buen amor*." In *Florilegium Hispanicum: Medieval and Golden Age Studies Presented to Dorothy Clotelle Clarke*, ed. John S. Geary and Charles B. Faulhaber, 139–150. Madison: Hispanic Seminary of Medieval Studies, 1983.

Usque, Samuel. *Samuel Usque's Consolation for the Tribulations of Israel (Consolaçam ás Tribulaçoens de Israel)*. 2nd ed. Philadelphia: Jewish Publication Society of America, 1977.

Valdeón Baruque, Julio. *Los conflictos sociales en los reinos de Castilla en los siglos XIV y XV*. Madrid: Siglo Veintiuno Editores, 1975.

Valdeón Baruque, Julio, Josep M. Salrach i Marés, and Javier Zabalo Zabalegui. *Feudalismo y consolidación de los pueblos hispánicos (siglos XI–XV)*. Barcelona: Labor, 1980.

van Bekkum, Wout. "O Seville! Ah Castile!: Spanish-Hebrew Dirges from the Fifteenth Century." In *Hebrew Scholarship and the Medieval World*, ed. Nicholas De Lange, 156–170. Cambridge: Cambridge UP, 2001.

van Gelder, Geert Jan. "The Conceit of Pen and Sword: On an Arabic Literary Debate." *Journal of Semitic Studies* 22.2 (1987): 329–360.

Vasvári, Louise O. "The Novelness of the *Libro de buen amor*." In *A Companion to the Libro de buen amor*, ed. Louise M. Haywood and Louise O. Vasvári, 165–181. London: Tamesis, 2004.

Vidal Manzanares, César. *España frente al Islam: De Mahoma a Ben Laden*. Madrid: Esfera de los Libros, 2004.

Viejo Sánchez, María Luisa. "El influjo de las construcciones hebreas de infinitivo absoluto en las construcciones sintácticas del tipo *fablar fablará, veer vimos* en las biblias medievales romanceadas." In *Actas del VI Congreso Historia de la Lengua Española,* ed. J. J. Bustos Tovar and J. Girón Alconcel, 1203–1214. Madrid: Arco Libros, 2006.

Vose, Robin. *Dominicans, Muslims, and Jews in the Medieval Crown of Aragon.* Cambridge: Cambridge University Press, 2009.

Wacks, David A. "Don Yllán and the Egyptian Sorceror: Vernacular Commonality and Literary Diversity in Medieval Castile." *Sefarad* 65.2 (2005): 413–433.

———. *Framing Iberia: Maqamat and Frametale Narratives in Medieval Spain.* Leiden: Brill, 2007.

———. "Ibn Sahula's Tale of the Egyptian Sorcerer: A Thirteenth Century Don Yllán." *eHumanista* 4 (2004): 1–12.

———. "Is Spain's Hebrew Literature 'Spanish?'" In *Spain's Multicultural Legacies: Studies in Honor of Samuel G. Armistead,* ed. Adrienne Martin and Cristina Martínez-Carazo, 315–331. Newark, DE: Juan de la Cuesta Hispanic Monographs, 2008.

———. "Reconquest Colonialism and Andalusi Narrative Practice in Don Juan Manuel's *Conde Lucanor.*" *diacritics* 36.3–4 (2006): 87–103.

———. "Toward a History of Hispano-Hebrew Literature of Christian Iberia in the Romance Context." *eHumanista* 14 (2010): 178–209.

———. "Vernacular Anxiety and the Semitic Imaginary: Shem Tov Isaac ibn Ardutiel de Carrión and His Critics." *Journal of Medieval Iberian Cultural Studies* 4.2 (2012): 167–184.

Waxman, Meyer. *Exile and Redemption in the Literature of the Jewish People* [Hebrew]. New York: Ogen, 1952.

Weiss, Julian. *The Mester de Clerecía: Intellectuals and Ideologies in Thirteenth-century Castile.* Woodbridge, UK: Tamesis, 2006.

Werblowsky, Tzvi. *Joseph Karo: Lawyer and Mystic.* 2nd ed. Philadelphia: Jewish Publication Society of America, 1977.

Whinnom, Keith. *La poesía amatoria de la época de los Reyes Católicos.* Durham: University of Durham, 1981.

White, Bob W. "Congolese Rumba and Other Cosmopolitanisms." *Cahiers d'Études Africaines* 42.168 (2002): 663–686.

White, Sidnie Ann. "Esther: A Feminine Model for Jewish Diaspora." In *Gender and Difference in Ancient Israel,* ed. Peggy Day. Minneapolis: University of Minnesota Press, 1989. 161–177.

Whitehouse, David. *Medieval Glass for Popes, Princes, and Peasants.* Corning, NY: Corning Museum of Glass, 2010.

Wilkinson, Alexander S. *Iberian Books: Books Published in Spanish or Portuguese or on the Iberian Peninsula before 1601.* Leiden: Brill, 2010.

Wolfson, Harry Austryn. "Maimonides on the Unity and Incorporeality of God." In *Studies in the History of Philosophy and Religion,* ed. Isadore Twersky and George Williams, 433–457. Cambridge, 1977.

Ya'iri, Abraham. *Hebrew Printing in Constantinople* [Hebrew]. Jerusalem: Magnes Press, 1967.

Yassif, Eli. *Tales of Ben Sira in the Middle Ages* [Hebrew]. Jerusalem: Magnes, 1984.

———. *The Hebrew Folktale: History, Genre, Meaning.* Bloomington: Indiana University Press, 1999.

Yellin, David. *Research on the Hebrew Poetry of Spain* [Hebrew]. Ed. Abraham Meir Habermann. Jerusalem: Reuven Mas, 1975.

Yellin, David, and Dan Pagis. *A Theory of Sephardic Poetry* [Hebrew]. Jerusalem: Magnes Press, 1972.

Ye'or, Bat. *The Dhimmi: Jews and Christians Under Islam*. Rutherford, NJ: Fairleigh Dickinson University Press, 1985.

Yerushalmi, Yosef Hayim. *From Spanish Court to Italian Ghetto*. New York: Columbia University Press, 1971.

———. *The Lisbon Massacre of 1506 and the Royal Image in the* Shebet Yehudah. Cincinnati: Hebrew Union College-Jewish Institute of Religion, 1976.

———. *Zakhor, Jewish History and Jewish Memory*. Seattle: University of Washington Press, 1982.

Young, Robert. *Postcolonialism: An Historical Introduction*. Oxford: Blackwell Publishers, 2001.

Zackin, Jane Robin. "A Jew and His Milieu: Allegory, Polemic, and Jewish Thought in Sem Tob's *Proverbios morales* and *Ma'aseh harav*." Doctoral dissertation. University of Texas at Austin, 2008.

Zemke, John. *Critical Approaches to the Proverbios Morales of Shem Tov of Carrión: An Annotated Bibliography*. Newark, DE: Juan de la Cuesta Hispanic Monographs, 1997.

Zink, Michel. *La Prédication en langue romane avant 1300*. Paris: Champion, 1976.

———. *The Invention of Literary Subjectivity*. Trans. Davis Sices. Baltimore: Johns Hopkins University Press, 1999.

Zurita, Jerónimo. *Anales de la Corona de Aragón, compuestos por Jerónimo Zurita*. Ed. Ángel Canellas López. Zaragoza: Institución Fernando el Católico, 1967.

Zwiep, Irene E. *Mother of Reason and Revelation: A Short History of Medieval Jewish Linguistic Thought*. Amsterdam: J. C. Gieben, 1997.

INDEX

DAVID A. WACKS

is Associate Professor of Spanish at the University of Oregon. He is
author of *Framing Iberia:* Maqamat *and Frametale Narratives in Medieval
Spain* and editor (with Michelle Hamilton and Sarah Portnoy) of *Wine,
Women, and Song: Hebrew and Arabic Literature in Medieval Iberia.*

CPSIA information can be obtained
at www.ICGtesting.com
Printed in the USA
LVHW092055040419
613062LV00004B/64/P

9 780253 015723